The Internet and the Law

The Internet and the Law

Kevin M. Rogers
Senior Lecturer in Law, University of Hertfordshire

palgrave
macmillan

This edition first published in 2011 by
PALGRAVE MACMILLAN

Palgrave Macmillan in the UK is an imprint of Macmillan Publishers Limited,
registered in England, company number 785998, of Houndmills, Basingstoke,
Hampshire RG21 6XS.

Palgrave Macmillan in the US is a division of St Martin's Press LLC,
175 Fifth Avenue, New York, NY 10010.

Palgrave Macmillan is the global academic imprint of the above companies
and has companies and representatives throughout the world.

Palgrave® and Macmillan® are registered trademarks in the United States,
the United Kingdom, Europe and other countries.

ISBN-13: 978–0–230–23567–0 paperback

This book is printed on paper suitable for recycling and made from fully
managed and sustained forest sources. Logging, pulping and manufacturing
processes are expected to conform to the environmental regulations of the
country of origin.

A catalogue record for this book is available from the British Library.

10   9   8   7   6   5   4   3   2   1
20 19 18 17 16 15 14 13 12 11

Printed and bound in the UK by MPG Books Group, Bodmin & King's Lynn.

If you would like to comment on this title, please write to
lawfeedback@palgrave.com.

To Lisa and Jacob

Contents

Acknowledgements

The challenges of constructing a book on the relationship of the Internet with law are apparent. There have been numerous times when either the technology or the law has changed, which has necessitated a change of direction in the writing. I am grateful to many students and colleagues at the University of Hertfordshire for their help during this process, particularly Maureen Johnson with whom I have had the pleasure of teaching much of the subject matter contained within this book over the past few years – we have learnt much from each other as we have gone through. Also to Charles Wild whose continual enthusiastic encouragement ensured the proposal of this text reached a conclusion.

It is also important to recognise friends and family who have witnessed both the joys and frustrations during this process. My parents, Malcolm and Rita, who have also shown continual interest in the book's development and were extremely helpful – particularly in the latter stages.

Finally, I owe a large degree of gratitude to my wife Lisa, for her patience and forbearance. In the final stages of the writing of this book, Lisa presented me with our gorgeous firstborn son, Jacob Arthur, and it is to these two very important people that I dedicate this book.

There is a companion website to accompany this book, which can be viewed at: http://www.palgrave.com/law/rogers. All weblinks mentioned in the text are listed here and regular updates will also be uploaded to this site.

Cases and Legislation Cited

Cases

UK legislation

EU and International legislation

1 Internet Infrastructure

This chapter will consider:

- Whether 'Internet law' is a subject in its own right.
- The development of the technology in this area, taking into account the Internet, email, m-commerce (e.g. smartphones) and other developing forms of technology.
- A general consideration of the advantages and disadvantages of this technology.
- In what ways is the law dealing with the challenges of technology?
- Who is currently responsible for running the Internet and whether the current status quo is appropriate.
- An appraisal of the role of ICANN in providing the top level of domain names, including its role within the '.xxx' top level domain name and the future proposals for reform.
- A brief consideration of domain names, domain name allocation and domain name dispute resolution.

The subject matter contained within this book did not exist in its own right until a little over fifteen years ago. The nature of communication and commerce has been revolutionised by cyberspace. This is not a location with physical borders that one can cross into, although it has a supranational existence. Cyberspace may be intangible, but Cyber Law, or Internet Law or Information Technology Law (or further derivations of) are now mainstream subjects at undergraduate and postgraduate level in universities around the world. One ignores the Internet at one's peril as the speed of its growth is immense. Connectivity is increasing and the range of applications continues to develop, meaning that the way we live our lives – from education to employment to communication – has altered beyond recognition. It is ill-advised to simply regard the Internet as an addition to other, more established areas of law. Indeed, the Internet is often the driver in dictating how the law needs to respond. Whereas in the past, nations have fought over national borders and the oceans, and more recently space,[1]

---

[1] Friedmann, T *The World is Flat: A brief history of the twenty-first century* (2005) Farrar, Straus and Giroux.

the battle in the twenty-first century is to ensure that the maximum benefit is received from the Internet, while seeking to contain it to fit in with perceived norms.

The challenges posed to legislation and faced by the law enforcement agencies appear regularly. One such example appeared in Italy during 2009, where three executives of Google were convicted of breaking Italian data protection law following the posting of a video online. The video showed the bullying of a young boy, who had autism, by a number of people. The bullying was filmed using a mobile telephone and was placed online in September 2006. It remained online for two months, until Google was contacted by police who asked it to take the offending publication down. Google complied with this request, although criminal proceedings were still commenced against four executives of Google on the grounds of criminal defamation and violation of data protection laws (specifically the illicit treatment of personal data). Although all were cleared of the charge of defamation, three of the four executives were found guilty of violating data protection laws and were given a six month suspended sentence. This was a controversial judgment, due in no small part to the E-Commerce Directive 2000/31/EC, which gives immunity against prosecution to those who provide platforms for users to place illegal material online. The view of the court was that Google profited from the uploading of the video; it presumably knew that illegal and undesirable videos would almost certainly be uploaded and yet it continued with this policy, apparently in pursuit of profit. The court was also critical of Google because they did not have a filter in place to weed out such material.[2] In this one situation alone, a wide range of legal issues are present, including privacy and the right of free speech; the regulation of user-generated content; the liability of Internet Service Providers and other platforms which host services; online bullying; defamation and data protection. To consider such issues discretely would be to the detriment of the researcher, student or academic. The Internet pulls these – and many other topics – together to form a rich and vibrant variety of legal topics under the one heading. This book will cover many of these topics. At the same time it is recognised that there are challenges to drafting such a product due to the rapid evolution of the Internet and the law. This book will consider issues relating to contracting – both how contracts are formed and what legal protection an online consumer can rely on. Payment and taxation issues will also be covered, along with a discussion on jurisdiction and choice of law. Two large topics which will be covered include privacy in its widest form (focusing upon defamation and data protection) and also online criminal behaviour. This can take a range of forms from hacking, to identity fraud, to

---

[2] For more on this case see: Sartor, G & Cunha, M V *The Italian Google-Case: Privacy, Freedom of Speech and Responsibility of Providers for User-Generated Contents* (2010) International Journal of Law and Information Technology, volume 18, number 4, pages 356–378.

harassment, while the proliferation of indecent or illegal content, such as indecent images of children also forms a substantial part of this section. A chapter
on Web 2.0 and social media is an important addition. The social networking
site Facebook has (at the time of writing) over 500 million users. This means
that approximately a third of the connected world (estimated at 1.6 billion
people) are on Facebook. The legal issues surrounding such a platform are
immense and the chapter considers a number of these issues.

A brief history of the Internet

The Internet has its origins in the United States of America and was piloted
during the Cold War. A new protocol of communication, ARPANET, was developed to speed up information exchange. Under this protocol, information sent
was broken down into smaller units and reconstituted once it reached the
recipient. Interested by the possibilities offered by such a network, academics
joined ARPANET and were quickly followed by American governmental departments. In time, ARPANET reached full capacity and was replaced by NSF-Net,
the network of the National Science Foundation, a governmental agency for
the financing of research. The connection of NSF-Net to other networks and
computers finally gave birth to the Internet at the start of the 1980s. The
Internet arrived in Europe in 1988 via the network EBONE, which links the
United States to Europe. The creation of hypertext linking by Tim Berners-Lee
in 1992, which led to the development of the World Wide Web, opened the
Internet to many more people.

The Internet is a framework that allows users to exchange information at a
distance, work, carry out research, discuss, transfer files as well as a range of
other activities. These are accomplished using a wide range of applications and
tools including: email, web, newsgroups, internet relay chat, social networking sites, distance working and file transfers. Recent years have seen the development of further applications, including VoIP (Voice over Internet Protocol)
and the development of m-commerce and wi-fi. In September 2010, the
Office for National Statistics cited United Nations figures, which said that at
the end of 2008, 1.6 billion people were connected to the Internet (this
equates to around a quarter of world's population).[3] As applications to
connect to the Internet continue to diversify, the number of people engaged
online will continue to rise. This is demonstrated in the research by the
increase in social networking sites, where around half of the population of the
United Kingdom has joined a social networking site, such as Facebook or
LinkedIn, and during 2010 Facebook announced that the number of users

---

[3] Office for National Statistics *E-Society: how the Internet has changed the UK* (22nd September
2010). Available at: http://www.direct.gov.uk/en/Nl1/Newsroom/DG_190990.

passed the 500 million mark, meaning that if it were a real country it would be the third largest country in terms of population on the planet![4] The Internet has introduced a new era for our consumer society. It allows us through its different applications and the World Wide Web to buy and receive services directly delivered online, to communicate with other people, to manage finance through online banking systems, to watch television programmes or download material as well as a range of other activities. Yet not all people have access to the Internet and cannot obtain the benefits the Internet provides. This could be due to cost, language[5], education or connectivity and is termed the 'digital divide'.

Internet governance: who runs the web?

The Internet opened up a whole new sovereignty debate. It exists over and above existing borders and individual nations are keen to ensure that they retain sufficient oversight of its development. With increased trade, communications and commerce, caused in no small measure by rise of the Internet, individual countries are concerned to ensure that the Internet (and power to exert a form of control over it) does not slip away from their control. To some degree, the development of 'Internet law' has been on a piecemeal basis with different countries enacting different laws to regulate different types of behaviour. The standard case cited in making this point is the French case of **France v Yahoo!**.[6] In this case, a French group protested about the sale of Nazi memorabilia on the Yahoo auction website. This was available on both the French and American site. While France has strict laws forbidding people to glorify the holocaust, the ability for a person to do this in America is protected by the First Amendment right of free speech. Instead of appealing in a higher French court, Yahoo took their case to an American court, which found in their favour and did not enforce the French decision.[7] Cross-border regulation is complex and competing desires between governments are not helpful to the situation.

---

[4] The Economist *Social networks and statehood: The future is another country* (22nd July 2010). Available at: http://www.economist.com/node/16646000.

[5] Although most of the Internet uses English as its language of communication, in May 2010 ICAAN introduced a system that allows full web addresses to be typed using no English characters. See BBC News *'Historic' day as first non-latin web addresses go live* (6th May 2010). Available at: http://news.bbc.co.uk/1/hi/technology/10100108.stm.

[6] (Superior Court of Paris) (22nd May 2000). The judgment is available at: http://www.juriscom.net/txt/jurisfr/cti/yauctions20000522.htm.

[7] The American judgment in **Yahoo! v La Ligue Contre La Racsime et L'Antisemitisme** (2001) C-00-21275 JT is available at: http://w2.eff.org/legal/Jurisdiction and sovereignty/LICRA v Yahoo/20011107 us distct decision.pdf. See also: Maier, B *How has the law attempted to tackle the borderless nature of the Internet?* (2010) International Journal of Law and Information Technology, volume 18, issue 2, pages 142–175.

There are further complexities as countries seek to regulate something that cannot be seen or grasped. The Internet has no physical territory and no government. There is no one body with which a single government can open diplomatic relations. A person cannot cross a border to enter 'cyberspace', indeed the Internet is said to exist supranationally, that is, above and beyond current physical geographic borders. Some governments are more restrictive in monitoring the websites that their citizens view, or even preventing access to certain websites. The action a government could take includes requiring bloggers to register with a government agency, taking screen shots of people's Internet usage to monitor what sites are being viewed and blocking access to particular sites or the entire system.[8] This has been seen in recent years where some countries have closed down servers and prevented their citizens from accessing the Internet – and specifically message boards and Twitter – to comment on contentious elections.[9] Other examples of state involvement include the search engine Google establishing an arm specifically for China in 2006. Google.cn was a compromise between the corporate giant and China that blocked references to certain websites. This rather uncomfortable state of affairs was never fully embraced by either party as in 2009 it was alleged that the Chinese government had denied access to other Google services. The tension came to a head in early 2010, when Google was the victim of a number of attempted hacks. These attempts were apparently traced back to the Chinese mainland and so in response Google removed the censors from Google.cn and routed all searches through servers in Hong Kong. This meant that in theory websites that had previously been censored were available to the Chinese population. In practice however, results that reached the citizen were still censored by Chinese firewalls.[10] This apparent stand-off between one of the biggest countries in the world and one of the largest companies in the world provides a further illustration of the complexities of censoring material or content online.[11] Other countries have adopted a generally relaxed approach to what they allow their citizens to view, although there are some exceptions to this, such as Saudi Arabia, which in 2010 planned to block the use of BlackBerry smartphones in its jurisdiction as the system was very difficult to monitor, which could in turn lead to a security risk. After some protest, the

---

[8] See BBC News *How governments censor the web* (22nd March 2007). Available at: http://news.bbc.co.uk/1/hi/technology/6475911.stm.

[9] For instance, see *Post-election clampdown in Iran* (15th June 2009). Available at: http://news.bbc.co.uk/1/hi/world/middle_east/8100310.stm.

[10] For more see: BBC News *China condemns decision by Google to lift censorship* (23rd March 2010). Available at: http://news.bbc.co.uk/1/hi/world/asia-pacific/8582233.stm.

[11] See also: OUT-LAW.COM news *China signals secrets clampdown* (4th May 2010). Available at: http://www.out-law.com/page-10987. This article reports that the Chinese authorities have pledged to take action against telecommunications companies that allow state secrets to pass through their networks. The difficultly for Internet Service Providers is that the government has provided a very broad definition of what amounts to a 'state secret'.

government decided to review its decision at a later date.[12] However, the competing desires of regulating content, while allowing the Internet to grow organically have not yet been fully reconciled.

This has been of particular interest and controversy, especially during the first decade of the twenty-first century with the United Nations-sponsored World Summit on Information Society meetings, although academically it has been of interest for a great deal longer. There are two main lines of thought as to the most appropriate way for the Internet to be governed: the cyber-libertarian approach and the cyber-paternalist approach. Both have their roots in American research from the mid-1990s. The cyber-libertarian approach was espoused by academics such as David Johnson and David Post.[13] This line of thought believes that the Internet is similar to the 'Wild West'. Law, rules and norms are secured by individuals freely deciding as a collective. Interference by governments is minimal (indeed decentralisation is a necessity) and the rights to freedom of speech and expression are paramount. This theory links the new technology with libertarian ideas such as freedom, society and markets, and that these rights should be protected in cyberspace. The opposite cyber-paternalist view is held by academics such as Joel Reidenberg.[14] Cyber-paternalists argue that although many sovereign borders are being 'eroded' by the Internet, other centralised regulatory control is being established in its place. Laws are imposed upon the network, not only by governments, but also by the capabilities of the technology and also, perhaps more importantly, by its own architecture, which provide boundaries over which people cannot cross. There are a couple of fundamental problems with both theories. Cyber-libertarians are hampered by the desires of sovereign states to exercise a form of regulatory control over the Internet, while cyber-paternalists are restricted by the fact that the Internet is indeed a free and open network and with this open network it is difficult to impose regulatory structures. As the Internet has developed, the desire of governments to exercise a form of online control appears to suggest that the cyber-paternalist theory of regulation carries the most weight.

As the Internet has an international reach, there is a lot of controversy over who is responsible for its 'management'. The Internet exists over and above national borders. The nature of the Internet is that it allows ideas and information to be passed around speedily and freely with only some limited regulation

---

[12] Woods, B *Saudis grants RIM a BlackBerry reprieve* (10th August 2010) ZDNet News. Available at: http://www.zdnet.co.uk/news/regulation/2010/08/10/saudis-grant-rim-a-blackberry-reprieve-40089785/.

[13] Johnson, D & Post, D *Law and Borders – The rise of law in Cyberspace* (May 1996), Stanford Law Review, Volume 48, number 5, pages 1367–1402.

[14] Reidenberg, J *Lex informatica: The formation of Information Policy Rules through Technology* (February 1998) Texas Law Review, Volume 76, Number 3, pages 553–584. For a more detailed analysis of both of these approaches to the governance of the Internet, the author recommends Andrew Murray's excellent book *The Regulation of Cyberspace,* Routledge Cavendish (2007).

(by Internet Service Providers, or national governments[15]). As the Internet developed from an American defence tool, mainly by default, the American Department of Commerce has 'overseen' the development of the Internet through the Internet Corporation for Assigned Names and Numbers (ICANN). ICANN is the body responsible for handing out top-level domain names and is the closest the Internet has to a 'government'. Handing out domain names may only seem to be a small job, however without a domain name a person or company does not have a presence on the web. ICANN's role has caused considerable disquiet among the international community as the perception has been that the United States runs the Internet. Accordingly, due to international recognition of the tense governmental nature of the information society and the effect it was having on the future of the world, in 2001 a two-year process was put into action to enable world leaders to consider a global vision to ensure an all-inclusive and equitable system. A two-stage meeting process was established. In 2003, the first stage was held in Geneva, Switzerland and the second stage at the end of 2005 in Tunis, Tunisia. The aim behind the first meeting in Geneva was to find a resolution to the contentious Internet governance conflict. The conclusion from this meeting was to create a committee to examine the area of Internet governance, involving definitions, public policy issues and strategic approaches. The Working Group on Internet Governance (WGIG) reported in June 2005 in their document entitled 'Report of the Working Group on Internet Governance'.[16] On page 4 of this report, Internet governance was defined as:

"... the development and application by Governments, the private sector and civil society, in their respective roles, of shared principles, norms, rules, decision-making procedures, and programmes that shape the evolution and use of the Internet."[17]

The report recommended four systems, or models, of governance, ranging from the creation of a new multi-stakeholder forum, to leaving the status quo in place. It was also noted that if the Internet structure is to successfully defeat problems, such as spam, cyber-crime, privacy and security concerns, then a degree of international co-operation is required. Alongside the official reasoning for the working group, the political edge to the issue was apparent. The dilemma was, and is, predominantly political in nature and one founded upon freedom of expression. Countries such as China, Brazil and Iran are seeking a greater say in the governing of the Internet and are seeking a move towards

---

[15] News stories relating to Internet suppression in Burma, China, Libya and Iran in recent years are examples of governmental regulation.

[16] Available at: http://www.wgig.org/docs/WGIGREPORT.pdf.

[17] Ibid. Page 4.

a multi-national, multi-stakeholder body and a move away from the ICANN method of regulation, overseen by the American Department of Commerce. Prior to the second stage of the summit in Tunisia in 2005, press briefings became very tense. A line was drawn in the sand between the Americans, who sought to retain management through ICANN, and other countries who sought a more fluid governance model, allowing them a greater input.

Two main issues were discussed at the November 2005 meeting: first Internet governance and secondly the 'digital divide' (ensuring access to the information society for the developing areas of the world). The agreement reached in Tunisia in relation to Internet governance allowed ICANN to retain oversight of the Internet, in relation to domain names. However, alongside ICANN, a non-binding Internet Governance Forum (IGF) was to be established including governmental stakeholders from around the globe. The aggressive metaphors from politicians that greeted this outcome were indicative of the international tension prior to the meeting. The IGF was set up to be a multi-lateral, multi-stakeholder non-binding body. Thus, the remit is broad, but the power is minimal. The United Nations has taken the lead in formulating this body, and in February 2006 organised a consultation in Geneva to discuss its structure. The first meeting of the IGF was held in Athens in 2006. The gathering has since been held annually: Rio de Janeiro in 2007, Hyderabad in 2008, Sharm El Sheikh in 2009 and Vilnius in 2010. The effectiveness of this body has been questioned and it did not remove the political questions over the role and position of ICANN. However, in 2009 it was announced that an Affirmation of Commitments had been signed between ICANN and the American government.[18] There were a number of facets to this agreement. It confirmed that ICANN was a private, not-for-profit organisation, which was independent and not controlled by any one entity. It was appropriate however that ICANN be reviewed regularly by the Internet community. Reaction to the agreement was generally positive as it showed that ICANN was still an appropriate body to oversee top-level domain names, while seeming to encourage a move away from direct governmental regulation. The principle is that the United States will become one country among many who has a regulatory oversight of the running of the Internet.

The triple-x decision

The political edge to the Internet governance dispute and the alleged political involvement was seen in the .xxx domain name dispute. Seen as a test case of ICANN's independence, the '.xxx' domain name courted considerable

---

[18] See: http://www.icann.org/en/announcements/announcement-30sep09-en.htm.

controversy. ICM Registry were seeking to introduce '.xxx' as a top-level domain name to allow a place for all sexually explicit and pornographic websites to be located. In May 2006, ICANN refused to grant permission for this top-level domain to be introduced and ICM Registry subsequently issued proceedings against three American government departments after the decision by ICANN. Their view was that the refusal of ICANN to allow this domain name demonstrated political involvement by the right-wing Bush Administration (through the Department of Commerce). On announcing that '.xxx' would not be adopted, ICM Registry, who had spent around $3 million over six years, began a legal campaign. They filed three lawsuits under various headings (under the Freedom of Information Act) to obtain proof that the American government interfered in the final decision. The first sought to obtain documents from the Department of Commerce (documents previously obtained showed that there was fierce lobbying by some right-wing Christian groups, however significant portions of this information had been blanked out). The second was for documents sent between US communications secretary John Kneuer and ICANN president Paul Twomey. ICM Registry was particularly interested in documentation from around the time that ICANN voted against the '.xxx' domain name and the Department of Commerce stated that ICANN could remain in charge of the Internet's foundations. The third request asked for copies of communication between the Department of Commerce and Internet naming authority IANA shortly after the Department of Commerce sent a letter to ICANN outlining its concerns for the '.xxx' domain. They also provided a 176-page Amended Request for Reconsideration of Board Action to ICANN. This dispute continued until June 2010, when it was announced by ICANN that following a successful appeal by ICM Registry they had given permission for the application for an .xxx domain name to be taken forward.[19]

Domain names

The discussion about who is responsible for governing the Internet is of critical importance. The body that runs the Internet has the responsibility for acting as 'gate-keeper' and provides the rules for saying who can have an online presence and who cannot. The role of gate-keeper was exemplified in the '.xxx' decision. Once an individual or company decides that they want an online presence, usually through a website, they will need to obtain a domain name. Domain names are the human-friendly forms of Internet addresses, which are

---

[19] See ICANN Press Release *ICANN approves Chinese Internationalised Domain Names: Board also moves forward on .XXX domain application* (25th June 2010). Available at: http://icann.org/en/news/releases/release-25jun10-en.pdf.

commonly used to find web sites.[20] Each domain name is linked to an Internet Protocol address which is numeric, and the user-friendly address is attached to this unique code and allows users to navigate around the Internet. The difficultly with the numeric system is that it is not easy for the consumer to remember and these addresses could be mistyped without an easy way of spotting the error. Therefore, the domain name system creates a word-based structure, which is much more user-friendly for the consumer. There are two main types of domain name: the top level domain, with prefixes such as '.com', '.org' and '.net' and the second level domain such as '.uk' and '.fr'. Domain names form the basis of other methods or applications on the Internet, such as file transfer or email addresses. There are three ways in which one can acquire a domain name. The first way is to register with the appropriate registry (for example, Nominet in the United Kingdom), secondly to pay for the services of a registration broker, or thirdly to buy the name from the existing owner. Formerly, domain names had been distributed on a first-come, first-served system; however ICANN and the United Kingdom's devolved body for responsibility for issuing domain names, Nominet,[21] has an organised system, with built-in dispute resolution schemes. The role of ICANN and Nominet in this context is critical because if multiple companies had exactly the same domain name address the Internet would soon come to a halt. At the time of writing, Nominet manages over eight million '.uk' domain names. Domain names are crucial to businesses and the registration of a memorable domain name is necessary to a successful business. Businesses may want to register their name or trademark to ensure that customers not using a search engine will be able to locate the company's website. However, difficulties have arisen with registering a domain name. In some situations, two companies have very similar names and need to negotiate who is able to use the preferred name, while more troubling is the pre-emptive registration of domain names for companies not yet online which are then sold on at a vastly inflated figure. This is clearly of less relevance now than it was ten to fifteen years ago as companies were only beginning to exploit the advantages of the Internet, although cybersquatting is an issue of importance when considering domain names. As the holders of these registrations, 'cybersquatters' could put the domain names up for sale at an auction, or offer them for sale directly to the company or person involved, at prices far beyond the cost of registration. Alternatively, a 'cybersquatter' could keep the registration and use the name of the person or business associated with that domain name to attract business for the

---

[20] See **Pitman Training Limited v Nominet** [1997] EWHC Ch 367, which provided some general coverage about what a domain name is. For analysis of this decision see: Waelde, C *Is the Dam about to burst? An analysis of domain name disputes in the UK* (1997) Journal of Information Law and Technology, issue 2.

[21] See: http://www.nic.uk.

potentially-offending site. In the United Kingdom, many disputes as to domain names are litigated within laws relating to unfair competition, such as passing off and confusion.[22] Passing off is an area of law that protects the goodwill of business and seeks to restrain one business from passing off its goods or services as being those of another. A passing off claim can protect names, logos, materials, advertising themes and any other part of a business's general 'get-up' that distinguishes its goods or services from those of others. A claim for passing off will be made out if a misrepresentation is made by a business to potential customers which causes confusion as to the origin or association of its goods and/or services, and it is reasonably foreseeable that the goodwill of another business will be injured by this confusion and is likely to suffer loss as a result. For instance in **Marks & Spencer plc v One in a Million**[23] the claimant pre-emptively registered the trademarked names of companies (such as Ladbrokes, Virgin and British Telecommunication) as domain names. They did not use these domain names as substantive websites, although later tried to sell these domain names on to the company that owned the trade mark.[24] Even though there was no attempt by the defendant to pass themselves off as the claimant, the court insisted that the domain names be handed over to the owner of the trade mark. There were a number of problems with this decision, one of which was that it allowed 'big companies' to monopolise domain names close to their own trademark. Other domain name disputes may be connected to trade mark infringement, contract (where available) and tort (unlawful inducement of breach of contract or conspiracy). A further case heard by the Court of Appeal was **Phones4U Limited v Phone4U.co.uk Internet Limited**.[25] In this case, the Court of Appeal overturned the decision of the High Court and held that although there was no infringement of trade mark, the defendant was guilty of passing themselves off as the claimant. The facts were that the Phone4U.co.uk domain name was registered by a man called Abdul Heykali, who asserted that he did not know about the high street store Phones4U, even though it was a high profile brand at the time. Initially the site simply advertised services, although in early 2001 he began to offer to

---

[22] This is when a domain name is so similar to a well-known product or service that it is likely to result in confusion in the mind of the public that the website they are accessing is the famous brand and not the product or service actually offered on the website.

[23] [1998] FSR 265.

[24] See also: **Erven Warnick v Townsend** [1979] AC 731 and **Harrods v UK Network Services** [1997] 4 EIPR D-106.

[25] [2006] EWCA Civ 244. For a case comment see: *Phones 4U Limited v Phone4U.co.uk Internet Limited* (2007) Reports of Patent, Designs and Trade Mark cases, volume 124, issue 3, pages 83–106. See also OUT-LAW.COM *Phones4u wins passing off appeal against phone4u* (23rd May 2006). Available at: http://www.out-law.com/page-6942-theme=print. A similar case is that of **Easyjet Airline Co. Limited v Tim Dainty (T/A Easy Realestate)** [2002] FSR 6 where the transfer of the domain name 'easyRealestate.co.uk' to EasyJet was ordered on the basis of passing off and an injunction was granted to prevent Realestate from using the prefix of 'easy'.

sell mobile phones online. Even though there was a disclaimer on the website disassociating itself from Phones4U, the court held that there was evidence of passing off, which was strengthened when it came to light that Heykali allegedly tried to sell his domain name to Phones4U.

In the event of a domain name dispute, parties are encouraged to use the Uniform Domain Name Dispute Resolution Policy (UDRP) adopted by ICANN. The UDRP was prepared by the World Intellectual Property Organisation (WIPO), which is the organisation mandated by its members to promote the protection of intellectual property worldwide and to develop uniform and mandatory procedures to deal with cross-border domain name disputes. However, it appears that cybersquatting in its purest form no longer poses the same level of threat. This is primarily due to the effective removal of the 'first come, first served' policy, and a degree of priority for trade mark owners when registering domain names. Due to a more rigorous domain name registration procedure, and suitable dispute resolution mechanisms, the 'traditional' domain name dispute of cybersquatting is becoming less prevalent.[26] Whilst trade mark infringement is still an issue, in the main these matters can be dealt with by reference to the Trade Marks Act. There are also occasional unique occasions where cybersquatting is still prevalent, such as the 2012 Olympic Games in London, as was seen in the WIPO decision of **The London Organising Committee of the Olympic Games and Paralympic Games Limited v H & S Media Limited**.[27] In this case, the claimant pre-emptively registered the domain name 'mylondon2012.com'. As H & S Media had no legitimate claim to this domain they were required to hand it to the organising committee of the London Olympics.[28] It also appears that in more and more cases, when a person accesses the Internet, there is a greater desire and readiness to go through a search engine, such as Google. This means that typing in the search query should direct you to the website you are searching for. Businesses that are technically aware started to use methods such as metatags on their website. These are words or phrases which are written into the web pages but are hidden from view. This means that when a search engine searches for a website using the search terms it may be able to detect a metatag on a different website and accordingly send the individual to that site. This is clearly important from the point of view of businesses who will be keen to ensure that they maximise the number of visits to their site. Although search engine algorithms are now very sophisticated, it used to be the case that

---

[26] For a detailed analysis of the changing nature of the domain name dispute see: Colston, C *Passing off: the right solution to domain name disputes?* (2000) Lloyd's Maritime and Commercial Law Quarterly, pages 523–529.

[27] WIPO Case No. D2010-0415 (29th April 2010).

[28] For more on this judgment see: Foong Tan, C *The London Organising Committee of the Olympic Games and Paralympic Games Limited v H & S Media Limited* (2010) E-Commerce Law Reports, volume 10, issue 3, page 3.

including a number of keyword metatags meant that on a search engine results page the company would feature higher up – or ideally at the top – of the results list. The question which arises however, is whether use of another person's or company's trade mark constitutes a trade mark infringement. There are two main cases which have reached the courts in the United Kingdom on this issue: **Reed Executive Plc and another v Reed Business Information Ltd and others**[29] and **Road Tech Computer Systems Limited v Mandata (Management and Data Services) Limited**.[30] In the Road Tech case, the claimant discovered that words which they had trademarked were being used by the defendant on their website as metatags with a view to diverting traffic away from the claimant's website to their own. The court held that there had been an infringement of trade mark and the claimant was awarded £15,000, although the main reason for this judgment was arguably due to the defendant admitting to the infringement. This decision can be contrasted with the decision in Reed, which concerned two companies: Reed Employment (who were an employment agency with nearly 20 years experience) and Reed Elsevier (who were a publisher, although on their website they advertised employment opportunities). The issue in this case was that Reed Elsevier placed metatags on their website, such as 'job', 'recruitment' and 'reed business information'. Reed Employment alleged that Reed Elsevier were guilty of infringing their trade marks. While the High Court held in favour of Reed Employment and held that there had been an infringement, the Court of Appeal overturned this decision and held that there had been no infringement. The reason the court gave for this is that the use of a trade mark as a metatag is wholly invisible and does not reach a third party. The trade mark had not been 'used'.[31] There is also no confusion because all the user is doing is causing a webpage to appear higher up a search engine results page. Furthermore, there could be no passing off as the website operated by Reed Elsevier always appears underneath the website operated by Reed Employment in search results. This decision was supported by the case of **Victor Andrew Wilson v Yahoo! UK Limited and Overturn Services Limited**[32] in which the court held in an obiter comment that the use of a trade mark as a metatag did not constitute a trade mark infringement.[33]

This issue is far from resolved, particularly as search engines such as Google offer sponsored keyword advertising – so called 'AdWords'. This means that a

---

[29] [2004] 4 All ER 942.

[30] [1996] F.S.R. 805.

[31] Section 10(1) of the Trade Marks Act 1994 states that a person infringes a registered trade mark if he uses in the course of trade a sign which is identical to the trade mark.

[32] [2008] EWHC 361.

[33] Further (loose) support is found in the European Court of Justice case of **Gillette Company v LA-Laboratories Limited Oy C-228/03** (17th March 2005). See case comment *Advertising consumable – using a competitor's trade mark: Case C-228/03 The Gillette Company v LA-Laboratories Limited Oy (ECJ (Third Chamber), 17th March 2005)* (2005) Communications Law, volume 10, number 2, pages 59–61.

company can pay for a sponsored link on the search engine results page, which will appear prominently on the results page. The positioning of the advertisement will depend on the relevance and the amount that the company has paid to Google. The recent European Court of Justice decision in **Portakabin BV v Primakabin BV**[34] considered this issue. The facts were that Primakabin used the trade mark 'Portakabin' as a keyword in their Google AdWords campaign. Portakabin naturally objected to this and they argued that there was an infringement of their trade mark. The court held that a company is allowed to use another person's trade mark as long as there is no confusion between the two companies. If it is likely that the use of the trade mark will lead to detriment to any of the functions of that mark, then there will be a violation of that trade mark. Companies that select AdWords which are trade marks of third parties need to ensure that there is no possibility of confusion when they select them, otherwise there may be an infringement of that trade mark.[35] This case followed the decision handed down by the Court of Justice of the European Union in March 2010 in **Google France v Louis Vuitton Malletier**[36], which held that the Google AdWords system does not breach trade mark law, although in some situations, such as confusion about who was behind the advertisement or the suggestion that there is an economic link between the third party and the owner of the trade mark, companies can stop their trade marks from being used. The court held that Google simply provides the platform to allow companies to do business and Google itself does not infringe trade marks. Many companies object to the AdWords system because it means if they want to sponsor their own trade mark so that it appears more prominently on the results page they will have to pay more as third party companies may be sponsoring the same trade mark to advertise a different company. Despite this concern and the concern of the courts, in August 2010 Google announced that they would be testing the interpretation of these decisions by allowing companies to use trade marks as keywords in their AdWords system and refusing to act on any complaint about an infringement of a trade mark through AdWords.[37]

Intellectual Property issues

The use of a metatag and the protection of trade marks is just one of the potential intellectual property considerations in the Internet arena. It is important

---

[34] C-558/08 (8th July 2010).

[35] See case comment by Palmer, S *C-558/08 Portakabin BV v Primakabin BV* (2010) E-Commerce Law Reports, volume 10, issue 3, page 24.

[36] Cases 236/08 – 238/08 (23rd March 2010).

[37] See OUT-LAW.COM *Google to allow trade marks as keywords across Europe* (4th August 2010). Available at: http://www.out-law.com/page-11278-theme=print.

that consumers are protected from purchasing goods which have been falsely advertised as something that they are not. There are a range of different methods of obtaining goods and services online. Information can be transported very easily online. This same information can also be produced and copied, which can in turn lead to breaches of intellectual property rights. A person who creates an original work can hold the copyright, which is protected by the Copyright, Designs and Patents Act 1988. Section 1 of the Act states that copyright is a property right over original literary, musical, dramatic or artistic works. This includes sound recordings and films. This property right gives the author the exclusive right to copy the work, to issue copies, to rent or lease the work, to perform or adapt the work and to communicate the work to the public.[38] The reverse of this is that the copyright owner also has the ability to prevent these actions being carried out by another person without the other person being granted a licence from the copyright owner.[39] In order for there to be a breach of copyright a defendant must have used the whole or a substantial part of the work. In **Baigent v The Random House Group Limited**[40] the Court of Appeal rejected the argument of the claimants that in writing books, such as 'The Da Vinci Code' Dan Brown had copied large parts of their idea. The challenge posed by the Internet to copyright protection has been seen in the incidences of file sharing and music downloads. A high profile incident involved the peer-to-peer sharing service Napster. The principle behind Napster was that users could share files of music and films with other users and therefore bypass the traditional markets for selling such songs or films. This led to significant copyright violations as users were sharing the copyrighted work of another person without a licence. This came to a head with the American case of **A & M Records, Inc. v Napster Inc.**[41] where a number of recording companies joined together to commence an action against Napster under the Digital Millennium Copyright Act claiming that the users were directly infringing the copyright of the author's work and that Napster were contributing to this infringement by providing the platform. They brought an action against Napster, as opposed to the users, as their view was that it was better to go for the platform rather than the individual file sharers. This approach worked and Napster had to file for bankruptcy in 2002, although subsequently reopened. A similar case involved the American company Grokster, who provided the software for users to share files. A large number of the files that were shared were downloaded illegally and in **MGM Studios Inc. v Grokster Limited**[42] the court held that providing the software

---

[38] Copyright, Designs and Patents Act 1988, sections 16–21.
[39] Copyright, Designs and Patents Act 1988, section 90.
[40] [2007] FSR 24.
[41] USDC ND Cal, 114 F.Sup.2d 896 (10th August 2000).
[42] 125.S.Ct 2764 (2005).

for the copyright infringement to occur was illegal. Grokster was forced to pay $50m to companies within the music industry and eventually closed down later in 2005.

A more recent example involved the Swedish Group 'Pirate Bay'.[43] Pirate Bay was established in 2003 and at the height of its popularity had in excess of 22 million users. Pirate Bay operated a search engine that allowed people to locate films, music videos and games. Content was not held on their website, although BitTorrent links were. BitTorrent software allows users to download the same file at the same time in a significantly quicker time than normal. Four members of the Pirate Bay group were prosecuted in Sweden for promoting copyright infringement by providing the facilities for people to download files, which were subject to copyright. They were found guilty and sentenced to imprisonment for one year and were fined the equivalent of £3m. On appeal in November 2010, their prison sentences were reduced slightly, although the fine was increased to just over £4m.[44] Despite this court hearing, the Pirate Bay website has continued to operate.

Providing the software for a user to illegally download material which is the subject of copyright is one example of how the protection of intellectual property rights on the Internet is challenging. Other Internet-specific challenges include hyperlinking or deep-linking to a direct page on another person's website. The difficulty with this is that directly linking to another person's site may be infringing the copyright of that person. One of the earlier cases in this area is **Shetland Times Limited v Jonathan Wills**.[45] The question the court needed to consider in this case is whether a link from the defendant's own news website to an internal page on the Shetland Times website constituted an infringement of copyright. The court held that there had been a copyright infringement under the Copyright, Designs and Patents Act 1988 and granted an injunction preventing the defendant from linking directly into internal pages of the claimant's website. However, the defendant was able to provide links to the defendant's homepage.[46]

The challenges of illegal file sharing were one of eleven topics considered in the Digital Economy Act 2010.[47] This Act followed the substantial Digital Britain Report in 2009[48], which made a number of recommendations to

---

[43] See: http://thepiratebay.org/

[44] See BBC News *Pirate Bay founders lose appeal* (26th November 2010). Available at: http://www.bbc.co.uk/news/technology-11847200.

[45] [1997] FSR 604.

[46] For more on this issue see: Sangal, T *IP issues in linking, framing and keyword linked advertising* (2010) Computer and Telecommunications Law Review, volume 16, issue 3, pages 64–67.

[47] Other topics include the role of OFCOM, video classification and the registration of Internet domain names.

[48] CM 7650. Available at: http://www.official-documents.gov.uk/document/cm76/7650/7650.pdf.

ensure that Britain is adequately equipped to deal with the digital age. The Act received Royal Assent in April 2010 and it contains 48 sections with a further two schedules. Sections 3–16 of the Act insert sections 124A–124N into the Communications Act 2003 and require OFCOM to produce guidelines for Internet Service Providers and those who hold copyright about how they deal with illegal file sharing. This has the aim of making it easier to track down and prosecute illegal file sharers. These guidelines allow those who hold copyright to make a list of addresses of people whom they believe are infringing their copyright. They would then send these addresses to the relevant Internet Service Provider. The cost for collecting the addresses of people infringing copyright rests with the copyright holder. On receipt of this list, the Internet Service Provider must then contact the subscriber who is infringing copyright along with a Copyright Infringement Report. The Internet Service Provider is required to keep a list of the recipients of these reports. Copyright holders are entitled to ask for this list, although the names should be anonymous. There are financial penalties for Internet Service Providers who fail to comply with these requirements. The more controversial part of the legislation is the available penalties for persistent infringers, which include technical restrictions, including preventing people from accessing the Internet by suspending their broadband connection.[49] It was partly due to the controversial nature of this legislation that a number of Internet Service Providers were granted a judicial review in November 2010 to consider the legality of the legislation. The Act will be reviewed in 2011 with a particular focus on whether the legislation contradicts the provisions in the E-Commerce Directive, which limit the liability of Internet Service Providers for information held on their systems.[50]

Key points:

- The Internet provides the forum for a wide spectrum of legal issues, such as the Google-Italy case. The range of challenges posed to the law by the Internet merit the subject being considered in its own right.
- The Internet started life as an American defence tool, although it has since developed into cyberspace as we know it today and has revolutionised the way in which people lead their lives.

---

[49] For more on the Digital Economy Act 2010, see the Explanatory Notes at: http://www.legislation.gov.uk/ukpga/2010/24/notes?timeline=true, and Farrand, B *The Digital Economy Act 2010 – a cause for celebration, or a cause for concern?* (2010) European Intellectual Property Review, volume 32, issue 10, pages 536–541.

[50] See: BBC News *Net providers get Digital Economy Act judicial review* (10th November 2010). Available at: http://www.bbc.co.uk/news/technology-11724760.

- Domain names are user-friendly addresses that allow people to have a presence online. The Internet Corporation for Assigned Names and Numbers (ICANN) has overall responsibility for the distribution of domain names.
- ICANN has been the subject of considerable controversy as the organisation comes within the remit of the US Department of Commerce, the perception being that the American government has too much involvement in the running of the Internet.
- The two-stage World Summit on Information Society Meetings (Stage 1 was held in Geneva in 2003, with the second stage being held in Tunis in 2005) sought a resolution to this difficulty.
- The .xxx domain name dispute is an example of alleged governmental involvement in the running of the Internet. Although this proposal was initially rejected, in 2010 ICANN agreed to create this new top-level domain.
- During the early stages of web development a series of problems occurred with domain names, which related to passing off, trade mark infringement and confusion. The main case in this area is **Reed Executive Plc and another v Reed Business Information Ltd and others**.
- The current approach of the court is that the use of a trade mark as a metatag is permitted as in **Victor Andrew Wilson v Yahoo! UK Limited and Overturn Services Limited**.
- Recent decisions by the European Court of Justice suggests that trade marks can be used as metatags and also in sponsored advertising as long as there is no confusion about where the advertisement comes from and it is clear that there is no economic connection between the third party and the trade mark.
- There have been a number of cases around the world where courts have demonstrated a dislike for, and have found against, a number of platforms that offer the ability for users to download material that is subject to copyright. Cases in this area include Napster, Grokster and more recently, Pirate Bay.

Further reading:

Books

- Murray, A *The Regulation of Cyberspace,* Routledge Cavendish (2007).

Published Papers

- Azmi, I D *Domain names and cyberspace: the application of old norms to new problems* (2000) International Journal of Law and Information Technology, volume 8, number 2, pages 193–213.

- Bond, R *Business trends in virtual worlds and social networks – an overview of the legal and regulatory issues relating to intellectual property and money transfers* (2009) Entertainment Law Review, volume 20, issue 4, pages 121–128.

- Chaudri, A *Metatags and banner advertisements – do they infringe trade mark rights?* (2004) Computer Law and Security Report, volume 20, number 5, pages 402–404.

- Daly, M *Trade Marks, Search Engines and Fair Play* (October/November 2005) Computers and Law, pages 32–36.

- Deveci, H *Domain Names: Has Trade Mark Law Strayed From Its Path?* (2003) International Journal of Law and Information Technology, volume 11, number 3, pages 203–225.

- Edwards, L *Mandy and Me: Some Thoughts on the Digital Economy Bill* (2009) ScriptEd, volume 6, issue 3.

- Huston, G *ICANN, the ITU and WSIS, and Internet governance* (2004) World Internet Law Report, Volume 11, Issue 4, pages 26–30.

- Kleinwachter, W *WSIS and Internet governance: the struggle over the core resources of the Internet* (2006) Communications Law, Volume 11, number 1, pages 3–12.

- Koempel, F *Digital Economy Bill* (2010) Computer and Telecommunications Law Review, volume 16, issue 2, pages 41–43.

- Lessig, L *The Zones of Cyberspace* (May 1996) Stanford Law Review, Volume 48, Issue 5, pages 1403–1411.

- Marsden, C T *Beyond Europe: The Internet, Regulation, and Multi-stakeholder Governance – Representing the Consumer Interest?* (2008) Journal of Consumer Policy, volume 31, pages 115–132.

- Murray, A D *The use of trade marks as metatags: defining the boundaries* (2000) International Journal of Law and Information Technology, volume 8, number 3, pages 263–284.

- Murray, A D *Free Expression and Censorship through Design Protocols: A Misapplication of the ICANN UDRP* (2002). Paper given at the 17th Annual BILETA Conference, Amsterdam and available at: http://www.bileta.ac.uk/Document%20Library/1/Free%20Expression%20and%20Censorship%20Through%20Design%20Protocols%20-%20A%20Misapplication%20of%20the%20ICANN%20UDRP.pdf.

- Rogers, K M *The Early Ground Offensives in Internet Governance* (2007) International Review of Law, Computers and Technology, Volume 21, Issue 1, pages 5–14.

- Weber, R *Transparency and the governance of the Internet* (2008) Computer Law and Security Report, volume 24, issue 4, pages 342–348.

Questions for consideration:

1.1.   Outline the advantages and disadvantages of the Internet.

1.2.   To what extent do you agree with the statement that the law relating to the Internet should be taught as a subject in its own right?

1.3.   Provide a timeline of the key events leading to the Affirmation of Commitments signed between ICANN and the American government.

1.4.   'Discussions concerning Internet governance are parochial. No-one really cares who runs the Internet as long as it works.'
To what extent do you agree with this statement?

1.5.   In May 2006, ICANN, the body responsible for top-level domain names, refused permission for a top-level '.xxx' domain name to be introduced. This decision was criticised for being politically motivated and for demonstrating overt American interference with the running of the Internet. This matter was continually debated and in June 2010, ICANN agreed to take forward the '.xxx' proposal. This issue alone demonstrates the importance of the subject of Internet governance, which is exemplified by the establishment of an Internet Governance Forum, which will undoubtedly prove to be a success in the long term.
Critically evaluate this statement.

1.6.   How has the nature of the domain name dispute evolved in recent years?

1.7.   The decision in **Reed Executive Plc and another v Reed Business Information Ltd and others** [2004] 4 All ER 942 recognised a completely new approach to domain name disputes. The legality of this new type of domain name dispute, involving so-called metatags, is still uncertain within the United Kingdom and the International community.
Discuss.

1.8.   'The sponsoring of trade marks in order to secure a sponsored link, which appears in a prominent position on a search engine results page is common practice. For instance, Google operates an AdWords system which allows companies to sponsor keywords. When these keywords are typed into the search terms box, the companies that have sponsored that particular keyword will appear on the results page ranked in terms of relevancy and who has paid the most money. The use of trade marks in this business is an issue of controversy and a number of cases on this issue have reached the European Courts. However, as it stands, the approach of the courts is to the benefit of companies, but to the detriment of protecting trade marks.'
Undertake a critical evaluation of this viewpoint.

1.9.   What approaches have been taken by courts around the world to plat-
        forms which provide a service for users to download copyrighted files,
        without actually hosting any of the illegal material themselves?

1.10.   Outline the provisions of the Digital Economy Act 2010 insofar as they
        apply to online copyright infringement. How robust do you consider
        these provisions to be?

All weblinks mentioned in the text can also be found at:
http://www.palgrave.com/law/rogers

2 Online Contracting

This chapter will consider:

- Whether computers can make contracts.
- An appraisal of traditional common law rules on contracting and an examination of their suggested application to modern forms of technology.
- The incorporation of terms and conditions in an electronic contract.
- The availability of online auction sites and how they are altering online purchasing.
- The requirements placed on online businesses by regulatory bodies and legislation.

Contracts play an essential part in everyday life, from the purchase of a small item in a supermarket to a multi-million-pound international transaction. The formalities to a contract have been commonplace in English law for some time and are a staple diet for all law students. Under English law, for a contract to be valid several conditions must be satisfied: there needs to be a clear offer made and an unequivocal acceptance given. There needs to be an intention to create legal relations on each side and each party to the contract is required to provide some form of consideration. The massive expansion of internet trading (often at the expense of more traditional methods) has led to much discussion on the law of internet contracts, the bulk of which has focussed on ensuring legal certainty in the formation of the contract, specifically, at what point a contract is concluded and how parties can ensure that the relevant terms and conditions are incorporated into the agreement. These are important issues. The moment an acceptance is given is the moment that a contract is actually in existence and also means that the ability to withdraw an offer has ended. Acceptance could also be a deciding factor in ascertaining jurisdiction or which terms and conditions are used in the performance of the contract and may have a bearing from the point of view of taxation. Answers to the questions of when an offer is accepted in an online contract and how to ensure that the relevant terms and conditions are incorporated have been rooted in the traditional common law approach. Before exploring whether the traditional rules are relevant for twenty-first century Internet commerce, it is important to be reminded of the foundations of English contract law.

Offer

An offer is made by an offeror and it is a clear indication to be bound by the terms of the offer, and becomes an agreement once the offeree (the recipient of the offer) has accepted. An offer can be communicated in a number of ways, including verbally, in written form or by electronic communications. For there to be a successful agreement, a clear, definitive offer must be made to another party or to the public at large in which case it is termed a unilateral offer as in the well-known case of **Carlill v Carbolic Smoke Ball Company**.[1] Generally, an offer can be withdrawn before a valid acceptance is made[2] but this revocation must be received by the offeree before the offer is accepted. An offer is terminated by a counteroffer,[3] but a request for further information does not negate the original offer. An offer should not be confused with an invitation to treat. The distinction between an offer and an invitation to treat is that an offer is a statement by which a person is willing to contract, whereas if a person is merely seeking to start negotiations, then that is deemed to be an invitation to treat. Examples of an invitation to treat include tenders, advertisements, calling for bids at an auction and goods on display in a shop window.[4] An invitation to treat is not intended to be legally binding but unfortunately might be construed by the customer as such.

Acceptance

An offer on its own cannot form a contract; there needs to be an acceptance. In the majority of cases, acceptance has to be communicated in order for it to be effective.[5] Unless specifically stipulated, acceptance can be made by any communication method that is reasonable. The acceptance must be a clear and unequivocal acceptance of the original offer (a mirror image acceptance must be made to the offer) and there must be an external form of assent on

---

[1] [1893] 1 QB 256.

[2] **Payne v Cave** (1789) 3 Term Rep 148.

[3] **Hyde v Wrench** (1840) 3 Beav 334.

[4] See: **Fisher v Bell** [1961] 1 QB 394 and **Pharmaceutical Society of Great Britain v Boots** [1952] 2 QB 795. In the latter case Lord Goddard CJ was of the view that exposing goods for sale merely indicates that he is willing to treat. It does not equate to an offer to sell. Furthermore, **Partridge v Crittenden** [1968] 2 All ER 421 held that an advertisement in a magazine was also an invitation to treat.

[5] See: **Powell v Lee** (1908) 99 LT 284.

the part of the acceptor. Silence cannot normally be conferred as acceptance.[6] There are exceptions to the rule that acceptance must be communicated in order to be effective, for instance if the parties have a long standing course of dealing or in circumstances where conduct could be held to constitute acceptance as in **Brogden v Metropolitan Railway Company**[7], **Graeme Grant v Russell Bragg**[8] and **RTS Flexible Systems Limited v Molkerei Alois Müller Gmbh & Company KG (UK Production)**.[9] In the RTS case, a contract was not actually signed and exchanged between the two parties, however the parties behaved as if it was. A dispute arose about the performance of part of the machinery involved. On appeal, the Supreme Court was asked to decide how much (if any) of the contract was in force. The court held that as both parties behaved as if the contract was in force, then the court should treat the contract as if it were fully agreed. One of the more obvious exceptions to the rule that silence cannot amount to consent is the 'postal rule' acceptance. The postal acceptance rule was established at the time when post was the main method of communication and stipulates that a contract is made when a posted acceptance is placed into a postbox. Even if the letter containing the acceptance is not delivered to the offeror a contract is still in existence provided the envelope is properly addressed and stamped and put beyond the reach of the acceptor.[10] This principle has its roots as far back as **Adams v Lindsell**[11] and also in **Byrne v Van Tienhoven**[12] in which Lindley J stated:

> "It may be taken as now settled that, where an offer is made and accepted by letters sent through the post, the contract is completed the moment the letter accepting the offer is posted, even though it never reaches its destination."[13]

The postal rule adds a degree of certainty to the contracting process as the contract is concluded the moment the letter is dropped into the box and enters the custodianship of the Post Office.[14] The rule exists because the moment the acceptor has put his acceptance in the post box, he has done an act which he cannot revoke; the postal services will not allow the sender to retrieve his letter from the post box and the letter will be delivered to the addressed destination.

---

[6] See: **Felthouse v Bindley** (1862) 142 ER 1037.

[7] (1877) 2 App. Cas. 666.

[8] [2009] EWHC 74 (Ch).

[9] [2010] UKSC 14.

[10] See: **Household Fire and Carriage Accident Insurance Company (Limited) v Grant** (1878–79) LR 4 Ex D 216.

[11] (1818) 1 B & Ald 681.

[12] (1880) 5 CPD 344.

[13] Ibid. page 348.

[14] See: **Re: London & Northern Bank** [1900] 1 Ch 220.

Thus public policy appears to necessitate certainty in this situation. However, what is the situation when there is no apparent intermediary? Naturally, it is possible to accept an offer where no intermediary is involved (for instance by telephone, fax or telex), but the postal rule is not applicable in these situations. Instead there is the instantaneous communication acceptance rule, as found in the cases of **Entores v Miles Far East Corporation**,[15] **Brinkibon Limited v Stahag Stahl und Stahlwarenhandelsgesellschaft mbH**[16] and **The Brimnes**.[17] The rule is that acceptance is deemed to have been communicated at the instant (the communication may not be instantaneous, but acceptance is assumed at the instant that the document is (presumed to be) received) when the offeror has, or can reasonably be presumed to have received it. This is because as the communication is instantaneous this is deemed to have the same effect as being physically in each other's company. Parker LJ in **Entores** stated:

> "So far as telex messages are concerned, though the despatch and receipt of the message is not completely instantaneous, the parties are to all intents and purposes in each other's presence just as if they were in telephonic communications, and I see no reason for departing from the general rule that there is no binding contract until notice of the acceptance is received by the offeror."[18]

The postal acceptance rule and the instantaneous communication acceptance rule have formed the basis of contract law studies for decades, but it is appropriate to reconsider their applicability in the light of the context provided by the Internet and other speedy methods of communicating. The courts have shown that they are not afraid to propose a move away from the traditional approach. For instance in **Holwell Securities Limited v Hughes**[19] the court was of the view that if the postal rule would lead to manifest inconvenience and absurdity they should be able to deviate from following its prescriptive nature and not slavishly follow the principle. More recently in **Apple Corps Limited v Apple Computer Inc**[20] the Chancery Division held that they could see no conceptual barrier to why a contract could not be formed in more than one jurisdiction. They acknowledged the general principle that when instantaneous communication is used in the creation of a contract the contract is made in the place that the acceptance is received, but noted that there could be situations where a contract could be made in two places at once and in these situations the court needs to be more flexible in analysing the creation of the contract.

---

[15] [1955] 2 All ER 493.
[16] [1983] 2 AC 34.
[17] [1974] 3 All ER 88.
[18] [1995] 2 All ER 493, at page 498.
[19] [1974] 1 All ER 161.
[20] [2004] EWHC 768 (Ch).

Communicating offers and acceptances online

There is no requirement for individuals to meet face to face in order to create a contract. The chief way for a company to advertise its products to individuals is by the creation of a website. These can be set up to demonstrate the full catalogue of products, while also providing the medium for consumers to purchase goods. A website can be a very cost-effective and relatively low maintenance method for a company or business to advertise its goods or services. Whether a website can itself, legally, make offers is less certain. To date there has been no case to provide direction on whether a website makes offers or invitations to treat. The presumption is that a website is similar to a shop window and so the goods displayed on the site are not an offer, but an invitation to treat. Accordingly, the website visitor would make an offer for an item he would like to purchase, which the business would then accept. This would appear to make some sense as it follows the traditional approach in the United Kingdom.[21] However, the situation is muddled somewhat by the instantaneous nature of the Internet. A consumer could place an order via a website and within a couple of moments the business is able to send a confirmation email acknowledging the order, means of payment and perhaps even some guidance on delivery times. Does a confirmation email constitute acceptance? In 1999 and 2002, this very issue was in the spotlight. In 1999, Argos inadvertently advertised a Sony television on their website for £2.99, instead of the recommended price of £299. Thousands of people placed an order for this television. Shortly after each order was received, Argos sent out a confirmation of order email to each customer, acknowledging the purchase of the television at the lower price of £2.99. After Argos noticed their mistake, they withdrew the television from sale immediately and refused to honour any of the orders. Despite legal action being threatened by annoyed customers, no case materialised and Argos refused to honour the television sales. These facts are almost identical to a situation involving Kodak in 2002. Kodak advertised a top-of-the-range camera on its website for £100 instead of the recommended price of £349. Again an email confirmation was sent by Kodak, but perhaps the difference in this case was that the confirmation referred to the contract being formed. After being threatened with legal action, Kodak eventually conceded and honoured all the orders placed for this particular product. It is unclear whether Kodak were fearful of the bad publicity arising from a court action, which they had no guarantee of winning or whether an internal review of their legal processes suggested that there were deficiencies with their website and terms and conditions. It seems that the difference in phraseology on the confirmation of order

---

[21] See cases such as: **Fisher v Bell** [1961] 1 QB 394 and **Pharmaceutical Society of Great Britain v Boots** [1952] 2 QB 795.

between these situations was critical to the differing approaches taken by these two companies to honouring the order. Sadly, from the point of view of legal certainty neither of these cases reached the courts, but the lesson for companies is to ensure that terms and conditions are specific enough to ensure that an order confirmation does not equate to an acceptance and a clause which states that the price which is advertised may be incorrect and the business reserves the right to correct the price and offer the good to the customer again at the accurate amount.[22] As seen in these incidents, acceptance in online transactions has the potential to be extremely controversial.[23] In e-commerce contracts the acceptance is usually communicated to a machine (the computer) or is made by a machine. This raises the question as to whether English law recognises a computer as a proper contracting party. In general, the law will attribute acts and omissions of a machine to the person who executes it.[24] The use of a computer to make a contract does not affect the validity of the contract – indeed we have been using machines (such as vending machines) to make contracts for many years. However, the difference with the Internet is that the contract is concluded remotely. In a face-to-face transaction these points do not usually give rise to difficulty, but where parties are dealing at a distance, as in online contracts, the exact point at which the contract is concluded can be controversial. Determining this is important for a number of reasons. First of all, it establishes when a negotiating party's right to unilaterally withdraw is lost. Secondly, it shows which acceptance is first in time if there are competing acceptances for a limited number of contractual opportunities, and finally, it establishes where the contract is concluded, which will be a key factor in determining which jurisdiction's law applies to the contract in cross-border transactions.

Online contracts can take a variety of forms, for instance electronic data exchange, contracts concluded through email, or contracts concluded through

---

[22] For more on these cases see: Howitt, P *The perils of online pricing* (2003) E-Commerce Law and Policy, volume 5, issue 4, pages 2–3; Rogers, K M *Snap! Internet "offers" under scrutiny again* (2002) Business Law Review, volume 23, issue 3, pages 70–72; Rogers, K M *Snap-Happy consumers leave Kodak in the Dark* (2002) Business Law Review, volume 23, issue 5, pages 112–114; Thompson, D *Contracting and advertising over the Internet – Argos's failure to honour Internet orders* (2000) International Journal of Electronic Commerce Law and Practice, volume 1, issue 1, pages 53–58; Jones, S *Forming electronic contracts in the United Kingdom* (2000) International Company and Commercial Law Review, volume 11, issue 9, pages 301–308; and Azim-Kahn, R & MacQueen, H L *The Argos free TV debate: two legal opinions* (1999) Electronic Business Law, volume 1, issue 9, pages 9–10.

[23] In June 2010, the supermarket Asda also found itself at the centre of a high profile website error as their website promised all first-time customers a £75 discount on their shopping. On noticing the error, they contacted all customers who had placed an order and told them that they would need to pay the full price or their order would be cancelled. See: BBC News *Asda apologies to customers for offering £75 discount* (14th June 2010). Available at: http://news.bbc.co.uk/1/hi/business/10312959.stm.

[24] **Thornton v Shoe Lane Parking** [1971] 1 All ER 686.

an interactive website (including click-wrap, which is a type of agreement often found on the Internet, usually used in the installation of software packages). Equally, as mobile commerce and other remote systems of communicating develop, methods of contracting are evolving at a considerable rate. Contract law has developed well-established rules for contract formation governing offer and acceptance, consideration and intention to create legal relations in relation to 'traditional' contract formation. However, when one stands back and looks at how contracts can be concluded electronically, an examination is needed as to whether the two main acceptance rules (postal rule and instantaneous communication rule) should apply to online contracts or whether a completely different system should exist.

Two main arguments have been put forward. First of all, that all Internet communication is instantaneous and thus subject to the instantaneous communication acceptance rule advocated in Entores and Brinkibon. This would mean that in all communication carried out on the Internet, a contract would be concluded at the time when the acceptance can reasonably be said to have reached the offeror. A second view is that a distinction should be made between contracts concluded by use of email and those concluded over the World Wide Web (such as through a website). The technical argument for the distinction between email and the World Wide Web is that email communication is not instantaneous as there is no direct link between the two people communicating by email. All email communication goes through a server, and the argument follows that as there is an intermediary (which could be argued to be akin to the Post Office) email communication cannot be instantaneous. Furthermore, once the 'send' button has been pressed by the sender there is very little, if anything, that can be done to retrieve the correspondence although the fact that some email users can retract sent emails before they have been received adds an unfortunate degree of uncertainty. The technicalities of sending an email differ slightly to that of an interactive website as with the latter, communication is usually facilitated directly between the parties along a telephone line. Accordingly, the argument advanced for acceptance by email is that the postal rule should be the applicable means of confirming when a contract is finalised. As an email is irretrievably routed through a third party server, once the sender has clicked the 'send' button there is nothing that they can do to get the email back. At the same time, for contracts concluded via an instantaneous click-wrap agreement, the instantaneous communication acceptance rule is advanced.[25]

---

[25] For more on the discussion on which rules should apply to online contractual acceptance see: Wang, F F *E-Confidence: offer and acceptance in online contracting* (2008) International Review of Law, Computers and Technology, volume 22, issue 3, pages 271–278; Capps, D *Electronic mail and the postal rule* (2004) International Company and Commercial Law Review, volume 15, issue 7, pages 207–212.

There are a number of problems with these proposals. First of all, the appropriateness of applying aged authorities (in some cases nearly 200 years old) to modern forms of communication by imposing a fringe technical distinction needs to be questioned. To date no court has considered whether the approaches should be adopted by the common law on a formal basis. Further, the technical distinction tends to pale into insignificance when the actual speed of sending an email is considered. Although email, strictly speaking, is not instantaneous it is still significantly faster than posting a letter. An email can be received in seconds and although it does go through a third party, the need for the postal rule to supply legal certainty is required to a much lesser extent, especially as senders can set up responses which will show whether the email has been sent, received, read or rejected.

A third way

It is suggested that perhaps the courts need to be a bit more courageous in dealing with the issue of online contract formation. Cases such as Holwell Securities and Apple (mentioned above) suggest that the courts have shown willingness to move away from the rigid traditional contract formation rules. During the 1970s there was a small handful of cases, which suggested that the courts should be willing to move away from traditional contractual formation rules and a move towards a more subjective approach which looked at the intention of the parties involved. The so-called 'battle of the forms' cases, such as **Butler Machine Tool v Ex-Cello Corporation**[26] and **Gibson v Manchester City Council**[27] were factually similar in that offers, counter-offers and substantial amounts of information passed between the parties involved and the court was required to confirm where in fact the contract had been created.[28] In **Tekdata Interconnections Limited v Amphenol Limited**[29] the Court of Appeal needed to examine whether a contract between two companies, who had a long term business relationship, was in fact in existence. The judge was of the view that the traditional offer and acceptance rules should be applied unless there was a clear indication from the documents passing between the parties that some other terms should be adopted. In this case, however the

---

[26] [1979] 1 All ER 965.

[27] [1979] 1 All ER 972.

[28] More recent 'battle of the forms' cases include: **Sterling Hydraulics Limited v Dichtomatik Limited** [2006] EWHC 2004 (QB) and **J Murphy & Sons Limited v Johnson Precast Limited** [2008] EWHC 3024 (TCC). Furthermore, the High Court has held in a preliminary hearing that if companies cannot agree whose terms and conditions should be applied then neither company's terms can be enforced. See: **GHSP INC v AB Electronic Limited** [2010] EWHC 1828 (Comm). In these circumstances it is the responsibility of commercial law to step in and ascertain liability and in this case the Sale of Goods Act 1979 was of relevance.

[29] [2009] All ER (D) 208.

court did rely on the traditional approach to contract formation and found against Tekdata.[30] Whether a more subjective approach to deciding if an online contract has actually been formed is to be favoured is a moot point. Arguably from a consumer protection point of view, it is imperative that the consumer knows exactly what they have agreed to. However, the range of technology and the ease of contracting with organisations around the world does necessitate that the courts offer greater flexibility in determining whether or not a contract is indeed in existence.

European Assistance: The European Union's e-Commerce Directive

The European Union's Directive on certain legal aspects of information society services[31], in particular electronic commerce, in the Internal Market (Directive on electronic commerce) was introduced in 2000.[32] It seeks to establish a framework for electronic commence to provide legal certainty for both consumers and businesses.[33] It covers a wide range of issues listed in Article 1(2), including the place and establishment of information society service providers, the liability of Internet Service Providers,[34] requirements placed on online service providers, commercial communications,[35] guidance on the creation of electronic contracts and codes to increase consumer protection online.[36] The overarching objective of the Directive is to allow information society services to move freely between member states.[37] The Directive does not

---

[30] For a detailed analysis of traditional contract formation and battle of the forms cases see: Mitchell, C. *Contracts and contract law: challenging the distinction between the "real" and "paper" deal* (2009) Oxford Journal of Legal Studies, volume 29, issue 4, pages 675–704.

[31] Ibid. Recital 17. The definition of an information society service already exists within European legislation as any service normally provided for remuneration, at a distance, by means of electronic equipment for the processing (including digital compression) and storage of data, and at the individual request of a recipient of a service.

[32] Directive 2000/31/EC on E-Commerce is available at: http://eur-lex.europa.eu/LexUriServ/LexUriServ.do?uri=CELEX:32000L0031:EN:NOT. For initial reaction to the Directive see: Rawson, S. *An emerging framework for electronic commerce: The EU Electronic Commerce Directive and related developments* (1999) International Company and Commercial Law Review, volume 10, issue 6, pages 171–175.

[33] Ibid. Recital 7.

[34] Ibid. Contained with Articles 12–15 and considered in more detail in this book in chapter 8 on Defamation.

[35] Ibid. Defined in Article 2(f) as any communication designed to promote the goods and services of a company. An offer and/or an invitation to treat made by an online business would be treated as a commercial communication.

[36] Ibid. Articles 16–20.

[37] Ibid. Article 1. Recital 59 furthers this principle by arguing that regulation at European level is necessary to avoid fragmentation of the internal market and to ensure that the European Union can place itself in a strong negotiating position in international forums. Whether this can be achieved with a minimum harmonisation directive is a moot point.

apply to taxation, issues covered by Directive 95/46/EC (Data Protection Directive) or Directive 97/66/EC (Directive on the processing of personal data in the telecommunications sector), cartel law, public authority, issues before a court relating to a client and their defence, or gambling.[38] The Directive was implemented into the United Kingdom by the Electronic Commerce (EC Directive) Regulations 2002[39] and the Regulations followed the terms contained within the original Directive very closely.

The terms of the Directive make provision for principles to be applied by member states to ensure that consumers who place online orders are protected. The underlying principle espoused in recital 7 is to ensure legal certainty and consumer confidence. The Directive is keen to remove as many obstacles to online contracting as possible. Member states are also required to amend legislation which may impose restrictions as to online contract formation.[40] Any legal obstacles to online contracting must be removed, although alterations must be in conformity with Community Law.[41] The key terms in the Directive that deal with consumer contracts are found within Section 3; specifically Articles 9–11.

Article 9 – Treatment of contracts

Article 9 emphasises the objectives behind the Directive and outlines that member states must ensure that their legal system allows contracts to be concluded by electronic means. It is important that legal requirements applicable to the contractual process neither create obstacles for the use of electronic contracts nor result in such contracts being deprived of legal effectiveness and validity on account of their having been made by electronic means. Article 9(2) does allow member states to derogate from this general principle in certain contracts, including those relating to: contracts that create or transfer rights in real estate, except for rental rights; contracts requiring by law the involvement of courts, public authorities or professions exercising public authority; contracts of suretyship granted on collateral securities furnished by persons acting for purposes outside their trade, business or profession; and contracts governed by family law or by the law of succession. It is the responsibility of the member state to indicate to the Commission (and update this list every five years) the types of contract that they feel fall within the exception.[42]

---

[38] Ibid. Article 1(5).
[39] Statutory Instrument 2002/2013. Available at: http://www.opsi.gov.uk/si/si2002/20022013.htm (Crown Copyright 2002).
[40] Recital 34. Some exceptions listed in recital 36 are permissible (examples include contracts involving the courts, public authorities or professions exercising a public authority).
[41] Recitals 37 and 38.
[42] Article 9(3).

The provisions of Article 9 added nothing new to the online formation of contracts within the United Kingdom. That contracts should be able to be concluded online was laid out by the (now annulled) Electronic Communications Act 2000, and indeed the UNCITRAL Model Law on Electronic Commerce 1996[43] also had an equivalent provision.

Article 10 – Information to be provided

This Article places an obligation on the member states to specify certain requirements for business-to-consumer contracts. The Directive has adopted a minimum harmonisation approach, meaning that the information that a service provider needs to supply is a bare minimum and also means that a member state can develop an extended approach, leading to different rules in different countries. In terms of the requirements of Article 10, the service provider needs to specify clearly, comprehensibly and unambiguously and prior to the order being placed by the recipient of the service various items of information such as the different technical steps to follow to conclude the contract, whether or not the concluded contract will be filed by the service provider and whether it will be accessible. The service provider also needs to explain the technical means for identifying and correcting any input errors prior to placing the order, and also the languages that can be used in concluding the contract.[44] It is incumbent on the service provider to ensure that the terms and conditions displayed online can be downloaded and saved for reproduction by the customer.[45] It should be noted that these provisions do not apply where the contract is made exclusively by the exchange of emails or equivalent individual communications.[46] They only apply to contracts made over the Internet (usually by a click-wrap method). Emails are to be treated differently because they are not 'real-time' communications in that they are not instantaneous as the email goes through a third party prior to reaching its destination. It would appear that the postal rule will apply to email acceptances but not click-wrap acceptances. However the reality, as discussed previously, is that email can be, and often is, as instantaneous as contracts made directly over the Internet and perhaps this artificial distinction needs to be removed.

---

[43] See: http://www.uncitral.org/uncitral/en/uncitral_texts/electronic_commerce/1996Model.html.
[44] Article 10(1)(a–d).
[45] Article 10(3).
[46] Article 10(4).

Article 11 – Placing of the order

This article outlines the requirements on business regarding consumer contracts. Parties to online contracts between businesses are able to agree to their own terms. The core principle is that where the recipient of the service places his order through technological means, the service provider has to acknowledge the receipt of the recipient's order without undue delay and by electronic means. In practice, this acts as a 'confirmation of order email' that a consumer would receive when they place an order for goods or services online. Article 11(1) continues by stating that the order and the acknowledgement of receipt are deemed to be received when the parties to whom they are addressed are able to access them. This appears to be adopting the principle behind the instantaneous communication acceptance rule as highlighted in cases such as Entores and Brinkibon, although there is one crucial difference as Article 11 is simply laying down principles for the front end of the contract – the offer, or the order. The confirmation is not an acceptance, but merely a confirmation to the consumer that they have ordered the correct item. Article 11(2) states that the service provider makes available to the recipient of the service appropriate, effective and accessible technical means allowing him to identify and correct input errors, prior to the placing of the order. Although this means that technical or input errors can be corrected at the start of the contract, we are not given adequate guidance on the precise moment the contract is formed. This is an important issue, as a contract cannot simply arise from a series of communications. The moment a contract is formed may also have bearing on the jurisdiction and the terms and conditions that are applied to the contact. By failing to address the exact point of acceptance in a contract there remains a glaring hole in the legislation. Therefore, there remains a gap in legal certainty in this area as to the moment an online offer is accepted.

Incorporation of contractual terms and conditions

The terms and conditions within a contract are vital in determining the rights and liabilities of both parties should a dispute arise. Therefore, one of the most important issues for an online trader is to ensure that its standard terms and conditions are properly incorporated into contracts with its customers. If the terms and conditions are not incorporated, the parties to the agreement will not be able to rely on them and this may lead to lengthy and costly legal proceedings. A number of methods are presently used to draw the website user's attention to the terms and conditions. These include a hyperlink to a separate webpage, a dialog box which the user needs to scroll though or simply putting all the terms and conditions in the middle of the page, which the user needs to assent to by ticking a box at the bottom of the page. The website owner needs to achieve a balance between maximising legal certainty by ensuring the terms and conditions are fully incorporated, whilst maintaining the commercial attractiveness of the website, as users may be more likely to avoid a website that is weighed-down with lengthy legal verbosity. This problem is becoming increasingly more complex for online retailers as websites are also being accessed by wireless devices such as a BlackBerry, iPhone or mobile phone, making it very difficult to bring to the consumer full notice of their terms and conditions. Reference to a source offline may not be sufficient. Despite a number of cases that deal with the online incorporation of terms and conditions in America, the position of the courts is still uncertain,[47] while in the United Kingdom the current approach still seems to be to rely on the traditional common law rules.

There are three main methods of incorporation recognised in England and Wales: by signature, by notice and by course of dealing. The easiest (and most certain) method of incorporating terms and conditions is through signature. Common law is clear when it states that an individual is bound by the contents of a document they sign even if they did not read it or understand it as was seen in the case of **L'Estrange v Graucob**,[48] which held that when a document containing terms and conditions is signed, the person who signed the document is bound by it, and it is wholly immaterial whether that person read the document or not.[49] Clearly in an online contract a document cannot be signed in the traditional sense. It is not clear whether a person clicking on an 'I agree' button, which indicates that they have read and agreed to the trader's terms and conditions, may be regarded as the equivalent of a signature for the purpose of this rule within England and Wales.[50] There are a number of options available to online businesses, which require a signed document (this is of

---

[47] See: **Ticketmaster Corp v Tickets.com** (2000) US Dist. Lexis 4553 and **Specht v. Netscape Communications Corp** (2002) 306 F3d 17. In the Ticketmaster case, the court held that terms and conditions were incorporated because there was a notice on the homepage stating that use of the website was subject to their terms and conditions. This can be contrasted with the decision in Specht where terms and conditions were held not to be enforceable. In this case users could download software. The website made no reference to terms and conditions on that page, although they did exist elsewhere on the website. This meant that a download could take place without a consumer ever agreeing to terms. The judge held that the terms and conditions had not been incorporated as they were not brought to the user's attention. In contrast to the uncertainty with terms and conditions on websites, the decision in **Moore v Microsoft Corporation** (15th April 2002) NY Sup Ct App Div 2nd Dept held that legal obligations were in existence if website used an 'I agree' button, which a consumer then clicked on.

[48] [1934] 2 KB 394.

[49] There are some rare exceptions to this. An example is if the signature is obtained by misrepresentation or by fraud as discussed by the Court of Appeal in **Curtis v Chemical Cleaning and Dyeing Company** [1951] 1 KB 805 and the person signing the document has to reasonably expect that the document contains contractual terms as in **Grogan v Robin Meredith Plant Hire** [1996] CLC 1127.

[50] The American approach suggests that an 'I agree' button is adequate for terms and conditions to be incorporated as seen in **Moore v Microsoft Corporation** (15th April 2002) NY Sup Ct App Div 2nd Dept.

more relevance to providers of legal services than it is to online shops[51]). These include sending the document electronically and asking the other party to print it off and sign it and resend it or the creation of a signature page. There have been a small handful of decisions that have considered the validity of an electronic signature; one such example was **J Pereira Fernandes SA v Mehta**.[52] The facts were that Mr Mehta was a director of Bedcare (UK) Ltd, which was supplied bedding products by J Pereira Fernandes. However, after Bedcare failed to pay debts of £24,709.53, Fernandes sought to have Bedcare wound up. When the winding up order was received by Bedcare, Mr Mehta asked one of his secretaries to send an email to the solicitors of Fernandes asking for the winding up order to be postponed for seven days. In return for the postponing of the hearing he purported to offer a personal guarantee of £25,000 to cover the outstanding debts and also agreed to draw up a repayment plan over a period of six months. Part of this guarantee included an undertaking not to sell, market or dispose of any company assets without prior consent from Fernandes. This email was sent by one of Mr Mehta's secretaries, although was not signed by Mr Mehta or his secretary. The header of the email said that the email was sent from *nelmehta@aol.com.* After receiving this email, the solicitors of Fernandes telephoned to accept this guarantee and forwarded the paperwork to Mr Mehta to formalise the agreement. However the paperwork was never returned. Subsequently, Bedcare was wound up and Fernandes tried to enforce the personal guarantee. The court refused Fernandes' application and held two points of interest based on the requirements of the section 4 of the Statute of Frauds 1677, which requires that guarantees be made in writing and signed by or on behalf of the guarantor. First of all, they confirmed that an email was adequate for a document to be 'in writing'. However, the fact that Mr Mehta (or his secretary) had not signed or initialled the bottom of the email meant that the document had not been signed and therefore the personal guarantee could not be enforced. Even though the sender's email

---

[51] This difficulty was seen in the case of **R (on the application of Mercury Tax Group Limited v Revenue and Customs Commissioners** [2008] EWHC 2721 (Admin) in which Mercury was a tax consultancy business and they offered a tax avoidance scheme to a number of their clients. The Inland Revenue Commissioners believed that this scheme had been dishonestly implemented and so applied for a warrant under the Taxes Management Act 1970 to enter Mercury's premises and search for documents. The Commissioners alleged that the main flaw in the arrangement was that the key documents had not been signed by the clients. The clients appear to have signed a draft document, but the signature page was subsequently transferred to a final document, which contained different details. Although the court held that the warrants were unlawful, they did hold that a document does need to be signed and executed by an individual in its final form. For more on this case see: Singleton, S *Signature of documents* (2009) Criminal Law and Justice Weekly, volume 173, issue 8, page 124 and Frickler, D & Saxton, L *Mercury Tax Group v HMRC and the importance of "execution formalities"* (2009) Butterworths Journal of International Banking and Financial Law, volume 24, issue 3, page 158 and Dowden, M *Signed, sealed and delivered …?* (2009) New Law Journal, volume 159, issue 7370, pages 731–732.

[52] (2006) 1 WLR 1543.

address appeared at the top of the page, the court was of the view that this was not part of the actual document and accordingly no signature had been attached to the guarantee. This principle was followed in the case of **Sean Lindsay v Jared O'Loughnane**[53] where the court confirmed that a representation made following section 6 of the Statute of Frauds Amendment Act 1828 (which was introduced to stop people from making casual statements regarding a person's financial probity) could be made by email, provided that the email included a written indication of who the sender of the email was. It seemed to the judge that an unsigned email was not sufficient.[54] Further, the decision in **Kim Andrew Orton v John Brook Collins**[55] confirmed that for an email signature to be valid the body of the email in these circumstances needs to contain the name of the guarantor. The difficulty with the decision in Mehta is that it appears to be out of step with equivalent international legislation[56] and also fully fails to address the issue of automatic signatures appearing at the bottom of each email sent.[57]

The second main method of incorporating terms and conditions into a contract is incorporation by notice. Parties can be bound in circumstances where they are given reasonable notice of the terms. For incorporation by notice to be valid, essentially three factors have to be satisfied. First of all the terms need to be incorporated within good time. In the case of **Olley v Marlborough Court Limited**[58] terms and conditions excluding liability to loss or damage to property which appeared on the back of a hotel door were held not to be incorporated. As the contract for a room had been agreed at the hotel front desk, the terms – which were not highlighted until the customer reached their bedroom – could not be said to have been incorporated.

Secondly, the notice has to be in a contractual document. There are a number of famous 'ticket cases' that consider this requirement.[59] In **Chapelton v Barry Urban District Council**[60] the Court of Appeal held that terms and conditions for the hire of deckchairs (that were printed on the back of the ticket) and which the owners of the deckchairs attempted to rely upon, were not enforceable as the ticket was simply a receipt for the money paid for the hire of the chair. There was a notice adjacent to the chairs, which contained no

---

[53] [2010] EWHC 529 QB.

[54] Ibid. Paragraphs 94–95.

[55] [2007] EWHC 803 (Ch).

[56] See Christensen, S, Mason, S & O'Shea, K *The international judicial recognition of electronic signatures – has your agreement been signed?* (2006) Communications Law, volume 11, issue 5, pages 150–160.

[57] For more see: Freedman, C & Hardy, J J *Pereira Fernandes v Mehta: a 21st century email meets a 17th century statute* (2007) Computer Law and Security Report, volume 23, issue 1, pages 77–81.

[58] [1949] 1 KB 532.

[59] For more on the ticket cases in general see: Strickland, C *Tickets please!* (February 2003) Legal Executive, pages 20–21.

[60] [1940] 1 KB 532.

limitation of liability clause. The Chapelton case can be contrasted with **Parker v South Eastern Railway**[61] in which the court held that a ticket received from the cloakroom of a railway company in return for the deposit of a coat was reasonable notice of terms and conditions as it contained the phrase 'see back' on the front of the ticket. On the reverse were clauses limiting the company's liability. A more recent case dealing with notice of terms and conditions, and specifically the application of website disclaimers is **Gary Patchett v Swimming Pool and Allied Trades Association Limited (SPATA)**.[62] In this case, Mr and Mrs Patchett wanted a swimming pool built and so they visited the website of the trade body SPATA to find a SPATA-registered member to build the pool for them. The website stated that full checks (including financial) were made on members and based on the information on the website, the Patchetts instructed a contractor to build a swimming pool for them at a cost of just over £55,000. This contractor was only an affiliate member and so was not subject to the same level of checks as full members. During construction the contractor became insolvent and the work was not completed, meaning that the Patchetts had to employ other contractors to finish the job costing them an extra £44,000. The Patchetts brought proceedings against SPATA for negligent misstatement and sought to recover their losses. The Court of Appeal (by a majority) rejected their argument. It was held that a duty of care is owed by a website to its visitors, but the existence of a disclaimer may reduce or exclude liability. In this circumstance, the website encouraged people to make further enquiries prior to contracting with a contractor. These further enquiries included obtaining an Information Pack from SPATA, which the Patchetts did not do. Following this case, it therefore appears that a simple disclaimer that appears on a website is sufficient to mitigate against any future potential liability.[63] The third requirement to ensure that terms and conditions have been incorporated by notice is that reasonable steps have to be taken to bring the contractual terms to the notice of the other party. In **Thompson v London Midland and Scottish Railway Co**[64] the court held that the railway company had taken reasonable steps to bring an exclusion clause to Thompson's attention by reference to the company's timetables, even though the plaintiff was unable to read. What amounts to reasonable notice can be affected by the nature of the clause or term in question. The more unusual or onerous it is, the

---

[61] (1877) L.R. 2 CPD 416.

[62] [2009] EWCA Civ 717.

[63] For more on this case see: Massey, R *Patchett v Swimming Pool and Allied Trades Association Ltd: making a splash – the contextualisation of website statements* (2010) Computer and Telecommunications Law Review, volume 16, issue 3, pages 78–80 and Farmer, S *Patchett v Swimming Pool & Allied Trades Association Ltd (Case Comment)* (2009) E-Commerce Law Reports, volume 9, issue 3, pages 16–17. For an additional Irish perspective: Austin, M *Negligent misstatement – where now following Patchett v Swimming Pool & Allied Trades Association?* (2010) Irish Law Times, volume 28, issue 8, pages 122–127.

[64] [1930] 1 KB 41.

more notice will be required. In **Thornton v Shoe Lane Parking**[65] the court held that a car park could not rely on a small statement on the ticket collected as the plaintiff drove into the car park. The statement directed customers to review conditions displayed within the premises, and one condition was that the car park was not liable for any customer suffering injury. However the car park had not done what was reasonably sufficient to bring the terms and conditions to Thornton's notice.[66]

The third and final main method of incorporating terms and conditions into a contract is incorporation by course of dealing. For online retailers contracting with customers this is clearly not the main method of incorporating terms into a contract. However, a term can be incorporated, even if not expressly referred to in a particular transaction, if there has previously been a long, regular and consistent course of dealing between the parties on the basis of that term. In **Photolibrary Group Limited (t/a Garden Picture Library) v Burda Senator Verlag GmbH**[67] the court held that even though a delivery note (containing details of the photographic transparencies and penalty clauses if the transparencies were lost) was not signed there was an established course of dealing between the parties to show that these terms had been adopted.[68] More recently, the Court of Appeal ruled that for a course of dealing to be relied upon, the constituent elements of a contract are still required to be in existence. In **University of Plymouth v European Language Centre Limited**[69] the European Language Centre used accommodation at the University of Plymouth for their summer language classes. During 2005, the University advised the European Language Centre through emails and over the telephone that there would be less space available in 2006 and estimated that only 200 beds would be available. In fact, the number of beds available was reduced to 100 and the language centre sued the university, arguing that a contract was in existence for 200 beds, per the earlier email and telephone communication. The Court of Appeal held that

---

[65] [1971] 2 QB 163.

[66] The principle that the courts will require greater efforts to be made in bringing more onerous or unusual terms to the attention of the other party have been seen in further cases such as **J Spurling Limited v Bradshaw** [1956] 1 WLR 461 and **Interfoto Picture Library Limited v Stiletto Visual Programmes Limited** [1989] QB 433. For more on this principle see: Macdonald, E *The duty to give notice of unusual contract terms* (September 1988) Journal of Business Law, pages 375–385. More recently, the Financial Services Authority stated that even if a consumer 'ticks a box' agreeing to unfair contract terms it does not mean that they can subsequently reject a customer's complaint about that unfair term. See OUT-LAW.COM *FSA backs OFT ban on 'read and understand' contract declarations* (18th June 2010). Available at: http://www.out-law.com/page-11149.

[67] [2008] EWHC 1343 (QB).

[68] Another example is found within **Hollier v Rambler Motors (AMC) Limited** [1972] 2 QB 71 which said that three or four contracts over a period of about five years was probably not sufficient to be a course of dealing for this purpose.

[69] [2009] EWCA Civ 784. See also **Bear Stearns Bank Plc v Forum Global Equity Limited** [2007] EWHC 1576 (Comm).

looking at the entire communication between the parties a contract had not been entered into and they had merely been negotiating prior to formalising the arrangement into a contact. Even though there had been a course of dealing between the parties running back to the late 1990s, in previous years that final arrangement included a detailed contract, which was not in evidence for the purposes of this dispute.

Whatever method an online retailer uses to ensure that their terms and condition are incorporated into the contract, there are certain mandatory terms that cannot be excluded, or where exemption is restricted. Specifically, these are the implied terms found within *inter alia* the Sale of Goods Act 1979 (including that goods will be of satisfactory quality and fit for purpose), the Supply of Goods and Services Act 1982 (including that services will be provided with due care and skill, in reasonable time and for a reasonable price) and the Unfair Contract Terms Act 1977.

Key points:

- Internet transactions continue to increase, with consumers attracted by the speed, convenience and low cost of purchasing online.
- To a large extent academic debate ascertaining when a contract is formed online is mainly based on applying traditional common law rules to the newer technology.
- It is presumed that a website that displays goods for sale is a similar arrangement to goods on display in a shop window, meaning that they are displayed as an invitation to treat (**Fisher v Bell [1974]**).
- The main area of academic discussion is about when an offer is accepted online. There are no definitive common law decisions on this currently, although the suggestion exists that the postal acceptance rule (as applied in **Adams v Lindsell (1818)**) should apply for email acceptances, while the instantaneous communication acceptance rule (as seen in **Entores v Miles Far Eastern Corporation (1955)**) should be used for contracts carried out over the Internet.
- Consider whether it is appropriate to have different rules for technologies based on only a minor technical difference.
- There have been a number of high profile problems, notably involving Argos and Kodak, about when an offer was accepted.
- The European Union's E-Commerce Directive provides some assistance to contract formation online. Articles 9–11 are the most important and require that member states remove legal barriers to online contracting.
- An obligation is also placed on service providers to acknowledge receipt of a consumer's order without undue delay and by electronic means. Although this helps consumers avoid input errors at the front end of the

contract, the legislation does not assist with the precise moment a contract is agreed and formed.

- It is also important that terms and conditions are fully incorporated into a contract. This will ensure that in the event of a dispute both parties will know their rights and liabilities.
- Again, the academic discussion on incorporation into online contracts tends to focus on applying the traditional common law rules of signature, notice and course of dealing.
- There have been some cases on incorporation of contractual terms in relation to the Internet – notably **J Pereira Fernandes SA v Mehta (2006)** and **Gary Patchett v Swimming Pool and Allied Trades Association Limited (SPATA) [2009].**

Further reading:

Books:

- Reifa, C & Hörnle, J *The Changing Face of Electronic Consumer Contracts in the Twenty-first Century: Fit for Purpose?* (2009) Chapter 2, in *Law and the Internet* 3rd Edition (edited by Lilian Edwards and Charlotte Waelde), Hart Publishing.
- Wang, F F *Law of Electronic Transactions – Contemporary Issues in the EU, US and China* (2010) Routledge Publishing.

Articles:

- Allen, T & Widdison, R *Can computers make contracts?* (1996) Harvard Journal of Law and Technology, volume 9, number 1, pages 26–52.
- Brownsend, R & Howells, G *When surfers start to shop: Internet commerce and contract law* (1999) Legal Studies, volume 19, number 3, pages 287–315.
- Del Ninno, A *The Rules for E-Contracts in Selected Member States: The Implementation of Directive 2000/31/EC* (September 2004) World Internet Law Report, pages 3–6.
- Deveci, H A *Cash back deals: con or contract?* (2009) Computer and Telecommunications Law Review, volume 15, issue 3, pages 60–66.
- Dickie, J *When and where are electronic contracts concluded?* (1998) Northern Ireland Legal Quarterly, volume 49, number 3, pages 332–334.
- Gilles, L E *Addressing the "cyberspace fallacy": targeting the jurisdiction of an electronic consumer contract* (2008) International Journal of Law and Information Technology, volume 16, issue 3, pages 242–269.
- Maidment, K *Deadline or guideline? – Stipulations as to time in IT contracts* (2006) Computer Law and Security Report, volume 22, issue 6, pages 481–485.

- Nicholl, C *Can computers make contracts?* (January 1998) Journal of Business Law, volume pages 35–49.

Questions for consideration:

2.1. Do you consider goods for sale on a website to be an offer or an invitation to treat? Give reasons for your answer.

2.2. The moment a contract is formed online is currently a point of conjecture based on traditional contract law acceptance rules. Explain how these traditional rules are being applied to Internet contracts.

2.3. How far would you agree with the statement that both Argos and Kodak should have honoured the agreements with their customers for the sale of the televisions and cameras respectively?

2.4. Outline the ways in which an online company could try to incorporate terms and conditions into an online contract.

2.5. Explain the traditional methods through which terms and conditions can be incorporated into a contract. Do you see any natural parallel with these methods and the attempts online traders are making to ensure the terms and conditions are incorporated?

2.6. Lisa purchases a mobile phone online from the (fictitious) company 'Phones4Uonline'. The website has written in bold at the bottom of each page "For our full terms and conditions please click on this hyperlink ..." Underneath this statement there is a hyperlink, which would take Lisa to the terms and conditions of 'Phones4Uonline'. However, Lisa's computer is old and slow and therefore she does not access the terms and conditions. Is Lisa bound by them?
Discuss. What could 'Phones4Uonline' do differently to ensure that the terms and conditions are clearly incorporated?

2.7. 'The Court of Appeal decision in **Patchett v Swimming Pool and Allied Trade Association [2009] EWCA Civ 717** leaves the law in no doubt as to how contractual terms are incorporated into online contracts'.
By reference to case law and academic opinion, undertake a critical assessment of this view.

2.8. 'The European Union's Directive on Electronic Commerce 2000/31/EC has ended all uncertainty regarding contract formation and incorporation of contractual terms online'.
Critically assess the above statement. Ensure you make reference to decided case law and academic opinion.

2.9.   After deciding to retire from the circus, Maureen wants to sell her ring-master's whip and hat. She decides to place an advert in a shop window advertising these two items for sale. The advert reads:

> "Ringmaster's whip and hat for sale – both are top-quality items and are being sold for £25.00."

The advert also contains Maureen's mobile phone and email address to allow people to contact her.

On Tuesday afternoon, Bethany is doing her weekly shop and notices the advert in the shop window. Bethany is very keen on purchasing the whip and hat as it would be an excellent addition to her fancy-dress box. Accordingly, Bethany rings Maureen on the mobile phone number provided on the advert to purchase the goods. Unfortunately, Maureen's mobile phone is turned off as she is attending a convention for retired clowns and circus performers. Therefore, Bethany leaves a message saying she would like to purchase the items for the asking price. The message is timed at 3.25pm on the Tuesday.

The same day, Gus is passing the shop on his way to the Bingo Club. He also notices the advert and also would like to purchase the items. Instead of going to the Bingo Club, he returns home and sends an email agreeing to purchase the whip and hat for the purchase price. The email is sent at 3.55pm, although does not arrive in Maureen's inbox until 4.15pm due to a large amount of local email traffic at that time.

Meanwhile, while at the convention for retired clowns and circus performers, Maureen meets Bill, who is a circus-performer with a European-wide profile. Coincidentally, Bill is looking to add to his circus equipment and needs a whip and a hat and therefore he agrees to purchase the items from Maureen for the advertised price at 4.00pm.

It is not until later that evening that Maureen discovers that Bethany, Gus and Bill have all agreed to purchase the whip and hat.
To whom is Maureen obliged to sell the whip and hat? Your answer must refer to case law and academic opinion.

2.10.   In her spare time, Kelly sells hair products for 'the discerning lady'. One afternoon, she rings the local paper and asks that they put the following advert in the newspaper:

> "For Sale: Hair Straighteners, very high-quality product, limited edition – I only have one pair to sell. Cost £89.99."

The advert is put in the paper, which is published on Thursday 17th May. Alongside the advertisement, there is Kelly's mobile number and email address.

On that Thursday morning, Nicola sees the advert in the paper and is very enthusiastic. She immediately finds her mobile telephone and rings Kelly. However, Kelly is not near her telephone and misses the call. Nicola leaves a voicemail message accepting the offer in the newspaper. The voicemail message is timed at 9.34am.

At 10.30am Colin, who is frantically looking around for a present for his girlfriend, reads the newspaper advert. He logs on to his computer and sends an email to Kelly also accepting her offer. However, the email is delayed in transmission and so does not reach Kelly's inbox until 11.12am.

At 11.20am, Kelly finds her mobile phone and notices that she has a voicemail message. She listens to it and hears Nicola's acceptance. Kelly then goes on to her computer to check her emails and reads Colin's acceptance.

Using academic opinion and case law, to whom is Kelly obliged to sell the hair straighteners?

All weblinks mentioned in the text can also be found at:
http://www.palgrave.com/law/rogers

3 Distance Selling

This chapter will consider:

- The advantages and disadvantages of online shopping.
- The aims of the original Distance Selling Directive 97/7/EC.
- The rules found within the United Kingdom's Consumer Protection (Distance Selling) Regulations 2000.
- Amendments to the regulations made to date.
- The provisions contained within the European Commission's Proposed Directive on Consumer Rights.

When a consumer contracts online there are some obvious differences to contracting face to face. There are clear advantages to shopping online, including the freedom to purchase an item from the comfort of a home or work computer. Internet purchasing also provides speed, convenience and competitive pricing. However, the disadvantages include the fact that the consumer has no real physical proximity to the seller and is unable to see the product at first hand. Additionally, the buyer may have less reassurance about where to return a product or complain to if the good/service is faulty, damaged or broken. There are natural concerns about the security of online payment and whether the good that is ordered will actually be delivered and conform to the order placed. When consumer and professional do not meet, the contract concluded at a distance arguably creates increased risks for the consumer. The consumer cannot check whether the goods will meet their requirements or ask direct questions about the products to the vendor. The difficulty comes when the product, which the consumer has ordered online, arrives but is different to what has been purchased, or is damaged or does not arrive at all. Whilst Internet shopping continues to expand as more and more consumers buy online, the number of consumers who are not fully aware of their rights compared with traditional sales is still high. In November 2009, the Office for National Statistics reported that Internet sales amounted to 9.8 per cent of non-financial service sales in 2008. This was an increase from 7.7 per cent in 2007.[1]

---

[1] Office for National Statistics *E-Commerce and information and communication technology (ICT) activity 2008 Statistical Bulletin.* Available at: http://www.statistics.gov.uk/pdfdir/ecom1109.pdf. These figures are comparable with similar research carried out by the Centre for Retail Research, see: http://www.retailresearch.org/reports/onlinetrends_2010.php.

The European Union's Directive 97/7/EC[2] on the Protection of Consumers in respect of Distance Contracts imposes requirements on business-to-consumer contracts concluded without the parties actually meeting. The Directive applies to contracts concluded within the European Union or European Economic Area. It purports to reinforce consumer protection and under Article 1 seeks to harmonise (or approximate) laws within the European Union in the area of distance selling. The Directive was the culmination of many years of discussion at European level and the recitals (especially recitals 5, 6 and 7) point to the extensive history to which this particular Directive is connected, with its roots going back to the mid 1980s. The Directive was implemented into the United Kingdom by the Consumer Protection (Distance Selling) Regulations 2000 and came into force on 31 October 2000.[3] This chapter will proceed by focusing analysis on the United Kingdom's regulations.

Application and scope

Regulation 3 sets out the core terms found within the legislation. A 'consumer' is defined as a natural person acting outside of their business, while a 'business' is to include a trade or profession. The complex, confusing and often inter-weaving nature of these two parties is prevalent throughout commercial and consumer law and these regulations are no exception as the distinction between a consumer and a business is still, in some situations, hard to discern. The case law in this area is very sketchy, particularly in grey areas, and decisions relating to whether a party should be regarded as a business or a consumer are often related to the specific circumstances, making definitive rules very difficult to ascertain. For instance, in **Stevenson v Rogers**[4] the court held that the one-off sale of a fishing boat was 'in the course of a business' as outlined in the Sale of Goods Act 1979. This case was later applied in **Feldaroll Foundry Plc v Hermes Leasing (London) Ltd.**[5] Questions relating to a business which is sell-ing items outside of their expertise (for instance, a solicitor selling office furni-ture) or an apparent consumer who sells a large amount of items on an online auction site ostensibly as a hobby activity remain without a clear answer and both could equally fall within the definition of a business or a consumer.[6]

---

[2] Available at: http://eur-lex.europa.eu/LexUriServ/LexUriServ.do?uri=CELEX:31997L0007:EN:HTML.

[3] Statutory Instrument 2000 no. 2334. Available at: http://www.opsi.gov.uk/si/si2000/20002334.htm.

[4] (1999) 1 All ER 613.

[5] [2004] EWCA Civ 747.

[6] For more consideration on the distinction between a business and a consumer see: Brown, I *Sales of goods in the course of a business* (July 1999), pages 384–389 and Twigg-Flesner, C *Companies "deal-ing as consumers" – a missed opportunity?* (January 2005) Law Quarterly Review, pages 41–43.

The regulations apply to distance contracts, which are defined in regulation 3 as:

> "any contract concerning goods or services concluded between a supplier and a consumer under an organised distance sales or service provision scheme run by the supplier who, for the purpose of the contract, makes exclusive use of one or more means of distance communication up to and including the moment at which the contract is concluded."

From the above definition four key factors need to be proven for the regulations to be relevant. First of all, the contract must be for a sale of goods or a service provision. Secondly, the contract must be between a business and a consumer. Accordingly, business-to-business and consumer-to-consumer contracts are excluded from the remit of the legislation. Thirdly, the contract must make exclusive use of distance communication up to and including the conclusion of the contract. If the business and consumer meet face to face at any point the regulations cease to be relevant. Finally the distance sale needs to be an organised sale, which means that one-off sales are not included, but call centres and websites selling goods or services to consumers are included. Schedule 1 of the regulations provides an indicative list of means of distance communication and refers to letters, telephone and electronic mail. Interestingly the list does not refer to, amongst other methods, the Internet, SMS, MMS or Voice over Internet Protocol or more recent technological advances. While an indicative list does allow flexibility in discerning whether a means of communication is 'distance', the list as written demonstrates the extent to which the initial Directive is technologically distinct from twenty-first century commerce.

The regulations do not have universal application to all distance sales as some contracts are excluded entirely from the protection offered by the legislation. Regulation 5 lists the excepted contracts, which are:

- Contracts for the sale or disposition of an interest in land;
- Construction of a building;
- Financial services;[7]
- Contracts concluded through an automated vending machine;
- Telecommunications operator through a public payphone; and
- Auctions.

Arguably, the main exception from the vantage point of Internet usage is that of auctions. Consumer usage of online auction sites such as eBay, eBid or

---

[7] Schedule 2 provides a non-exhaustive list of financial services and includes banks and investment advisors. Distance financial services have their own body of legislation, for instance Directive 2002/65/EC on the Distance Marketing of Consumer Financial Services.

OnlineAuction has grown dramatically. Individuals are invited to sign up to an account and can then sell items in one of two (main) ways, either by the traditional auction method, whereby the seller will put a length of time on the auction and the highest bidder 'wins' the item at the end of that time and after paying the agreed sum, or a 'buy now' concept whether the seller can put a price on an item, which the buyer can choose to purchase immediately. The total exception of auctions from the terms of the regulations means that individuals are not entitled to rely on the protection the legislation affords. This is to the detriment of the consumer as they are easy prey for unscrupulous sellers as methods of defrauding people through online auction sites continue to evolve.[8]

As well as the total exceptions, regulation 6 outlines contracts to which regulations 7 to 20 (the provisions relating to prior information and the right to withdraw) shall not apply. These are the so-called partial exceptions. Regulations 7–20 do not extend to timeshare arrangements and contracts for the supply of food or beverages or other goods intended for regular consumption supplied to the consumer by a regular roundsman.[9] Somewhat ironically, considering the technological context that the legislation is used and applied to, this final exception was thought to apply predominantly to doorstep milk and bread deliveries. However, this could be extended to the more contemporary 'regular roundsman' to include deliveries made by large supermarkets after a customer has placed an online order. Despite the continuing popularity of online grocery shopping it seems that individuals may not be offered any protection by the legislation.

Further partial exceptions include contracts for accommodation, transport, catering and leisure services to be provided on a particular date or within a certain timeframe.[10] It was in this area that the European Court of Justice made its first ruling on the legislation in the case of **EasyCar (UK) Ltd v Office of Fair Trading**.[11] This case concerned whether the partial exception found within Article 3(2) of the Directive (implemented into the United Kingdom as regulation 6(2)(b)), which relates to *inter alia* contracts for the provision of transport services, extended to car hire services. EasyCar (part of the Easy Group) operated an Internet-only car hire service on a 'book-early pay-less' model. This is a well-used business model that allows consumers to obtain goods or services

---

[8] For instance see: BBC News *Man fined over fake eBay auctions* (5th July 2010). Available at: http://www.bbc.co.uk/newsbeat/10508913. In this example, Paul Barrett from County Durham was fined £3,000 and ordered to carry out 250 hours of community service after being found guilty of fixing an online auction on eBay by bidding on the items that he had placed online.

[9] Regulation 6(1) and 6(2)(a).

[10] Regulation 6(2)(b).

[11] Case 336/03 (2005) All ER (EC) 834. See also *Case Comment: Car-hire exempted from Distance Contracts Directive* EU Focus (2005), 163, pages 12–13 and Unberath, H and Johnston, A *The double-headed approach of the ECJ concerning consumer protection* (2007) Common Market Law Review, volume 44, issue 5, pages 1237–1284, especially pages 1279–1281.

at a more competitive price the earlier they book. The question arose, however, whether there was still a right for the consumer to cancel the contract within the permitted timeframe and obtain a full refund. The Office of Fair Trading argued that EasyCar should provide customers with the opportunity to cancel the arrangement within seven days (as permitted by Article 6 of the Directive) as the car hire is a vehicle to travel in and not a transport service. EasyCar took a different view and were of the opinion that car hire was a transport service and consumers should not have the opportunity to cancel. EasyCar conceded that they had a cancellation policy that allowed consumers to cancel, but without obtaining a refund except in extreme circumstances (including terrorism, serious illness or natural disaster). The European Court of Justice had no definition of 'transport service' to rely on as no case law on this issue was in existence. Accordingly, they decided that the term should have its usual meaning and held that consumers should not be able to rely on the cancellation right. The European Court of Justice held that in everyday language a 'transport service' should include a method of transport and should not be restricted to simply a service which moves a person from one place to another.

Analysis on the relative merits of this decision is divided. One school of thought is that this decision is sound and based on good commercial sense.[12] By refusing the consumer the opportunity to cancel this type of agreement the decision is, in effect, protecting the book-early, pay-less business model. If consumers had the ability to cancel, businesses would be unable to maintain this plan as they would have unreliable and potentially changeable data as to remaining capacity. The decision avoids this uncertainly and means that suppliers can be certain about remaining available capacity. An opposing view[13] is that the decision in EasyCar focuses more upon the exception, rather the primary aim of the initial Directive, specifically to protect the consumer. Accordingly the protection provided to consumers is weakened. The transport service exception is one of several exceptions and these are headings (for instance accommodation, catering, leisure services) for which the majority of consumers will use the Internet – to book a holiday or hotel, to organise travel or to book a ticket for a sports match. That said, it seems that by refusing the right to cancel in this particular circumstance, competition among suppliers to provide cheaper plane seats or hire cars is maintained to the long term advantage of the consumer.

---

[12]   See: Walker, C *ECJ: Online car rentals exempt from cancellation rights* E-Commerce Law and Policy (April 2005), pages 3–4.

[13]   Advocated in Hall, L *Cancellation rights in distance-selling contracts for services: exemptions and consumer protection* Journal of Business Law (September 2007), pages 683–700.

Requirements prior to contract conclusion

In an arrangement where the Distance Selling Regulations are applicable, requirements are also placed on the business prior to the conclusion of the contract. Under regulation 7 the seller has to provide certain information to the buyer, specifically:

* The identity of the supplier and his address (if payment is required in advance);
* A description of the goods/services;
* The price (including any taxes);
* Delivery costs (if applicable);
* The arrangement for payment, delivery and performance;
* The existence of a right to cancel;
* The cost of using the distance communication;
* The period for which the price remains valid;
* The minimum duration of the contract (if applicable).

If the ordered good or service is not available, there is also the option for the supplier to advise the consumer of any substitutions. Regulation 7(2) stipulates that all the information listed above must be provided in a clear and comprehensible manner in a way which is appropriate to the distance communication being used and with due regard to the principles of good faith. 'Good faith' is a quintessentially European concept that has only recently been welcomed into the United Kingdom.[14] Furthermore, regulation 8 outlines further requirements for the provision of this information, and details about cancellation (if this right exists, pursuant to regulations 5 and 6). The supplier also has to provide information about exercising the right to cancel, the geographical address of the business for the consumer to address any complaints, after-sales services and guarantees and the conditions for cancelling. This information must be provided either before the delivery of the good or during the performance of the service. Failure to include this information will lead to the period of time for which cancellation can be effected (lengthening to a maximum of 3 months and 7 days[15]). This information is to be provided in "writing or in another durable medium".[16] This necessity seems somewhat quaint. To require

---

[14] In *Walford v Miles* (1992) 2 AC 128, Lord Ackner stated at page 138 that "... *the concept of a duty to carry on negotiations in good faith is inherently repugnant to the adversarial position of the parties when involved in negotiations ... A duty to negotiate in good faith is as unworkable in practice as it is inherently inconsistent with the position of a negotiating party ...* [and accordingly] *... has no legal content."* See Berg, A *Promises to negotiate in good faith* (July 2003), Law Quarterly Review, pages 357–363.

[15] Regulation 11(4).

[16] Regulation 8(1).

that all consumers receive more information than they would easily obtain during a face to face transaction seems to be a backwards step in facilitating fast and convenient purchasing online. Although the information does not have to be in writing, it does add a further burden to the supplier. However, the aim of the original Directive is to put consumers (as best it can) in the same position as a face to face buyer. Therefore, by providing the consumer with a body of information they are arguably in a stronger and more knowledgeable position if something were to go wrong with the good or service.

The right to withdraw

Regulations 10–18 contain the provisions on withdrawal and cancellation. Arguably, these provisions form the lynchpin of the regulations. Consumers in the United Kingdom are allowed to cancel a distance contract, as defined in regulation 3, for no reason whatsoever within seven days from the conclusion of the contract.[17] The consequence of the cancellation, as outlined in regulation 10(2) is that the contact will be deemed as not being made and the parties should be returned to their position prior to the creation of the contract. For the cancellation to be valid, a clear intent to cancel must be made by the buyer to the supplier (or supplier's nominee) in writing or other durable medium within the cancellation period. Under regulation 10(4) consumer is deemed to have served notice, if the intention to cancel is left at the last known address of the supplier, or is posted to the same address, or if the buyer sends an email or a fax to the supplier. The commencement and rules of the cancellation periods are slightly different for contracts relating to goods and contracts for the provision of services. Under regulation 11, a consumer has seven working days to inform the supplier that they wish to cancel a contract for goods. The seven days commences the day after the day that the buyer received the goods. However, there is the potential for the cancellation period to be extended to three months and seven days if the supplier does not provide the information required under regulation 8. The right for the consumer to cancel a good is completely extinguished three months and seven days after the good is delivered. Regulation 12 covers similar provisions for the cancellation of a contract for services. The cancellation period commences the day after the day on which the contract was concluded. An extension of the right to cancel of three months and seven days is also available if the information required by regulation 8 has not been provided. This provision was a little unfair on suppliers as it gave the potential for consumers to cancel a service even after the service had been concluded. This issue was considered in the reform proposals,

---

[17] Cancellation periods in the rest of Europe differ from seven days to 15 days.

forwarded by the then Department of Trade and Industry, and was amended in 2005 so that the cancellation right was extinguished on completion of the service.[18] Under regulations 14 and 15[19] after cancellation, the parties must be put back into the same situation they were in before the contract. This includes a requirement on the supplier to return any monies paid by the consumer for the good or service within 30 days, beginning on the day that the cancellation notice was given. In return, in contracts for the sale of goods, it is the responsibility of the consumer under regulation 17 to retain possession of the goods and take reasonable care of them until they can be returned to the supplier.

Regulation 13 provides a list of contracts where the cancellation right shall not be available unless the parties have agreed otherwise:

- The supplier of a service has complied with regulation 8 and the service has commenced prior to the end of the cancellation period;
- The goods or services are subject to fluctuations of the financial market and out of the control of the supplier;
- Goods are to the personal specifications of the buyer;
- Audio, video or unsealed computer software materials;
- Newspapers, periodicals or magazines;
- Lottery or betting services.

These are in place predominantly to protect the supplier from undue costs arising from a cancellation for personalised items or goods which are time-specific and a buyer no longer wants.

The liability for the costs of returning the goods was laid out in the initial Directive and recital 14 states clearly that the consumer is liable only for the direct cost of returning the goods. All other sums must be refunded by the supplier to the buyer.[20] In 2003, the company Virgin Wines Online was

---

[18] The Consumer Protection (Distance Selling)(Amendment) Regulations 2005, Regulation 2(3)(b).

[19] Regulation 15 applies to credit agreements.

[20] This principle was confirmed by the European Court of Justice in the case of **Verbraucherzentrale ordrhein-Westfalen e.V. v Handelsgesellschaft Heinrich Heine GmbH** Case C-511/08 (2009/C 32/30). This case was a reference for a preliminary ruling from the German courts asking whether the terms of the Distance Selling Directive (specifically Article 6) prevented national legislation from allowing online businesses the right to refuse the refund of delivery charges to the consumer, even if they have legitimately withdrawn from the contract. This case concerned a delivery charge of €4.95 and German legislation stated that the delivery charges did not need to be refunded. The European Court of Justice rejected this approach, saying that a business was obliged to return all sums paid by the consumer including the delivery fee. The court was of the view that if this was not the case they may dissuade consumers from exercising their right to cancel and would also place the balance of risk for transporting the goods firmly on the side of the consumer. The only charge that may be made to a consumer is the cost of returning the goods to the supplier. For more see: OUT-LAW.COM News *Online retailers cannot deduct delivery fee when making refunds* (15th April 2010). Available at: http://www.out-law.com/page-10919.

required to amend its terms and conditions, following an approach by the Office of Fair Trading. It was noted that the terms and conditions stated *inter alia* that the delivery charge for sending the goods to the consumer was non-refundable after cancellation and that cancellation (which could only be effected by telephone or email) was only possible after a number of conditions had been met. There were also terms which allowed Virgin Wines to take longer than 30 days to deliver the goods. These terms were contrary to the provisions in the legislation and were revised by the company.[21] However, there is a secondary issue with consumers returning goods, particularly if they have received some form of benefit from the item in question. Since the regulations came into force various business groups, particularly those in the vehicle industry, have been voicing concern at the cancellation right of consumers. They argued that a consumer could purchase, for instance, a car, use it and then return it within the cancellation period and receive all monies back. They argued that the ability for a consumer to cancel a contract for a car up to seven days after the contract was concluded was to the detriment of the seller. This is because the value of a car depreciates very quickly, and if this is coupled with usage of the vehicle for a few days prior to cancellation, the seller could find that a car is being returned to them worth significantly less than when it left the showroom. In response to these concerns the Office of Fair Trading produced guidance for the industry in May 2005.[22] This 'question and answer' styled guidance sets out the requirements placed on businesses that sell vehicles exclusively through distance means of communication. Concerning the issue of cancellation, the guidance states clearly that even though the car may lose value immediately after sale and registration, this is unlikely to affect the physical condition of the car. There is a requirement on the consumer to take reasonable care of the vehicle and so if the car has been damaged, the consumer may be liable for the damage, but they would not forfeit their right to cancel.[23] Accordingly, suppliers would remain responsible for bearing the risk although could be awarded compensation in the event of the good being damaged. The issue of compensation for loss of value was considered in a preliminary reference made to the European Court of Justice by a German court in the case of **Pia Messner v Firma Stefan Krüger**.[24] In this case, the applicant (a consumer) purchased a second-hand laptop computer from the defendant, who ran an online mail order company. This purchase was made in

---

[21] OFT Press Release PN 58/03 *Virgin Wine gives consumers a fairer deal online* 14 May 2003. Available at: http://www.oft.gov.uk/news/press/2003/pn 58-03.

[22] OFT Guidance *Cars and other vehicles sold by distance means: Guidance on compliance* (May 2005). Available at: http://www.oft.gov.uk/shared oft/reports/consumer protection/oft689.pdf.

[23] Ibid. Pages 18 and 21.

[24] C489/07 [2009] All ER (D) 57 (Sep). For more on this case see: Rott, P *The balance of interests in distance selling – case note on Pia Messner v Firma Stefan Krüger* (2010) European Review of Private Law, volume 18, issue 1, pages 185–194.

early December 2005. The terms and conditions of the sale gave a 14 day cancellation window for the consumer and in the event of cancellation the consumer was required to return the goods to the supplier. There was an additional clause in the terms, which stated the consumer was obliged to pay compensation for any depreciation in the value of the goods from the point of sale to their return. In August 2006, the computer became defective and the consumer notified the supplier of this and requested it to be repaired, which the supplier agreed to do, but at a cost to the consumer. Dissatisfied with this response, in November 2006 the consumer advised the supplier that he would be cancelling the contract and wanted a full refund of the purchase price. Under the Distance Selling Directive, consumers have seven days within which they can cancel the contract. If the prior information is not provided, the cancellation window can be extended under Article 6 by a further three months. However, under German law the cancellation right does not expire until notice of the right to cancel is given by the supplier to the consumer. In the current case, as this notice had not been given, the option to cancel was still available to the consumer almost a year later. The question referred to the European Court of Justice was whether a seller may claim compensation from the consumer for the consumer's use of a good if they later legitimately cancelled the agreement. The court considered the cancellation provisions in Article 6, which forbids a penalty or charge to be levied against a consumer unless it is a cost directly associated with the return of the goods. The Directive does not include definitions of either a 'penalty' or a 'charge', but the European Court of Justice adopted a narrow definition, saying that charges may not be levied against a consumer apart from the direct cost of returning the good to the supplier. Accordingly, in this case compensation was not available to the supplier even though the consumer obtained considerable usage from the laptop. The court was of the view that to allow otherwise would damage the aims of the legislation in terms of consumer protection. If consumers were liable to pay compensation for use of a good prior to cancellation, it may induce reticence on the part of the consumer to check, inspect or test the items, as use of the good in this way might decrease its value. Furthermore, it could dissuade the consumer from withdrawing from the contract entirely out of fear of the potential for a compensation claim from the supplier.

The restrictive approach taken by the European Court of Justice and the Office of Fair Trading in terms of compensation for use of goods prior to cancellation does appear to be somewhat harsh on the supplier. Suppliers could potentially be liable for considerable sums of money, or have a good returned to them which has significantly depreciated in value, if a consumer chooses to cancel a contract within the cancellation window after receiving some benefit from the item in question. Potentially an online consumer has more margins for fussiness or fickleness than a face to face consumer as they can return an item for no apparent reason providing the latest date for withdrawal has not passed. The Sale of Goods Act 1979 has no equivalent provision. However, the aim of the legislation is (as best it can) to put the distance consumer in the same position as if they were dealing face to face. In distance contracts, the consumer is the more vulnerable party and is in a more disadvantaged position than the supplier. If the decision in Pia Messner had been decided in the alternative it could have potentially had a broader impact on online sales: consumers may have been less inclined to transact electronically as the protection available to them have been reduced. It is therefore argued that the decision of the European Court of Justice should be welcomed as it maintains the level of protection offered to the online consumer, thus making online commerce – in terms of available legislative protection – as attractive to the consumer as possible.

The impact on businesses is not only felt in terms of the potential depreciation of goods sold and later returned, but also in terms of taxation. In the Scottish case of **The Commissioners of Customs and Excise v Robertson's Electrical Limited**[25] the court held that VAT on goods purchased online is payable on the day they were paid for by the consumer and not at the end of the seven day cancellation period. This is of particular relevance if the seven days cross over an accounting period. This is an important decision in terms of ensuring that companies adequately manage their cash flow. The consequence of this decision is that it is possible for a customer to order and pay for a good online at the end of one financial accounting period and then to cancel the order (under regulation 10) at the beginning of the next financial accounting period. This means that the business will be liable for not only refunding the customer, but also paying the VAT on the good purchased. The business will then need to reclaim the VAT paid, leading to a greater administrative burden being placed upon the business.

The protection provided to a consumer by virtue of these regulations is safeguarded by regulation 25, which states that a contractual term is automatically void if it is in conflict with the protection provided by the regulations. Additionally, under regulation 19, a supplier has 30 days within which they must complete the contract. If the good cannot be delivered or service is not available during this time, the supplier is under an obligation to inform the consumer of this and reimburse any monies paid.

Initial amendments and regulatory guidance

In January 2004, the then Department of Trade and Industry published a consultation document on proposals to change the regulations entitled

---

[25] [2005] CSIH 75.

"Consumer and Competition Policy – Consultation on proposed changes to the Consumer Protection (Distance Selling) Regulations 2000".[26] The consultation aimed at finding solutions to make the regulations clearer, more workable and less costly for suppliers and consumers. The consultation closed on 23rd April 2004 and received 43 responses from businesses, trade associations, consumer organisations, law firms and professional bodies. The consultation focused on three distinct areas. First of all, whether to extend the scope of regulation 7 to require the information provided to the consumer prior to the contract to cover either the existence or absence of a right to cancel, and in the case of services whose performance is to start within seven days, information that the right to cancel will expire once performance begins. Under the original Directive, consumers only needed to be advised if they had a right to cancel and the proposal was to advise consumers if they did not have a right to cancel. Secondly, to require consumers to be given, during the performance of a service, information (in writing or another durable form) about the loss of cancellation rights once performance of the service begins. At present this information must be provided prior to the conclusion of the contract (regulations 8 and 12) and the ability for a consumer to cancel a service during its performance could be detrimental to the supplier. Finally, the third area of consultation was whether to allow consumers to cancel contracts by use of telephone, which was not included in the list found in regulation 10 of appropriate ways to cancel. Out of the three areas of consultation, the government opted to amend only the second element and this meant that cancellation would still be possible after performance had begun, if the consumer had not received notification of their cancellation right beforehand. However this right to cancel would end once the service had been performed. The other two areas of consultation (advising a consumer if a cancellation right does not exist and allowing consumers to cancel a contract by telephone) were not adopted. It was felt that in both of these situations there was scope for confusing the consumer in advising that a cancellation right does not exist and also scope for technical errors and evidential problems if a contract were cancellable by telephone. The changes were announced by the Department of Trade and Industry on 22nd October 2004 and were included in the Consumer Protection (Distance Selling) (Amendment) Regulations 2005.[27] Shortly after this in September 2006, the Department of Trade and Industry and the Office of Fair Trading issued a joint publication entitled *A guide for businesses on distance selling*[28] which sought to provide guidance to businesses on the regulations and advice on how to

---

[26] Available at: http://webarchive.nationalarchives.gov.uk/tna/+/http://www.dti.gov.uk/ccp/consultpdf/distselcon04.pdf.

[27] Statutory Instrument 2005/689. Available at: http://www.opsi.gov.uk/si/si2005/20050689.htm.

[28] Available at: http://www.oft.gov.uk/advice_and_resources/resource_base/legal/distance-selling-regulations.

comply with them. In this context of legislative reform and updated regulatory guidance, the Office of Fair Trading launched a study in April 2006 to examine whether consumer protection laws were providing adequate protection to online consumers.[29] It was set up to focus on four key areas: whether consumers were confident in shopping online, whether they received the correct level of regulatory protection, whether consumers were aware of their rights when they shopped online and whether businesses were compliant with the entire regulations for distance marketing and selling to consumers. A substantial 176-page report entitled *Internet Shopping: An OFT Market Study* was published in June 2007.[30] The main headlines of the report suggested that awareness of consumer protection legislation in this area was low and that consumers had many fears pertaining to online security and privacy threats when purchasing goods or services on the Internet. As part of the follow up to this report, the Office of Fair Trading decided to undertake a review of the top online retail websites selling to United Kingdom consumers to ensure that the level of protection available was in line with the consumer protection legislation.[31] The need for consumers to receive greater education about the legislative protection that is available when purchasing goods and services online was the basis of a later consultation paper issued by the Office of Fair Trading in July 2010.[32] The consultation was part of a wider strategy to encourage consumer protection groups to work more closely together in securing the protection of consumers who transact online. There were three main focuses contained within the consultation. First of all, the need to provide greater education for consumers to ensure that they are aware of their rights. Secondly, promoting compliance by businesses, and finally to develop effective enforcement regimes for businesses that do not comply with the rules. The consultation closed in October 2010.[33]

European reform

The domestic reporting and research was overshadowed somewhat by an extensive review at European level. In September 2006, the European Commission issued a consultation on the implementation of the Distance

---

[29] OFT Press Release 81/06 *OFT launches fact-finding market study of internet shopping* (27th April 2006). Available at: http://www.oft.gov.uk/news-and-updates/press/2006/81-06.

[30] Available at: http://www.oft.gov.uk/shared_oft/reports/consumer_protection/oft921.pdf.

[31] For the initial results of this sweep see: Massey, R *United Kingdom: Office of Fair Trading retail web sweep: summary of findings* (June 2008) E-Commerce Law and Policy, volume 10, issue 6.

[32] Office of Fair Trading *E-Consumer Protection: A Public Consultation on Proposals* (July 2010). Available at: http://www.oft.gov.uk/shared_oft/consultations/eprotection/oft1252con.pdf.

[33] See also: OUT-LAW.COM News *Consumer regulator outlines plans to protect online shoppers* (22nd July 2010). Available at: http://www.out-law.com/page-11243-theme=print.

Selling Directive,[34] which considered how the Directive had been implemented into European member states. The immediate conclusion of this paper was that although the Directive was likely to be flexible enough to withstand changes in technology, there were problems within the legislation with the wording, for instance 'durable medium', 'regular roundsman' and key definitions such as 'consumer' and 'business'. The responses to this consultation were published in November 2007[35] and they were fed into the more substantial review of the *Consumer Acquis*.[36] This review stretched back to 2004 and had the aim of simplifying the European legislative framework seeking to protect consumers. The review covered eight directives, which were all focused on consumer protection[37] and the aim was to provide an equivalent level of protection for consumers in all of the areas reviewed. At the time, there were a number of differences in the available protection provided to consumers through these directives (for instance withdrawal rights in the various directives differed, as did the available remedies) and the Consumer Acquis sought to modernise the legislative framework and to improve the regulatory environments for both consumers and professionals. An extensive series of consultation questions was included which looked at a wide range of issues, starting at whether a full or minimal harmonisation approach was desirable, definitions of key terms such as 'consumer' and 'professional', potential consequences for businesses that do not provide the prior information, whether the 'cooling-off' period should be uniform across all consumer protection legislation and what, if any, costs should be levied on a consumer who does withdraw from a contract during the cancellation window. The consultation closed on 15th May 2007 and more than 300 responses were received. The majority of responses were positive towards the proposals and in the light of these responses and other stakeholder events held during 2007, the European Commission

---

[34] European Commission Communication on the protection of Consumers in respects of Distance Contracts (September 2006) COM (2006) 514 Final. Available at: http://eur-lex.europa.eu/LexUriServ/LexUriServ.do?uri=CELEX:52006DC0514:EN:NOT.

[35] Summary of Responses to the Consultation on Distance Selling Directive 97/7/EC contained in Communication 2006/514/EC. Available at: http://ec.europa.eu/consumers/cons_int/safe_shop/dist_sell/sum_responses_consultations_en.pdf.

[36] The Green Paper on the Review of the Consumer Acquis COM (2006) 744 Final was published in February 2007.

[37] Specifically: Directive 85/577/EEC to protect the consumer in respect of contracts negotiated away from business premises, Directive 90/314/EEC on package travel, package holidays and package tours, Directive 93/13/EEC on unfair terms in consumer contracts, Directive 94/47/EC on the protection of purchasers in respect of certain aspects of contracts relating to the purchase of a right to use immovable properties on a timeshare basis, Directive 97/7/EC on the protection of consumers in respect of distance contracts, Directive 98/6/EC on consumer protection in the indication of the prices of products offered to consumers, Directive 98/27/EC on injunctions for the protection of consumers' interests and Directive 1999/44/EC on certain aspects of the sale of consumer goods and associated guarantees.

published its proposal for a Directive on Consumer Rights.[38] This proposal intends to merge four directives[39] into one set of rules.[40]

Proposed Directive on Consumer Rights

The Proposed Directive on Consumer Rights seeks to update, simplify and complete the legislation surrounding business-to-consumer transactions. At the start of this process it was noted that there was a range of often overlapping legislation that invariably led to high compliance costs for businesses. The proposal seeks to provide a balance between protecting consumers, while at the same time ensuring that the context in which businesses operate remains competitive.[41] It seeks to achieve this in a number of ways. The initial proposal took a different legislative approach to the previous legislation in that it was horizontal in nature and was one of full harmonisation, as opposed to minimum harmonisation. This meant that all European member states were to be obliged to adopt the provisions of the Directive and ensure that their own laws were not in conflict by offering either less or greater protection. This was one of the more controversial aspects of the plan as it could be seen as an intrusive mode of operating, which fails to respect well-established legal traditions within individual member states. Full harmonisation is somewhat risky. An example within the Distance Selling Directive is the indicative list of what constitutes a distance means of communication contained within in Schedule 1. This list failed to include *inter alia* the Internet, BlackBerry, SMS or m-commerce. Although this was only an indicative list, it pointed to the time when the Directive was in the planning stages during the 1980s and also demonstrates how legislation in this area can become dated very quickly as technology continually evolves. However, providing for maximum harmonisation does make cross-border trade easier for the business as they will not be required to learn the laws of each member state to ensure that they are complying with the rules of a country outside of their home jurisdiction. It was for these reasons and the complexity of getting the maximum harmonisation approach approved within the European legislators that in March 2010, Viviane Reding

---

[38] COM (2008) 614 Final 2008/0196. Available at: http://ec.europa.eu/consumers/rights/cons_acquis_en.htm.

[39] The four directives are: Directive 85/577/EC on Doorstop Selling, Directive 87/7/EC on Distance Selling, Directive 93/13/EC on Unfair contract terms and Directive 99/44/EC on the Sale of consumer goods and guarantees.

[40] A connected, although separate, development in this area is the European Commission's work towards harmonising contract law within the European Union. See *European Commission's Green Paper on policy options for progress towards a European Contract Law for consumers and businesses* COM (2010) 348 Final (1st July 2010). Available at: http://ec.europa.eu/dgs/justice/summary/summary_intro_en.htm.

[41] Proposed Directive on Consumer Rights, Recital 4.

(the European Union's Commissioner with responsibility for consumer law), announced that the maximum harmonisation element of the legislation was being withdrawn. The expectation was that by watering down the provisions of the legislation in this regard the European Parliament would be more willing to support the proposals.[42] The proposed Directive also aims to enhance consumer confidence, increase cross-border trade, introduce tighter regulation in the sector, provide consumers with more information about the rights that are available to them and explanations on how these rights are to be exercised and to increase legal certainty.

Scope, definition and obligations

Article 1 outlines the scope of the proposed Directive and states that it seeks to ensure the proper functioning of the internal market and provide a high level of consumer protection. This will be achieved by approximating (or harmonising) laws within the European Community, which is considered to be important due to the fragmented nature of consumer protection legislation within different member states.[43] Article 2 provides the key definitions. A consumer is defined as a natural person who is acting outside his "trade, business, craft or profession."[44] This seems relatively clear and easy to understand as far as it goes, however no real consideration is given to an individual who purchases a good for their business, but does not have any real knowledge or experience about the good in question. For instance, a solicitor who purchases office computers may have limited expertise in this area, but would not have protection from the proposals as they are unlikely to classify as a consumer. Equally, a solicitor who may offer legal advice through his website may choose to sell some office furniture through the same website. It is not overly clear whether this person is selling in the course of a business. Also, an individual who sells lots of items on (for instance) an online auction website may only be selling items in their spare time, but this can be quite lucrative for them. It is not clear at which point this 'consumer' becomes a 'trader'. A 'trader' is defined as someone "acting for purposes relating to his trade, business, craft or profession or anyone acting in the name of or on behalf of a trader."[45] The definition of a 'trader' seems to be an addition to the consumer/business distinction, yet with the definition provided it is not clear whether employees will be personally liable for breaches of the proposed Directive, if they act on behalf of their employer.

---

[42] For more on this alteration see: OUT-LAW.COM News *Commission surrenders on full consumer law harmonisation* (19th March 2010). Available at: http://www.out-law.com/page-10842-theme=print.

[43] Article 4 states that member states are unable to introduce any other consumer protection measures, although this is likely to be revised following the move away from full harmonisation.

[44] Article 2(1).

[45] Article 2(2).

The definition of a distance contract is defined in Article 2(6) and covers contracts for goods or services where the trader makes exclusive use of one or more means of distance communication. It may seem a tad pedantic however, if this is a draft Directive to protect consumers; surely there needs to be a requirement that the consumer also makes exclusive means of distance communication? A distinction is made between a distance contract and an 'off-premises' contract. The latter is where a trader may enter into a contract with a consumer away from their place of business, but in the physical presence of the consumer.[46] A 'distance communication' is where a contract is concluded without the "simultaneous physical presence of the trader and the consumer".[47] The immediate point to note with this definition is the removal of the need for it to be an 'organised distance sale' as required under the Distance Selling Directive. This is to be welcomed as providing broader protection for the consumer as there is no longer the requirement that a distance sale is an organised distance sale and so one-off sales are now covered. An indicative list of means of distance communication has not been included. Annex 1 of the Distance Selling Directive contains an indicative list of means of distance communication, but while such a list may be of assistance as a guide, it can become dated very quickly, as was seen with the distance selling legislation. Other interesting definitions include that provided for 'durable medium'. This is defined as:

> "... any instrument which enables the consumer or the trader to store information addressed personally to him in a way accessible for future reference for a period of time adequate for the purposes of the information and which allows the unchanged reproduction of the information stored."[48]

This definition of 'durable medium' is expanded by recital 16, which says that the information can be provided on paper, USB sticks, CD-ROMs, DVDs, memory cards and the hard drive of a computer. However, conspicuous by their absence are emails and also voicemails. By not including them within the recital there is some uncertainty as to whether these methods of communication would count as a durable medium. The definition of an auction is also of note and refers to a competitive bidding procedure, where the highest bidder is bound to purchase the goods or services. The definition also refers to a fixed price offer, which is not an auction, even if the consumer has the option of concluding the purchase of the item through the same procedure.[49] The draft Directive therefore proposes a difference between 'traditional' online auctions

---

[46] Article 2(8).
[47] Article 2(7).
[48] Article 2(10).
[49] Article 2(15).

and online auction sites that operate a 'buy it now' procedure where consumers can opt to purchase a good at a stated price. At first glance, this distinction is to be welcomed as there was a considerable degree of confusion as to their legal nature and which, if any, consumer protection legislation extended to the given auction scenario, although the apparent arbitrary distinction could cause confusion to both businesses and consumers further down the line. A final definition of note is that of a 'good' itself. Article 2(4) refers to a good as any moveable, tangible item. Whilst this may appear to be a wide definition, it does appear to exclude digital services, such as music downloads and software that can be downloaded directly on to a computer.

Article 5 maintains the requirement for the trader to provide information to the consumer prior to the conclusion of the contract. This information includes the main characteristics of the product, the address and identity of the trader, the price (including taxes), the arrangements for payment and delivery, the existence of a right to withdraw (where applicable), the existence of any after-sales services and guarantees, the duration of the contract, the obligations of the consumer and whether any deposit is required. The list repeats the requirements under the Distance Selling Directive with a couple of additions. The business is required to provide this information to the consumer if it is not "already apparent from the context".[50] This phrase is concerning, seems a little vague and is potentially the cause of litigation if a consumer claims not to have been advised of this information whilst the trader believes that the consumer should have obtained all the information from their negotiations. Additional alterations from the pre-existing legal landscape are the penalties for failure to provide the information. The existing extension to the right to withdraw is retained (see below), while Article 6(1) further states that if consumers do not receive the information about additional charges, as required in Article 5(1)(c), then consumers will not be obliged to pay these charges. The information required under Article 5 needs to be provided in plain and intelligible language and also needs to be legible and delivered using a durable medium (the problems with the definition of the term 'durable medium' are discussed briefly above).[51] The pre-contract information must also be provided in a way appropriate to the means of distance communication used.[52] If the contract is being concluded by a means which allows for limited space or time to display the information (for example SMS), then the trader needs to provide the main characteristics of the product and the total price. The remainder of the information should follow in an appropriate manner.[53] It is not clear, however, how

---

[50] Article 5(1).
[51] Article 11(4).
[52] Article 11(1).
[53] Article 11(3).

the information is to be arranged, either on the receiving machine with limited space or when it follows at a later date.

The right to withdraw is outlined in Articles 12–20. The exceptions to the right to withdraw are found in Articles 19 and 20. Article 19 states that the right to withdraw does not extend to contracts for services where performance has begun (with the consumer's express consent) before the end of the four-teen day period, contracts where the price fluctuates, goods that are made to the consumer's specifications, the supply of wine (where the price was agreed at the conclusion of the contract), the supply of sealed audio or visual record-ings or computer software, the supply of newspapers, periodicals and maga-zines, gaming and lottery services and contracts concluded at an auction.[54] Article 20 lists the partial exceptions, in that Articles 8–19 do not apply to contracts for the sale of immovable property, contracts concluded by an auto-mated vending machine, contracts through a telecommunications operator by public payphone, contracts for foodstuffs or beverages brought by a trader on frequent and regular rounds in the neighbourhood.[55] There is also a partial exception to the withdrawal right for distance contracts for accommodation, transport, car rental services, catering and leisure services, with a specific time and date.[56] These exceptions seem to have a large degree of familiarity about them in that they seem to be a reproduction of the original Distance Selling Directive. In terms of protecting a consumer this appears to be somewhat of a missed opportunity. The protection afforded to consumers is weakened by the exceptions which remain in Article 19 and 20. The exemptions listed within Article 19 are very wide and cover the majority of occasions a consumer goes online (booking a holiday, ordering food from a major supermarket, buying an aeroplane ticket, online auctions etc.). Accordingly the draft Directive offers only very limited rights to the consumer, without a great deal of difference to the exceptions that were in existence beforehand.

The mechanism for withdrawing from a contract can be located in Article 12 and the initial parameters provide the consumer with fourteen calendar days in which they can withdraw from a distance contract without giving any reason. The fourteen day period commences from the day on which the consumer (or the consumer's agent) acquires each of the goods ordered.[57] In contracts where the consumer orders more than one good and the goods arrive separately, recital 26 is quite clear when it states that a withdrawal right is in existence for each good. (Article 13 states that if the consumer is not advised about their right to withdraw, the period of withdrawal will expire after three months). The increased time a consumer has to withdraw from the

---

[54] Article 19(1) (a–h).
[55] Article 20 (1) (a–d).
[56] Article 20(3).
[57] Article 12(2).

contract is clearly positive for the consumer, although is perhaps less helpful for businesses, particularly if a sale and a withdrawal happen either side of a VAT/tax cut-off date. Furthermore, there is the ongoing issue of goods that reduce in value very shortly after purchase – a car being a good example. If a consumer purchases a new car and drives it for twelve days and then wishes to return it, the car has obviously depreciated in value, which the seller may be unable to reclaim. Article 17 attempts to answer this query by providing that consumers have fourteen days in which they are required to return the goods. The consumer will only be charged the direct price of returning the goods, unless the goods have diminished in value resulting from use beyond that which was needed to ascertain the nature and functioning of the goods.[58] This issue is potentially litigious as the difficulty remains as to how the exact amount of the 'diminished value' is to be ascertained and whether a consumer has used a good beyond the level required to ascertain its functionality. If a consumer wishes to withdraw they need to advise the trader of their decision within fourteen days in a durable medium.[59] In the Distance Selling Directive, a list is provided containing the ways in which a consumer can advise the business that they wish to withdraw, however in the draft Directive this is not provided. Indeed, it leaves open the possibility that a consumer will be able to withdraw by telephoning the trader, which could lead to problems further down the line if a dispute arises with each party having difficulty proving that a telephone call cancelling the contract was made. It was for this reason that the 2005 amendment to the Distance Selling Regulations did not extend to allowing consumers to cancel by telephone. It can also be inferred that simply returning the goods to the trader may not constitute an adequate withdrawal. The draft Directive does however (in Annex 1) provide a standard withdrawal form, which a consumer can use to cancel a contract. This seems a little unnecessary and perhaps a tad patronizing. But if this is the direction the legislation wishes to go, it may be beneficial to add a reference or invoice number space, so it would be easier for the business to locate the order with a degree of precision. After a withdrawal notice has been made (by whatever means), the consumer has fourteen days to return the goods to the trader. The cost of returning the goods is borne by the consumer and whilst this may be fairly straightforward with smaller goods, obvious problems arise with larger goods, which are likely to be significantly more expensive to return. There is also the question of the balance of risk and where the transfer of risk occurs from the consumer returning the goods to the trader receiving them. Once the withdrawal notice has been made the trader has thirty days to reimburse the money paid by the consumer for the good or service.[60] It is also interesting to note that there is

---

[58] Article 17(1) and (2).
[59] Article 14(1).
[60] Article 16(1).

no minimum price threshold for withdrawal. Currently, a contract can only be cancelled if the good or service is worth more than £35. Arguably removal of this threshold may place a large burden upon traders.

The proposed Directive as it stands is a little disappointing as it (in many ways) is simply a 'copy and paste' of the old distance selling regime and retains a large body of exceptions to the standard protection in areas (such as travel, accommodation, food and drink) where consumers are very active online. Also, the draft Directive does not assist with the moment a contract is formed. This is not adequately addressed in other legislation either and it seems a little odd to have a range of criteria for forming a distance contract and rights that exist afterwards, without outlining the moment a contract is formed. The United Kingdom government has been consulting widely on its proposed implementation. In November 2008 the then Department of Business, Enterprise and Regulatory Reform issued a consultation on the plans.[61] It invited interested parties to comment on over sixty questions. Over fifty responses were received from business groups, academics, consumer associations and other interested stakeholders and the government (through the newly formed Department for Business, Innovation and Skills) published its response in July 2009.[62] At the same time, the European Union Committee of the House of Lords also published their report on the proposals.[63] The views held in both the response by the government and by the House of Lords were similar in nature. Both expressed their support to the European Commission in their aims of simplifying the law in this area and removing inconsistencies, while increasing the protection available to consumers. The full harmonisation approach was generally welcomed, although there was concern expressed that it meant further rules could not be added[64] despite the sentiments of recital 8, which state that full harmonisation will increase legal certainty for both consumers and businesses. Indeed, the full harmonisation approach could in some areas reduce the available protection to consumers. Yet, despite the advantages of full harmonisation, this approach was dropped. Concern was also expressed that the draft Directive as it stands may not fully achieve its aims in enhancing cross-border trade. Indeed in 2009 the European Commission published a report which stated that only 6–7 per cent of consumers from the European Union

---

[61] DBERR, *Consultation on EU Proposals for a Consumer Rights Directive* (November 2008). Available at: http://www.berr.gov.uk/consultations/page48780.html.

[62] BIS, *Government Response to the Consultation Document on the EU Proposals for a Consumer Rights Directive* (July 2009). Available at: http://www.berr.gov.uk/consultations/page48780.html.

[63] House of Lords European Union Committee *EU Consumer Rights Directive: getting it right* (July 2009) 18th Report of Session 2008-09. Available at: http://www.parliament.the-stationery-office.co.uk/pa/ld200809/ldselect/ldeucom/126/126i.pdf.

[64] Indeed, the ECJ in case C261/07 and C299/07 VTB-VAB NV v Total Belgium NV and Galatea BUBA v Sanoma Magazines Belgium NV held that member states cannot introduce any further measure to a full harmonisation directive, even if the aim is to increase consumer protection.

engage in cross-border e-commerce.[65] It does not matter how effective the consumer protection regime is because cross-border trade will not increase until issues relating to language, culture, physical distance and technical specifications are addressed. The draft Directive needs to consider some of these fundamental issues before achievement of this aim will be fully realised. Another consideration with the proposal is that it does not include business-to-business contracts. Whilst the Distance Selling Directive does not include such contracts within its remit a discussion needs to be had about whether this is an appropriate stance to continue, particularly when a large multi-national firm contracts with a small enterprise.

Current analysis suggests that this draft Directive will not be implemented until 2013 at the earliest. While discussion at national and European level continues changes will inevitably be made to the proposal as it stands. However it is clear that in the not-so-distant future the consumer protection landscape for online sales will alter – exactly by how much remains to be seen.

Key points:

- European Directive 97/7/EC on Distance Selling was implemented into the UK as the Consumer Protection (Distance Selling) Regulations 2000.
- It seeks to provide protection to consumers who contract online, or by other means of distance communication.
- The regulations apply to business-to-consumer contracts for goods or services agreed exclusively through an organised distance sale.
- It provides rules for ensuring that consumers are provided with key information prior to the conclusion of the contract and in the majority of cases have opportunity to withdraw from the contract up to seven days after the goods have been delivered.
- There are a number of contracts which fall completely outside the remit of the legislation. These are found in regulation 5 and include contracts for the sale of land, construction, financial services and auctions.
- A number of partial exceptions are found within regulation 6 and these are contracts for *inter alia* accommodation, transport services, leisure provisions and deliveries by a regular roundsman.
- Regulations 10–18 provide the ability for a consumer to cancel a contract within seven days. Both parties must be returned to the position they were in prior to the formation of the contract.

---

[65] European Commission Staff Working Document *Report on cross-border e-commerce in the EU* (March 2009). Available at: http://ec.europa.eu/consumers/strategy/docs/com_staff_wp2009_en.pdf.

- The withdrawal period can be extended to three months and seven days if the business fails to provide the consumer with the pre-contract information that is set out in regulations 7 and 8.
- In 2004, the then Department of Trade and Industry consulted on the regulations, which led to minor changes being introduced by the Consumer Protection (Distance Selling) (Amendment) Regulations 2005.
- The European Commission's review of the Consumer Acquis led to the forwarding of the Proposed Directive on Consumer Rights.
- This proposes a number of changes in the consumer protection legislation in this area, including an extension to the withdrawal period to fourteen days and changes in key definitions.
- The proposal was initially a full harmonisation measure, meaning that member states will be unable to legislate for less or greater consumer protection. However in early 2010, the European Union's Commissioner with responsibility for consumer protection, Viviane Reding, announced that this principle was being removed in the hope that it would ease its passage through the European Parliament.
- Current predictions suggest that the proposed Directive will be introduced by 2013.

Further reading:

- Hall, L *Cancellation rights in distance-selling contracts for services: exemptions and consumer protection* (September 2007) Journal of Business Law, pages 683–700.
- Helberger, N *Making place for the iConsumer in Consumer Law* (2008) Journal of Consumer Policy, volume 31, pages 385–391.
- Hörnle, J *Is an Online Auction an 'auction' in law?* (2007) Electronic Business Law, volume 8, issue 12, pages 7–9.
- Jolly, I *The UK Distance Selling Regulations: A Guide for Business* (October 2005) World Internet Law Report, pages 3–5.
- Mak, C *Fundamental Rights and the European Regulation of iConsumer Contracts* (2008) Journal of Consumer Policy, volume 31, pages 425–439.
- Massey, R *Sales for the next century: Europe's draft Directive on consumer rights* (2009) Computer and Telecommunications Law Review, volume 15, issue 2, pages 23–25.
- Ramberg, C *Internet Marketplaces – The Law of Auctions and Exchanges Online* (2002) Oxford University Press.
- Stone, K *Distance Selling changes aim to clarify cancellation right* (August 2005) E-Commerce Law and Policy, pages 3–5.

- Twigg-Flesner, C & Metcalfe, D *The proposed Consumer Rights Directive – less haste, more thought?* (2009) European Review of Contract Law, volume 6, issue 3. Available at SSRN: http://ssrn.com/abstract=1345783.

Questions for consideration:

3.1. List some of the advantages and disadvantages of online shopping.

3.2. What is a distance contract, as defined in the Consumer Protection (Distance Selling) Regulations 2000?

3.3. What types of contracts are excluded from the regulations?

3.4. What information does a supplier need to provide to a consumer prior to the conclusion of the contract? How does this information need to be provided?

3.5. Explain how a consumer can withdraw from a distance contract.

3.6. Who bears the cost for returning the good to the supplier?

3.7. Outline some of the main differences between the Distance Selling Directive and the Proposed Directive on Consumer Rights.

3.8. 'The Consumer Protection (Distance Selling) Regulations 2000 is arguably the main piece of legislation offering protection for people who transact on the Internet. However, without any doubt the Regulations are weak and offer consumers very little protection.'
To what extent do you agree with this statement?

3.9. Matthew is the managing director of an online company. He has been in operation for over five years and has built up a successful customer base within the United Kingdom. Last Christmas particularly saw a large increase in their sales. Matthew is eager to ensure that his customers are treated fairly and legally and he goes to considerable length to maintain the goodwill of the business. However, he has had a few unhappy customers speak to him on separate occasions, about the following issues:

a. Lisa sent an email on Thursday 10th May to Matthew saying that she would like to return the goods to Matthew that she purchased on Monday 7th May (three days earlier) because she did not like them. Matthew operates a non-return policy.

b. Colin has written to Matthew complaining about the cost of delivery for a good he ordered. Colin includes a copy of some preliminary information sent to him by Matthew, which includes no reference to delivery costs at all. Colin wants to return the good. He purchased the good just over two weeks ago.

c. Matthew sends out calendars to each of his good customers around Christmas. Sally has complained about the invoice that came along with the calendar requesting payment of £15.99 (including taxes and delivery costs) within 28 days. Sally is particularly annoyed as she did not ask for the calendar.

d.   John telephoned Matthew two days after buying a good wanting to cancel it. Once again Matthew refused.

Matthew would appreciate any assistance you could offer him about any other legal requirements placed upon him by the **Consumer Protection (Distance Selling) Regulations 2000** *and any relevant provisions since the regulations were slightly amended.*

Two weeks later, Matthew speaks to you again and mentions that he is considering going into the online car-hire business. Do you have any additional advice for him?

3.10.   'The draft Directive on Consumers Rights introduced by the European Commission in 2009 makes wholesale changes to the protection afforded to the consumer who engages in online purchasing. It is without doubt that the nature of this protection is clearly to the advantage of the consumer who will be in a significantly better position than under the current Distance Selling Directive regime.'

To what extent do you agree with this statement?

All weblinks mentioned in the text can also be found at
http://www.palgrave.com/law/rogers

4 Online Payment, Gambling and Taxation

> **This chapter will consider:**
>
> - The methods in which a consumer and businesses can pay for online transactions.
> - Traditional and more modern methods of payment.
> - The legal issues surrounding taxation of online purchases.
> - The requirements to tax, the easier availability of tax havens and approaches to the relative privacy attached to tax returns.
> - The original E-Money Directive 2000/46/EC, its deficiencies and whether the new E-Money Directive 2009/110/EC provides an adequate legal framework for the e-money industry.
> - The provisions of the Payment Services Regulations 2009 and how they relate to e-money.
> - An explanation of reasons behind the growth of online gambling and the advantages and disadvantages when compared with traditional forms of gambling.
> - The relevant provisions contained within the Gambling Act 2005.

Online transactions

The nature of payment is evolving. Banks no longer have the monopoly on payment transactions as cheques and cash continue to reduce in usage. The Internet has overseen a shift in culture from traditional payment methods to evolution of a 'cash-less' society, where credit and debit cards, e-money and other payment systems (including pre-paid cards and specialist payment transfer providers) are being used to a greater degree. In April 2010, the Payments Council[1] published a wide-ranging report entitled 'The Way We Pay: The UK's Payment Revolution'.[2] It reported that during the first decade of the twenty-first

---

[1] An organisation that seeks to set the strategy for payment within the United Kingdom – see http://www.paymentscouncil.org.uk.
[2] Available at: http://www.paymentscouncil.org.uk//files/payments_council/the_way_we_pay_2010_final.pdf.

century the methods people used to make payment changed dramatically. Internet banking increased along with the use of payment cards, particularly debit cards. The use of a cheque is becoming a rarity, with only 0.8 per cent of retail transactions paid for in this way, which led the Payments Council to announce that cheques would be phased out by 2018. It was also predicted that by 2015 less than half of transactions will be paid for using cash due to a continual increase and improvement in technology allowing for swift and secure payment. E-commerce by its very nature demands effective and robust mechanisms for ensuring that payment is successfully made. Online payments need to be safe, secure and immediate to ensure that there are no delays in the transfer or delivery of the goods. There are also issues relating to a need for trust in the system and accessibility to ensure that a critical mass of consumers use any given system. A payment system which has incidents of security breaches is not going to be accepted by a financially conservative and risk-averse general public. The vast majority of online contracts demand that a form of financial payment is made, although no single system for making online payments currently exists. Instead there is a range of systems – both modern and traditional – employed by businesses and consumers to allow payment to be made. Even though the 1990s saw a growth in payment systems and other methods of storing value equivalent to cash[3] (caused largely by the dot com boom), these new systems have failed to really take off and the most widely used online payment method continues to be the credit card. This chapter will consider why this is the case. It will also examine other online payment mechanisms and will consider the relative successes of these systems.

Traditional payment methods

Payment by cash is seen as absolute and has many advantages. Cash is accepted anywhere and although different currencies exist, many companies are happy to accept other major currencies and so the Euro, the Australian and American Dollar and the British Pound are readily available and transferrable.

---

[3] One such example was the Mondex smart card developed by the National Westminster Bank in 1990 and later sold to MasterCard. This was a members-only organisation that provided chipped cards and allowed members to transfer money from one person to a recipient by placing the card into a card reader, which then transferred the money instantly. The advantages of the Mondex card was that it was safer than carrying currency (although if lost the result is the same for the owner), it could operate online, was portable, and users retained anonymity. However, in order for a user to 'top-up' a Mondex card they needed to have access to a particular type of ATM machine and the card could then only be used in stores that had signed up to the scheme and had the required reader for the card. For these reasons, the Mondex system did not really take off, although the principles behind it did form the basis of Transport for London's Oyster Card System. For information on the current structure of Mondex see: http://www.mondex.com/.

There is no transaction charge when payment is made by cash[4] and a person using this as a means of payment is able to conceal their full identity. There are disadvantages to this form of payment though. Although security methods continue to improve, cash is susceptible to forgery and a person may be in receipt of a forged note and will be unable to do anything about this. Also, cash is very easy to lose and once lost there is nothing that a person can do to get the money back. In terms of e-commerce cash is wholly impractical as it is inadvisable to send cash in the post (even by special or recorded delivery) and the advantages of online shopping are removed if the buyer visits the business in question to make payment. For these reasons, credit and debit cards are the most widely used and popular method of payment for online transactions. Credit cards can be issued by credit card companies as well as by banks. This differs somewhat to debit cards, which are issued by the cardholder's bank and take the money directly from the account of the buyer into the account of the seller. Strictly speaking, a credit card does not provide payment but debt substitution, as the credit card company promises to pay for the item instead of the consumer. There are many advantages to their usage. The use of credit cards in the United Kingdom is widespread. They are very widely accepted and trusted and consumers are protected under the terms of section 75 of the Consumer Credit Act 1974. The principle of section 75 is that if a consumer purchases goods or services by credit card and there is a subsequent breach of contract, or it became apparent that the sale was induced by a misrepresentation, then the consumer will have a claim against not only the supplier, but also against the credit card company. This is not a uniform rule as there is the requirement that the sale needs to be between £100 and £30,000 and must have been paid for using a credit card (debit cards are not covered by this section). The consumer protection law in this area has recently undergone a degree of European-level reform with Directive 2008/45/EC on credit agreements for consumers,[5] although the provisions of section 75 have been retained.[6] This means that if a consumer makes a purchase using a credit card and the item is not delivered or the supplier becomes bankrupt then the consumer can reclaim their money from the credit card company. The provisions of the 1974 Act were also strengthened by the House of Lords, which

---

[4] A usual exception to this is when payment is made internationally. Current money transfer systems include BACS and CHAPS. These are clearing houses for money transfers, but a user needs a bank account in order to take advantage of these systems. Two main types of bank transfers are standing orders (regular payments of the same amount) and direct debits (different amounts on a regular basis). These systems are used for, amongst other things, paying wages and utility bills. See the judgment of Staughton J in **Libyan Arab Foreign Bank v Bankers Trust** [1989] QB 728, which considers the nature of a bank transfer.

[5] Available at: http://eur-lex.europa.eu/LexUriServ/LexUriServ.do?uri=OJ:L:2008:133:0066:0092:EN:PDF.

[6] Although Article 2(2)(c) of Directive 2008/48/EC covers credit agreements up to 60,000, which is higher than that provided by the Consumer Credit Act 1974.

held that the protection extended to foreign transactions as well as purchases made within the United Kingdom.[7] Credit cards allow consumers to purchase goods or services very easily with a period of interest-free credit before the amount is required to be paid back. A credit card has a credit limit, which is the maximum amount of money a person may take out on that card and if this limited is exceeded, the credit card company will usually impose a weighty financial penalty and higher rates of interest. Despite this, they are easy to use, and security is improving. Since February 2006, all credit cards within the United Kingdom are required to be 'chip and pin' enabled. This means that when purchasing a good in a shop, instead of signing to pay for the goods and your signature being checked against the signature on the back of the card, a customer enters their four digit PIN. This has seen a noticeable drop in credit card fraud in a shop context, although a rise in 'cardholder not present' credit card fraud has been noticed.[8] Once payment is made by a credit card, it is deemed to be absolute. In other words, a seller cannot pursue the buyer for payment. This was one issue discussed in the case of **Re Charge Card Services Ltd.**[9] The main focus of the case was whether a charge card was an absolute or conditional payment. The argument in the case was that there is a general principle in English law saying that if there is any risk of non-payment the payment remains conditional until the money is transferred. Therefore, a cash sale would be an example of an absolute payment as once the cash payment is received by the seller there is no risk of the payment not being made. The court held that whilst the general principle was accurate the extension of the principle to the charge card was inappropriate. Like a credit card, a charge card payment is absolute and the supplier would be unable to pursue the customer in the event of the card issuer becoming insolvent. The reasoning of the court was that the supplier would be unable to trace the address of the user as no address was provided. Further, the advantages of this system would be under-mined if the payment was only held to be conditional. There are a number of disadvantages to credit card use however. Their very nature means that they cannot be owned and used by anyone under the age of 18. Children and teenagers (who are an important consumer base for many businesses) are unable to use credit cards, thus preventing them from engaging in online commerce with this medium. Furthermore, while credit cards are generally 'free' for the consumer to use, a charge is levied against the business receiving the payment (this is usually a small percentage of the total payment). Some

---

[7] **Office of Fair Trading v Lloyds TSB Bank Plc** [2007] 3 WLR 733.

[8] Other security problems with the 'Chip and Pin' system, including cloning and tricking the card reading terminal, have been highlighted. See: BBC News (Watts, S) *New flaws in chip and pin system revealed* (11th February 2010). Available at: http://www.bbc.co.uk/blogs/newsnight/susanwatts/2010/02/new_flaws_in_chip_and_pin_syst.html and BBC News *Net card fraud 'underestimated'* (23rd April 2008). Available at: http://news.bbc.co.uk/1/hi/business/7362055.stm.

[9] (1987) Ch 150.

companies may pass this on to the consumer, but regardless of whether the charge is passed on or not, the very nature of the charge means that credit cards are an uneconomic means of making small or micropayments. Although businesses can circumvent the micropayment difficulty by requesting consumers pay a 'subscription' fee, which can be topped up when it has diminished, this is not an ideal solution as it requires consumers to provide money to a company for services which they may (or may not) take advantage of in the future. Furthermore, while credit cards are continually becoming less susceptible to fraud, new methods of obtaining details are always developing, whether through shoulder surfing (looking over someone's shoulder while they enter their PIN), cloning a credit card or by 'phishing' for details.

Other payment systems have been piloted over the past couple of decades. These include digital or e-money, Internet Cash, Cyber Cash and Net Cheque.[10] A specific example of the digital or e-money is that of Digicash, which was established in the early 1990s. This had the potential of being a pure online payment system, as users would obtain software that placed an electronic wallet on the hard drive of their computer. This would be kept secure by use of encryption. Users could then electronically purchase Digicash, which would be sent (in encrypted form) to the electronic wallet. After purchasing a good or service, the user could then transfer electronically its value to the supplier. There were many advantages to this system. The money was divisible and anonymous meaning that it had very similar qualities to traditional cash, and there was also no fee for transferring the money. Further, in the event of forgery the encrypted files containing values of money could be deactivated to prevent theft. Yet the use of these – and many other – systems has dwindled. One of the main difficulties faced by Digicash was that it was not very portable and the electronic wallet was linked to the hard drive of a computer meaning that users could only access it from one machine. Like Mondex (considered above) it never really took off, leading to Digicash filing for bankruptcy in 1998. In general though, there are two main reasons for the failure of these newer online payment methods. First of all they did not achieve universal recognition and secondly, because this universal recognition had not been achieved these systems could not realise full acceptability. Businesses are reticent to invest in software and machinery to operate a payment system that only has limited uptake by consumers. Equally, consumers are unwilling to engage with payment systems that are new due to security risks and lack of universal recognition. Arguably, the fact that many of these online payment systems were introduced by private companies with no track record did not install confidence from the start. Although these systems had some advantages (for instance, being able to make micropayments) the failures in these e-money

---

[10] For more on these online payment systems see: Wild, C, Weinstein, S, MacEwan, N *Internet Law* Old Bailey Press 2005, particularly pages 124–133.

systems meant that the systems were never considered an absolute discharge for payment. However, some newer payment systems have been able to jump these hurdles into both acceptability and universality. One such example is that of Paypal, which even though a private company has established itself as a leader in its field. Starting in 1999 Paypal was initially used for consumer-to-consumer payments, although business-to-consumer payments followed shortly afterwards. The turning point in Paypal's history came in October 2002, when the online auction site eBay purchased Paypal for $1.5bn dollars. Paypal had become the payment system of choice for over 50 per cent of eBay users and this payment system found itself in competition with eBay's then payment system of Billpoint. Today Paypal is eBay's payment system of choice – at the time of writing there are over 185 million accounts and payment can be accepted in 19 currencies in over 100 countries. The reach of Paypal is continuing to grow and in 2009, it became the only payment system for the purchase of BlackBerry Applications. Setting up a Paypal account is straightforward. A user enters a few personal details and then verifies their identity. Payment into the Paypal account is made directly from the user's bank account or credit card by direct debit. The advantages of this system are plentiful. No specific software is required, payments between Paypal accounts clear instantly and it is very easy to use. Further advantages that Paypal holds over credit cards are that it is able to cope with small and micropayments and there is also no age restriction placed upon users.[11] Paypal has not been without its share of controversy as it has in the past frozen customers' accounts for long periods of time without sufficient warning or reasoning and has also had to alter its dispute resolution schemes following complaints and occasional litigation.

The E-Money Directives 2000/46/EC and 2009/110/EC

As online payment systems (successful and otherwise) increased, the European Commission was keen to establish a context within which e-money providers could operate. On 18th September 2000, Directive 2000/46/EC on the taking up, pursuit of and prudential supervision of the business of electronic money institutions was passed.[12] The aim behind this Directive was to harmonise the regulatory supervision of, and to increase public confidence in, e-money issuers by providing strict standards that e-money institutions needed to follow.[13] An

---

[11] For more on Paypal see: Gonzalez, A G *PayPal: the legal status of C2C payment systems* (2004) Computer Law and Security Report, Volume 20, Issue 4, pages 293–299.

[12] Available at: http://eur-lex.europa.eu/LexUriServ/LexUriServ.do?uri=OJ:L:2000:275:0039:0043: EN:PDF.

[13] Recital 5 of 2000/46/EC speaks about the importance of providing a regulatory framework so that e-money usage can achieve its full potential and technological development is not restrained.

electronic money institution was defined in Article 1(3)(a) as an undertaking or other legal person, other than a credit institution, which issues means of payment in the form of electronic money.[14] This definition was closely linked to the requirements for an e-money institution contained within Article 1(5), which restricted the activities of their business to a number of very discrete areas. First, to administer and issue e-money. Second, to the provision of closely related financial and non-financial services such as the administering of electronic money by the performance of operational and other ancillary functions related to its issuance, and the issuing and administering of other means of payment but excluding the granting of any form of credit. Finally, to store data on electronic devices on behalf of other undertakings or public institutions. The effect of these restrictions was emphasised in the final sentence of Article 1(5), which stated that e-money institutions were not allowed to have a holding in any other undertaking except where they formed an organisational or ancillary function to the e-money that had been issued. The effect of this was to bar companies (with the exception of credit institutions, such as banks) from operating as an e-money institution as well as operating in different areas of the economy. This meant that in order to be an e-money institution you either had to be a bank (or other credit issuing company) or a bespoke e-money institution. The rationale behind this was to protect large banks, while also allowing small e-money institutions to develop and innovate in this area.

However, the reality was somewhat different. Although restricting the ability of companies to become e-money institutions had good intentions, the requirements placed on e-money institutions were extremely onerous, meaning that very few new e-money institutions were encouraged into the market. Article 4 outlined these requirements, which included the need for e-money institutions to have a minimum capital requirement of €1m[15] and to retain a higher level of operating funds, equivalent to 2 per cent of the higher of the current amount or the average of the preceding six months' total amount of their financial liabilities related to outstanding electronic money.[16] Furthermore, Article 5 stipulated that the e-money providers also needed to have investments of no less than their financial liabilities in low risk accounts. The European Commission had tried to achieve a balance between providing confidence for consumers to enable them to engage with e-money, while trying to secure the financial probity of e-money institutions. However, this was

---

[14] Electronic money was defined in Article 1(3)(b) as momentary value as represented by a claim on the issuer which is: stored on an electronic device, issued on receipt of fund of an amount not less in value than the monetary value issued, and accepted as means of payment by undertakings other than the issuer. However, no definition of electronic device was provided.
[15] Directive 2000/46/EC, Article 4(1).
[16] Directive 2000/46/EC, Article 4(2).

not achieved and when the European Commission provided their report[17] on the effectiveness on Directive 2000/46/EC[18] it was found that since the implementation of the Directive only nine independent e-money institutions had come into existence. The report offered further criticisms of the legislation regime, including that realisation that the e-money market had developed more slowly than anticipated and that no single, clear e-money system had been achieved. There also seemed to be confusion about the business advantages for engaging in the e-money market as the stringent requirements placed upon e-money institutions acted as a disincentive. It was also noted that different implementation methods of the Directive within member states did not assist in achieving harmonisation in this area. However, one of the more interesting conclusions from the report was that the Directive was no longer in line with the technological direction that electronic payment systems had taken. Instead of e-money institutions dictating the pace and systems, credit and debit card usage had continued to increase, and smartcards within particular areas (such as the Oyster Card) had also increased. A further development was the increase of payment by mobile phone and other forms of m-commerce. It was uncertain whether the provisions of the E-Money Directive extended to mobile devices. The evaluation was roundly critical of the legislation as it stood, and therefore the European Commission launched a substantial review which aimed to update the regulation of e-money institutions.[19] The European Commission published its report in July 2006 into the earlier review on the E-Money Directive. Further consultation and review occurred until October 2009, when the new E-Money Directive was issued.[20]

Recital 2 of Directive 2009/110/EC was forthright in suggesting that the old E-Money Directive 2000/46/EC was responsible for hindering the emergence of a true single market for e-money services, while recital 4 stated that the rules for e-money institutions needed to be reviewed to ensure a level playing field for all payment services providers. The result was a directive that provided much more flexibility and openness for companies to engage in providing e-money.[21] A key difference within the new Directive is that the definition of an e-money institution has been widened and is defined as a legal person who has been authorised to issue e-money. This definition needs to be read in conjunction with

---

[17] *Evaluation of the E-Money Directive 2000/46/EC* for the DG Internal Market, The European Commission (17th February 2006). Available at: http://ec.europa.eu/internal_market/payments/docs/emoney/evaluation_en.pdf.

[18] As was required under Article 11 of Directive 2000/46/EC.

[19] European Commission Staff Working Document *Review of the E-Money Directive (2000/46/EC)* SEC(2006) 1049. Available at: http://ec.europa.eu/internal_market/payments/docs/emoney/working-document_en.pdf.

[20] Directive 2009/110/EC on the taking up, pursuit and prudential supervision of the business of electronic money institutions. Available at: http://eur-lex.europa.eu/LexUriServ/LexUriServ.do?uri=OJ:L:2009:267:0007:0017:EN:PDF.

[21] The original E-Money Directive 2000/46/EC has now been repealed.

Article 6(1), which provides a lengthy list of other activities that e-money institutions may get involved in, including the provision of payment services[22], granting credit, offering organisational or ancillary services relating to the provision of e-money, and finally (and most crucially), any other legitimate business activity. Immediately, the restrictiveness of the new Directive's predecessor, which required e-money institutions to stay exclusively with this pursuit, has been removed. This in turn has the advantage of making the entire industry much more competitive and opens the market to many more companies who may wish to get involved, who are now able to offer mixed services. This is not the only rule which has been watered down, as the requirements relating to the liquidity of the e-money institution are significantly less stringent, although Article 5 does provide a fairly complex list of requirements concerning the financing of the e-money institution.[23] The issue of whether m-commerce is covered by the legislation has been addressed by the Directive and recital 6 states that

> "the Directive does not apply to the purchase of digital goods or services, where, by virtue of the nature of the good or service, the operator adds intrinsic value to it, e.g. in the form of access, search or distribution facilities, provided that the good or service in question can be used only through a digital device, such as a mobile phone or a computer, and provided that the telecommunication, digital or information technology operator does not act only as an intermediary between the payment service user and the supplier of the goods and services."

This is a situation where a mobile phone or other digital network subscriber pays the network operator directly and there is neither a direct payment relationship nor a direct debtor–creditor relationship between the network subscriber and any third-party supplier of goods or services delivered as part of the transaction. This recital means that purchases such as an application for a mobile phone or a digital download are outside of the remit of the legislation. These will instead fall within the Payment Services Directive, which is discussed below.

Payment Services Directive 2007/64/EC

Directive 2007/64/EC on payment services within the internal market stemmed from a European Commission initiative to regulate electronic means of payment within the European Union. Directive 2007/64/EC was passed in

---

[22] As listed in Annex 1 of the Payment Services Directive 2007/64/EC (see discussion below).
[23] These requirements are brought in line with the Payment Services Directive 2007/64/EC.

2007 and sought to make electronic payments more efficient and to remove barriers to payment systems.[24] The Directive was implemented into the United Kingdom as the Payment Services Regulations 2009 and came into force in March 2009. The Directive sought to be a maximum harmonisation measure and at the heart of the legislation lay three core principles. First of all, the creation of an authorisation scheme for providers of payment systems;[25] secondly to harmonise the business rules that apply to payment service providers; and thirdly to open up payment systems within the European Union.[26] Further objectives included the aim to increase competition, enhance efficiency and also to provide a level playing field for all payment institutions. The regulations cover all payment service providers, including banks, building societies, credit institutions and electronic money institutions. Within the United Kingdom, the Financial Services Authority is the body appointed to authorise providers (although the Office of Fair Trading, Her Majesty's Revenue and Customs and the Financial Ombudsman Service also have roles in this area). It is the responsibility of the Financial Services Authority to establish a register of payment service providers and set out the conditions and procedure for registration.[27] There are two main sections to the regulations – the rules for payment service providers and the rules they need to follow to conduct their business, including whether charges can be made for services and the liabilities in the event of a non-payment. An e-money institution would be required to register under these provisions[28] and Part 5 of the regulations details the information requirements placed upon these institutions in terms of the details they are required to give users. A payment service provider will need to either register, or be fully authorised to the Financial Services Authority. If the average value of payments is less than €3m a month and they are not engaging in cross-border payments, the organisation will need to register with the Financial Services Authority. However, if the payment value is more than €3m and the organisation seeks to engage in cross-border commerce in other member states, they will then need to obtain full authorisation.

The effect of the Payment Services Directive 2007/64/EC and the new E-Money Directive 2009/110/EC is that there are now three levels of payment service providers, with banks at the top, e-money institutions in the middle and all other payment providers at the bottom. The result is that there are different

---

[24] Directive 2007/64/EC is available at: http://eur-lex.europa.eu/LexUriServ/LexUriServ.do?uri=OJ:L:2007:319:0001:01:en:HTML.
[25] An exhaustive list of what amounts to a 'payment service' is found within Schedule 1, Part 1 of the regulations.
[26] See The Payment Services Regulations 2009 No. 209 Explanatory Note. Available at: http://www.legislation.gov.uk/uksi/2009/209/note/made.
[27] Payment Services Regulations 2009, Part 2.
[28] Failure to do so is a criminal offence under Part 9.

capital requirements for e-money institutions and other payment institutions.[29] However (as discussed previously) the nature of electronic payment has taken a different course to that which was anticipated, with continued usage of credit and debit cards and greater reliance on m-commerce to make payments. It remains to be seen whether the new legislative landscape will allow new methods of online payment to flourish, or will continue to restrict their growth by rigid regulatory rules.

Online gambling

Adequate payment methods are needed for a range of online activities, with one of the more popular being online gambling. Gambling has been present throughout history and has appeared in many different forms. It is clear the Internet did not create this activity, although the ease of access and the convenience offered has widened participation.[30] Prior to the Gambling Act 2005, there was a range of enacted legislation that sought to regulate gambling activities. These Acts included the Betting, Gaming and Lotteries Act 1963, the Gaming Act 1968, the Lotteries and Amusements Act 1976 and the Betting and Gaming Duties Act 1981. These statutes legislated for lotteries, betting, prize competitions and wagers, but they were not enacted with technology in mind, such as television, the Internet and mobile devices. The nature of gambling has altered with the developments in new technology and allows people to bet not only on the result of, say, a game of football, but also the first goal, first scorer, time of the first goal, the number of corners, and the timing of any penalty. Advertisements for these gambling activities were very high profile during the 2010 FIFA World Cup held in South Africa. These wagers can be placed not only before the game, but also during the game and from the comfort of the participant's own home. The advantages and disadvantages of online gambling are well rehearsed and are very similar to those for almost any online activity, from shopping and communicating to online banking. Instead

---

[29] The Payment Services Directive has requirements for a minimum capital requirement of between €20,000–125,000. The effect of this was to make the capital requirements placed upon e-money institutions in the E-Money Directive 2000/46/EC look overly stringent. This was another driver in the reform proposals leading to the new E-Money Directive 2009/110/EC, which has more relaxed capital requirements.

[30] The industry statistics for 2008/09 published by the Gambling Commission reported that from March 2008 to March 2009 around 9.9 per cent of adults had engaged in some form of remote gambling. This was a slight rise (9.7 per cent) from the year before and a reasonable increase from the year before that (7.7 per cent in 2007). Remote gambling by use of a computer or laptop was the most popular method (8.2 per cent of respondents), while 2.8 per cent of people gambled remotely using a mobile device. See Gambling Commission *Industry Statistics 2008/09* October 2009. Available at: http://www.gamblingcommission.gov.uk/pdf/Gambling%20Industry%20Statistics%202008%202009%20-%20update%20-%20October%202009.pdf.

of being constrained to one venue, such as a bookmakers or a casino, gambling has been democratised and is accessible at all times by anybody. Online gaming sites are very attractive and enticing and offer a broader range of activities than would be found in an average casino. Coupled with the increase of online banking and the ease of use of other payment methods, it has become increasingly straightforward to engage in this activity. Online gaming is also attractive to the operators as overheads are lower, meaning that they can offer better odds than could be offered in a normal casino. However, age verification is notoriously difficult to achieve, and there are limited safeguards to prevent people from becoming addicted to a particular pursuit. The Gambling Act 2005 received Royal Assent in April 2005 after a lengthy passage through Parliament.[31] Prior to the consultation procedure, the government ordered a comprehensive review on the gambling industry and in 2001, Alan Budd published his Gambling Review Report (the Budd Report) which reviewed the entire gambling industry.[32] This report highlighted a number of concerns, including that the law relating to gambling activities was old and piecemeal in nature, that there had been a societal change in attitude to gambling and that developments in technology meant that the legislation was no longer sufficient to regulate gambling in its fullest form. Subsequently, in 2002 the Secretary of State for Culture, Media and Sport, Tessa Jowell, published the government's proposals for future gambling legislation reform, which was also a response to the Budd Report. This response of the government also included a draft bill.[33] This eventually led to the Gambling Act 2005, which repealed all the old legislation[34] and introduced a new codified system which sought to provide a comprehensive legislative landscape for gambling to operate within. The approach of the Gambling Act is regulatory in nature and covers all gambling activity, with the exception of the National Lottery and spread betting.[35] Section 1 sets out the stance of the Act and outlines the three main tenets to the new regime. First of all, it seeks to prevent gambling from being linked to crime and disorder, secondly it aims to ensure gambling is carried out in a fair and open way, and its final objective is to protect children and vulnerable adults from being harmed or exploited through gambling.[36]

The 2005 Act outlined the core methods of gambling to ensure its scope was as encompassing as intended. A lottery is defined by section 14 and

---

[31] It came into force in September 2007.

[32] Department for Culture, Media and Sport *Gambling Review Report* (2001). Available at: http://www.culture.gov.uk/reference_library/publications/4642.aspx.

[33] Department for Culture, Media and Sport *A Safe Bet for Success – modernising Britain's gambling laws* (2002). Available at: http://www.culture.gov.uk/reference_library/publications/4754.aspx.

[34] Gambling Act 2005, Schedule 17. Over 50 pieces of legislation have been either totally or partially repealed.

[35] The National Lottery is regulated by the National Lottery Act 1993, while spread betting is a regulated activity which falls within the remit of the Financial Services and Markets Act 2000.

[36] Gambling Act 2005, Section 1 (a–c).

provides definitions for both 'simple' and 'complex' lotteries. The core elements of a lottery are that a person is required to pay in order to participate in the arrangement, secondly there is a distribution of prizes and finally there must be a process that awards these prizes wholly by chance. The main difference between simple and complex lotteries is the number of processes which are gone through to determine the eventual winners. A process which requires any skill, judgment or knowledge cannot be classified as a lottery. The core definition has not altered and has its roots established in common law.[37] Furthermore, the legality of prize competitions is also confirmed in section 339, as long as the activity does not constitute gaming, betting or participating in a lottery. Section 9 provides examples of what constitutes 'betting', including making or accepting a bet on the outcome of a race, competition or other event, or the likelihood of an event occurring, or whether something is true or not, while in section 6 'gaming' is defined as playing a game of chance for a prize. This is different to a lottery as there is an element of skill as well as chance involved. However, one of the main developments introduced by the 2005 Act is the addition of 'remote gambling', which is defined in section 4. Remote gambling covers all types of gambling carried out by remote communication. A remote communication includes the Internet, television, telephone, radio and any other electronic or other technology which can facilitate communication.[38] Under section 4(3), the Secretary of State has the ability to determine whether or not new technology can be added to come within the parameters of a remote communication. This provides the legislation with a degree of flexibility to respond to the evolving nature of technology. The Secretary of State is also able to issue regulations relating to the advertisement of remote gambling.[39] However, this is only likely to occur if the self-regulatory system (considered in more detail in chapter 5 on Online Marketing), is considered to be ineffective. Under section 330, it is an offence to advertise unlawful gambling.[40]

One of the major changes offered by the Act was the establishment of a Gambling Commission. The Gambling Commission falls within the remit of the Department of Culture, Media and Sport and is the body with the responsibility of regulating gambling and granting licences to gambling operators. It is an offence for a person to facilitate gambling unless he has obtained a licence authorising the activity and the activity is carried out in accordance with the requirements of the licence.[41] A person who provides a remote gambling service, which

---

[37] **Readers' Digest Association Limited v Williams** [1976] 3 All ER 737.
[38] Gambling Act 2005, section 4(2).
[39] Gambling Act 2005, section 328.
[40] A defence is provided for Internet Service Providers, which is similar to that contained within the E-Commerce Directive 2000/31/EC.
[41] Gambling Act 2005, section 33. A person who is found guilty under this section is liable for a sentence of up to 51 weeks imprisonment, or a fine, or both.

has one or more pieces of equipment situated within Great Britain, will also be required to obtain a licence.[42] The role of the regulator matches the initial aims of the legislation: to be fair and open, to remove association from criminal activity and to protect children and vulnerable adults. On the latter objective, the Gambling Act has a range of measures to protect children from engaging in online gambling. Section 46 makes it an offence to invite, cause or permit a child (under 16) or young person (under 18) to gamble. A person guilty of this offence is liable for a term of imprisonment not exceeding 51 weeks, or a fine, or both. Section 63 does provide a defence if the person took all reasonable steps to determine the age of the child or young person and reasonably believed that that the person was not a child or young person. If a licensed gambling outlet subsequently becomes aware that a child or young person has used their facilities for gambling, the stake must be returned as soon as is reasonably practicable and any prize given to the player does not need to be returned.

The approach taken by the United Kingdom government in regulating, as opposed to restricting or outlawing the practice of gambling, is quite probably due to the vast revenue streams which are available through this medium, and the difficulties in realistically enforcing bans and other restrictions. It is notoriously difficult to ban activities online as the system operates over and above existing geographical borders. If online gambling were to be banned, then this activity would simply move to off-shore locations, out of reach of the legislature, meaning that they would be unable to protect individuals or obtain the income through taxation.[43] Players would simply move to sites where no regulation existed, which could mean that no redress would be available in the event of the fraudulent obtaining of a participant's money. The government is of the view that it is better to have a licensed system of reliable sites which are attractive to participants and under the scrutiny of the regulatory bodies, that generate revenue and control criminal activity such as money laundering or unscrupulous gaming practices. However, the regulatory regime needs to be robust and favourable enough to the gambling company (and the participant) to want them to locate within the United Kingdom, while encouraging companies already operating off-shore to

---

[42] Gambling Act 2005, section 36. 'Equipment' can include anything used to store information relating to a person's participation in the gambling, or that presents to a user a virtual game, race or event by reference to which the gambling is conducted, or a facilities to determine the result or something which stores information relating to the result.

[43] This was seen in the United States of America, as they prohibited online gambling through the Unlawful Internet Gambling Enforcement Act, which was enacted in October 2006. See: Hamilton, M & Rogers, K M *Internet gambling: Community flop or the Texas Hold'em poker rules* (2008) International Review of Law, Computers and Technology, volume 22, number 3, pages 223–230. However, recent reports suggest that the US is considering changing this approach to regulate, instead of prohibit, online gambling. See: Goodman, M *Odds-on for legal online gaming in US* (20th June 2010) The Sunday Times, Business Section, pages 1, 10.

consider relocating to the United Kingdom. To strengthen the success of remote gambling within the United Kingdom, the Department of Culture, Media and Sport issued a consultation paper in March 2010.[44] The consultation paper suggested that the regulatory regime was a positive addition to the law in this area, although a number of difficulties still existed. It was noted that a number of online gambling companies are located off-shore and beyond the reach of the Gambling Act and the Gambling Commission's regulatory control. This had the potential for reducing the potential protection available to consumers and also meant that these companies were not compelled to report certain information, such as unusual betting practices. Furthermore, different regulatory approaches within the European Union means that no one uniform level of protection exists for the British consumer who engages with online gambling and there is confusion about where to direct complaints. Rules to prohibit money laundering are by no means uniform, which means that it could potentially be easier for criminal gangs to exploit them. A number of proposals were forwarded, including requiring all remote gambling operators who either directed their activities to the British market, or had some of their equipment based within Britain, to obtain a licence from the Gambling Commission; altering the rules on advertising remote gambling services; and plans to increase compliance with the Gambling Commission from within the industry. The consultation period closed on 18th June 2010, shortly after the 2010 general election. At the time of writing, the Coalition Government's response to the consultation paper's findings is still awaited.

Taxation

Many of the payments that we make or the income that we receive is subject to taxation. Income tax is a levy on our salary, while Value Added Tax (VAT) is payable on many items that are purchased, and businesses are taxed through a range of corporation taxes. E-commerce can be carried out in a plethora of ways: through emails, websites, distance selling and digital downloads, among others. The liability to be taxed is not dependant on how a company or individual operates, but depends simply on the financial results. Whether e-commerce itself should be taxed at all is a question worth considering; as more and more transactions are carried out online, national governments will want to ensure that they also reap the benefits of a connected world. A range of different activities are carried out online, many of which incur some form of

---

[44] Department of Culture, Media and Sport *A Consultation on the Regulatory Future of Remote Gambling within the United Kingdom* (22nd March 2010). Available at: http://www.culture.gov.uk/images/consultations/remotegambling_consultation.pdf.

taxation liability in the 'real world'. These include auctions, sales of goods and services, distribution of music, films and television programmes, gambling websites and educational services. There are complexities with taxation in the Internet setting. A person may be transacting anonymously, which may make enforcement difficult. Additionally, ascertaining the precise amount of tax owed by any online trader is not without problems, as the Internet does not commend itself to leaving a paper trail, making it difficult to work out the level of taxation a person is liable for. Although it does seem that initial concern about the ability of governments to be able to tax online activity adequately seems a little misplaced, there are a number of difficulties that are still being addressed. A business can be established in (or moved to) a tax haven, a country which has a much more relaxed taxation system than, say, the United Kingdom or the United States of America. This means that a business can locate itself in one of these jurisdictions and market their goods to the whole world, while avoiding paying substantial tax on their profits. There is the added problem of companies incurring liability for taxation in more than one country, or at a more local level individuals engaging in profit-making activity online (through an online auction site or virtual world) and not disclosing their income to the relevant authorities. On an international level the Organisation for Economic Co-operation and Development (OECD) deals with taxation and it operates following five fundamental principles of taxation: neutrality, efficiency, certainty and simplicity, effectiveness and fairness and flexibility. These principles were established in the Ottawa Taxation Framework in 1998.[45] As well as identifying key principles for taxation of e-commerce, a number of challenges were also presented. These challenges include: the service the taxpayer receives, how the collection of taxation is controlled, the administration of taxation collection (including the identification of companies and individuals and the provision of the information required), how consumption taxes are managed and, finally, international agreement and co-operation. This section will consider the basic taxation landscape in the United Kingdom and will highlight some of the core issues in taxing online activity.

Within the United Kingdom, Her Majesty's Revenue and Customs (HMRC) is responsible for tax collection by virtue of the Taxes Management Act 1970. Annual Finance Acts, usually based upon the Budget presented to the House of Commons by the Chancellor of the Exchequer provide the legislative backdrop for the amount of taxation to be collected. A taxation cycle is one year in length. For the individual the financial year starts on 6th April and concludes on

---

[45] A report by the Committee on Fiscal Affairs to the Ministers of the OECD Ministerial Conference (1998) *Electronic Commerce: Taxation Framework Conditions*. Available at: http://www.oecd.org/dataoecd/46/3/1923256.pdf.

5th April the following year. The financial year for a company normally commences on 1st April and concludes one year later on 31st March. The amount of taxation owed is based upon a number of thresholds expressed in percentage terms against the amount of income earned. There are two main ways in which an individual can be taxed within the United Kingdom. The chief way is through Pay As You Earn (PAYE), which is where income tax, along with National Insurance is deducted at source. This is the easiest way for taxation to be collected. For individuals who are self-employed, or have a second employment or other tax-related complications, a self-assessment needs to be made. This is where the individual will outline all their earnings and other financial incomes in any one financial year, which will allow HMRC to establish that individual's tax liability. An individual is able to appeal against the charges to either the General or Special Commissioners. These hearings are similar to a standard court hearing, although the stringent evidence rules do not apply and the rules relating to costs are also different. A right of appeal exists from the Commissioners to the High Court, Court of Appeal and ultimately the Supreme Court.

The taxation landscape for a business is different. When setting up a business, the owner has to choose between setting up as a sole trader, entering into a partnership, a limited liability partnership (LLP) or incorporating as a limited liability company (Ltd). The advantage of establishing either an LLP or Ltd company is that theoretically liability is limited to the amount of money which has been invested into the company. In many cases however, directors and managing partners are required to provide personal guarantees for loans. The favoured corporate model is the Limited Company. At law a company is a separate legal entity from the people who set the company up.[46] Accordingly, a company has the capacity to sue and be sued[47], own property[48], employ people[49] and continue after the original members have left the company. A company is also a taxable entity in its own right, whereas sole traders and partnerships are not. The nature of this taxation is through corporation tax, which is paid upon company profits. The rate of corporation tax from April 2010 is 28 per cent, although this is reducing to 24 per cent by 2014 as a result of the Emergency Budget introduced by the Coalition Government in June 2010. This is still significantly lower than the higher rate of income tax, which at the time of writing is 50 per cent. Company profits are only taxable once, even if they are reinvested back into the company. The minor exception is dividends, which are payments made to shareholders (at the discretion of the directors) out of

---

[46] **Salomon v Salomon** [1893] AC 22.
[47] **South Hetton Coal Co. Ltd v North-Eastern News Association Ltd** [1894] 1 QB 133.
[48] **Macaura v Northern Assurance** [1925] AC 619.
[49] **Lee v Lee's Air Farming** [1961] AC 12.

the profits of the company. The shareholders who receive the dividends are liable for tax on the payments.

The tax system within the United Kingdom for an individual is based on an individual's place of residence.[50] An individual based in the United Kingdom, but with employment in different parts of the world will still be taxed on his entire income. Tax liability for companies depends upon whether they were established in the United Kingdom (and so registered at Companies House) or whether their central control and management is based in the United Kingdom. The case of **De Beers Consolidated Mines Ltd v Howe**[51] demonstrated how an ostensibly South African company was held to be resident in the United Kingdom, as the majority of directors lived there and board meetings were regularly held in London. The more recent case of **Wood v Holden**[52] reached a similar conclusion as the majority of decisions made within this particular company were taken in the United Kingdom. The approach to corporate taxation liability within the United States is slightly different in that it is based wholly on the location of the company's incorporation.

One of the key challenges for taxing goods and services sold online is how to attach VAT (or the relevant sales tax, depending on the countries involved) to online sales. Again, in the United Kingdom, HMRC is responsible for collecting VAT. The general principle is that a person who buys goods from overseas will be liable for tax at their own domestic rate. After the Emergency Budget in June 2010, the Coalition Government increased the level of VAT from 17.5 per cent to 20 per cent from January 2011. Therefore, if a person based in London buys a good from a country outside of the European Union they will be liable to pay VAT at the current level in the United Kingdom, plus any import duty, if relevant. With traditional international sales, the way in which HMRC collected the duties was by requiring that senders of goods filled in a form outlining the cost of the item, which would then allow HMRC to work out the level of tax owed. If necessary they could retain the good until payment had been made. There are a number of difficulties with this method. It relies very much on the honesty of the sender to list accurately the value of the good and it is also very heavy on manpower requirements. The development of the Internet saw a further difficulty as there is no inter-mediary involved in certain sales, for instance, in digital purchases such as software. A form could be filled in, but there would not be an appropriate place for the form to be viewed by customs as the software can be sent directly from the supplier to the end user. This meant that it was possible for

---

[50] **Levene v Inland Revenue Commissioner** [1928] AC 217, HL.
[51] [1906] AC 455.
[52] [2006] STC 443.

people to circumvent the taxation system. Two pieces of European legislation (which need to be read together) assist in this area. First of all, the Sixth Council Directive 77/388/EEC on the harmonisation of the laws of the member states relating to turnover taxes (the 6th VAT Directive)[53] and Directive 2002/38/EC on the VAT arrangements applicable to radio and television broadcasting services and certain electronically supplied services.[54] Recital 2 of Directive 2002/38/EC states that it is desirable, for the good of the internal market, to have a harmonised set of rules relating to the applicability of VAT to electronically supplied services. An illustrative list of what constitutes an electronically supplied service is found within Annex 1 of the Directive and includes: website supply, web hosting, distance maintenance of programmes and equipment, supply of software and updating thereof, supply of images, text and information and making databases available, supply of music, films and games, including games of chance and gambling games, and of political, cultural, artistic, sporting, scientific and entertainment broadcasts and events and supply of distance teaching. A recent case in the First-Tier Tribunal (Tax Chamber) further held that a company which operated an electronic money system that allowed consumers to make purchases online was also the provider of an electronically supplied service.[55] The consequence in this case, and also the consequence of being classified as an electronically supplied service is that goods are taxed in the place of consumption, rather than the place of sale. This means that in the sale of a digital download they should be taxed where the consumer accesses and uses the purchased software. This approach is clearly more beneficial for suppliers based within the European Union[56] and it places them on a level footing with other suppliers, who may locate themselves in so-called tax havens, where the level of tax is low or even zero.

The reality is that online taxation is hugely complex as individuals can engage in a range of different activities in different jurisdictions. The approach of the legislature seems more responsive than pre-emptive and it is likely that, with countries such as India, China and African nations becoming big players on the Internet scene, the rules relating to online taxation will become more complex.

---

[53] Available at: http://eur-lex.europa.eu/LexUriServ/LexUriServ.do?uri=CELEX:31977L0388:EN:HTML.

[54] Available at: http://eur-lex.europa.eu/LexUriServ/LexUriServ.do?uri=OJ:L:2002:128:0041:0044:en:PDF.

[55] **Smart Voucher Limited v Revenue and Customs Commissioners** [2010] S.T.I. 1398.

[56] Although the principles relating to recovery of intra-European Union trade, as highlighted in Darnley, A *Cross-border VAT: all change* (2009) Computer and Telecommunications Law Review, volume 15, issue 6, pages 137–138, need to be borne in mind.

Key points:

- The range of services that are offered over the Internet necessitate a broad range of payment methods to enable consumers to fully engage.
- The use of a credit card by a consumer to make online payments is the most widespread online payment method. The reason for this is that credit cards are universally accepted and offer a degree of security and protection, which is contained within section 75 of the Consumer Credit Act 1974.
- Conversely, other online payment methods have generally failed to get off the ground as they do not attract the same acceptance and universal applicability.
- There are some exceptions to this, with Paypal being a case in point. This payment system is the system of choice for eBay, making its usage more accepted.
- The Internet provides both gambling operators and participants with a range of advantages in engaging in an ancient activity in a modern, dynamic setting. Online gaming sites are attractive, convenient and easy to use, facilitated by a range of attractive online payment mechanisms.
- A number of disadvantages to online gambling also exist. These include difficulty in verifying age and having limited safeguards in place to protect people from addiction.
- The Gambling Act 2005 makes wholesale changes to the gambling legislation landscape within the United Kingdom. It repeals dozens of earlier statutes and regulates all online gambling, with the exception of the National Lottery and spread betting.
- The Department of Culture, Media and Sport concluded a consultation on the regulatory future for remote gambling with a number of proposals, including widening the net of suppliers who needed to register with the Gambling Commission.
- Online taxation is a complex area, with a number of unanswered questions. Different rules apply for businesses, which may be liable to corporation tax, and individuals, who may be liable to income tax.
- The Sixth VAT Directive and Directive 2002/38/EC on the VAT arrangements applicable to radio and television broadcasting services and certain electronically supplied services alter the rules relating to the applicability of VAT on purchases to the place of consumption instead of the place of sale. The consequence of this is that EU suppliers are protected as they are given a level playing field with non-EU suppliers.

Further reading:

- Anni, P *Payment Services Directive: A Detailed proposal by the European Commission for a New Legal Framework* (2006) Journal of International Banking Law and Regulation, volume 21, page 344.
- Chambers, C & Willcox, C *Gambling on compliance with the new 2005 Act: do organisations fulfil new regulations?* (2009) International Review of Law, Computers and Technology, volume 23, number 3, pages 203–215.
- Haloin, R & Moore, R *Developments in electronic money regulation – the Electronic Money Directive: A better deal for e-money issuers?* (2009) Computer Law and Security Review, volume 25, issue 6, pages 563–568.
- Kierkegaard, S *Payments in the internal market and the new legal framework – EU law: harmonising the regulatory regime for cross-border payment services* (2007) Computer Law and Security Report, volume 23, issue 2, pages 177–187.
- Kohlbach, M *Making sense of Electronic Money* (2004) Journal of Information, Law and Technology, Issue One.
- Light, R *The Gambling Act 2005: Regulatory Containment and Market Control* (2007) Modern Law Review, volume 70, issue 4, pages 626–653.
- Littler, A *Regulatory perspectives on the future of interactive gambling in the internal market* (2008) European Law Review, volume 33, issue 2, pages 211–229.
- Mansour, Y *The E-Money Directive and MNOs: Why it All Went Wrong* (2007) Paper presented at the 2007 BILETA Conference, University of Hertfordshire. Available at: http://www.bileta.ac.uk/Document%20Library/1/The%20 EMoney%20Directive%20and%20MNOs%20-%20Why%20it%20 All%20Went%20Wrong.pdf.
- Rees, P & Hodgkinson, D *E-Money regulation: all change?* (2007) Computer and Telecommunications Law Review, volume 13, issue 1, pages 1–3.
- Reid, A *Is society smart enough to deal with smart cards?* (2007) Computer Law and Security Report, volume 23, issue 1, pages 53–61.
- Steennot, R *Allocation of liability in case of fraudulent use of an electronic payment instrument: The new Directive on payment services in the internal market* (2008) Computer Law and Security Report, volume 24, issue 6, pages 55–561.
- Turner, M *Is shopping online now risk free for UK consumers?* (2006) Computer Law and Security Report, volume 22, issue 4, pages 333–337.

Questions for consideration:

4.1. What types of issues need to be addressed before an online payment system is fully utilised by businesses and consumers?

4.2.   Discuss the various forms of e-money. Critically evaluate the likelihood of success of these methods within the United Kingdom.

4.3.   To what extent are newer forms of electronic finance likely to challenge the dominance of the credit and debit card?

4.4.   Outline the advantages of purchasing a good online by use of a credit card instead of a debit card. Your answer must refer to the Consumer Credit Act 1974.

4.5.   Outline the provisions within Directive 2000/46/EC on E-Money which posed difficulties to the development of e-money systems.

4.6.   What requirements does the Gambling Act 2005 place upon suppliers of remote gambling services?

4.7.   To what extent will the proposals contained within the Department of Culture, Media and Sport's consultation paper on the regulatory future of remote gambling within the United Kingdom strengthen the protection given to consumers who engage in this activity?

4.8.   List some of the complexities involved in taxing e-commerce activities.

4.9.   How far do the Sixth VAT Directive and Directive 2002/38/EC on the VAT arrangements applicable to radio and television broadcasting services and certain electronically supplied services adequately solve the previous problems of how and when to apply VAT to purchases made online?

4.10.   'The original Directive 2000/46/EC on E-Money aimed to regulate and enhance consumer confidence in the use of e-money. It provided a rigorous regulatory regime on e-money institutions, but did not achieve its desired effect. Indeed it hindered, rather than encouraged, the development of e-money systems. The subsequent review and reforms contained within the new E-Money Directive 2009/110/EC will reverse this direction and will undoubtedly lead to an increase in the uptake of e-money systems within the European Union.'
Undertake a critical evaluation of this view.

All weblinks mentioned in the text can also be found at
http://www.pagrave.com/law/rogers

5 Online Marketing

This chapter will consider:

- The development of the Internet as a marketing medium and some of the marketing methods used on the Internet.
- The traditional methods of regulating Internet advertisements including the role of self-regulatory systems.
- The relative advantages and disadvantages of unsolicited bulk commercial email (often known as 'spam').
- The approach of the Privacy and Electronic Communications Directive 2002/58/EC in tackling both spam and cookies.
- Reforms to Directive 2002/58/EC in relation to spam and cookies.

The Internet has opened many possibilities for individuals or businesses to advertise and offer products online or through wireless devices. There is an increasing variety of ways for a business to advertise online (occasionally called 'webvertising'); these include websites, banner advertisements, pop-ups (or pop-unders), email and (increasingly) social websites such as Facebook. The power of Google and other search engines has transformed the manner in which businesses can advertise goods and services. The wealth of advertising opportunities leads to greater purchasing choice for the consumer, with search engines able to rank results not only in order of popularity, but also with reference to the preferences of the user.[1] However, with the rapid increase in online marketing comes the competing desire to protect the individual from unscrupulous marketers. These marketers may misuse or abuse a customer's data by sending advertisements in which the consumer has negligible or no interest. This chapter will look at the methods of advertising on the Internet and will examine the current legislative and regulatory approaches adopted to safeguard consumers. The bulk of this section will focus upon the phenomenon

---

[1] In February 2010, three companies lodged a formal complaint with the European Commission arguing that the way in which Google ranks its search results is anti-competitive and in breach of competition law. See OUT-LAW.COM news *Companies ask EU Commission to step in on Google search ranking complaint* (24th February 2010). Available at: http://www.out-law.com/page-10784-theme=print. At the time of writing, the results of this complaint are not known.

of unsolicited bulk commercial email (colloquially known as 'spam') and will consider why spam is such a critical issue on the Internet today that legislation has been established in an attempt to provide a regulatory framework for it.

The rise and fall of the 'dot com'

The Internet as we know it today is central to the conduct of e-commerce in the twenty-first century business world, yet this rise as a central facilitator of commerce has not been a journey without difficulties. During the late 1990s and early 2000s, the Internet as a marketing and commercial medium really began to take off. Companies advertised on the Internet, spending vast quantities of money in the process, all within a comparatively short period of time. The so-called dot com bubble was created by many entrepreneurs seeking to make their fortune, leading to reports of $2bn entering Silicon Valley companies each week in the late 1990s. However, very few people realised what they were getting into. In hindsight it is easy to see how vastly inflated the prices of some companies were. The online companies Amazon and Yahoo! both went live in 1995. Yahoo! floated on the stock market in 1996 and on the first day of trading its share price tripled. In 1999 Jeff Bezos (the founder of Amazon) was said to be worth in excess of $10bn, while 20 dot com companies paid around $3m each for a 30-second television advert during an American Super Bowl match in 2000.

The fallacy of the extravagance behind online commerce was seen initially in 2000 as the dot com bubble burst and many companies became bankrupt, while others were clearly overvalued. Many online companies disappeared overnight and numerous jobs were lost. Various reasons have been mooted for the boom of 'dot com'. There was a clear misconception of the potential revenue available from webvertising; coupled with this, it was clear that the marketing was vague and massively overhyped – nobody, especially the investors, really knew the power of the Internet or had any idea what they were getting into. The power of the herd was plain to see as many people were pulled in by the directional pull of the masses towards these new dot coms believing them to be the 'next big thing'.[2] The subsequent bust of the dot com market had severe repercussions for website designers, advertisers, creative agencies and other stakeholders as a critical source of income was abruptly reduced. Investors who had had their fingers burnt thought twice about investing in online companies, while a number of high profile dot coms became

---

[2] See Ashton, J *Dotcom comes of age* The Sunday Times (Business Section) 28th February 2010, page 5. The theory of the 'pull of the masses' driving the direction of the Internet was also considered in Keen, A *The Cult of the Amateur: How Today's Internet is Killing our Culture and Assaulting our Economy* Nicholas Brealey Publishing (2007).

bankrupt. Perhaps for the first time, the shortcomings in many dot com business models had been highlighted and it took a while for trust to be restored. Yet this period was not a disaster for the online market as services such as online banking and insurance, auctions and the music industry became mainstream and available to the online consumer. They have continued to have a strong online presence. In 2005, the Daily Telegraph pointed to research carried out by the Office of National Statistics, which showed that the value of online advertising had reached the heights achieved during the peak of the dot com bubble (approaching £1bn.[3]) Arguably, a dot com bubble has returned with the purchase by Google of YouTube for $1.65bn and Rupert Murdoch's News Corporation purchasing MySpace for $580m in 2006, although perhaps the difference this time is that there is a greater appreciation of the value of these websites because both YouTube and MySpace had established themselves online.[4] Furthermore, in October 2010 the domain name 'sex.com' was bought at auction for $13m dollars. Previously, the highest amount paid for a domain name for $16m for 'insure.com' in 1999 – at the height of the dot.com boom.[5]

Online marketing: advantages and disadvantages

The characteristics of the Internet, such as its international nature and the dematerialisation of goods and services, create new challenges. On the one hand, usage of the Internet often involves a multiplicity of states, laws, individuals, companies and cultures. These are often competing in nature and conflicts are highlighted and confronted every day. One problem is that what may be socially accepted in one part of the world may not be in another, for example, the eulogy of Nazism is a crime in France, but is tolerated in the United States under the First Amendment right of free speech. In a real world, composed of physical borders, it is difficult to face the phenomenon of internationalisation without physical borders, which is the essence of the Internet. On the other hand, the international dimension of the Internet offers unlimited opportunities to reach a global customer base. This can be done at a reduced cost, as there is no need to open physical branches abroad to obtain a presence in that location. Although a website on its own is not enough to be successful, it is possible to

---

[3] The Daily Telegraph *Profits are back to the good old days* 5th October 2005.
[4] See: BBC News *Google buys YouTube for $1.65bn* (10th October 2006). Available at: http://news.bbc.co.uk/1/hi/business/6034577.stm and BBC News *Has the dotcom boom returned?* (10th October 2006). Available at: http://news.bbc.co.uk/1/hi/business/6036337.stm and BBC News *Whatever happened to the dotcom millionaires?* (9th February 2010). Available at: http://news.bbc. co.uk/1/hi/technology/8505260.stm.
[5] See BBC News *Sex.com internet domain name sold for $13m* (21st October 2010). Available at: http://www.bbc.co.uk/news/technology-11596477.

reach customers who would probably be inaccessible were the company simply using more traditional forms of commercial marketing.

Online traders want to make use of the advantages of the Internet. The Internet supplier is able to reach a global customer base and offer goods and services at a more competitive price, often due to economies of scale and lower financial overheads (for example, through the lack of an expensive high street presence). How these traders advertise, negotiate with customers and invite offers for their products is key to their survival. The vast majority of companies will have a website and through this will be able to invite offers, communicate with customers, display their goods and take online payment for items purchased. The flexibility of a website is essential for the success of the business and so usability and accessibility are the basic elements required for consumers to return to sites. Additionally, secure payment systems and robust procedures for safeguarding the details of customers are also required to ensure that the goodwill of customers is retained. If a company can get the 'virtual face' established, the financial rewards will follow. Figures published in early 2010 by the Centre for Retail Research suggest that consumers in the United Kingdom spent £38bn online in 2009, which equates to around 10 per cent of total retail sales during the year. The Centre's prediction for 2010 suggests that online retail sales within the United Kingdom will continue to increase and be worth around £42.7bn.[6]

A website may not only be displaying details of just that one company. A website owner may be able to raise additional revenue by selling space on his site for other companies to place banner advertisements. A banner advertisement is often found towards the top, side or bottom of a webpage and it will be advertising a different company or service. A user can click on this banner advertisement and be taken to the website being advertised. A website owner may enter into a contract with a second company wishing to place a banner advertisement on his website, which may include payment for the number of 'clicks' that particular advertisement receives. It is this system that makes banner advertisements one of the biggest providers of income in the sector. Many adverts also have pop-ups or pop-unders attached to them. These are advertisements that literally pop up (or pop under) in a new window on your computer screen while you are on a particular webpage. They will be advertising a different good or service, often one which has been pre-selected based on the preferences of the users. They are eye-catching and can be misleading as a person may click the 'X' in the top right hand corner to remove them, but in fact may find themselves being directed to the advert's website.[7]

---

[6] See Centre for Retail Research *Online Trends 2010*. Available at: http://www.retailresearch.org/grtb_globaltrends.php.

[7] See: Tyacke, N *Internet Law – The legality of Internet "pop-up" ads* (2005) Computer Law and Security Report, Volume 21, issue 3, pages 262–265.

A more recent strategy for maximising advertising revenues is through behavioural advertising. This is where websites can monitor the activities of a consumer and then build up a profile of the types of websites that they visit. This allows advertisements to be targeted to that particular individual. For example, if a person visits a large number of websites about cars, they will almost inevitably find that a large number of the banner advertisements or pop-ups they see are advertising car websites. There are several key legal issues inherent in this marketing method, relating to both privacy and data protection. The Article 29 Working Party published an opinion of behavioural advertising in June 2010, which highlighted a number of key issues that needed to be addressed, such as whether children should be targeted by such advertisements.[8]

Traditional methods of advertising control

The United Kingdom has a range of strict legislative and statutory controls that regulate both traditional advertising and also more dynamic direct advertising carried out over the Internet. Running alongside the legal controls is a stringent range of self-regulatory systems. The Advertising Standards Authority is an independent watchdog responsible for maintaining high standards of advertising within the United Kingdom.[9] Part of its role is to adjudicate on situations where marketers appear to be acting in contravention of the relevant laws and industry codes. The main industry codes are the British Codes of Advertising, Sales Promotion and Direct Marketing. These are more commonly known as the CAP Codes. They are comprehensive sets of rules that provide basic principles for those engaged in advertising. The Code is enforced by the Committee of Advertising Practice, which is a self-regulatory body. The Code exists in addition to the law, and seeks to fill gaps or loopholes while providing for a more effective way of resolving disputes by avoiding costly litigation. Although not part of legislation, the Codes are followed by the vast majority of marketers. There are three key principles at the heart of the Codes, which are that advertisements must be legal, decent, honest and truthful; they should be prepared with a sense of responsibility to consumers and to society and should also be in line with the principles of fair competition generally accepted in business.

---

[8] Article 29 Data Protection Working Party *Opinion 2/2010 on online behavioural advertising* WP171 00909/10/EN. Available at: http://ec.europa.eu/justice home/fsj/privacy/index en.htm. 00909/10/EN.

[9] There are other similar industry groups, which offer guidance or regulate online direct marketing, such as the Direct Marketing Association (who operate a code of best practice for electronic commerce), the Interactive Advertising Bureau UK (a trade association for those involved in interactive advertising, electronic commerce and online marketing) and ADMARK, which is an opt-in system for marketers to say that their advertisements are legal, decent, honest and truthful and in return they can display the ADMARK logo on their website. There is also what is colloquially know as 'netiquette'. This is an unofficial, self-regulatory practise of Internet users. It is akin to regulation by convention.

On 16th March 2010, the Advertising Standards Authority announced (after a substantial two year consultation exercise that received over 30,000 responses) that a new set of codes would be introduced, and they came into effect on 1st September 2010 as the twelfth edition of the Codes.[10] The main changes contained within this edition made the Codes more accessible and easier to understand by using a clearer format and greater consistency throughout the document. Introduced for the first time were rules surrounding corporate and social responsibility and also advertising to children; guidance on consumer protection and sector specific rules were also amended.[11] The new codes do not extend to marketers' own marketing communication as this is being considered elsewhere by the Advertising Standards Authority.[12]

Alongside the traditional controls within the United Kingdom, the Federation of European Direct Marketing (FEDMA) exists at a European level to provide guidance to direct marketers. In 2000 they published their own guidance for companies involved in e-commerce and interactive marketing.[13] The aim of the code is to increase consumer confidence in transacting online, while enhancing the good business practice of the direct marketing industry.

Advertising by email

Over one quarter of the world's population is currently online.[14] This means that email is an easy way by which marketers can reach a wide audience. Businesses are able to tailor the emails they send to their customers to try to achieve the highest possible take-up rate by consumers. Email is a very effective way of marketing – easy to send, cheap and speedy, particularly as broadband services are increasing in their coverage. Partly for this reason, millions of unsolicited bulk or 'spam' emails are sent out on a daily basis. The term 'spam' is derived from a Monty Python comedy sketch where the characters make repetitive over-use of the term in a restaurant setting. While understanding the provenance of the term is fairly straightforward, achieving a definitive recognised definition of

---

[10] See Advertising Standards Authority News *New Advertising Codes Launched* (16th March 2010). Available at: http://www.asa.org.uk/Media-Centre/2010/New-Advertising-Codes-Launch.aspx.

[11] The Direct Marketing Association has also amended its guidance to include direct marketing to children. See: *Direct Marketing Association Code of Practice* (4th Edition, July 2010). Available at: http://www.dma.org.uk/membership/mem-code.asp.

[12] For more see: Committee of Advertising Practice *New UK Advertising Codes*. Available at: http://www.cap.org.uk/The-Codes/CAP-Code.aspx.

[13] Federation of European Direct Marketing *FEDMA Code on E-Commerce and Interactive Marketing* (September 2000). Available at: http://www.oecd.org/dataoecd/12/21/2091875.pdf.

[14] See: Internet World Stats: Usage and Population Statistics *Internet Usage Statistics: The Internet Big Picture World Internet Users and Population Stats* (taken at 31st December 2009). Available at: http://www.internetworldstats.com/stats.htm.

spam is more complex. A comprehensive definition has been sought for some time[15], but broadly speaking a commercial email communication becomes spam when it contains advertisement(s) – often offensive, misleading or fraudulent in nature – which are sent indiscriminately in bulk to random email inboxes. This email is often – although not exclusively – pornographic, commercial, political, sexual or financial in nature. By its nature, spam is annoying and offensive to many people. It clogs up inboxes and slows the overall speed of the Internet. It is not targeted to any individual, but to a mass of people and businesses, which means both that children are often exposed to these emails and that the productivity of businesses is reduced. Those who send spam (usually called 'spammers') can manufacture millions of email addresses by using a simple piece of software and then send the emails out. It is argued that (due to its annoying nature) spam is one of the main disincentives for engaging with the Internet and is partly responsible for a reduction in consumer confidence in the Internet. Furthermore, as spammers employ a 'machine gun' approach to sending these emails, they can end up in the inbox of a business as well as a private individual. This inevitably leads to lost productivity for businesses as workers need to spend some time reading and deleting them. While (costly) spam filters are the norm, they are not the panacea to the problem and employees often have to check the 'junk mail' box to ensure that important emails have not been misplaced. In practice, the burden of the cost of spam is placed upon the recipient as opposed to the sender, as recipients need to purchase the software to block spam, and the online storage to process it. Further, legitimate advertisers also suffer as consumers become blinded by constant marketing communication and often delete genuine advertising emails without reading them. Burdens are also placed on Internet Service Providers, who need to spend resources in trying to eradicate the problem to avoid losing customer goodwill.

Spamming is an international problem, not purely American or British. It is these reasons which have led the European Union, the United States, Australia and many other countries to pass anti-spam legislation with the intention of putting an end to spam. Some of this legislation will be examined shortly. However, before looking at the legislative responses it is worth considering why spam is still an issue. Opinion about spam is (generally) very negative as it causes local and global problems, yet the amount of spam sent continues to rise. It is very difficult to place an exact figure on the amount of spam email

---

[15] See for example: Chissisk, M & Kelman, A *Electronic Commerce – Law and Practice* 3rd Edition (Sweet & Maxwell, 2002), Chapter 10, pages 241–256, Butler, M *Spam – The meat of the problem* (2003) Computer Law and Security Report, Volume 19, Number 5, pages 388–391 and Chetwin, M & Clarke, B *The relative effectiveness of technology legislation in curtailing spam* (2004) Computer and Telecommunications Law Review, volume 10, issue 8, pages 192–197.

sent, although it is estimated to be in the region of 90 per cent of total email traffic and shows no sign of reducing.[16]

The creativity of spammers is continually evolving: for example, spam often uses words spelt in their phonetic sense and also employs the use of more pictures to bypass spam filters. But if reaction is so poor and opinion so negative why does spam continue? If spam is genuinely the problem it has been presented as being, why does the tide of this communication not cease as spammers discover there is no real market? The answer lies partially in the economics. The sheer volume of spam that can be sent means that a spammer only needs a miniscule response rate, which may yield credit card numbers or bank account details to be able to fraudulently obtain some considerable money.[17]

The European approach to tackling spam

The European Union's Directive 2002/58/EC on the processing of personal data and the protection of privacy in the electronic communications sector (Directive on Privacy and Electronic Communications) received a fanfare introduction as being the key piece of legislation in the fight against spam.[18] The legislation updated the earlier Directive 97/66/EC by providing a broader scope to cover the Internet, email and other communication technologies. The scope of the Directive is outlined in Article 1, which states that the Directive:

> "... harmonises the provisions of the Member States required to ensure an equivalent level of protection of fundamental rights and freedoms, and in particular the right to privacy, with respect to the processing of personal data in the electronic communication sector and to ensure the free movement of such data and of electronic communication equipment in the Community."

From this it can be seen that the Directive is intended to be a harmonising measure and seeks to ensure that the rules across the European Union are uniform in tackling spam. Its primary aim is to provide a balance between

---

[16] See for instance: BBC News (Waters, D) *Spam overwhelms email messages* (8th April 2009), available at: http://news.bbc.co.uk/1/hi/technology/7988579.stm, which reported (based on a Microsoft Security Report) that potentially up to 97 per cent of global email traffic was spam.

[17] For more on the economics of spam see the joint research project by the International Computer Science Institute, Berkeley and the Department of Computer Science and Engineering, University of California, San Diego *Spamalytics: An Empirical Analysis of Spam Marketing Conversion* (October 2008). Available at: http://www.icsi.berkeley.edu/pubs/networking/2008-ccs-spamalytics.pdf.

[18] Directive 2002/58/EC is available at: http://eur-lex.europa.eu/LexUriServ/LexUriServ.do?uri=CELEX:32002L0058:EN:HTML.

upholding individual privacy and allowing for free movement of information – including the ability for a company to advertise their products. Recitals 40 to 45 provide the background to the provisions relating to spam.[19] Recital 40 states:

> "Safeguards should be provided for subscribers against intrusion of their privacy by unsolicited communications for direct marketing purposes in particular by means of automated calling machines, telefaxes, and emails, including SMS messages."

A key objective of the legislation is introduced within Recital 42, which states that consumers should only receive direct marketing after they have given their prior consent.[20] Recital 17 suggests that consent should have the same meaning as contained within the Data Protection Directive 95/46/EC, which is that the consent can be given by any appropriate method and should be freely given, specific and informed and with the option of opting-out at a later date.[21] The recital also suggests that consent could be provided by ticking a box on a website. A final recital worthy of note is 43, which explains why it is necessary to prohibit false identities and return addresses (of organisations issuing marketing messages), to allow the enforcement of rules on unsolicited messages to be effectively enforced.

The Directive was implemented into the United Kingdom as The Privacy and Electronic Communications (EC Directive) Regulations 2003 and they came into force on 11th December 2003.[22] The regulations virtually adopt verbatim

---

[19] Although contained within the body of the legislation, strictly speaking recitals do not form part of the legislation and act more as 'explanatory notes'.

[20] The definition of 'direct marketing' is not contained within the Directive on Privacy and Electronic Communications. Section 11(3) of the Data Protection Act 1998 does state that direct marketing is the communication, by whatever means, of any advertising or marketing materials which is directed to particular individuals. The Information Commissioner has also provided guidance on the Privacy and Electronic Communications (EC Directive) Regulations 2003. These state that direct marketing is not simply offering goods and services, but also extends to the promotion of the aims or objectives of an organisation, which means that emails promoting a charity or a political objective could also be included. See: http://www.ico.gov.uk/for organisations/data protection/ the guide/principle 6/preventing direct marketing.aspx. This is a very broad definition and has extended to the use of automated telephone systems used by some political parties to contact potential voters.

[21] In February 2007, the Advertising Standards Authority adjudicated on the company World Networks. World Networks sent a number of text messages to people who were ostensibly customers of Orange offering them an upgrade on their mobile phone. The problem was that although the message appeared to come from Orange, this was not the case and although recipients were told that they could opt out, in practice there was no clear or simple means of doing so. The adjudication found World Networks to be acting in contravention to the Privacy and Electronic Communications (EC Directive) Regulations. See: http://www.asa.org.uk/Complaints-and-ASA-action/Adjudications/ 2007/2/World-Networks/TF ADJ 42217.aspx.

[22] Statutory Instrument 2003/2426. These regulations are available at: http://www.opsi.gov.uk/ si/si2003/20032426.htm.

the terms laid out in the Directive. Regulation 2 provides the definitions for terms, which run throughout the regulations. While 'electronic mail' and 'communication' are defined,[23] there is no mention of 'spam', 'junk email' or 'unsolicited commercial email'. This is problematic because if this legislation is to carry the fight against spam, it is suggested that a definition of this term would be beneficial. The heart of the legislation is found in regulations 22 and 23, which deal specifically with the transmission of unsolicited communication by email. Regulation 23[24] provides that:

> "A person shall neither transmit, nor instigate the transmission of, a communication for the purposes of direct marketing by means of electronic mail –
> (a)   where the identity of the person on whose behalf the communication has been sent has been disguised or concealed;
> (b)   where a valid address to which the recipient of the communication may send a request that such communication cease has not been provided."

Regulation 23 requires that all communications for the purposes of direct marketing shall provide a clear and genuine identity of the sender and shall also include a valid return address. There are a couple of problems with this regulation. First of all, the legislation is a little narrow as it only applies to emails which are for direct marketing and so may not extend to emails which are religious or political in nature.[25] Secondly, and perhaps more importantly, there is a presumption on the part of the authors of this legislation that all people who send email for direct marketing purposes aim to do so within the parameters of the law. Following this presumption to its natural conclusion, the belief that all direct marketing is sent by legitimate, law-abiding businesses is a little naïve as the majority of spam comes from a small group of criminals who are very difficult to trace. They may route their communications through different servers in different countries, making detection very difficult to achieve for law enforcement agencies. The criminal spammer is clearly going to be less inclined to ensure they provide a legitimate subject line and return address as

---

[23] 'Electronic mail' is defined as: means any text, voice, sound or image message sent over a public communications network which can be stored in the network or in the recipient's terminal equipment until it is collected by the recipient, while 'communication' is defined as: any information exchanged or conveyed between a finite number of parties by means of a publicly available electronic communications service. This does not include any information conveyed as part of a broadcasting service to the public over an electronic communications network except to the extent that the information can be related to the identifiable subscriber or user receiving the information.

[24] This implemented Article 13(4) of Directive 2002/58/EC.

[25] Although as suggested above, the Information Commissioner has provided a broader definition of what amounts to direct marketing.

it would make their detection easier.[26] Therefore it seems the effectiveness of this regulation is only effective in terms of legitimate senders of commercial communication, who will want to ensure that customers can easily make contact with them though a valid return address.

However, the central plank in this piece of legislation that is aimed at tackling spam is Regulation 22.[27] This regulation sets out the legitimate methods by which unsolicited email for direct marketing purposes may be sent. Regulation 22(2) states that the sender must obtain *consent* from the recipient before a commercial email is sent. This means that the recipient must opt in to receiving this communication. This is problematic in itself, due to the undefined nature of 'unsolicited'. Furthermore, 'consent' itself is not defined in the regulations. Recital 17 of the Directive explains that consent means that same as in the Data Protection Directive 95/46/EC (which was implemented into the United Kingdom as the Data Protection Act 1998), which requires the consent to be freely given, specific and informed. But the waters are muddied a little as the Data Protection Directive and the Data Protection Act refer to two types of consent. If a data subject allows an organisation to process his personal data he needs to give his 'consent'.[28] However if he is allowing an organisation to process his sensitive personal data, the data subject is required to give his explicit consent.[29] Both Directive 95/46/EC and the Data Protection Act are silent as to the difference between these two standards of consent and it is not clear which is applicable in relation to the spam regulations. However, the phrase of particular interest in considering the nature of consent is that the recipient has *"... previously notified"* the sender that he consents to the sending, which perhaps indicates a higher level of consent than merely implied by conduct. While the exact definition of consent in the regulations is arguably not very helpful, the regulations continue by providing methods by which a recipient is deemed to have consented. Regulation 22(3) reads:

"A person may send or instigate the sending of electronic mail for the purposes of direct marketing where –
(a)   that person has obtained the contact details of the recipient of that electronic mail in the course of the sale or negotiations for the sale of a product or service to that recipient;

---

[26] As an aside, a term requesting that commercial communication should be appropriately titled was found in The Electronic Commerce (EC Directive) Regulations 2002. This states that where an unsolicited commercial communication is sent, it must be *"... clearly and unambiguously identifiable as such as soon as it is received"* (Regulation 8).
[27] This implemented Article 13(1–3) of Directive 2002/58/EC.
[28] Schedule 2 of the Data Protection Act.
[29] Schedule 3 of the Data Protection Act.

(b)   the direct marketing is in respect of that person's similar products or services only; and;

(c)   the recipient has been given a simple method of refusing (free of charge except the costs of the transmission of the refusal) the use of his contact details for the purposes of such direct marketing, at the time that the details were initially collected, and, where he did not initially refuse the use of the details, at the time of each subsequent communication."

It can be seen from this regulation that the default position employed by the legislation is that this type of communication can be sent as long as an individual has consented. Regulation 22(3) (a) and (b) provide a method by which it can be inferred that an individual has consented. Before examining these requirements for sending such email, the High Court in **Microsoft Corporation v McDonald**[30] considered *inter alia* the definition of 'instigate' and what is meant by instigating the sending of a direct marketing email. The facts of this case were that Microsoft set up a large number of bogus email addresses. McDonald operated a website that offered email lists to direct marketers, with comments on the website saying that all the websites were from people who had consented to receiving direct marketing email and were all looking forward to receiving exciting offers. Some of the email addresses that Microsoft had set up appeared on the lists offered for sale by McDonald and it was perfectly clear that as the email addresses were bogus there could be no consent to their usage. Even though Mr McDonald had not personally sent spam emails, the judge was of the view (in the absence of Mr McDonald, who did not turn up to court) that the encouragements placed on his website were sufficient for him to have 'instigated' the sending. The judge suggested that:

"... to urge or to incite somebody to do something requires something more than the mere facilitation of the action concerned; it requires in my judgment, some form of positive encouragement."[31]

The three methods for a recipient to consent to receiving direct marketing via email will now be examined individually. First of all there is the requirement for an existing customer arrangement. This term allows for senders of directing marketing communication to retain details of past or current customers to enable them to use their email address to forward future advertisements.

---

[30] [2006] All ER (D) 153. For more on this case see: Wilson, C *The UK fight against spam: Microsoft Corporation v Paul Martin McDonald* (2007) Computer Law and Security Report, volume 23, issue 2, pages 128–129 and Rogers, K. M. *Spam Nation* (2007) 157 New Law Journal.

[31] Ibid, paragraph 13.

However, unsurprisingly – from the point of view of defeating spam – this has its critics. While the (then) Department of Trade and Industry consulted widely on the wording of this term it is suggested that the final product is weakened by the addition of the phrase "… or negotiations for the sale". This phrase is not found in the Directive. An existing customer relationship is deemed to exist after a business has sold an item to a consumer or negotiated for the sale of goods or a service. The Information Commissioner, who has responsibility for enforcing these regulations, has maintained that the sale does not need to be completed for this exception to apply. If this is the case, the question needs to be asked just how far does a negotiation need to have progressed for this exception to be valid? It is not clear whether a simple request for further information would be sufficient or whether some form of bartering over price is required. Equally, it is uncertain whether a consumer who purchases a good online, then exercises his right to cancel the good within seven days[32] would fall within this category or not.

The second requirement is that the direct marketing must be in respect of similar products or services only. This permits direct marketers to send email to a customer with whom they have an existing consumer-business relationship, for items which are similar to a product or service which the consumer has previously purchased or negotiated to purchase. Whilst this forms a level of protection for the consumer, the critical issue is what a person (who does not object to receiving future advertising emails from any Internet company) would 'reasonably expect' the future advert to contain. Specifically, what would be classified as a 'similar product or service'? This is especially challenging when considering large supermarkets that sell everything from traditional food and drink to electrical goods, periodicals, toys, clothes and even financial services. In this case if an individual purchased food from a supermarket would that supermarket then be able to send direct marketing communications regarding all the other goods, products and services that they offer? In his guidance on the regulations, the Information Commissioner states that his office will be taking a 'purposive' approach and will place the emphasis on action upon the consumer.[33] If the consumer feels that adverts are being sent which are beyond what he would 'reasonably expect', he would be able to opt out from receiving them. The Information Commissioner is of the view that respectable marketers would want to avoid this, as it would limit their potential audience for advertising and would potentially damage customer goodwill.

The final requirement imposed by this part of the legislation is that the recipient has a simple means of refusing (or opting out of receiving) such

---

[32] Consumer Protection (Distance Selling) Regulations 2000, regulations 10–18.
[33] See Information Commissioner's Guidance available at: http://www.ico.gov.uk/for_organisations/privacy_and_electronic_communications.aspx.

emails. The regulations are not clear, and little has been written on the meaning of this term and how it applies to senders and recipients alike. The Information Commissioner suggests however that this term allows a recipient to opt out of receiving direct marketing email, even after providing initial consent. Furthermore, they argue that enforcement proceedings will be taken against those businesses that refuse to positively act upon a recipient's request, although to date no action has been taken by the Information Commissioner's office. One case that the Advertising Standards Authority has considered on the issue of opt-outs involved ING Direct. ING sent out a direct mailing (including a newsletter outlining some recent products) to customers who had previously opted out of receiving direct marketing. An included letter stated that if they had changed their mind about receiving such marketing material they could contact the consumer services helpline to be placed back on to the recipient list. The adjudication by the Advertising Standards Authority was that ING Direct had breached the CAP Code by sending marketing communication to customers after they had opted out.[34] A similar case involving Virgin Media Limited was heard by the Advertising Standards Authority in July 2010. The facts were that Virgin Media sent an email promoting the latest offers to a customer who had previously opted out of receiving direct marketing. Virgin Media argued that the email was announcing an ownership change within the company and that customers may wish to opt back in once they were informed. The Advertising Standards Authority rejected this argument and found that Virgin Media had breached the Code.[35]

The basic rule provided by Regulation 22 is that unsolicited direct marketing email may not be sent to an individual unless they have consented to receiving it. This allows individuals the ability to decide whether or not they wish to receive it and if they do they may 'opt in'. However, Regulation 22(3) provides methods by which a person may give consent, which allows direct marketing email to be sent to a passive recipient. If an individual has contacted a business for any reason, that individual is therefore likely to receive such communications. Thus, the regulations have provided what many commentators call a 'soft opt-in'.[36] This is due to the ease by which an individual may find

---

[34] See: Advertising Standards Authority Adjudication on ING Direct N. V. (5th March 2008). Available at: http://www.asa.org.uk/Complaints-and-ASA-action/Adjudications/2008/3/ING-Direct-NV/TF ADJ 44091.aspx. A similar case involving opting out by text message was the Advertising Standards Authority Adjudication on Claim Management UK Limited (24th June 2009). Available at: http://www.asa.org.uk/Complaints-and-ASA-action/Adjudications/2009/6/Claim-Management-UK-Ltd/TF ADJ 46452.aspx.

[35] ASA Adjudication on Virgin Media Limited (28th July 2010). Available at: http://www.asa.org.uk/Complaints-and-ASA-action/Adjudications/2010/7/Virgin-Media-Ltd/TF ADJ 48855.aspx.

[36] For example, see: Henderson, B R Opt-in or Opt-out. Are these the only options? (May 2005) Journal of Internet Law pages 1, 12–18 and Boardman, R Direct marketing – The new rules (2004) Hertfordshire Law Journal, Volume 2, Issue 1, pages 3–30.

that they have opted in to receiving this type of communication. There are further deficiencies in these regulations, however it seems the critical issue with this entire piece of legislation is that the European Union and the United Kingdom have (while trying to balance privacy and business needs) attempted to regulate, rather than outlaw spam. The legislation makes no distinction between honourable businesses legitimately marketing their products and hardened spammers, who ignore the law and are probably hidden from the law enforcement agencies. The regulations can only really impact on legitimate businesses, which are not the major problem. A legitimate business is not going to ignore a request from an individual asking for their details to be removed from the company's mailing list database, as the company would not want to lose the goodwill of the customer or run the risk of potential enforcement proceedings by the Information Commissioner for failing to comply with the regulations. However, when the sender is an individual in an upstairs room, on his own, or even someone from outside the European Union, who willingly flouts the law in the hope of making a profit, the situation is completely different. They will disregard any request for a person's details to be removed and possibly bombard that individual with more spam, as they are certain that they have reached an active email address. It seems the regulations may have inadvertently provided a degree of legality for spam, instead of making it illegal. Therefore, while spam still makes money and it is financially beneficial for a spammer to send spam, the law can be ignored or loopholes can be found and exploited. Furthermore, the regulations only extend as far as individual subscribers and not users (Regulation 22(1) and the definitions provided in Regulation 2(1)(h)) and they do not apply to businesses. This means that spammers can legitimately send spam to millions of people, providing they use their work email address, as opposed to their private address.

The final consideration in relation to these regulations are the potential remedies for recipients and sanctions for those marketers who flout the rules. Regulation 30 is the relevant section and states that:

"(1) A person who suffers damage by reason of any contravention of any of the requirements of these Regulations by any other person shall be entitled to bring proceedings for compensation from that other person for that damage.
(2) In proceedings brought against a person by virtue of this regulation it shall be a defence to prove that he had taken such care as in all the circumstances was reasonably required to comply with the relevant requirement."

Regulation 30(1) states that an individual is entitled to bring proceedings against any person who suffers any damage. The difficulty here is quantifying the nature of the damage; on the face of it, receiving a number of unsolicited commercial emails does not constitute damage in the traditional sense of the word. Refusal to comply with the regulations is a criminal offence, with a penalty of a £5,000 fine (in a Magistrate's Court) or unlimited if the trial takes place in a higher court. The Information Commissioner enforces the regulations, yet from the wording he would have a very difficult job to prove beyond all reasonable doubt that there had been a breach, as the defence is "... *that he had taken such care as in all the circumstances ...*" (Regulation 30(2)). This is a very broad defence and it is suggested that it would limit potential convictions, as a spammer would only need to show that he had taken reasonable care. The decision in the aforementioned case of **Microsoft v McDonald** is also helpful in terms of available remedies as it confirms that an Internet Service Provider can bring an action under the regulations, which is a small extension from the initial view that only the subscriber to the service could commence an action. Furthermore, the decision provides a slightly wider scope for remedies and extends to allowing for injunctions to prevent the action from continuing. To date, the Information Commissioner has not succeeded in any prosecutions under these Regulations. However there have been two successful private prosecutions. The first was brought by Nigel Roberts against Media Logistics, a company based in Scotland. Mr Roberts was awarded £300 in damages in December 2005.[37] The second was heard in Scotland and concerned a person called Gordon Dick. He was awarded £750 (plus costs) against an Internet company, which had harvested his email address and sent him (and over 70,000 other people) unsolicited emails.[38] However, the Information Commissioner has had some success in prosecuting senders of unsolicited faxes.[39]

The Advertising Standards Authority is generally robust in bringing action against those who break the rules relating to email advertising (for instance, where the advertisement itself breaks advertising standards, as opposed to being just unsolicited). They follow both the CAP Codes and also the relevant legislation and have had greater results. Once such case focused on a company called Metrodome Group Plc and their viral marketing campaign promoting the film 'Shifty'. This campaign allowed people to 'stitch up' their friend by submitting their friend's email address to the company. Metrodome would then forward an email to this address saying that they were the subject of a criminal investigation into the use of illegal drugs and that they need to participate in counselling and weekly drug testing to reduce the risk of prosecution. Once they clicked through on the relevant link they were then told that they had been 'stitched up' by a mate. There were a number of problems with this

---

[37] For more on this case, see Mr Robert's website at: http://spamlegalaction.pbwiki.com/.

[38] Like Nigel Roberts, Mr Dick has set up his own website, available at: http://www.scotchspam.com/transcom.html. (See also The Times *Courts orders firm to spam spam victim £750* (6th March 2007).

[39] See: OUT-LAW.COM *Under-caution spam faxer fined over £6000* (20th April 2009). Available at: http://out-law.com/page-9958-theme=print.

advert. First of all, the sender had not received the consent of the recipient. Secondly, it was not clear who the email was from, and finally the email did not state that it was a marketing communication.[40]

Traditional remedies against spammers in the United Kingdom

It is possible that a number of traditional statutes may also be of relevance when dealing with spam in the United Kingdom. For example, spamming may constitute a trespass or unlawful interference with goods in the possession of another in violation of Section 1 of the Torts (Interference with Goods) Act 1977. Spamming may also violate the Computer Misuse Act 1990 (as amended by the Police and Justice Act 2006). Although created over twenty years ago primarily in response to the problem of hacking, section 3 may be particularly relevant in relation to Denial of Service attacks. The decision by the Court of Appeal in **Director of Public Prosecutions v Lennon**[41] (in which Mr Lennon sent over 500,000 emails to his former employers which clogged up their email system) is a useful example. This was held to be a breach of section 3 as the purpose was unauthorised (for more on this case please see chapter 10 on Internet crime). Finally, there may be an available action for trade mark violation if the spam sent uses someone else's email address or domain name, misleading recipients into believing that the owner of the trade mark was responsible for the spam.

The American approach to tackling spam

The European Union is not alone in creating legislation to try to eradicate spam. The United States of America, which is consistently the top producer of spam in the world, has also enacted legislation to tackle the problem. This chapter will continue by examining the relative strength of the provisions and provide a comparison with the European legislation.

On 16th December 2003 the President of the United States signed the Controlling the Assault of Non-Solicited Pornography and Marketing Act (2003) (CAN-SPAM Act). Until 2003, there were 36 different state laws relating to spam in America. The first was in Nevada in 1997, which provided that recipients should be able to opt out of receiving spam. However, despite all

---

[40] See: ASA Adjudication on Metrodome Group Plc (6th May 2009). Available at: http://www.asa.org.uk/Complaints-and-ASA-action/Adjudications/2009/5/Metrodome-Group-plc/TF_ADJ_46218.aspx.

[41] [2006] EWHC 1201 (Admin).

these laws, spam within the United States continued to increase. The likely reason for this was that each statute imposed different standards and legal requirements. As there was no uniform approach, spammers could 'state-hop', finding the best legislation for their purposes. The signing of the CAN-SPAM Act concluded almost six years of debate on this issue. Yet, the effectiveness of the final result is still doubted. In every society there needs to be a balance between a person's right to privacy and the right to have freedom of speech. Spam is relevant in this area as it sits on the borderline between a person's right to privacy and the freedom of expression afforded to businesses. The problem with 'privacy' is that there is not a specific definition of privacy, particularly as it depends on the context of the situation. In the European Union, the balance is played out in the European Convention on Human Rights[42] (Article 8 provides for a respect for a private life, whereas Article 10 allows for a freedom of speech). Although the European Union is bound by freedom of speech, it tends to regard the right to privacy as the stronger right. This is seen in the approach adopted towards spam in the Directive on Privacy and Electronic Communications (as discussed above), which has the default position of spam being unlawful unless the sender meets a number of requirements.[43] The default position is different in the United States. In contrast to the European Union the rights of business or the organisation take precedence over the consumer. This has its roots in the First Amendment, which states *"Congress shall make no law ... abridging the freedom of speech"*.

The contrasting approaches between these two pieces of legislation can be seen in the introductions to the two Acts. Recitals 5 and 6 of the European Union's Directive explain that the underlying aim of this legislation is to uphold consumer confidence. In contrast, Article 2(a)(1) of the American CAN-SPAM Act talks about the importance of email and how it assists the e-commerce world to grow. Immediately there is a sharp conflict. The European Union's focus is on upholding consumer confidence, while America seeks the development of the e-commerce world by allowing businesses to freely advertise. Accordingly, the favoured approach in America to free speech over privacy rights has meant that an anti-spam law in America was very slow in coming. However, it is suggested that such a law gained rapid impetus after the announcement of a proposed anti-spam law in California which was remarkably strict. It proposed an opt-in to receiving spam email and provided for very harsh sanctions, which had the potential for nationwide applicability. This caused a great deal of consternation, particularly by the Direct Marketing Association, who considered that their right to free speech was being damaged by limiting the potential utilisation of advertising methods the Internet presented. In 2003 alone, nine Bills were presented

---

[42] Incorporated into the United Kingdom by the Human Rights Act 1998. Available at: http://www.hmso.gov.uk/acts/acts1998/19980042.htm.
[43] Regulations 22 and 23.

before Congress, as lobbying by businesses and advertisers against the Californian Bill intensified. When the CAN-SPAM Act came onto the books it was broadly welcomed, mainly because its provisions were less rigorous than those in the Californian Bill. It could be argued that the CAN-SPAM Act was introduced as the 'lesser of two evils', and potentially would not be in existence today, had the Californian Bill not forced the hand of business.

Provisions and definitions

The overriding purpose of the Act, as stipulated in the heading of the Act, is to "... *regulate interstate commerce by imposing limitation and penalties on the transmission of unsolicited commercial electronic mail via the Internet.*" The CAN-SPAM Act omits to provide a clear definition of 'spam' and the closest the Act gets to relevant definitions is found within section 3(2)(A), which provides that a 'commercial electronic mail message' is any electronic mail message which has the primary purpose of being a commercial advertisement or promotion of a commercial product or service. To be covered by the Act, it seems that spam must be commercial in nature, yet it appears that spam can only be commercial in nature. It would be deemed commercial when the recipient is likely to conclude that the email contains an advertisement. The consequence of this approach is that email which is political or religious in nature could fall outside of the ambit of the Act. The presumption contained within the Act is that all emails sent are legitimate, unless they fail to meet one of the criteria in the Act. The criteria – or obligations created – are as follows:

"i   It must be sent in bulk."
If an email is to be caught under CAN-SPAM, it must be sent in bulk. The Act prescribes this in Section 4(d)(3) as more than 100 electronic mail messages in a 24-hour period, more than 1,000 messages in a 30-day period or more than 10,000 messages in one year. This provision is important. The CAN-SPAM Act recognises the importance, convenience and efficiency of email and the authors did not want to legislate in such a way that restricted the benefits of email and hence gave a threshold before email could be termed as spam.

"ii   The recipient must not have given his affirmative consent."
Affirmative consent is defined in Section 3(1) of the Act and states that:

"The term 'affirmative consent', when used with respect to a commercial electronic mail message, means that:
(a)   the recipient expressly consented to receive the message, either in response to a clear and conspicuous request for such consent or at the recipient's own initiative; and

(b)   if the message is from a party other than the party to which the recipient communicated such consent, the recipient was given clear and conspicuous notice at the time the consent was communicated that the recipient's electronic mail address could be transferred to such other party for the purpose of initiating commercial electronic mail messages."

Accordingly, emails to which the recipient has consented to will not be construed as spam. This is similar to the position within the European Union.

"iii   The email is not a transactional or relationship message"
This is defined in some detail in Section 3(17)(A–B). It seeks to protect customer–business relationships already in existence. By protecting existing relationships, the CAN-SPAM Act shields legitimate companies from falling under the Act. As legitimate companies are more likely to want to comply with the law to avoid adverse publicity and losing the goodwill of customers, existing relationships are protected.

"iv   The Primary purpose must be commercial in nature."
As highlighted, CAN-SPAM focuses upon commercial emails. It is possible therefore that the terms of the Act do not extend to religious or political email, or email that does not seek to obtain money from the recipient.

"v   The sender must be promoting his products or those of a third party."
This builds upon the need for email to be commercial in nature before coming under the terms of CAN-SPAM. Furthermore, if a third party business has agreed for their products to be advertised, they too could come under the Act, even though they were not the sender.[44] This provides added protection for the consumer.

Therefore, it can be seen that before the CAN-SPAM Act can come into play, email must be sent in bulk, and have a primary purpose of advertising a commercial product. Spam is defined in CAN-SPAM by a process of elimination, and will not come under the Act, unless this first stage is met.

Requirements and prohibitions

After the first stage of whether an email has the potential of coming under the CAN-SPAM Act, the Act moves on to provide requirements that all emails sent in America must contain. Failure to include these requirements in an email will

---

[44] See Section 3(16)(B) and also Section 6.

lead to the email being termed as spam, and thus liable to the penalties under the Act, which are both criminal and civil in nature. Section four of the Act entitled 'Prohibition against predatory and abusive commercial email' provides for the general offences which could lead to a criminal conviction. Paraphrased, it is a criminal offence to:

(a)   hijack a computer and send multiple commercial emails from it;
(b)   send multiple commercial emails with the intention of misleading or deceiving recipients;
(c)   falsify header information;
(d)   set up a false email account to send multiple commercial emails; and
(e)   falsely represent oneself as a registrant and send multiple commercial email from such addresses.

The penalties for breaching these requirements are a fine (which increases depending upon the volume sent) and up to five years imprisonment.[45] The other requirements and sanctions are as follows:

i.   Prohibition of false or misleading transmission information (section 5(1))
The transmission information (or header information) can be used by the recipient to trace the sender of the email. The authors of the CAN-SPAM Act recognised that legitimate businesses would want to put their correct details on the email, to enable customers to be able to contact them. As well as providing accurate header information, senders are obliged to ensure that there is a valid return address to which recipients can send responses.[46]

ii.   Prohibition of deceptive subject headings (section 5(2))
Section 5(2) of the Act stipulates that it is unlawful to initiate a commercial email if:

> "... such person has actual knowledge, or knowledge fairly implied on the basis of objective circumstances, that a subject heading of the message would be likely to mislead a recipient ... about a material fact regarding the contents or subject matter of the message."

Therefore, the contents of an email should be accurately reflected in the subject line. Furthermore, if the email is sexual in nature, the subject line must contain a reference to this.[47] Such email should have the prefix 'SEXUALLYEXPLICIT' at

---

[45] Section 4(b).
[46] Section 5(3).
[47] Section 5(d).

the front of the subject line. Failure to comply with this requirement, could lead to a criminal conviction.

iii.   Prohibition of transmission of commercial electronic mail after objection (Section 5(4))

It is contended that this provision is pivotal to CAN-SPAM and its potential for assisting the international effort to eradicate spam. The term reads:

> "If a recipient makes a request using a mechanism provided pursuant to paragraph (3) [inclusion of return address] not to receive some or any commercial electronic mail messages from such sender, then it is unlawful –
> (i)   for the sender to initiate the transmission to the recipient, more than 10 business days after the receipt of such request ..."[48]

The CAN-SPAM Act provides for an 'opt out' to receiving unsolicited commercial email. Furthermore, the email must contain a clear and conspicuous return email address for the opt-out to be carried out.[49]

In circumstances where the sender of the email is not a legitimate business, it is suggested that to opt out is time-consuming for consumers and futile, since general advice given to consumers about limiting potential spam email is not to reply to spam as it provides acknowledgement that the email address is a valid address.

The key provisions of the CAN-SPAM Act, somewhat controversially, override state legislation[50] and the Federal Trade Commission has responsibility for the enforcement of the Act, alongside individual states. A strength contained within the Act is that Internet Service Providers are able to bring an action.[51] This is a positive step as Internet Service Providers are likely to have the motivation and the financial backing to forward actions. The ability for an Internet Service Provider to bring an action has been replicated in the United Kingdom in the Microsoft judgment, although it seems that this is a rare similarity between the approaches of the two jurisdictions.

It is contended that lots of international legislation (which in many cases conflicts, or at least has different emphases) will not on its own lead to spam becoming a thing of the past. Indeed a more co-ordinated effort is required, including in legislation, enforcement (and ensuring that enforcement agencies have sufficient resources to deal with the hardened criminal spammer), technology and education, for spam to be removed from inboxes. However,

---

[48] Section 4(A).

[49] Section 5(3).

[50] Section 8(b)(1) – there are some exceptions to the *prima facie* rules listed in Section 8(b)(2), which in some cases are harsher than at federal level.

[51] Section 7(g).

considering the covert methods that spammers use to send the communication, it may well be that this is not a realistic possibility.

The use of cookies in online marketing

A more discreet online marketing method is the use of cookies. Cookies are files which attach themselves to the hard drive of a computer and then monitor and track the usage of the Internet by the user. Over a period of time a picture is put together of the main Internet sites the user visits, which enables directed advertising to be targeted to that particular person. Cookies are necessary to the running of the Internet and have been commonplace for some time. If a website is accessed on a regular basis from a home computer, for instance your webmail account or online banking service, a cookie will remember your username from the last time you entered it, so that you only need to enter your password to access your accounts. There are two main types of cookies. The session cookie is temporary and is erased after use (or when the user exits the site). It tracks a user's behaviour during the session on a particular website, but does not track someone's general Internet usage over a period of time. A persistent cookie is permanent until it is deliberately erased or it expires. It can have the ability to track a user's website viewing habits to enable more targeted advertising.

Cookies form a large part of the memory of the Internet and operate as the identification card for Internet users, thus avoiding lengthy login procedures when accessing a commonly-used website. Cookies are also used when a customer visits a website such as Amazon and places goods into a 'virtual shopping basket', allowing individuals to continue browsing through the rest of the site. Once the customer has finished browsing and proceeds to the checkout, the website remembers which goods they have clicked on by use of a cookie. This increases the speed with which an individual can use the Internet. As mentioned, cookies assist websites in their advertising to consumers, and it enables advertisers to monitor advertising sent to individuals to ensure they are not sent the same advert many times. By watching the viewing habits of an individual, relevant pop-ups or banner advertisements can be displayed which are more suitable to the viewer; in effect the advertiser builds up a profile of the web user.

Despite the fact that cookies have an important role in the running of the Internet and are essential to e-commerce, they present some key problems, most notably to the privacy rights of an individual. It is possible that through cookies a profile of a user can be built up. At the same time, excessive use of cookies could lead to the user's computer working towards full memory capacity, thus slowing the speed of the computer. One of the problems with companies making use of cookies is that individuals could potentially lose control of their personal details. The Data Protection Act 1998 states that individuals have the right to request the personal data held about them and data controllers are under an obligation to keep data up to date. This is not guaranteed with the use of cookies, as there is limited protection for the data held.

The key piece of legislation for regulating the use of cookies, alongside the Data Protection Act, is Directive 2002/58/EC on Privacy and Electronic Communications. As highlighted above, this Directive is vital in the European Union's fight against spam or unsolicited commercial bulk email, yet alongside this it deals with the use of cookies. During the consultation period for the Directive it appeared that cookies would be completely banned. However, by the time the Directive was published, the situation had swung full circle. Recital 24 states:

> "So-called spyware, web bugs, hidden identifiers and other similar devices can enter the user's terminal without their knowledge in order to gain access to information, to store hidden information or to trace the activities of the user and may seriously intrude upon the privacy of these users. The use of such devices should be allowed only for legitimate purposes, with the knowledge of the users concerned."

The recital presents more questions than it answers. On the one hand it states that cookies and equivalent pieces of equipment can be an intrusion into the privacy of an individual, while on the other hand states they can be used for 'legitimate purposes'. The question as to what is a legitimate purpose is answered to some extent by Recital 25:

> "... such devices, for instance so-called 'cookies' can be a legitimate and useful tool, for example, in analysing the effectiveness of website design and advertising and in verifying the identity of users engaged in online transactions. Where such devices ... are intended for a legitimate purpose, such as to facilitate the provisions of information society services, their use should be allowed on condition that users are provided with clear and precise information in accordance with Directive 95/46/EC."

The definition of a legitimate purpose is somewhat vague. This is not helpful as it is likely to cause confusion over what is and what is not a legitimate purpose. However, the recital continues by stating what rights an Internet user should have in relation to cookies:

> "... Users should have the opportunity to refuse to have a cookie or similar device stored on their terminal equipment. This is particularly important where users other than the original user have access to the terminal equipment ... Information and the right to refuse may be offered once for the use

of various devices to be installed on the user's terminal equipment during the same connection and also covering any further use that may be made of those devices during subsequent connections."

It appears that users can refuse a cookie, but the recital states that they may only have one opportunity. This 'once-and-for-all' agreement is weaker than in earlier drafts, as previously consent for using a cookie had to be obtained each time such a device was used. Recitals 24 and 25 are developed further by Article 5(3) of the Directive, which states:

"Member States shall ensure that the use of electronic communications networks to store information or to gain access to information stored in the terminal equipment of a subscriber or user is allowed on condition that the subscriber or user concerned is provided with clear and comprehensible information in accordance with Directive 95/46/EC, *inter alia about the purposes of the processing, and is offered the right to refuse such processing by the data controller*. This shall not prevent any technical storage or access for the sole purpose of carrying out or facilitating the transmission of a communication over an electronic communications network, or as strictly necessary in order to provide an information society service explicitly requested by the subscriber or user."

The combined effects of the above provisions in relation to cookies are six-fold. First of all, they can only be used for legitimate purposes; secondly in accordance with Directive 95/46/EC the user must be provided with clear and comprehensible information about the purpose of processing; thirdly the user must have an opportunity to refuse a cookie (to 'opt out'); fourthly this opt-out opportunity may be offered on a one-off basis; fifthly the method of opt-out must be as user friendly as possible; and finally a service can be conditional on the acceptance of a cookie, as long as it is used for legitimate purposes. The Directive was implemented into the United Kingdom as the Privacy and Electronic Communication (EC Directive) Regulations 2003. Regulation 6 and 7 are of particular interest to cookie usage. Building upon the terms of the Directive, Regulation 6 (which implemented Article 5(3)) states that:

"... a person shall not use an electronic communications network to store information, or to gain access to information stored, in the terminal equipment of a subscriber or user unless the requirements of paragraph 2 are met ... that the subscriber or user of that terminal equipment –

(a)   is provided with clear and comprehensible information about the purposes of the storage of, or access, that information; and

(b)   is given opportunity to refuse the storage of or access to that information."

The requirements found within the Directive that if a cookie is to be used, clear and comprehensible information must be provided alongside an option to opt-out of the cookie are mirrored within the regulations.

Reform of the Directive on Privacy and Electronic Communication 2002/58/EC

Directive 2002/58/EC is a key piece of legislation providing rules for sending unsolicited commercial communication and use of cookies. In October 2009, the European Commission adopted changes to the Directive.[52] One of the main changes is the introduction of a data security breach notification law for telecommunications companies,[53] although there are changes for both the rules relating to cookies and commercial communications. Member states are required to implement these changes by May 2011.

The rules relating to websites that use cookies are the more substantive change under the reforms. Currently, cookies can be used for legitimate purposes as long as the users of the website are provided with clear and comprehensive information about the use of the cookie and are given an adequate means of opting out. The difficulty with this is that websites would insert the cookie on the hard drive of the user's computer and would either provide the opportunity to opt out afterwards, or contain details of how to opt out (or reject the cookie) within the website's terms and conditions. In practice, the section was not really applied. Article 5(3) (discussed above) is to be amended so that before a cookie is stored in the terminal equipment, the user is provided with clear and comprehensive information and has given the website operator his consent to the cookie being used. This is a substantial shift in approach and is controversial. First of all, the very nature of the process of storing a cookie on terminal equipment necessitates that personal data will be processed prior to the consent of the user being obtained, although the phrasing of the new section does not state explicitly that the consent needs to be given prior to the use of the cookie. Secondly, it is not clear whether this provision applies to all cookies, or to all cookies and spyware, or just those cookies that process personal data. Finally, the nature of consent is unclear. It is not certain how 'pro-active' the consent needs to be. For example, if a user does not refuse use, can the website automatically assume that the user has consented, or does the consent need to clear and unequivocal? It is not clear

---

[52] The amending Directive also makes changes to Directive 2002/22/EC on universal service and users' rights relating to electronic communications networks and services and Regulation 2006/2004 on cooperation between national authorities responsible for the enforcement of consumer protection laws and is available at: http://register.consilium.europa.eu/pdf/en/09/st03/st03674.en09.pdf.

[53] This is considered in more detail in chapter 7 on Data Protection.

how the website owner is to obtain the necessary consent from the user. This will not be confirmed until member states implement the amended Directive. The initial difficulty with this amendment is that every website that uses cookies will need the consent of the user. This could even extend to websites that count or monitor the number of users.[54] The reforms to this area of law are still subject to considerable controversy.[55]

There are some minor changes to the sending of commercial communications. First of all, Recital 67 is introduced to make it clear that Regulations 22 and 23 apply not only to the use of email, but also SMS, MMS and other forms of technology. Furthermore, Article 13 is extended and Article 13(6) seeks to make it easier for those adversely affected by a breach under this Article to commence legal proceedings. The right of an Internet Service Provider to bring an action against a spammer is enshrined in legislation (the case of **Microsoft v McDonald**, discussed above, concluded that an Internet Service Provider would also be able to commence legal proceedings). However it is not clear the extent to which member states will interpret the phrase 'any person adversely affected', as this could include businesses that receive large volumes of spam email. Despite a wider net of people who could commence legal proceedings against a spammer, the effectiveness of these provisions is likely to be rooted in the enforcement regime and the Information Commissioner will need to push for greater funding and personnel to be successful.

Key points:

- The Internet provides a range of ways in which an online company can advertise their products, including websites, banner advertisements, commercial email and pop-ups.
- The use of search engines has also revolutionised advertising with companies able to pay search engine providers to achieve a higher search ranking and also have their website ranked in order of popularity in terms of hits.
- Spam emails are one of the main difficulties with the Internet as they slow down the speed of communicating and contain information that is often offensive in nature. Yet there is also profitability behind this form of communication as spammers are able to make money.
- The Directive on Privacy and Electronic Communications 2002/58/EC is the main piece of legislation within the European Union addressing the

---

[54] See OUT-LAW.COM editorial: Robertson, S *Consent will be required for cookies in Europe* (9th November 2009). Available at: http://www.out-law.com/page-10510-theme=print.

[55] See for instance: OUT-LAW.COM *Cookie compliance: privacy regulators make the best of a bad law* (29th June 2010). Available at: http://www.out-law.com/page-11185-theme=print.

problem of spam. It was introduced into the United Kingdom as the Privacy and Electronic Communications (EC Directive) Regulations 2003.

- Regulations 22 and 23 are the main provisions relating to spam. Regulation 23 states that commercial email may not be sent with a misleading subject line or no return address. The rationale for this is to ensure that the legislation can be effectively enforced against offenders, as stated in Recital 43.
- Regulation 22 is of most importance to spam and states that a recipient needs to consent to receiving the communication. This regulation also provides for a 'soft opt-in' in that a person is deemed to have consented if they have previously provided their contact details in the course of a sale or negotiations of a sale, the communication is for similar products or services and the recipient has a simple means of opting out.
- Enforcement is dealt within Regulation 30. The Information Commissioner's Office has responsibility for enforcing the provisions, yet the penalty of £5,000 is relatively small.
- There have only been a couple of private prosecutions to date, although the Advertising Standards Authority has adjudicated in some similar cases in its enforcement of the CAP Codes.
- Cookies are small files which attach themselves to the hard drive of a user's computer. They 'remember' certain details, although various privacy concerns exist.
- Generally, cookies can be used as long as the recipient is given clear and comprehensive information about their usage and has been given the option to opt out.
- The European Commission is reforming the provisions in the Directive on Privacy and Electronic Communications to require the website to obtain the user's consent to cookie usage. This is a shift from offering the user the right to refuse the storage of the cookie after receiving clear and comprehensive information about the purposes of the cookie.

Further reading:

Books

- Asscher, L F & Hoogcarspel, A A *Regulating Spam: A European Perspective after the Adoption of the E-Privacy Directive* (2006) T M C Asser Press, ISBN 90-6704-220-X.

Articles

- Boardman, R *Direct marketing – The new rules* (2004) Hertfordshire Law Journal, Volume 2, Issue 1, pages 3–30.

- Cheng, T S L *Recent international attempts to can spam* (2004) Computer Law and Security Report, volume 20, number 6, pages 472–479.
- Debussere, F *The EU E-Privacy Directive: A monstrous attempt to starve the cookie monster?* (2005) International Journal of Law and Information Technology, Volume 13, Number 1, pages 70–97.
- Fritzmeyer, W & Law, A *The CAN-SPAM Act – Analysed from a European Perspective* (2005) Computer and Telecommunications Law Review, Volume 11, Issue 3, pages 81–90.
- Garrie, D B & Wong, R *Privacy in electronic communications: the regulation of VoIP in the EU and the United States* (2009) Computer and Telecommunications Law Review, volume 15, issue 6, pages 139–146.
- Hedley, S *A Brief History of Spam* (October 2006) Information and Communications Technology Law, volume 15, number 3, pages 223–238.
- Kierkgaard, S M *How the cookies (almost) crumbled: Privacy and lobbyism* (2005) Computer Law and Security Report, Volume 21, Issue 4, pages 310–322.
- Kosta, E, Valcke, P and Stevens, D *Spam, spam, spam, spam ... lovely spam! Why is Bluespam different?* (2009) International Review of Law, Computers and Technology, volume 23, issues 1 and 2, pages 89–97.
- Rogers, K M *Viagra, viruses and virgins: A pan-Atlantic comparative analysis on the vanquishing of spam* (2006) Computer Law and Security Report, Volume 22, Issue 3, pages 228–240.
- Schryen, G *Anti-Spam Legislation: An Analysis of the Laws and Their Effectiveness* (March 2007) Information and Communications Technology Law, volume 16, number 1, pages 17–32.

Questions for consideration:

5.1. What are some of the key ways of advertising online?

5.2. In what ways does unsolicited bulk email damage consumer confidence in the Internet?

5.3. To what extent do the traditional methods of regulating advertisements successfully apply to webvertising?

5.4. What role does the Advertising Standards Authority have within the United Kingdom in relation to direct marketing?

5.5. The provisions found in the United Kingdom's Privacy and Electronic Communication (EC Directive) Regulations 2003 and those found in the American Controlling the Assault of Non-solicited Pornography and Marketing Act 2003 (CAN-SPAM Act) will ensure that spam will soon be a thing of the past.
Critically evaluate the above statement.

5.6. In what situations may a business send direct marketing email in the United Kingdom?

5.7. Explain the nature and usage of a cookie.

5.8. What is the difference between an opt-in and an opt-out system?

5.9. James is the managing director of a company based in the United Kingdom, which sells an extensive range of equipment for tourists. He has a substantial warehouse, which includes items as large as caravans and as small as a map and compass. His business is successful and he has made considerable money from his venture.

   In recent years, James has developed a fascination with the Internet and has spent a great deal of time considering how he can develop his customer base and the profitability of his company by utilising the Internet to a greater degree. He has established a website which has received several orders, but still James is not satisfied.

   One evening, James has the idea of emailing people to advise them of the latest offers and products that he has available. He ponders this thought for a while and comes up with the following strategies:

   • To email all people who have purchased any good from his website and advise them that he has in stock the latest AX-1009 Tent, which is a brand-new, top-of-the-range tent; and

   • To purchase a piece of software that can manufacture email addresses and then send out a general advertising email to all the email addresses that this piece of software provides, listing basic details about his company and some special offers the company is currently running.

   Two days later, Rebecca, a former customer of James, receives the email from James advertising the AX-1009 tent. Rebecca is unhappy because she did not expressly say to James that he could use her email address to email her.

   The same day, Lauren, who has never even heard of James' company, receives the email from him advertising his company. Lauren is also very unhappy at this email, which she sees as an invasion of her privacy.

   Both Rebecca and Lauren approach you as they have heard that you are studying law. Please advise both Rebecca and Lauren on the legal position of these advertising emails and any potential remedies that are available.

5.10. Directive 2002/58 is to be applauded as being a significant legal framework that specifically deals with the use of cookies. The privacy issues are recognised and a satisfactory approach is taken to protect the fundamental right of privacy, while allowing businesses to pursue their legitimate interests.

Undertake a critical evaluation of this view. Does your answer change if the reforms due to be implemented into the United Kingdom by May 2011 are introduced as currently drafted?

All weblinks mentioned in the text can also be found at:
http://www.palgrave.com/law/rogers

6 Jurisdiction and Choice of Law

This chapter will consider:

- The Internet-specific problems in the broad arena of private international law, specifically in ascertaining jurisdiction and deciding on the choice of law and enforcing judgments.
- The main pieces of relevant legislation in this area (specifically, the Rome Convention (and the new Rome I) and Brussels Regulation 44/2001).
- Issues relating to choice of law and domicile.
- The types and advantages and disadvantages of online alternative dispute resolution schemes.

Introduction

As discussed elsewhere in this book, the supranational nature of the Internet provides a wealth of new opportunities in terms of communication and commerce. The very design of the Internet requires that international borders are crossed and individuals can enter the website belonging to a company or individual in another country with relative ease. It is not uncommon for two contracting parties to be located in different countries. With the continual increase in Internet traffic, the potential for trans-border disputes also increases. These disputes may be caused by a breach of contract (for example, a product which was ordered online failed to turn up or was not the product that was ordered) or tortuous (e.g. defamation). If the benefits of the Internet are to continue to be enjoyed, it is important that a body of rules exists to provide legal certainty for how these disputes may be heard. This has the dual aim of protecting the interests of businesses by ensuring that they are not discouraged from engaging in Internet commerce, while also (and perhaps more importantly) providing protection for consumers who transact online. Obviously the first point of call in deciding where a dispute will be heard is to look at the contract between the two parties. However, if the 'jurisdiction clause' is vague or unenforceable or if the contract is between a business and a consumer, rules need to be in place to provide the guidelines for resolving the dispute. In the rather complex choice of law and jurisdiction discussion there are two main questions which need to be asked (and which will be addressed in this chapter). First of all, which country's court has jurisdiction to hear a dispute and secondly, which country's law is to be applied? Whilst in the majority of cases the answer to these two questions will be the same one country, there are exceptions to this. In addition to these rules for resolving disputes, enforcement capabilities need to be considered, as there is little point in obtaining a judgment in a third country, only to discover that the effect of the judgment cannot be relied upon by either the individual or company concerned. To this end, alongside the enforcement of judgments, this chapter will also consider the scope of alternative online dispute resolution schemes. The rationale for these is clear in that they avoid the need for often lengthy and costly court proceedings. In the first instance though, it is necessary to consider issues pertaining to jurisdiction or, in the event of a dispute, where the action will be heard. The main piece of European legislation in this area is Council Regulation (EC) 44/2001 on jurisdiction and the recognition and enforcement of judgments in civil and commercial matters, also known as the Brussels Regulation.[1]

The Brussels Regulation 44/2001

The Brussels Regulation originated from an ad hoc Working Party, which was established in 1997 to consider revisions (due in no small part to the rise of Internet) to the Brussels Convention (1968) and the Lugano Convention. Later the same year, the Working Party published its proposals[2] and on 30th November 2000 the European Council adopted the Brussels Regulation, which came into effect on 1st March 2002. This regulation applies to disputes that arise from within European member states. Where disputes occur outside these states, but within the European Free Trade Association (which includes European member states, plus Norway, Switzerland, Iceland and Liechtenstein) then the Lugano Convention would be of relevance.[3] However if the dispute is between an individual within the United Kingdom and another outside the European Community then English common law would be relevant.[4]

The main objective of the European Community is to achieve a free market where goods, services, capital and persons can move freely from one member

---

[1] Available at: http://europa.eu/legislation summaries/justice freedom security/judicial cooperation in civil matters/l33054 en.htm.

[2] See: *Towards greater efficiency in obtaining and enforcing judgments in the European Union* (COM(97)609 final – OJ C33 of 31/01/1998).

[3] Available at: http://curia.europa.eu/common/recdoc/convention/en/c-textes/ lug-textes.htm.

[4] Regulation 44/2001, Article 4.

state to another. The objectives of the Brussels Regulation, which are set out within the recitals reflect this EC objective. Recital 1 sets out that judicial co-operation is essential to the continued success of the internal market and that a uniform set of rules to govern jurisdiction and recognition of judgments within the European Community are necessary to avoid any disruption to the development of the internal market.[5] Additionally, these rules are required to be highly predictable with the default position of jurisdiction being decided by the domicile of the defendant (with a small body of exceptions, notably for consumers).[6] The scope of the Brussels Regulation is set out in the early substantive Articles. Article 1 states that the scope of the regulation extends to "civil or commercial matters" only.[7] This is a wide parameter within which the regulations can have effect and the vast majority of contracts made over the Internet will be civil or commercial in nature. The decision by the European Court of Justice in **LTU v Eurocontrol**[8] provides some instruction as to the interpretation of civil or commercial matters. The European Court of Justice suggested that in deciding whether a dispute is civil or commercial in nature, consideration must be given to both the objectives and scheme of the convention (instead of just one individual country) and the general principles that arise from the national legal systems.[9] The regulations also provide some guidance on the types of contracts which do not come within the ambit of the regulations. Specifically:

- the status or legal capacity of natural persons;
- rights in property which arise out of a matrimonial relationship;
- wills and succession;
- bankruptcy or proceedings relating to the winding-up of a company or legal person;
- judicial arrangements, compositions and other analogous proceedings; and
- social security and arbitration.[10]

Once the applicability of the regulations has been finalised, they will override any provision of national law.

The basic default principle of the Brussels Regulation is set out in Article 2. The principle is that the member state in which a defendant is domiciled

---

[5] Recital 1.

[6] Recital 11.

[7] Brussels Regulation Article 1(1).

[8] [1976] ECR 1541 – note that this decision was reached under the 'old' 1968 Brussels Convention, although this in itself is not a problem (as Recital 19 states that there should be continuity between the old Brussels Convention and the new Brussels Regulation).

[9] Ibid. Paragraph 5.

[10] Brussels Regulation Article 1(2) (a–d).

(whatever their nationality or citizenship) exercises jurisdiction. This means that the defendant can be sued in the courts of that country, even if they are not a national of that country and regardless of the type of action. It is interesting to note that this starting point is wholly dependant upon the domicile of the defendant. Even though in some Internet contracts different servers in different countries around the world may be used, the applicability of the regulation depends upon the domicile of the defendant involved and has no interest in the various technical deviances that may have been attempted. Therefore, the general principle is that if a person is domiciled in a member state and the matter concerned is civil or commercial, the regulations will apply. There are, of course, exceptions to this general principle. These are found in Article 5, which says that a person domiciled in one member state, may be sued in another member state in cases involving *inter alia* a civil claim for damages, a tort, employment contracts, insurance matters and consumer contracts. Consumer contracts will be considered in greater detail below.

Deciding domicile

Article 59 in the 44/2001 Regulation states simply that in deciding the domicile of a party it is the responsibility of the court which is hearing the action to use the internal law of that country to decide where domicile is found. If the court of a member state which is hearing the action cannot find domicile then the court can apply the law of a second member state to establish whether the individual is domiciled in that second member state.[11] In other words, if the rules of one member state say that a person is domiciled in that country then the domicile of that individual is found in that member state. From the point of view of the United Kingdom, the relevant statute in deciding domicile is the Civil Jurisdiction and Judgments Act 1982.[12] A two-stage test is outlined in this Act, which needs to be applied to an individual by a court seeking to decide on their domicile. First of all, if a person wants to prove domicile they need to be a resident in the United Kingdom and, secondly, the nature and circumstances of their residency needs to show a substantial connection to the United Kingdom.[13] If the court cannot prove domicile in the United Kingdom, they are able to use the law of another member state to decide if the individual is domiciled in that other member state (as per Article 59). Failure to prove domicile in either the United

---

[11] Brussels Regulation Article 59(2).

[12] As amended by Civil Jurisdiction and Judgment Order 2001 (Statutory Instrument 2001/3929).

[13] Civil Jurisdiction and Judgments Act, section 41(2). This second part of the test is presumed to be answered in the positive if the individual has been living in the United Kingdom for more than three months – section 41(6).

Kingdom or another member state would show that both the Brussels Regulation and Lugano Convention would not be relevant in that given circumstance and so common law would apply. The Civil Jurisdiction and Judgments Act also allows a United Kingdom court to decide the domicile of an individual from outside of the European Community. Again, a two-stage test is outlined. First of all the individual should be a resident in the non-member state and secondly the nature and circumstance of that residency should indicate that he has a substantial connection with that state. There is no requirement on the United Kingdom court to use the domicile rules from the non-member state country in deciding on the individual's domicile.

The rules outlined above relate to the finding of the domicile for an individual. The rules differ somewhat if the defendant is a company or other legal person. In these circumstances, domicile is located where the company has its statutory seat, or central administration or its principal place of business.[14] If a United Kingdom court needs to find the domicile of a company or legal person, again the Civil Jurisdiction and Judgements Act lays out a two-stage test. The first requirement is that the company was incorporated within, and has a registered office or other official address in the United Kingdom. Secondly, the central management and control of the company is exercised in the United Kingdom.[15] Unlike an individual, a company may be domiciled in more than one member state.[16] If the United Kingdom court does not find domicile, section 43(6) allows the court to see if the company is domiciled in another member state. In these circumstances, domicile in an alternative member state may be found if the company was established in that member state and its central management and control is located in that member state. Again, it is interesting to note that the domicile rules have no interest at all in the usage of servers or other technology; they are solely dependant upon the physical location of the company.

If domicile of either an individual or a company can be found within a member state then in the event of an online dispute the defendant can be sued in that member state.[17] There are a number of exceptions to this principle, which are contained within Article 5. These exceptions are that the defendant may also be sued in the member state where the performance of the obligation was to have occurred or where the products should have been delivered

---

[14] Brussels Regulation Article 60(1). This could include a company's registered office, although by 'principal' place of business it is likely that this will mean the most important, as opposed to the main place of business, which is from where control is exercised – see **Ministry of Defence and Support of the Armed Forces for the Islamic Republic of Iran v FAZ Aviation Limited** [2007] EWHC 1042 (Comm).

[15] Civil Jurisdiction and Judgments Act 1982, section 42(3).

[16] Brussels Regulation Article 60(1)(a–c).

[17] Brussels Regulation, Article 2(1).

to, or where the service was due to be carried out.[18] Whilst the distinction between goods and services is to be welcomed here, it remains unclear as to where the place of performance for digital services (purchased from a different member state) is located. There is further uncertainty if there has been a breach of obligation in more than one location. A further exception exists within Article 23, which allows parties the right to what is known as prorogation of jurisdiction, or the right to choose the court the dispute will be heard in.[19] This will be valid provided that the agreement is evidenced in writing, or is produced in a form that the parties have agreed to and established between themselves, or is in a standard form and the parties ought to have been aware of its existence.[20] This ability to choose the court may, however, be superseded by the actions of the two parties. In some cases, after a dispute arises between two parties, each party may commence an action in the court of their domicile, which is occasionally known as parallel proceedings. The difficulty with parallel proceedings is that two courts in two different countries may reach wholly incompatible conclusions. Therefore, as only one court can hear the action at any one time, it is incumbent on the second court to adjourn the hearing, while the first court determines jurisdiction.[21] Once jurisdiction has been decided then it is the responsibility of that court to hear the action. The case of **Erich Gasser GmbH v MISAT SRL**[22] demonstrates this principle. The claimant was an Austrian company that sold clothing to an Italian company. The defendant brought an action in Italy against the claimant seeking to have their contractual relationship terminated. In response, the claimant instigated proceedings in Austria for unpaid invoices. The European Court of Justice held that the Austrian court must stop hearing the action, while the Italian court determined the relevant jurisdiction. This would be the case even if an exclusive jurisdiction agreement was in place. Once the jurisdiction was determined then the court of that country could proceed to hear the action.[23] The objective behind this principle is to prevent conflicting judgments, although an unwelcome consequence is that a party to the dispute may commence an action in a foreign court with the intention of delaying matters. The other party

---

[18] Brussels Regulation, Article 5(1). This article applies in matters relating to a contract – see **Martin Peters v Zuid** Case 34/82 ECR I-987.

[19] This is also known as a jurisdiction agreement.

[20] Article 23(2) allows for communication by electronic means which provides a durable record to be equivalent to writing and, as long as the formal requirements are adhered to, the validity of the agreement is presumed, as in **Transporti Castelletti SpA v Trumpy SpA** Case C-159/97 [1997] ECR 1597.

[21] See also Brussels Regulations Articles 27–29.

[22] (2003) All ER (D) 148.

[23] This principle was endorsed in **Turner v Grovit** (2004) All ER (EC) 485. In this case, the claimant applied to the English court to request that parallel proceedings in Spain be restrained. On appeal to the European Court of Justice by the House of Lords it was confirmed that it is the responsibility of the first court to decide upon jurisdiction.

to the dispute will be required to contest the competence of that particular court from hearing the action leading to an increase in costs and time.[24]

Business-to-consumer contracts

The above discussion has focused predominantly upon business-to-business disputes. However, the Brussels Regulations set out specific rules for disputes which are between businesses and consumers. The rationale for this is that in the vast majority of cases the consumer is the weaker party, both in terms of financial resources and in their ability to understand foreign legal systems. Therefore Articles 15–17 provide rules for consumers to ensure that they receive special protection with the aim of removing any of the consumer's discouragement from being able to sue.

Article 15(1) defines a consumer as a person who is acting outside of his trade or profession. This definition remains the same as that which appeared in the 1968 Brussels Convention and the limited case law that exists provides a very narrow interpretation of this term. In **Beniscasa v Dentalkit**[25] the European Court of Justice held that a contract was a consumer contract only when it satisfied the private consumption needs of an individual who was believed to be the weaker party. The difficulty with this narrow interpretation is that it does not assist professionals who are acting outside of their immediate area of expertise, for example a solicitor who wants to sell computer equipment through his firm. His profession would be that of a solicitor, yet by selling computers through his business it is unlikely that the solicitor would constitute a consumer for the purposes of the Brussels Regulation, even though his knowledge of computer systems may be very limited. Equally, a private doctor who purchases a vehicle to allow him to visit patients at home in the course of his employment, while also using the same vehicle for transporting his family, would also be unlikely to be counted as a consumer. As well as demonstrating that an individual is a consumer, to demonstrate that the arrangement is a consumer contract it must also be for the sale of goods on instalment credit terms, or be a contract for a loan repayable on instalments (or other form of credit), or the contract must have been concluded with a person who pursues commercial or professional activities within the member state of the consumer's domicile or, by any means, directs such activities to that member state.[26] This final element demonstrates the attempt by the European Council

---

[24] For more analysis on this decision see: Furmston, M & Chuah, J (ed.) *Commercial and Consumer Law*(2010) Pearson Education Limited, Chapter 10, particularly pages 584–587.

[25] [1997] Case C-269/95 ECR I 3767.

[26] Brussels Regulation, Article 15(1).

to extend the provision of this legislation to the Internet. A business-to-consumer contract can be in existence if the business 'pursues commercial or professional activities' within the member state where the consumer is domiciled, or 'directs such activities' to that member state.[27] It seems that the insertion of the provision (particularly the use of the phase 'by any means') was an attempt to ensure that this legislation applied to transactions over the Internet. However no further guidance on the definition of these terms seems to exist. Arguably if a website is created and can be accessed from all around the world, then a person is pursuing commercial activities there, or at the very least is directing such activities to that country. However, it seems that the potential scope of this section is not as broad as it could be perceived to be. For a consumer contract to be demonstrated, a company needs to do more than simply create an attractive website, even if the language used and the currency applied correspond to the second country. The pursuit of a commercial activity in a member state must have a specific relation to the contract in dispute. The consequence of this is that companies may choose to avoid pursuing commercial activities in countries which have a complex legal system. This means that even though their website could be accessible by a consumer in that country the elements relating to consumer contracts would not come into play. A second problem is that 'directs such activities' is not defined in either the Brussels Regulation 44/2001 or its predecessor. As highlighted above, the relative accessibility of a website is likely to be insufficient. Again it seems that a greater involvement in the dispute itself is required, beyond a mere passive website, but the exact level of interactivity required within a particular country is not certain. The flip-side of this narrow interpretation is that it provides safeguards to the business that has an online presence by ensuring that they will not face potential actions in every court in the European Community.

If a contract is held to be a consumer contract then Article 16 provides that in circumstances where a consumer wishes to bring an action against a business in another member state, the consumer may use the court of their domicile (provided that the business has directed activities to that country) or the court of the business's domicile.[28] The reality of the situation is that a consumer, often constrained by limited finance and understanding of the complexities involved, will very rarely apply to a court in a different country, favouring instead to go to their local court. However, if the action is to be brought against a consumer by a business then the consumer can only be sued in the court of the member state where the consumer is domiciled.[29] Article 17 provides exceptions to these rules and allows for parties to choose the court where the dispute may be heard. The principles contained in Article 16 may be

---

[27] Brussels Regulation, Article 15(1)(c).
[28] Brussels Regulation, Article 16(1).
[29] Brussels Regulation, Article 16(2).

departed from by agreement between the two parties only after the dispute has arisen, or if the agreement allows the consumer to bring proceedings in courts other than those indicated in the section, or which is entered into by the consumer and the other party, both of whom are domiciled in the same member state, which means the jurisdiction of the member state prevails.[30] This prevents businesses from imposing onerous terms and conditions on the consumer prior to the conclusion of the contract.

In situations (in both business-to-business and business-to-consumer disputes) where domicile is found to be outside of the European Community, then Article 4 states it is up to the jurisdiction rules of that member state to decide where a dispute will be heard.

Enforceability of judgments

Once the jurisdiction has been found and the case has been decided it is not always the case that the losing party in the litigation will voluntarily comply with the order of the court. This problem can be particularly acute in international litigation where the court order being enforced is from a court in a different country. In English common law, a judgment will be recognised if it is a final and conclusive judgment, for a fixed sum (not being a form of taxation or a penalty). Furthermore, the judgment must be given by a court with recognised international jurisdiction and there should be no available appeal to the judgment. If a judgment is being appealed, it may still be possible to enforce the ruling, although it is more likely that the proceedings will be paused until the appeal is decided.[31] Questions of enforcement are clearly very important, as a party does not want to go through the expense and difficulty of litigation only to discover that the losing party has no available assets in that particular country, or any ability or interest to meet the demands of the court. It is sometimes necessary to use enforcement mechanisms to ensure the court order is complied with. The Brussels Regulation provides guidance for recognising judgments delivered in other member states. The starting point is given by Article 33, which says that a judgment given in one member state shall be recognised within all other member states. No special procedure is required for recognition to occur, although it does need to have been declared enforceable in the first member state.[32] This links into the first recital of the Brussels Regulation, which places a large emphasis on judicial co-operation. Exceptions to this general principle are found in Article 34 and a judgment shall not be recognised in a second member state if the decision is manifestly contrary to

---

[30] Brussels Regulation, Article 17(1–3).
[31] See: **Colt Industries Inc v Sarlie (No. 2)** [1966] 3 All ER 85.
[32] Brussels Regulation, Article 38.

public policy, or if the decision was given in default of performance (or the defendant did not have sufficient time to arrange his defence), or the judgment was irreconcilable with a decision between the same parties in that second member state, or finally, that it is reconcilable with an earlier judgment involving the same action and the same parties. Article 36 also outlines that a judgment given in one member state may not be reviewed as to its substance by a second member state. Therefore, if a party is seeking to enforce a judgment given by the courts in one member state in another member state, Article 53 simply requires the person to provide an authentic copy of the judgment to the court in the country where the decision is requiring enforcement. Interestingly, contrary to English common law, there is no requirement that the judgment is final.

Choice of law

Closely aligned to discerning the relevant jurisdiction in any given case is the issue of the choice of law the parties to the contract have agreed to. The purpose of ascertaining the choice of law is to determine which national law will be applied to decide the case. The Rome Convention 1980[33] was introduced into a pre-Internet era and at a time when international disputes were only likely to be between large businesses or organisations. It introduced standard rules for choice of law between European member states and at its heart had several key policy ideals, including party autonomy, flexibility, legal certainty and protection of weaker parties. As it is a European measure, its interpretation is ultimately left to the discretion of the European Court of Justice. The changing nature of twenty-first century business, with consumers having significantly more power and choice due to the development of e-commerce, increasingly meant that the legislation in this area was not fit for purpose and more responsive rules were required to ensure that consumers – as well as large corporations – were given adequate legal protection. Partly in response to this, Regulation (EC) No 593/2008 on the law applicable to contract obligations ('Rome I') came into force in December 2009.[34] It applies to all European member states (with the exception of Denmark, which had previously opted out) and covers all contracts entered into after 17th December 2009.[35] Article 24 in Rome I states that the regulation replaces the Rome

---

[33] Implemented into the United Kingdom as the Contracts (Applicable Law) Act 1990.

[34] Regulation 593/2008 is available at: http://eur-lex.europa.eu/LexUriServ/LexUriServ.do?uri=OJ:L:2008:177:0006:0016:EN:PDF.

[35] The Rome Convention applies to contracts entered into before this date. If the Rome Convention does not apply, then common law rules need to be used.

Convention on the law applicable to contractual obligations.[36] Rome I applies to rules relating to choice of law within the European Union. For a consumer based in the United Kingdom, if they have contracted with a professional outside of the European Union, then the Civil Procedure Rules apply. The rationale for these rules in Rome I is that in many cases the consumer is the weaker party and so needs additional protection by legislation.

Article 1 states that the regulations apply to situations involving a conflict of laws in a contractual obligation in civil and commercial matters. A lengthy list of contracts which are excluded from the remit of the legislation is also provided, although this is not really of direct relevance to business-to-consumer Internet transactions. The default position of the regulations is found in Article 3(1) and states that a contract shall be governed by the choice of law expressly chosen or clearly demonstrated by the parties. Thus in many Internet terms and conditions the sentence 'this contract will be governed by English law' will point towards an express choice of law clause. This upholds the principle of party autonomy from the original Rome Convention. Article 3 also clarifies earlier uncertainty by saying that the choice of law clause could only be made expressly, either within the terms of the contract or the circumstances of the case. The parties can also choose to apply a choice of law to all, or part, of the contract. If parties to a contract have failed to specify a choice of law in their contract under Article 3, then Article 4 is of relevance. Article 4 provides a number of different permutations in situations where the parties have failed to select a choice of law and in these circumstances a number of presumptions are made. For instance, a contract for the sale of goods shall be governed by the law of the country where the seller has his habitual residence[37] and a contract for the provision of services shall be governed by the law of the country where the service provider has his habitual residence.[38] Further, a contract for the sale of goods by an auction shall be governed by the law of the country whether the distributor has his habitual residence.[39] This clause could be of relevance to those engaging in Internet auction sites. These presumptions are

---

[36] C027/34, January 1998. Available at: http://europa.eu/legislation_summaries/justice_freedom_security/judicial_cooperation_in_civil_matters/l33109_en.htm.

[37] Article 4(1)(a). Recital 39 states that for the sake of legal certainty there should be a clear definition of the term 'habitual residence'. Article 19 seeks to provide this clarity by saying that the habitual residence of a company shall be the place of its central administration and the habitual residence of a person acting in the course of his business shall be his principal place of business (Article 19(1)). If the contract is concluded through a branch or agency, then the place where the branch or agency is located shall be the habitual residence (Article 19(2)). Article 19(3) continues by saying the relevant moment in time in ascertaining this shall be the time of the conclusion of the contract. Such a precise definition did not exist under the previous Rome Convention, so this is beneficial in providing greater certainty.

[38] Article 4(1)(b).

[39] Article 4(1)(g).

relatively easy to apply, but if these presumptions do not provide certainty as to which national court has the competency to hear a case then Article 4(2) states that the contract shall be governed by the law of the country where the party required to effect the characteristic performance of the contract has his habitual residence.[40] Yet both Article 4(1) and 4(2) can be trumped by the displacement principle in Article 4(3). In circumstances where it is manifestly clear that the contract is more closely connected with a country other than that indicated by Article 4(1) or 4(2) then the law of that country shall apply.[41]

The default position found within Articles 3 and 4 is moved away from in the event of a business- (the regulations use the word 'professional') to-consumer contract. Article 6 governs the choice of law applicable to consumer contracts. The immediate difference between Rome I and the Rome Convention is that the Convention was limited to contracts for goods or services only. Rome I offers no such limitation. The guiding principle in Article 6(1) is that the choice of law of the contract shall be the law governed by the country where the consumer has his habitual residence. There are two conditions to this. First of all, the professional needs to have pursued his commercial or professional activities in the country where the consumer has his habitual residence, and secondly the professional has directed such activities to that country, or to several countries including that country. If these two conditions are met then the consumer protection rules in the consumer's member state will apply. These are known as mandatory rules. However, a professional and consumer may agree to vary the choice of law as provided by Article 6(2), but Article 6(1) states that this choice must not have the effect of reducing the protection afforded to the consumer. In other words, a professional cannot contract with a consumer and insert a choice of law clause which provides less protection to the consumer than that consumer's country of habitual residence provides. For example, a consumer in the United Kingdom would not be able to contract out of provisions contained within the Sale of Goods Act 1979, or the Consumer Protection (Distance Selling) Regulations 2000. The ability for a professional and a consumer to decide upon their own choice of law does ensure that a sufficient degree of party autonomy is retained.[42] If the requirements in Article 6(1) (a) and (b) (relating to the professional directing his activities to a particular country) are not fulfilled, then Article 6(3) states that the choice of law shall be determined by aligning the contract to one of a number of standard contracts listed within Article 6(4). There are five examples listed (including a contract for services where the services are to be supplied to the

---

[40] See **Intercontainer Interfrigo (ICF) v Balkenende** Case C-133/08 [2010] All ER (EC) 1.

[41] Recitals 20 and 21 provide more insight to the meaning of 'closely connected'. Furthermore in the event that a state has more than one legal system (for instance, the United Kingdom), Article 22 states it shall be left to the discretion of that member state to determine which legal system applies.

[42] A court may refuse to apply the mandatory rules if they are contrary to public policy as in **Royal Boskalis Westminster NV v Mountain** [1999] QB 674.

consumer in a country other than his habitual residence and a contract relating to a right *in rem* in immovable property), although the disappointing factor
from an e-commerce angle is that none of them are of much relevance to the
Internet. Finally, Article 27 states that by June 2013, the European Commission
should submit a report on the application of Rome I. Part of this report should
be focused upon the coherence of the consumer protection provisions and an
evaluation of the effectiveness of the rules contained within Article 6.

In February 2010, the Ministry of Justice issued guidance on Rome I.[43] This
guidance aimed to provide a summary of the main provisions in the regulation
and the rules that allow courts within the European Union the ability to select
which national rules have the competency to hear any given dispute.

Although the theory may be good, in practice there are a number of basic
problems that no amount of legislation can solve. The choice of law rules are
notoriously complex and they differ from one member state to the next, as
each member state was required to implement them in their own way.
Accessing and utilising these rules will inevitably incur significant financial cost
on the part of the consumer. Costs will also increase with visits to the other
member state to progress the case and it is likely that documents may need
translating into a language that the consumer can understand. The delay and
frustration that is encountered in the hearing may be replicated at a later date
if the consumer is successful in their action, yet finds they need to spend yet
more time and money in trying to get the judgment enforced in the other
member state.

Alternative dispute resolution

The reality with most of the above discussion however is that in the majority of
cases individuals, particularly consumers, are unlikely to want to pursue an
action in the courts, particularly if it involves foreign jurisdictions, which will
take a considerable amount of time, money and effort. As the use of e-
commerce increases, disputes between contracting parties – including those
involving consumers – will become more frequent. It is important therefore
that there are effective alternative online dispute resolution schemes in place to
provide individuals the necessary access to justice, while protecting businesses
from the unfavourable publicity that a legal action may bring. As consumers
are unable to deal face to face with the supplier (in an online business-to-
consumer contract), a forum for hearing disputes is important to safeguard
consumer confidence in the Internet. The European Community is a firm
supporter of the creation of more accessible dispute resolution schemes.

---

[43] Ministry of Justice *Guidance on the law applicable to contractual obligations (Rome I)* February
2010. Available at: http://www.justice.gov.uk/publications/contractual-obligations-rome.htm.

Indeed, the E-Commerce Directive 2000/31/EC of 8th June 2000 states that member states shall avoid obstacles to the use of alternative disputes resolution systems.[44] However, one of the criticisms which can be levelled against the Brussels Regulation is that it does not introduce a framework for alternative dispute resolution. This is disappointing, especially considering the fact that in the event of a dispute very few consumers will want to gamble on taking a big business to court.

There are a number of online dispute resolution methods that individuals can use.[45] One example includes mediation, which is a voluntary process where the two parties and a third party (who acts as an independent person) will try to find a compromise.[46] The independent party may meet with the parties individually and try to arrange a face-to-face meeting (which could be carried out by webcam) to try to reach an agreement. This agreement may form the basis of contract to prevent either party from reneging on the conclusion. The European Union has demonstrated its support for the increase in mediation by the introduction of Directive 2008/58/EC on certain aspects of mediation in civil and commercial matters.[47] This Directive recognises the cost-effectiveness and swift nature of mediation and also suggests that parties are more likely to remain on good terms following mediation than they would through formal litigation[48] and further recognises that use of modern technology should not be removed from the mediation process.[49] The Directive encourages the training of mediators[50] and also allows courts to recommend mediation to parties involved in a dispute[51] and ensures that a system is in place to allow mediation conclusions to be enforceable.[52] The European Commission is required to provide a review on the implementation and effectiveness of this Directive by 2016. Online mediation is a much cheaper way of reaching an agreement than through costly litigation, although it does require the consent of both parties to commence the process.

A further alternative dispute resolution scheme is that of arbitration, which is where an independent third party listens to both sides and then reaches a decision. There is more flexibility than with a judicial hearing, as the parties can choose both the arbitrator and also the grounds on which a decision will be

---

[44] E-Commerce Directive 2000/31/EC, Article 17.

[45] For more on online dispute resolution systems see: Dieguez, J P C *A European Perspective on consumer ODR* (2009) Computer and Telecommunications Law Review, volume 15, issue 4, pages 90–100.

[46] Mediation differs from conciliation in that a conciliator will listen to both sides of the dispute and then arrive at a reasoned opinion, which will form the basis of the final settlement.

[47] Available at: http://www.arbitration-adr.org/mater/Directive%202008-52-EC_en.pdf.

[48] Directive 2008/58/EC, Recital 6 and Article 1.

[49] Directive 2008/58/EC, Recital 9.

[50] Directive 2008/58/EC, Article 4.

[51] Directive 2008/58/EC, Article 5.

[52] Directive 2008/58/EC, Article 6.

made.[53] In contrast to mediation, once an arbitration procedure has commenced, parties are unable to pull out. Arbitration is also easier to manage online than mediation as the independent third party does not need to spend as much time with the parties in dispute; an arbitrator's role is to hear both sides of the story and then reach a measured conclusion and much of this can be carried out electronically.

Other minor alternative dispute resolution schemes include: self-help, negotiation or chargeback. Chargeback seeks to protect from consumers from fraudulent use of their credit or debit card and reverses the payment in these situations.[54] The advantages of all these methods of online dispute resolution are that they are invariably cheaper, more flexible than and not as formal as traditional legal proceedings. However, both parties do need to agree to such a method, which may not always be possible if one party refuses to co-operate. Many online organisations have installed their own online dispute resolution system, to ensure that if something goes wrong, the users and the company are protected. A good example of this is eBay. If a dispute arises between a buyer and seller on eBay, rather than abandoning the dispute, eBay suggests that you use an independent mediator to resolve the dispute. The whole mediation process takes place online and is initiated by filing a case. The mediator will not make a decision; rather they will aid both parties to reach an agreement. This can lead to an amicable resolution for both parties as well as the removal of negative feedback on an eBay account if one of the parties has been hasty in leaving such feedback. The process typically takes two weeks and is free, but a nominal fee is charged to involve a mediator. Mediation is more suitable for trade involving higher-value items such as computers and cars, but is only effective if both parties are willing to co-operate and negotiate.

Key points:

- It is important that a strong body of legislation is in place, in relation to where disputes will be held and the choice of law which shall be relevant, to deal with online disputes. These rules need to provide flexibility, yet also predictability to ensure that the advantages of online commerce are not overshadowed by uncertain legal processes in the event of a cross-border dispute.
- The Brussels Regulation 44/2001 applies to contracts for civil or commercial matters.

---

[53] See: **Channel Tunnel Group v Balfour Beatty** [1993] AC 334.

[54] For more on Chargeback see: Edwards, L & Wilson, C *Redress and Alternative Dispute Resolution in EU Cross-Border E-Commerce Transactions* (2007) International Review of Law, Computers and Technology, volume 21, issue 3, pages 315–333.

- The basic starting point is set out in Article 2 and states that the action shall be heard in the court of the defendant's domicile. The location of a server or other Internet equipment is not of relevance here.
- If a court is required to determine the domicile of an individual that court should apply the internal rules of that member state. Furthermore, if two courts in two different member states are hearing the case at the same time, the second court must postpone their hearing to allow the first court to decide upon jurisdiction.
- The rules for business-to-consumer contracts are found within Articles 15–17. A consumer is defined as someone who is acting outside of their trade or profession, but this does not provide protection to people who, whilst ostensibly acting within their business, are engaged in an activity outside of their expertise.
- The other requirement for a business-to-consumer contract is that the business needs to pursue their commercial or professional activities within the member state where the consumer is domiciled, or 'directs such activities' by any means to that member state; it is unlikely that the simple existence of a website will fulfil this requirement as most websites are available virtually anywhere.
- Article 33 states that a judgment handed down in one member state shall be (subject to a handful of exceptions found within Article 34) enforced in other member states. To achieve this, an authentic copy of the judgment must be provided.
- Rome I came into force at the end of 2009 and replaces the earlier Rome Convention of the law applicable to contractual obligations 1998.
- Parties to a contract are able to determine the choice of law of the contract. This must be expressly stated within the contract.
- The default position in these regulations is located in Article 3 as parties to a contract can expressly choose the choice of law governing the contract.
- If the parties have not selected a choice of law, then Article 4 lists a number of standard contracts. If a choice of law still cannot be established then the national law with competency shall be the one with which the contract is manifestly most closely related to.
- Article 6 provides the rules for choice of law in consumer contracts. A consumer contract shall be governed by the consumer's national law provided that the professional has pursued his activities in the country where the consumer has his habitual residence and the professional has directed such activities to that country.
- A business and a consumer can negotiate an alternative choice of law clause providing that it does not reduce the amount of legal protection that they would receive in the country of their habitual residence.

Further reading:

Books:

- Clarkson, C M V & Hill, J *The Conflict of Laws* (2006) Oxford University Press, 3rd Edition.
- Cortes, P *Online Dispute Resolution for Consumers in the European Union* (2010) Routledge.
- Fawcett, J, Carruthers, J & North, P *Cheshire, North and Fawcett: Private International Law* (2008) Oxford University Press, 14th Edition.
- Hartley, T *International Commercial Litigation: Text, Cases and Materials on Private International Law* (2009) Cambridge University Press.

Articles:

- Foss, M & Bygrave, L A *International Consumer Purchases through the Internet: Jurisdictional Issues pursuant to European Law* (2000) International Journal of Law and Information Technology, volume 8, number 2, pages 99–138.
- Gilles, L E *Addressing the "cyberspace fallacy": targeting the jurisdiction of an electronic consumer contract* (2008) International Journal of Law and Information Technology, volume 16, issue 3, pages 242–269.
- Gillies, L *A Review of the New Jurisdiction Rules for Electronic Consumer Contracts within the European Union* (2001) Journal of Information, Law and Technology, issue 1.
- Hartley, T C *"Libel tourism" and conflict of laws* (2010) International and Comparative Law Quarterly, volume 59, issue 1, pages 25–28.
- Johnson, D & Post, D *Law and borders – the Rise of Law in Cyberspace* (1999) Stanford Law Review, volume 48, pages 1367–1402.
- Kohl, U *The Rule of Law, Jurisdiction and the Internet* (2004) International Journal of Law and Information Technology, volume 12, number 3, pages 365–376.
- Lando, O & Neilsen, P *The Rome I Regulation* (2008) Common Market Law Review, pages 1687–1725.
- Mitrani, A *Regulating e-commerce, e-contracts and the controversy of multiple jurisdiction* (2001) International Trade Law and Regulation, volume 7, issue 2, pages 50–60.
- Oren, J *International jurisdiction over consumer contracts in e-Europe* International and Comparative Law Quarterly (2003), Volume 52, Issue 3, pages 665–695.
- Tang, Z *An effective dispute resolution system for electronic consumer contracts* Computer Law and Security Report (2007), Volume 23, Issue 1, pages 42–52.

- Tellini, D E *Applicable law and electronic consumer contracts: a European perspective* International Company and Commercial Law Review (2005), Volume 16, Issue 1, pages 1–7.
- Zekos, G I *State Cyberspace Jurisdiction and Personal Cyberspace Jurisdiction* (2007) International Journal of Law and Information Technology, volume 15, issue 1, pages 1–37.

Questions for consideration:

6.1. What complexities does the Internet introduce in relation to choice of law and jurisdiction in business-to-consumer contracts?

6.2. Outline the rules for deciding domicile in the Brussels Regulations 44/2001 for both an individual and a company or other legal body.

6.3. How is a consumer defined in Article 15 of the Brussels Regulation 44/2001? What difficulties are there with this definition?

6.4. What needs to be shown and what are the rules for jurisdiction in a business-to-consumer contract?

6.5. How can a consumer enforce a judgment given in one member state in another member state? Does the regulation achieve its aim of facilitating judicial co-operation?

6.6. Article 3 of Rome I states that the choice of law shall be governed law expressly chosen or clearly demonstrated by the parties. If this is not clear, how is the choice of law determined?

6.7. What flexibility does Rome I provide in business-to-consumer contracts where the parties want to negotiate the choice of law?

6.8. Undertake a critical evaluation of whether the provisions in the Brussels Regulation 44/2001 and Rome I are effective enough to encourage consumers to engage in e-commerce.

6.9. 'Despite effective legislation that provides guidelines for determining choice of law and jurisdiction issues within the European Union, it is clear that litigation remains a costly and time-consuming activity that very few consumers are going to be willing to engage in. It is therefore necessary that a range of alternative dispute resolution schemes exist to provide recourse for the online consumer in the event of a dispute.' *Outline the main methods of the alternative dispute resolution schemes and evaluate whether the advantages of these systems outweigh the disadvantages.*

6.10. 'The truth of the matter is simple. It does not matter how robust and up to date rules relating to jurisdiction and choice of law are, a consumer is going to exercise great reticence before commencing

legal proceedings against a company from another member state. It is clear that the only way forward in resolving consumer disputes arising from failed Internet transactions is to focus more attention on alternative dispute resolution schemes. These provide the greatest assistance to consumers seeking redress.'
Undertake a critical evaluation of this viewpoint.

All weblinks mentioned in the text can also be found at
http://www.palgrave.com/law/rogers

7 Data Protection

The interoperability of computers and their international connectivity has revolutionised the flow of informational data. Automated filing systems have a significantly superior storage ability compared with traditional filing systems. Vast amounts of information can be held on these systems and the technology allows many more transactions to be carried out at a significantly faster speed. The 'power' available through these databases is colossal as they can provide a company with large amounts of information about any one person. A supermarket loyalty card is a good example. A customer is required to hand over their personal details (such as name, address and date of birth) to sign up to a scheme. In return the customer receives a loyalty card with which they can 'earn' points based on the amount of their purchases. These points can be converted into money to spend either in the store or in the form of vouchers for use elsewhere. The perception of receiving a 'good deal' is the front the supermarket offers. However, behind the scenes the supermarket can obtain information about your shopping habits (for instance, where you shop and at what time of the day) and it holds information about the types of products and services you regularly purchase. This in turn enables the supermarket to build up a profile of you, including characteristics like whether you are a pet owner (the regular purchase of dog food would be an indicator of this) or whether you have children (the purchasing of nappies may be an indicator here). This allows the supermarket to direct advertisements and targeted 'special offers' to you. New challenges for protecting personal information are continuing to emerge due to the development of information and computing systems and the increase in surveillance technologies. The number of databases in existence is continuing to grow and the threats posed to this data (held by both public and private bodies) are real. Ascertaining a precise value on personal data is notoriously difficult, but information is power and it is vital that significantly robust legislation is in place to safeguard the use of such data.

Since 1998, the Human Rights Act has placed the right to a private life on to the statute books as a fundamental human right and means that individuals can assert their right to a private life in their local courts. There is a range of case law in this area, which this book does not go into in detail. In the same year, the Data Protection Act[1] was introduced, received Royal Assent on 16th July 1998 and came into force on 1st March 2000. The Act regulates the processing of information relating to individuals in the United Kingdom and replaces the former Data Protection Act 1984. The 1998 Act was introduced following European Directive 95/46/EC on the protection of individuals with regard to the processing of personal data and on the free movement of such data.[2] Calls for a European-wide directive on protecting personal information stretch back to the mid 1970s and the underlying aim of the final Directive (which was a partial harmonisation measure) was to create a balance between protecting the privacy of an individual (or 'data subject') in terms of the handling of their information, while ensuring that authorities and organisations have the ability to legitimately utilise the data at their disposal.[3] The Directive sought to provide a balance between these two competing aims by removing obstacles to inter-state economic activity and harmonising the level of privacy protection at a European level. The legislation gives an individual the ability to control information which is held about them by the organisation. Prior to this Directive there was a wide range of levels of privacy protection within member states, which had the potential of restricting inter-state transmission of this data.

Within the United Kingdom, the Act applies if either the person who determines the purposes for processing the data (the 'data controller'), or equipment used for the processing is situated in the United Kingdom.[4] An example of jurisdiction being decided by virtue of the equipment used is found in the case of **Michael Douglas v Hello! Ltd (No.2).**[5] This was one of the infamous

---

[1] Available at: http://www.opsi.gov.uk/Acts/Acts1998/ukpga_19980029_en_1.

[2] Available at: http://ec.europa.eu/justice_home/fsj/privacy/docs/95-46-ce/dir1995-46_part1_en.pdf.

[3] See Recitals 7 and 8.

[4] Data Protection Act 1998, Section 5.

[5] [2003] EWCA Civ 139.

series of cases involving publication of the wedding pictures of Michael Douglas and Catherine Zeta-Jones by *Hello!* Magazine after the rights to take pictures of the wedding had been awarded to *OK!* Magazine. The Court of Appeal held (overturning an earlier decision[6]) that the use by *Hello!* of an ISDN line to send pictures through was analogous to fax transmission. Therefore, despite the fact that the photographer and his equipment were from the United States of America, the Act did have jurisdiction in this case as the data had been processed in the United Kingdom.[7] The Data Protection Act 1998 is arguably the key Act in relation to maintaining the privacy of an individual's data, and is particularly important when the use of the Internet is considered and the ease of passing information about a person through cyberspace.

The Data Protection Act is relevant when personal data relating to a living individual is processed by automated means, or that forms part of a relevant filing system. Key definitions are provided in Section 1. 'Data' is clearly a central definition in the understanding of the Act and it means information which:

(a)   is being processed by means of equipment operating automatically in response to instructions given for that purpose;
(b)   is recorded with the intention that it should be processed by means of such equipment;
(c)   is recorded as part of a relevant filing system or with the intention that it should form part of a relevant filing system; or
(d)   does not fall within paragraph (a), (b) or (c) but forms part of an accessible record, as defined by section 68 (Section 1(1));
(e)   is recorded information held by a public authority and does not fall within any of paragraphs (a) to (d).[8]

Yet it is the interpretation of key terms within this definition that has caused some difficulty. This controversy will now be examined.

Judicial interpretation

One of the more controversial elements of the data protection landscape is the manner in which the judiciary within the United Kingdom has defined some of the key terms within the Act. The judicial approach to the Data Protection Act 1998 is somewhat restrictive and problematic. In November 2005, Dr Mark Walport was the author of a report entitled *Better use of personal information:*

---

[6] [2002]EWHC 2560 (High Court).
[7] [2003] EWCA Civ 139. See paragraphs 45–47.
[8] This subsection was added by section 68 of the Freedom of Information Act 2000.

opportunities and risks. This report recognised that use of personal data by governmental departments had wide-ranging benefits, however, a number of risks were inherent in its use. In his report he stated:

> "The legislative regime is critical to this area [intra-governmental data sharing], but it is complex and not well understood, in particular the Data Protection Act. Greater clarity is needed urgently: the large amount of guidance, often at a departmental level serves simply to confuse."[9]

This chapter will consider the interpretation by the judiciary of the key terms of the Data Protection Act. The basic definitions are found within section 1 of the 1998 Act.

Data Controller

The data controller is a natural or legal person, public authority, agency or any other body who (either alone or jointly with others) is responsible for determining the purposes behind the processing of personal data. According to the Article 29 Working Party, a person who determines the purpose of processing is *de facto* the data controller.[10] It is the responsibility of the data controller to notify the Information Commissioner that processing of personal data is taking place and also the type of information and reasoning for the processing. The provisions relating to notification are found within Part III of the Act and are discussed in more detail below.

Data Processor

A data processor is a natural or legal person (other than an employee), public authority, agency or any other body who processes personal data on behalf of the data controller. The existence of a data processor depends on the decisions taken by the data controller and so is a separate entity from the data controller, although processes personal data on his behalf.[11]

---

[9] Council for Science and Technology Report *Better use of personal information: opportunities and risks* (November 2005), page 2. Available at: http://www.cst.gov.uk/cst/reports/files/personal-information/report.pdf.

[10] Article 29 Data Protection Working Party *Opinion 1/2010 on the concepts of "controller" and "processor"* 16th February 2010. Available at: http://ec.europa.eu/justice_home/fsj/privacy/docs/wpdocs/2010/wp169_en.pdf. See also: OUT-LAW.COM *Privacy chiefs define 'data processor' and 'data controller'* (March 2010). Available at: http://www.out-law.com/page-10836-theme=print.

[11] Ibid.

Data Subject

A data subject is an individual who is the subject of personal data. Part II of the Act provides data subjects with a number of rights over their information, relating to data access and rights of correction and erasure of inaccurate data. Examples of a data subject could include an employee or a university student.

Personal Data

The definition of 'personal data' is central to the whole understanding of the scope of protection provided to an individual by the Act. This is because 'personal data' is the starting point for discerning the applicability of the data protection rules. Section 1(1) defines personal data as:

> data which relate to a living individual who can be identified –
> (a)   from those data, or
> (b)   from those data and other information which is in the possession of, or is likely to come into the possession of, the data controller,
> and includes any expression of opinion about the individual and any indication of the intentions of the data controller or any other person in respect of the individual.[12]

From the above definition the Act outlines a number of main elements as to what constitutes personal data. First of all, the information relates to a living individual. Secondly the living individual is one who can be identified from those data or data which is likely to come into the possession of the data controller. There are two issues of importance here. In the equivalent provision (Article 2(a) in Directive 95/46/EC) the definition is extended to include 'identifiable persons' as well as identified persons.[13] Although this distinction may be based upon semantics, arguably the inclusion of 'identifiable' within the Directive gives personal data a wider definitional scope than in the Act as the latter suggests there needs to be a greater certainty in the identification of an individual, while the Directive appears to allow some flexibility by providing that the person only needs to be identifiable. Additionally, the concept of 'likely to come into the possession of the data controller' is not within the Directive. A person may be identifiable indirectly if the data controller is able to use additional information alongside the pure personal data. The final element in this definition is that personal data can extend to opinions held about the data

---

[12] Data Protection Act, 1998 Section 1(1).

[13] Article 2(a) continues by expanding on the concept of an 'identifiable person' and states "... *an identifiable person is one who can be identified, directly or indirectly, in particular by reference to an identification number or to one or more factors specific to his physical, physiological, mental, economic, cultural or social identify.*"

subject and/or indication of intention. At the outset it seems the United Kingdom's implementation of Directive 95/46/EC is more restrictive than the European Union had intended. This apparent restrictive approach has been followed by the judiciary and the reverberations from the Court of Appeal decision in **Durant v Financial Services Authority**[14] continue to be felt to this day. Mr Durant had been in a long-standing dispute with Barclays Bank and after he had failed in a litigation attempt, he attempted to obtain records held by the bank, which he thought would enable him to reopen the case or examine the conduct of the bank with a view to taking further action. He was unsuccessful and so turned his attention to the Financial Services Authority (FSA)[15] and commenced proceedings against the regulator to try and obtain documents which he believed had been transmitted between the bank and the FSA. The Court of Appeal rejected Durant's application and in offering a seminal judgment decided that personal data should be given a narrow definition. The view of the court was that the information that the FSA held was not personal data and it was merely about the situation involving Mr Durant; in other words it focused on the complaints that Mr Durant made, as opposed to the claimant himself. The view of the Court of Appeal was that personal data needs to go beyond merely retelling the involvement of an individual in an event and the right of subject access under section 7 is not applicable simply if a person is just mentioned in a document – information does not become personal data simply because a person is mentioned within it. The Court provided a two-stage approach to assist in the defining of personal data. This is not a test *per se*, but guidance for deciding whether the data is personal data. Specifically:

1. The data is "biographical in a significant sense, that is, going beyond the mere recording of the putative data subject's involvement in a matter or event which had no personal connotations, a life event in respect of which his privacy could not be said to have been compromised."
2. Secondly "… whether the information has the putative data subject as its focus rather than some other person with whom he may have been involved or some transaction or event in which he may have figured or have had an interest such as, in this case, an investigation into some other person's or body's conduct that he may have instigated."[16]

Personal data clearly extends to personal identifiers, such as a person's name and address. It could also extend to IP addresses. In the Durant judgment, the Court of Appeal decided that the information the FSA held was not biographical of Mr

---

[14] [2003] EWCA Civ 1746.

[15] This body was set up under the Financial Services and Markets Act 2000 to regulate the financial services industry within the United Kingdom.

[16] *Supra* n.12, paragraph 28.

Durant significantly and he was not the focus of the information. The focus of the information was the complaints he had made. Furthermore, the information must affect a person's privacy, whether in his family or personal life or even in his professional or business capacity. The decision therefore was focused on the need for the data to "... relate to" an individual.

Since the decision in Durant, a number of cases have been heard by the courts which appear to be continuing the restrictive interpretation of the term 'personal data', such as **Johnson v Medical Defence Union**[17] and **Smith v Lloyds TSB Bank Plc.**[18] In Johnson the claimant was a surgeon who had been a member of the Medical Defence Union (MDU). As a member, Mr Johnson had access to a range of services and was able to obtain discounted professional insurance. However, in early 2002, the MDU refused to renew Mr Johnson's membership based on the outcome of a risk assessment scoring system (to which Mr Johnson was not privy) that the company used. Mr Johnson was concerned that the refusal of the MDU to grant him membership and insurance would damage his professional credibility and so he used the data subject access provisions contained within section 7 to try to obtain documents which would reveal the reasoning behind the MDU's decision. Although he received some documentation, he was of the view that not all the relevant data had been disclosed and therefore he commenced proceedings under section 7 to compel the MDU to fully comply with his request as well as an application for damages under section 13. However, the court was of the view that the MDU had applied the Data Protection Act correctly. In his judgment, Mr Justice Laddie stated that the documents were not 'personal' as they were not focused on Mr Johnson himself, but his application for membership and insurance.[19]

The decision in Smith had a very similar outcome. This case arose from an ongoing argument about bankruptcy and possession litigation. Mr Smith made an application under section 7 to obtain documents to assist him in his litigation, which he believed the bank held about him. However, the judge (interestingly, Mr Justice Laddie presided in this case as well as the Johnson case) was of the view that the data requested was not 'personal' as it related to loan applications and not to Mr Smith himself. Mr Justice Laddie went on to say:

"... it is clear that the documents held by Lloyds and the information contained within them are not personal to Mr Smith in the relevant sense.

---

[17] [2004] EWHC 347 (Ch).

[18] [2005] EWHC 246 (Ch). For analysis of the immediate case law surrounding the Durant decision see: Watts, M *Information, data and personal data – reflections on Durant v Financial Services Authority* Computer Law and Security Report (2006), Volume 22, Issue 4, pages 320–325 and Jagessar, U & Sedgwick, V *When is personal data not "personal data" – The impact of Durant v FSA* Computer Law and Security Report (2005), volume 21, Issue 6, pages 505–511.

[19] (2004) EWHC 347 (Ch), paragraphs 38–49.

The files that do exist all relate to the loans ... although it is true that Mr Smith is mentioned in them ... Indeed, if one stands back and looks at what Mr Smith is trying to obtain by means of these proceedings, it is not documents about him but it is documents which deal with the terms of an alleged oral agreement."[20]

However, it is submitted that the more recent High Court decision in **Ezsias v Welsh Ministers**[21] provides a suggestion of the reasons behind the restrictive interpretation provided by the courts. In this case Mr Ezsias, a consultant with North Glamorgan NHS Trust, was dismissed from his employment as a surgeon. In support of his appeal against his dismissal he requested documents which related to his case from a number of different bodies, including the NHS Trust, the Welsh Assembly and individual Assembly Members. Although the decision in Durant was upheld,[22] it is arguable that part of the reason for the restrictive approach in defining personal data is the judiciary's dislike of a data subject using section 7 for broader purposes, such as assisting with other (potentially spurious) legal actions. Judge Hickinbottom, in reference to section 7, stated:

"Mr Ezsias has exhibited fundamental misunderstanding of those rights ... He correctly emphasises that the right of access to information under the 1998 Act is a free-standing right. There is no exemption from the requirements under the Act where proceedings are pending ... There is a fundamental distinction between the right of access to data in the hands of another person for the purposes of protecting privacy, and the right to disclosure of documents ... The purpose of the Act is to protect that privacy. To use the provisions of the Act to seek disclosure of documents generated as the result of the applicant's own complaint, in order to further a legal claim of the applicant against a third party is a legal abuse."[23]

Reading between the lines, it seems that the underlying rationale to the restrictive approach is that there needs to be a harmful effect on an individual's privacy as opposed to simply document disclosure. Regardless of whether the approach of the judiciary in defining personal data is due to a desire to have a narrow definition of the term, or due to a dislike for using the Data Protection Act in furthering speculative future legal action, anticipation was growing towards the end of 2008, with rumours abounding that the definition of

---

[20] [2005] EWHC 246 (Ch), paragraph 32.
[21] [2007] All ER (D) 65.
[22] Ibid. Paragraphs 50–67.
[23] Ibid. Paragraphs 50, 51, 53 and 66 respectively.

personal data provided in *Durant* would be challenged in the House of Lords[24] in the Scottish case of **Common Services Agency v Scottish Information Commissioner**.[25] This case concerned the refusal of an NHS agency to reveal statistics about childhood leukaemia figures, which were requested under the Freedom of Information Act 2002 by a member of the Scottish Parliament, who was researching the health effects of children being located near to nuclear facilities. The Agency refused to release the data, arguing that as there were such a small number of individuals involved that there was the potential to be able to indirectly identify those involved, even though the data had been anonymised by a process called barnardisation. The view of the Common Services Agency was that as the individuals could be indirectly identified, the data held was personal data and therefore was exempt from release under section 38 of the Freedom of Information Act. In a two-day hearing in April 2008, the House of Lords considered that if the barnardisation of this data did make the information anonymous it could no longer be classified as personal data. At the same time, if the information could not be adequately anonymised, then the data could be classified as personal data and the Agency would not be required to release it. The House of Lords noted that anonymised data would undoubtedly relate to an individual (or individuals), but for it to be personal data it also had to identify individuals. Accordingly, the judgment was for the question of identifiability to be referred back to the Scottish Information Commissioner to determine, as a question of fact, whether or not the information was sufficiently anonymised for it not to be personal data or whether it could be sufficiently disguised for release of the information under the Freedom of Information Act to be permitted. The Law Lords were also of the view that as this information was connected to medical records, it would be classified as sensitive personal data and therefore they considered that there was no need for them to review the Court of Appeal's decision in **Durant**.[26]

There are a number of core criticisms with the restrictive approach adopted by this range of case law.[27] Arguably the judgments restrict the scope of the

---

[24] Mr Durant himself had an application to the House of Lords for an appeal against the Court of Appeal's decision rejected on 29th November 2005, as he could not demonstrate a likelihood of success.

[25] [2008] 1 WLR 1550.

[26] Ibid. Page 1573, paragraph 74.

[27] It is important to note at this point that there is an argument that the Court of Appeal's decision in *R v Rooney [2006] EWCA Crim 1841* indirectly goes against the tide of the main body of case law in defining personal data. This case concerned a police employee in the personnel department, who used her access to the police computer system to find out where her sister's former partner (also a police officer) had relocated to. Although this case did not expressly make reference to *Durant*, the information disclosed (in this case the name of a town) is not (following *Durant*) information that is either significantly biographical nor has the individual as the focus, yet even so the court found Rooney guilty of unlawfully obtaining and disclosing personal data or the information contained within personal data under section 55 of the Data Protection Act as the court was of the view that the name of the town was information within personal data. Rooney was fined with costs awarded

Act, as the central definition of 'personal data' is narrowly defined.[28] This is problematic for individuals seeking a data subject access request under section 7 and potentially tips the balance of the legislation away from the protection of personal privacy[29] towards the data controllers. It is also contended that the judicial interpretation of personal data is much narrower than the initial Directive intended, which defines personal data as *"relating to an identified or identifiable natural person ('data subject')"*.[30] In 2004, the European Commission issued the United Kingdom Government with a 'letter of formal notice'. This has never been published, although it is believed that the narrow definition of personal data was one of the issues that the Commission was concerned about.

The approach of the judiciary in apparently restricting the term 'personal data' has led to wider complications. The Article 29 Working Party was set up by the European Commission to provide advice and expert opinion on the scope of the provisions contained within the Directive. This group is made up of the data protection authorities from the member states. The group allows for co-operation between the supervisory agencies within the European Union although it is independent. It makes recommendations about definitions, implementation and reform proposals.[31] In considering the definition of personal data as outlined in the Directive, the Working Party pointed to four 'building blocks' which make up the definition: specifically 'any information', 'relating to', 'an identified or identifiable' and 'natural person'.[32] They also highlighted three key elements that need to be present for data to be held as personal data. First of all, the content of the data needs to be about a particular data subject, second, this data is then processed by the data controller and finally, the result of the processing would impact upon the data subject. The Working Group also added that the data does not need to focus on the data subject. The Working Party contended that together these elements will assist in determining whether or not data is 'personal data' and was in favour of a wider definition as espoused by the Directive, a different position to that adopted by the

---

against her. A brief commentary on the case by Boardman, R & Dewi, R can be found in E-Commerce Law Reports (2006), Volume 6, Issue 4, page 19.

[28] See: Turle, M *When data gets personal* New Law Journal (15th October 2004), Volume 154, page 1514.

[29] Article 1(1) of the Data Protection Directive 95/46/EC states that *"… Member States shall protect the fundamental rights and freedoms of natural persons, and in particular their right to privacy with respect to the processing of personal data"*.

[30] Directive 95/46/EC Article 2(a).

[31] See the European Commission's pages on the Article 29 Working Party for more details of their role and responsibilities. Available at: http://ec.europa.eu/justice_home/fsj/privacy/workinggroup/index_en.htm.

[32] See: Article 29 Data Protection Working Party *Opinion 4/2007 on the concept of personal data* 20th June 2007. Available at: http://ec.europa.eu/justice/policies/privacy/docs/wpdocs/2007/wp136_en.pdf.

United Kingdom judiciary, which provided a narrower set of conditions in Durant by the Court of Appeal. In response to conflict between the Durant decision and the opinion of the Article 29 Working Group, in August 2007 the United Kingdom's Information Commissioner released Technical Guidance to assist in determining what constitutes personal data.[33] This replaced the earlier guidance, and although not binding on the courts, the guidance provides some assistance with interpretation. The guidance is written in the form of a yes/no flow-chart looking at the following eight areas:

1. Identifiability
2. Meaning of 'relates to'
3. Data 'obviously about' or 'not obviously about' a particular individual
4. Data linked to an individual
5. The purpose of the processing
6. Biographical significance
7. Does the information concentrate on the individual?
8. Processing which has an impact on individuals

The aim of this guidance is that by being able to answer 'yes' or 'no' to each of the questions, it should be ascertainable whether or not data is personal data. The guidance also provides advice for miscellaneous situations which may involve personal data, for instance personal data about more than one individual, complaint files, anonymising data and disclosing information. The guidance makes some interesting 'obiter' comments, for instance data, which may not be personal now, may become so as technology develops and also data may still be personal data even if the individual's name is not mentioned. The rationale for this is that the identifiability of an individual should not be determined simply on the standard of the ordinary man in the street, but should be the standard of the determined individual, which could include an investigative journalist, stalker or industrial spy. In other words, how easy is it for these determined individuals to identify a person from the information available? It is interesting to note, as an aside, that in ascertaining identity, the question uses the word 'identified' and does not extend as far as 'identifiable', which is used in the Directive. The key problem with this guidance is that it sought to be a compromise between the expansive view of the definition of personal data (as favoured by the Article 29 Working Party) and the narrower approach adopted by the United Kingdom's judiciary. This dichotomy of view-point demonstrates the difficulty currently being experienced in defining this term. The Information Commissioner appears to have aligned himself closer to

---

[33] Information Commissioner's Office *Data Protection Technical Guidance: Determining what is personal data* (2007). Available at: http://www.ico.gov.uk/upload/documents/library/data protection/detailed specialist guides/personal data flowchart v1 with preface001.pdf.

the view of the Working Party than with the decision in Durant and to have suggested that the principles contained within the Durant decision should only be applied to data subject access requests under section 7. Until a resolution is reached, the scope of the Data Protection Act – particularly from the point of view of the data subject – will be uncertain, which could lead to less legislative protection for the individual when their personal data is being processed.

Processing

Personal data is not the only key definition that has been narrowly defined by the courts. While the data controller is responsible for determining the purposes of processing and the processing of the data itself, he may employ data processers to process data on his behalf. The definition of 'processing' has a controversial history. The long running saga of **Johnson v Medical Defence Union Limited**[34] appears – by a majority decision – to offer a narrower definition for the term 'processing' than the Act provides. The facts of the case are as previously stated, however in this particular appeal, Mr Johnson was arguing that the processing that had been carried out on his data was done so unfairly and this led to the MDU refusing his application for insurance. Section 1(1) of the DPA defines processing extremely widely as:

> "'processing', in relation to information or data, means obtaining, recording or holding the information or data or carrying out any operation or set of operations on the information or data, including –
> (a) organisation, adaptation or alteration of the information or data,
> (b) retrieval, consultation or use of the information or data,
> (c) disclosure of the information or data by transmission, dissemination or otherwise making available, or
> (d) alignment, combination, blocking, erasure or destruction of the information or data."

From the parameters of the definition, processing seems to be able to encompass almost any action to the data – as long as a schedule 2 or schedule 3 ground for processing has been met and the Information Commissioner had been notified of the processing by the data controller. The definition is significantly wider than that previously defined in the 1984 Act.[35] The majority

---

[34] [2007] EWCA Civ 262.
[35] Data Protection Act 1984, section 1(7). The case of *R v Brown (Gregory Michael) (1996) 2 WLR 203* is a good example of the limited definition. In this case, Mr Brown was a police officer, who used the police computer to check on the vehicles of people who owed money to his friend. His friend ran a debt collecting agency. Brown used the computer twice, on one occasion no personal information was brought up on to the screen. The House of Lords held that a person would need to do more with the data than simply bring it up on to a computer screen.

judgment was offered by Buxton LJ, who based his judgment upon the phrase-ology on Article 3 of the original Directive 95/46/EC which outlines that the scope of the legislation extends to the processing of personal data by (either wholly or partly) automatic means.[36] In the present case the processing was carried out by a person, who manually selected information from a file to make a decision and therefore, the conclusion of Buxton LJ was that no processing had taken place as it was not automated. The dissenting judgment was made by Arden LJ who argued that as the information was recorded by automatic means 'processing' had occurred. Comment on this case is varied. Cullen (2007) argues that the majority decision is a demonstration of the reluctant approach the courts take to data protection and suggests that the minority view offered by Arden LJ contains significantly more pragmatism.[37] Cullen continues by suggesting that the current approach of the courts to the Data Protection Act is damaging the effectiveness of the legislation. Wright and Hodgkinson (2007) take a different view to Cullen and contend that the deci-sion is helpful for data controllers who regularly make non-automated deci-sions about data subjects and give the example of an employer/employee relationship where employers may often have to make non-automated assess-ments on employees, such as those relating to promotions and appraisals.[38]

Relevant filing system

The decision in Durant was not only limited to the definition of personal data, but also discussed the meaning of a 'relevant filing system', which is defined in s1(1) of the Act as:

> "... any set of information relating to individuals to the extent that, although the information is not processed by means of equipment operat-ing automatically in response to instructions given for that purpose, the set is structured, either by reference to individuals or by reference to criteria relating to individuals, in such a way that specific information relating to a particular individual is readily accessible."

The Act only applies to personal data that is held in a relevant filing system. This applies to computer files and manual files, although in the current context the court was examining manual files. The Court of Appeal in Durant stated:

---

[36] Article 3(1).

[37] Cullen, S *Johnson: Implications of the Johnson case on the Data Protection Act* Data Protection Law and Policy (June 2007) Volume 4, Issue 6.

[38] Wright, T & Hodgkinson, D *Data Processing: Johnson v The MDU: 'processing' under the DPA* E-Commerce Law and Policy (May 2007), Volume 9, Issue 5.

"... Parliament intended to apply the Act to manual records only if they are of sufficient sophistication to provide the same to similar ready accessibility as a computerized filing system. That requires a filing system so referenced or indexed that it enables the data controller's employee responsible to identify at the outset of his search with reasonable certainty and speed the file or files in which the specific data relating to the person requesting the information is located ... without having to make a manual search of them."[39]

Accordingly, the recipient of a request for personal data must know that there is a system in place which allows for the retrieval of the file directly relating to an individual. Furthermore, the content of the file needs to be sub-divided so that the searcher can go directly to the correct category, without having to leaf through the papers. Chronological order is not adequate for a relevant filing system. The Court of Appeal held that the FSA's files on Mr Durant's complaints were neither structured nor referenced with Durant's personal data in mind, nor was the information about him that he requested readily accessible. Therefore, his claim failed.

The Information Commissioner's Office and its powers

Although exploring the core definitions of the Data Protection Act may seem somewhat pedestrian, it is of utmost importance when examining the scope of the Act and the responsibilities placed on data controllers. The first responsibility is that if an organisation holds and processes personal data, they are obliged to notify the Information Commissioner.[40] Failure to do so is a criminal offence.[41] This notification needs to include specific registrable details (including the name and address of the data controller, a description of the personal data, the reasons for it being processed, a description of any recipients and details if the data is to be transferred outside of the European Economic Area). A general description of the security measures that are in place to protect the personal data should also be provided. This information will then be entered on to the Public Register of Data Controllers. The cost of notification is £35 for the majority of organisations and this fee and the notification procedure is repeated annually. However, from October 2009, a two-tier notification system was introduced. For companies with a turnover in excess of £25.9m and over 250

---

[39] [2003] EWCA Civ 1746, paragraph 48.

[40] Part III of the Act, particularly sections 16–21.

[41] Section 21, Data Protection Act 1998. A defence is available under section 21(3) if the person who is charged with an offence can show that they exercised all due diligence to comply with the duty.

members of staff the cost of notification increased to £500 per year.[42] The same fee will apply to a public authority with more than 250 employees. The fee of £35 will be retained for smaller companies and organisations, and charities.

The Information Commissioner has a number of key roles. He is responsible for enforcing the Data Protection Act and promoting good practice. He is also required to keep the register of notifications, to serve information or enforcement notices, to prosecute breaches of the Act and, where necessary, to liaise with European colleagues. The powers available to the Information Commissioner's Office extend to Information Notices,[43] which require the company or organisation to supply information to the Information Commissioner relating to a matter under investigation, and Enforcement Notices,[44] which are documents similar to an injunction demanding that a company or organisation change its practices. It is only upon breach of the Information or Enforcement Notice that a criminal offence is committed under section 47.[45] If a criminal offence is deemed to have been committed, the Information Commissioner may then prosecute those involved. The Information Commissioner's Annual Report for 2006/07 showed that there were fourteen successful prosecutions during this period, with the main penalty being a fine of around £200–300 per offence.[46] This level of prosecution seems to have remained constant as in the 2008/09 Annual Report fourteen prosecutions were reported, with a similar level of financial sanction. A similar number of organisations were the recipient of a warrant allowing the Information Commissioner's Office to inspect premises.[47] The limited strength of this sanction can be compared with other regulators, for instance the Financial Services Authority. In December 2007, the Financial Services Authority fined Norwich Union £1.26m for failing to take reasonable care in its

---

[42] See Data Protection (Notification and Notification Fees) (Amendment) Regulations 2009.

[43] Section 43, Data Protection Act 1998. An additional tactic used by the Information Commissioner is to get a company acting in breach of the Act to sign an undertaking. This is a document produced by the Information Commissioner's Office, which is signed by the organisation acting in breach of the Act, to promise to improve their practice. By ensuring that a 'senior member' of the company or organisation sign the document the Information Commissioner can be sure that changes can be introduced top-down within a company. Furthermore, if the Information Commissioner seeks to issue an Enforcement Notice further down the line, he will have additional evidence in support of this course of action.

[44] Section 40, Data Protection Act 1998. These are usually reserved for serious breaches (for example, breaches of security or for failing to deal with a subject access request adequately), or where the data controller is being unco-operative.

[45] Section 47(3) provides a defence to an individual who exercised all due diligence to comply with the notice in question.

[46] Information Commissioner's Office *Annual Report 2006/07*, July 2007. Available at: http://www.ico.gov.uk/upload/documents/annual_report_2007_html/index.html, pages 56–57.

[47] Information Commissioner's Office *Annual Report 2008/09*, July 2009. Available at: http://www.ico.gov.uk/upload/documents/library/corporate/detailed_specialist_guides/annual_report_2009.pdf, pages 41–45.

organisation of risk management systems.[48] The system Norwich Union employed allowed fraudsters to use publicly available data (including names and dates of birth) to impersonate customers and obtain other sensitive data from its call centres. Furthermore, in the last few years, the Financial Services Authority has also fined BNPP Private Bank £350,000 for having weak anti-fraud systems,[49] Nationwide Building Society £980,000 for information security lapses, the most high profile being the theft of a laptop containing sensitive customer details,[50] Capita Financial Administrators £300,000 for poor anti-fraud controls over customer accounts[51] and most recently in June 2010 they levied their largest ever fine of £33.32m against JP Morgan for failing to protect client money by segregating it appropriately.[52] Other regulators in different sectors also have considerable power when it comes to penalties, yet historically the Information Commissioner has only had Information and Enforcement Notices at his disposal, followed by the possibility of taking comparatively low-level legal action against the perpetrator. The apparent weaknesses with this system were that although the Information Notice requested that data controllers provide information about their data security practices, there was no investigative power for the Information Commissioner provided by the legislation.[53] Furthermore, in some situations, enforcement actions and prosecutions (including any appeal) took several years to reach a conclusion. Criticism of this system was widespread[54] and it was within this context that the government introduced the Criminal Justice and Immigration Act 2008, which received Royal Assent on 8th May 2008. The Act makes considerable changes to large portions of the criminal justice system in the United Kingdom,

---

[48] FSA Press Release *FSA fines Norwich Union £1.26m for exposing its customers to the risk of fraud* 17th December 2007. Available at: http://www.fsa.gov.uk/pages/Library/Communication/PR/2007/130.shtml.

[49] FSA Press Release *FSA fines BNPP Private Bank £350,000 for weak anti-fraud controls* 10th May 2007. Available at: http://www.fsa.gov.uk/pages/Library/Communication/PR/2007/060.shtml.

[50] FSA Press Release *FSA fines Nationwide £980,000 for information security lapses* 14th February 2007. Available at: http://www.fsa.gov.uk/pages/Library/Communication/PR/2007/021.shtml.

[51] FSA Press Release *FSA fines Capita Financial Administrators £300,000 in first anti-frauds control case* 16th March 2006. Available at: http://www.fsa.gov.uk/pages/Library/Communication/PR/2006/019.shtml.

[52] FSA Press Release *FSA levies largest ever fine of £33.32m on J. P. Morgan Securities Limited for client money breaches* (3rd June 2010). Available at: http://www.fsa.gov.uk/pages/Library/Communication/PR/2010/089.shtml.

[53] The Information Commissioner's ability to search, enter and inspect premises is not absolute and he is required to obtain the permission of the court under Schedule 9. The warrant will name the persons who are able to enter the premises. Once access has been gained, the Information Commissioner has the ability to confiscate items of interest (for instance, a computer) to allow for a detailed search. This power is provided under section 50 of the Criminal Justice and Police Act 2001.

[54] See, for instance, House of Lords Science and Technology Committee Report on Personal Internet Security 10th August 2007, particularly page 53, paragraph 5.57, which refers to the powers of the Information Commissioner as being "handicapped", "cumbersome" and "inadequate". Available at: http://www.parliament.uk/parliamentary_committees/lords_s_t_select/internet.cfm.

and section 77 is relevant to the current discussion. This amends section 55 of the Data Protection Act and makes it an offence for a person to knowingly or recklessly (and without the consent of the data controller) obtain or to disclose personal data or to disclose the personal data to another person. This breach needs to be deliberate or reckless and applies in circumstances where the data controller knew, or ought to have known that there was a risk that the contravention would occur and that the contravention would lead to substantial damage or substantial distress and the data controller did not take reasonable steps to prevent the contravention. The use of the word 'substantial' in relation to the damage or distress caused may be misleading in suggesting how widely used this provision will be. As an act in contravention of the Data Protection Act can be committed recklessly, this provision has the ability to apply at an early stage. For instance, as the Information Commissioner is of the view that computer passwords and encryption are standard security measures, a simple failure in these areas could lead to a monetary penalty being issued. The inserted Sections 55A and 55B of the Data Protection Act came into force in April 2010 and state that a person who is guilty of an offence will be liable, on summary conviction, to imprisonment, or to a fine not exceeding the statutory maximum or to both, and on conviction on indictment, to imprisonment for a term not exceeding the specified period or to a fine or to both. The maximum prison sentence is two years. These penalties can only be levied against the data controller. Previously, section 55 of the 1998 Act merely stated that contravention of the section meant that an offence had been committed and allowed the Information Commissioner to issue an Enforcement Notice or on rare occasions take further legal action. The inserted sections provide the Information Commissioner with additional power in terms of a prison sentence and the ability to fine. If the Information Commission seeks to apply a monetary penalty there is a procedure that the Information Commissioner needs to follow. He needs to provide the data controller with a Notice of Intent. This will state that the Information Commissioner is considering levying a financial penalty and explain the reasoning. The data controller then has 21 days in which they can respond. After the 21 days has expired, the Information Commissioner then has six months to decide whether to issue a penalty or not. If a data controller does receive a penalty notice they have two choices. If they make prompt payment within 28 days, they will receive a 20 per cent discount. They can also choose to appeal, although if they do they will lose their prompt payment discount. Needless to say, the Information Commissioner's Office welcomed the amendments to the law, and after the legislation received Royal Assent, David Smith, the Deputy Information Commissioner stated:

"This change in the law sends a very clear signal that data protection must be a priority and that it is completely unacceptable to be cavalier with

people's personal information. The prospect of substantial fines for deliberate or reckless breaches of the Data Protection Principles will act as a strong
deterrent and help ensure that organisations that their data protection obligations seriously."[55]

This amendment to the law had not been expected by experts and it is possible that this will become a wide offence as the Information Commissioner can
use the power when a data controller has deliberately or recklessly breached
any of the eight Data Protection Principles. In November 2009, the government issued a consultation paper on the maximum monetary penalty that
should be able to be applied for a breach of this section.[56] Included within this
was the principle that the monies raised should go into a consolidated fund
managed by the Treasury, to ensure that there is no incentive for the
Information Commissioner to pursue individuals under this section in order to
generate funds for the Commission. There were calls during the early stages to
wait for the recommendations from the various reports relating to data security,[57] although these calls seem to have been ignored, and the government's
consultation, which closed on 21st December 2009 proposed a maximum
penalty of £500,000[58] and in January 2010, the government confirmed this
would be the maximum amount.[59] The Information Commissioner's published
guidance outlining how this would work and how to decide whether to
penalise a data controller with a financial penalty, stated that they should
consider the seriousness of the breach, the likelihood of damage and distress
to those affected, whether the breach was deliberate or reckless and a consideration of the action the organisation had taken to protect the information that
it held. The guidance also stated that monetary penalties and Enforcement
Notices could be issued together, although the Information Commissioner
could not use this new monetary policy for an offence committed before April
2010 as it is not a retrospective provision.

The Coroners and Justice Act 2009 also strengthens the power of the
Information Commissioner to audit data controllers. Previously, the

---

[55] ICO Press Release *ICO welcomes new powers to fine organisations for data breaches* 9th May 2008.
Available at: http://www.ico.gov.uk/upload/documents/pressreleases/2008/criminal justice and
immigration act.pdf.

[56] ICO Guidance *Data Protection Act 1998: Information Commissioner's guidance about the issue of
monetary penalties prepared and issued under section 55C (1) of the Data Protection Act 1998.* Available
at: http://www.ico.gov.uk/upload/documents/library/data protection/detailed specialist guides/
ico guidance monetary penalties.pdf.

[57] As an overview, please see: OUT-LAW.COM Press Release *Information Commissioner gets power
to fine for security breaches* 12th May 2008. Available at: http://out-law.com/page-9110-theme=print
(13th May 2008).

[58] See: Ministry of Justice *Civil Monetary penalties – setting the maximum penalty* CP48/09.
Available at: http://www.justice.gov.uk/consultations/civil-monetary-penalties-consultation.htm.

[59] The Data Protection (Monetary Penalties) Order 2010.

Information Commissioner could only audit a data controller with their consent. The Act inserts sections 41A–C into the Data Protection Act and provides the Information Commissioner with the ability to audit government departments, although it is likely that with the introduction of secondary legislation other public bodies and private bodies at high risk (meaning that they process large amounts of personal data and a high level of damage may arise if there is a breach of the principles) will be added to the remit of the Information Commissioner. The audit powers extend as far as allowing the Information Commissioner access to premises, collection and viewing of documents and the ability to take items of interest away for inspection. Interestingly, any documents obtained in this search may not be used as evidence in awarding a monetary penalty under Section 55A.

The eight Data Protection Principles

Once registered, and once an organisation is processing personal data, eight principles, known as the 'Data Protection Principles' and which are found in Schedule 1 of the Act need to be adhered to. In effect the principles constitute a list indicating 'good practice' for handling data, but are at the heart of data protection law, particularly the first principle which is an overriding provision. These eight principles will now be discussed in turn.

Principle One: Personal data shall be processed fairly and lawfully

This principle states that personal data shall be processed fairly and lawfully. What makes processing 'fair' or 'lawful' is not defined by the Act, although it extends as far as ensuring that the data was obtained fairly and that no person was deceived or misled as to the purpose of processing. The case of **Innovations (Mail Order) Limited v Data Protection Commissioner**[60] demonstrated this point as the mail order company shared customer data with third parties. It was not until an order had been acknowledged that the customer discovered that this was in fact the case. The Data Protection Registrar (the forerunner to the Information Commission) held that this was not fair processing and the customers should be told about this at the time of collection. Equally, in **British Gas Trading Limited v The Data Protection Registrar**[61] British Gas appealed against an Enforcement Notice issued by the Registrar after they had sent a leaflet providing details of their other services

---

[60] Case DA/9231/49/1.
[61] 25th March 1998, unreported.

and a letter saying that they were going to share customer records with third parties unless customers wrote back asking to be removed from this system. The court held that this ability to opt-out was not sufficient as British Gas held a monopoly over gas supplies and customers had to give their details to this company. A more recent case, which (although focusing on section 77 of the Consumer Credit Act 1974) had some interesting things to say about this first principle was **Phillip McGuffick v The Royal Bank of Scotland plc**.[62] The facts were that Mr McGuffick entered into a credit agreement with a bank for just over £17,000. He shortly fell into arrears and the bank sent his file to a debt collection agency. Under section 77 of the Consumer Credit Act, McGuffick asked for a copy of the agreement and statement of account from the lender. The consequence of this was that any enforcement should be suspended until the consumer is in receipt of the requested documents. However, despite the requirement for enforcement proceedings to cease, the bank continued to advise credit reference agencies of the default in payment and McGuffick argued that this was in breach of the first data protection principle. This argument was easily rejected by the court, which said that as banks and other financial institutions have a duty to ensure responsible lending this action was not against the spirit of this principle. The collection of the data and subsequent use must be legitimate and the data subject should also be provided with details of the processing, including the identity of the data controller, the purpose of processing and any other relevant information.[63] If the data is stored on an online database, the data subject should also be informed of this.[64]

The core requirement of this principle is that the personal data should not be processed unless one of the conditions of Schedule 2 is met. Schedule 2 lists the conditions relevant for processing personal data, which are:

- The data subject has consented to the processing;
- The processing is necessary for the performance of a contract;
- The processing is necessary for legal compliance;
- It is in the vital interests of the data subject;

---

[62] [2009] EWHC 2386 (Comm).

[63] See Schedule 1, part II.

[64] A significant breach of this principle was discovered in 2009, when Ian Kerr pleaded guilty to running a secretive operation to vet people for employment in the construction industry. He set up a company called 'The Consulting Association' and for an annual fee charged to major construction companies he allowed them to view the list to see if a prospective employee had been blacklisted. The people on this list had no idea that the list existed, or that they appeared on it – the data was clearly not being processed fairly or lawfully. The Crown Court fined him £5000, plus costs. It is interesting to note that Mr Kerr was not punished for breaching any of the data protection principles because at that time no punishment was available. Instead they prosecuted him for failure to notify as a data controller. If a similar case were brought today it is likely that section 55A would be utilised, which covers knowing or reckless breaches of the Act. See the Information Commissioner's press release on this story at: http://www.ico.gov.uk/upload/documents/pressreleases/2009/kerr_sentencing_160709.pdf.

- The processing is for judicial/governmental purposes;
- The processing is necessary for legitimate purposes pursued by the data controller.

Clearly, one of the more popular grounds for processing is that the data subject has consented to the processing; hence the large number of contracts which contain a tick-box section for individuals to indicate that they consent to their personal data being processed – from entering employment to the purchasing of a mobile telephone. However, to add a small degree of confusion, the Act also uses the concept of Sensitive Personal Data. This is defined by Section 2 of the Act as information relating to an individual regarding their:

- Racial or ethnic origin;
- Political opinions;
- Religious beliefs;
- Trade Union membership;
- Physical or mental health;
- Sex life; or
- Criminal record.

This is an exhaustive list, but also provides an indication of the age of the Act by what is not included. Information relating to, for example, financial and banking records and genetic or biometric details are not included within the heading of sensitive personal data.[65] It is arguable that these types of data are more sensitive than some of the headings contained within the section 2 list. This aside, if the data which is being processed is sensitive personal data, then a condition in Schedule 3 of the Act must be met.[66] Specifically:

- The data subject has given his explicit consent;
- The processing is necessary for the purposes of employment obligations on the controller;
- It is in the vital interests of the data subject or another person (if the controller cannot reasonably get consent from the data subject);
- It is carried out by a non-profit-making organisation, which exists for religious, philosophical, political or trade union purposes. This data should only relate to members of the association and should not be passed to third parties;

---

[65] For more on this issue, see: McCullagh, K *Data Sensitivity: resolving the conundrum* Paper presented to the 22nd Annual BILETA Conference, held University of Hertfordshire April 2007. Available at: http://www.bileta.ac.uk/Document%20Library/1/Data%20Sensitivity%20-%20resolving %20the%20conundrum.pdf.

[66] Or a ground contained within the Data Protection (Processing of Sensitive Personal Data) Order 2009 (S.I. 2000/417) is met.

- It is necessary for legal compliance;
- It is necessary for the administration of justice;
- It is necessary for medical purposes and is undertaken by a health professional or equivalent person;
- It is necessary to maintain equal opportunity records, which is done with appropriate safeguards; or
- It is to be processed following an order from the Secretary of State.

The definition of consent found in Schedule 2 and 3 is somewhat controversial. There is currently no definition of consent contained within Schedule 2. Article 2(h) in the original Data Protection Directive 95/46/EC suggests that a data subject's consent is 'any freely given specific and informed indication of his wishes by which the data subject signifies his agreement to personal data relating to him being processed'. However, to confuse the issue further, if the personal data is of a sensitive kind, then a criterion in Schedule 3 needs to be met. This time the data subject must have given his 'explicit' consent. Once again, there is no express definition of this term, and therefore there is a degree of uncertainty as to the level of consent required. It seems that 'explicit' consent needs some express action on the part of the data subject, but if this is the case, it may follow that consent for under Schedule 2 may merely be implied.[67]

Principle Two: Personal data is only obtained for one or more specified and lawful purposes

This principle states that data may only be obtained and processed for lawful reasons which have been given to the Information Commissioner under the notification procedures found within Part III of the Act. The grounds for processing must be clearly specified and the data should not be processed in a manner that is incompatible with the declared purposes. This is an important principle for online companies to bear in mind as the Internet allows personal data and information to flow freely and it is important that checks are put in place to ensure that the processing of the data does not extend beyond its specified purpose. Invariably, an organisation that notifies the Information Commissioner that they are to process personal data will ensure their notification covers as many different grounds for processing as possible, although this

---

[67] There is a small body of UK case law on the nature of consent. In **Re Caughey ex parte Ford** (1896) LR1 Ch.D 521 the Court of Appeal held that consent cannot have been given by somebody who was unaware of the situation. Additionally, in **Attorney-General v Jonathan Cape Limited** (1976) 3 WLR 606 the Queen's Bench Division of the High Court stated that consent needs to be affirmative.

principle does seek to provide transparency so that the data subject, Information Commissioner and the data controller are all fully aware of the reasoning behind the processing.

Principle Three: Personal data shall be adequate, relevant and not excessive

This is the first of three principles which relate to the management of the data by the data controller and principle three requires the data controller to ensure that the data being held is adequate, relevant and not excessive. For instance, a data controller may not hold information that is not needed at that time, but may potentially be useful in the future. The exact concept of adequacy and relevance is a matter of interpretation and definition. The case of **Runnymede Borough Council v Data Protection Registrar**[68] was a decision under the old 1984 Act and related to the collection of the Poll Tax. The court held that holding details of the type of property an individual lived in was too excessive and so was not required to be held on the computer. More recently, the Court of Appeal considered a case that covers this principle and also principles four and five. The decision in **Chief Constable of Humberside v Information Commissioner**[69] continued the discussion of the provocative issue of whether the police are able to retain the criminal history of individuals who have spent their conviction. In this case, the Information Commissioner issued Enforcement Notices against five different chief constables requesting that minor convictions (some of which related to incidents in the 1970s and 1980s and some of which were carried out during the data subject's teenage years) relating to five different individuals should be deleted. The difficulty faced by these five individuals was that when they applied for a job requiring a Criminal Records Bureau (CRB) check, these 'old' offences were being highlighted, even though (in one situation), the police force had said that the conviction would be erased once the individual reached the age of 18. The Information Commissioner argued that retaining details of these offences was contrary to the provisions of the Data Protection Act 1998, specifically data protection principle three (data held should not be excessive) and principle five (data should not be kept for longer than necessary). However, the Court of Appeal disagreed and held that the Enforcement Notices should be quashed as it is up to the data controller (in this case the respective chief constable) to determine the purposes of processing and retention. Provided they felt that there was a worth and value to having a conviction held on record that should be just reason. Indeed, Article 8(5) of the original Data Protection Directive 95/46/EC

---

[68] (1990) 30 R.V.R. 236.
[69] [2009] EWCA Civ 1079.

does allow member states to keep a complete register of criminal convictions "… *only under the control of official authority*". Additionally, the Court of Appeal was of the view that there is no statutory constraint on any individual or company as to the purposes for which he or it is entitled to retain data. The one caveat to this is that the purpose has to be lawful, in order to comply with the first data protection principle that the data should be processed fairly and lawfully. In this case, the chief constable had listed 'vetting and licensing' as one of their processing purposes (this is required by the current CRB regime) and therefore the court considered that the processing by the police was carried out in line with their core purposes. An appeal to the Supreme Court was refused, although there are indications that the claimants will seek to take their case to the European Court of Human Rights.

Principle Four: Personal data shall be accurate and, where necessary, kept up to date

Under this principle, a data controller is obliged to take reasonable steps to ensure that the data he holds is accurate and current. Section 70(2) of the Act explains that data items are inaccurate if they are incorrect or misleading as to any matter of fact (accordingly opinions held about a data subject cannot be inaccurate). A data controller will not be acting in contravention of this principle if the data they are holding was received from the data subject or a third party provided they have taken reasonable steps to ensure the accuracy of the data or they have included a note with the inaccurate data indicating that the data subject has challenged the accuracy of the data held. The High Court considered the applicability of this principle in **Christopher John Quinton v Robin Heys Pierce.**[70] Mr Quinton was a Conservative candidate for a seat on a local council in Oxfordshire. The incumbent was the Liberal Democrat defendant Mr Pierce. Quinton sued Pierce for defamation after a number of election leaflets had been produced which made allegations against him. This action was unsuccessful and therefore Quinton commenced an action alleging that there had been a breach of the fourth data protection principle as the information was personal data and therefore as it was being processed there was a duty on the data controller to ensure that the information was accurate. This was also rejected as the information contained within the leaflets was broadly accurate. Furthermore, it would be unusual to require a competitor in an election to provide advance warning of a piece of election material, which may paint the opponent in a negative light.

---

[70] [2009] EWHC 912 (QB).

Principle Five: Personal data shall not be kept for longer than is necessary

This principle places an obligation upon data controllers to ensure that they securely dispose of all personal data once the purpose for which it was required has been concluded. The Information Commissioner recommends a regular systematic review of all data held to ensure that any personal data is still required. Although this may seem slightly bureaucratic, such an exercise will ensure that an organisation has up to date information, which will ensure the data can be used most effectively. However, it is prudent to ensure a balance is achieved as it is possible that some data may have a further use at a later point (although organisations will need to ensure that they comply with the second data protection principle of obtaining personal data for only one or more specified and lawful purposes). The precise answer to how long data should be kept for does depend on the type of data being held and the processing purpose. Various pieces of legislation may provide assistance with determining how long data may be kept prior to disposal in certain circumstances[71] and the European Court of Justice has stated that it is the responsibility of member states to set limits for retention of data and a suitable balance must be found between protecting the privacy of an individual and not placing too great a burden on the data controller to retain the information.[72] Timeframes for retaining data differ depending upon whether the data held relates to employment, finance or taxation or legal matters.

Principle Six: Personal data shall be processed in accordance with the data subject's rights

The Data Protection Act does not merely impose obligations upon those who process data, but also provides rights for the data subject. Under section 7, a data subject has the right to contact the data controller at the organisation which they believe holds personal data about them and request to see data held. This request must be in writing. The organisation may levy a fee of £10 for this, but must respond within 40 calendar days. The 40-day period includes weekends and bank holidays and commences once the data controller has received sufficient information about the personal data that is requested and

---

[71] For instance the Limitation Act 1980 states that an action founded on a simple contract needs to be brought within six years of the accrual of the cause of action (section 5), while actions relating to the recovery of land need to be brought within twelve years (section 15). These may act as indicators for how long particular personal data should be retained by an organisation.

[72] See: **College van burgemeester en wethouders van Rotterdam v M. E. E. Rijkeboer** (2009) Case 533/07).

the necessary fee. A data controller is also able to ask the data subject to verify their identity. The data controller must provide the data subject with a description of the personal data held in relation to him or her, a copy of any information held and information which is needed to make the copy intelligible. The data subject must also be provided with information about the grounds for processing, the likely recipients and the logic used behind any automated decisions that may be taken about them. There are a number of exemptions, which could be relied upon by the data controller to withhold the release of information. These exemptions include *inter alia* if the release would reveal confidential references that were written by the data controller, or that the detection of a crime would be prejudiced, negotiations and management forecasts. Furthermore, if a data subject makes repeated subject access requests then the data controller would have the right not to respond. Although the data subject access request is arguably the main right a data subject has, there are other statutory rights contained within the Act. These include the right to prevent processing that will cause damage or distress,[73] the right to prevent processing for direct marketing purposes,[74] a right to an explanation about how automated decisions are made,[75] a right to compensation if damage has been caused due to a data controller not fulfilling their obligations under the Act,[76] a right to correction, erasure or destruction of inaccurate data,[77] and finally a right to request an assessment by the Information Commissioner on the legality of the processing.[78] Data subjects are unable to contract out of these rights.

Principle Seven: Personal data is kept secure using technical and organisational methods

Arguably, the principle of keeping personal data secure using technical and organisational standards has attracted the highest profile over the past few years. Since the loss by HM Revenue and Customs in 2007 of two discs containing the personal and bank details of all child benefit recipients, data

---

[73] Data Protection Act 1998, section 10. The case of **Phillip McGuffick v The Royal Bank of Scotland plc** [2009] EWHC 2386 (Comm) (mentioned above in relation to Principle One), also considered the use of section 10, as McGuffick's solicitors had sent a Section 10 Notice to the lender requesting that the processing of McGuffick's data should cease, although the letter did not give the reasons for this. The court held that in these circumstances, a data controller should not be able to hide behind a technical breach of the requirements of the legislation if they were acting in clear breach of the Act (although they were also reluctant to allow data subjects to serve these notices without adequate reasoning).

[74] Ibid. Section 11. The Act states that data subjects should be provided with an 'opt-out' to allow them to remove themselves from mailing lists.

[75] Ibid. Section 12.

[76] Ibid. Section 13.

[77] Ibid. Section 15.

[78] Ibid. Section 42.

security breaches have been big news stories. The two discs are still lost and this security breach was one in a long line of data protection breaches to hit HMRC in recent years.[79] Other examples of high profile data breaches include the loss by the Driving Standards Agency of data relating to three million people about to take their driving theory test,[80] nine NHS trusts losing data relating to thousands of patients[81] and sporadic disappearances of laptops in both the public and private sector.[82] In light of the HMRC security breach, the Poynter Report was commissioned and was published in June 2008.[83] This inquiry was set up to establish the circumstances that led to the significant loss of personal data and highlight lessons that should be learnt. In all, 45 recommendations were made – all of which were accepted by HMRC. The first recommendation was that information security should be acknowledged as a corporate objective by HMRC and objectives to achieve this should be set out.[84] This recommendation was in the light of the report's finding that information security was not a priority within the organisation. Indeed staff tended to "… *prioritise operational delivery over information security*".[85] Higher up the chain of command there appeared to be a lack of communication and poor accessibility of relevant policies and procedures, partly due to time constraints and also due to a lack of appreciation of the potential seriousness of an information security breach. Working to improve the perceived importance of the security of data may be beneficial – although a little obvious following the media's crusade against such breaches.

A data security breach can happen for a number of reasons. It could be that data (or equipment storing data) is stolen, or is accessed by an unauthorised person and disclosed to a third party, or that computer systems are hacked into. Information security breaches can often lead to embarrassment for the organisation concerned as well as significant distress to the data subject(s) whose data has been mislaid. The Information Commissioner is keen to ensure that data is kept as secure as possible; evidence for this is seen by the requirements contained within the notification formalities, which request details of security measures in place. In considering the appropriateness of security measures, the

---

[79] For the initial BBC Press Release see: *UK's families put on fraud alert* (20th November 2007). Available at: http://news.bbc.co.uk/1/hi/uk_politics/7103566.stm.

[80] BBC News *Millions of L-Driver details lost* 17th December 2007. Available at: http://news.bbc.co.uk/1/hi/uk_politics/7147715.stm.

[81] BBC News *Nine NHS trusts lose patient data* 23rd December 2008. Available at: http://news.bbc.co.uk/1/hi/uk/7158019.stm.

[82] Indeed, as far back as 2003, the BBC reported that 1 in 17 of public sector workers had either lost their laptop or it had been stolen. See: *Government laptops 'not secure'* 15th September 2003. Available at: http://news.bbc.co.uk/1/hi/technology/3109602.stm.

[83] HM Treasury *Review of information security at HM Revenue and Customs (Final Report)* June 2008. Available at: http://www.hm-treasury.gov.uk/independent_reviews/poynter_review/poynter_review_index.cfm.

[84] Ibid, page 89.

[85] Ibid, page 37.

Information Commissioner recommends that regard should be paid to the implementation cost, the technological developments (i.e. what technology is available to protect data), the nature of the data (sensitive personal data should require greater protection than personal data) and the harm that may result if the data is lost or unlawfully processed. The European Court of Human Rights has also adopted a very wide expectation of what an organisation needs to do in order to comply with this principle. In **I v Finland**[86] the applicant was a nurse specialising in eye care who worked in a hospital. She contracted HIV and needed to be treated at the same hospital. Based on comments that were made to her she formed the impression that her medical records had been accessed by her colleagues. The log kept by the hospital only detailed the last five accesses and only noted the accessing by department, as opposed to the person. This meant the hospital was unable to show who had accessed her file. Initially the Finnish court said that as access by unauthorised persons could not be proved there was no case to answer. However, the European Court of Human Rights held that there was a positive duty to secure data – particularly if the data held is sensitive personal data. There is a clear link with Article 8 in the European Convention on Human Rights and confidentiality of health records is fundamental to right to a private life. Therefore, practical and effective protection is needed to safeguard against the misuse of personal data.

Principle Eight: Personal data is not to be transferred out of the European Economic Area unless there is an adequate level of protection for data subjects

This principle seeks to protect data subjects from having their data transferred outside the remit of the legislation to a country which may have a significantly less stringent approach to protecting personal data than the European Economic Area. The European Economic Area encompasses the European Union, as well as Norway, Iceland and Liechtenstein. There are a number of exemptions to this principle, which are listed in Schedule 4. Amongst other grounds, this principle does not apply if the data subject has provided their consent for their personal data to be transferred outside of the European Economic Area, the transfer is necessary for the performance of a contract or it is necessary for legal proceedings. There are clearly a number of countries who are key players on the world stage, who are not located within the European Economic Area and do not have an adequate level of protection.[87] The United

---

[86] (2008) Application 20511/03.

[87] See the European Commission website to find the list of countries outside of the European Economic Area that currently offer an 'adequate level of protection' to personal data: http://ec.europa.eu/justice_home/fsj/privacy/thridcountries/index_en.htm.

States is a good example, meaning that until recently transfers of personal data to the United States were illegal. To try to rectify this difficulty, on 26th July 2000, and after two years of negotiation, the compromise position of Safe Harbour was reached.[88] This is a voluntary system allowing American companies and organisations to sign up to the scheme to say that they are meeting basic data protection principles, similar to those in the European Union. To join Safe Harbour a company must:

- Comply with the principles of Safe Harbour;
- Make a public statement affirming compliance with the principles;
- Self-certify compliance to the United States Department of Commerce.

There was a very slow uptake to Safe Harbour, with only a few dozen companies in the first six months, arguably due to the annoyance of American businesses in having to comply with the European Union's direction. Although interest is increasing there is still only a relatively small number of companies who have signed up. There are seven main principles of Safe Harbour, which relate to notice, choice, transfers, access, security, data integrity and enforcement. In October 2004, a European Commission Working Group examined the success of the Safe Harbour scheme. In a document entitled: *The implementation of Commission Decision 520/2000/EC on the adequate protection of personal data provided by the Safe Harbour privacy Principles and related Frequently Asked Questions issued by the United States Department of Commerce* they made a number of conclusions. These were:

1. Safe Harbour is beginning to be embraced by the American business community, although a greater uptake is needed;
2. However, there are a number of organisations who have signed up to Safe Harbour but who do not have a privacy policy, which is in contravention of the agreement;
3. The Department of Commerce, responsible for enforcing Safe Harbour is carrying out their function well, although they need to make certain changes to their website;
4. There are some problems with alternative dispute resolution schemes.

The Commission also questioned whether the Federal Trade Commission is competent to deal with international data flow where the data relates to

---

[88] Commission Decision 520/2000/EC of 26th July 2000 pursuant to Directive 95/46/EC of the European Parliament and of the Council on the adequacy of the protection provided by the Safe Harbour privacy principles and related frequently asked questions issued by the US Department of Commerce. Available at: http://eur-lex.europa.eu/LexUriServ/LexUriServ.do?uri=CELEX:32000D0520: EN:NOT.

human resources. This is an issue, considering that around 30 per cent of the companies who have signed up to Safe Harbour have done so for human resources purposes.

Exemptions

The provisions contained within the Data Protection Act do not apply in all circumstances. Part IV of the Act (sections 27–39) lists a number of situations where the Act does not apply. Section 28 allows for an exemption on the grounds of National Security. This is has a very wide definition and provides exemption from virtually the entire Act. The Secretary of State is required to certify that a given situation is exempted from the requirements of the Act. A person who is affected by the granting of a certificate by the Secretary of State is able to appeal to the General Regulatory Chamber[89], which will decide the appeal following similar principles to that of judicial review. Section 29 provides that personal data collected for crime and taxation purposes are exempt from the first data protection principle and also section 7, while section 30 lists an exemption for health, education and social work purposes, which gives the Secretary of State the ability to request that data be withheld from a person if its disclosure would be seriously harmful to that person or a third party. Section 31 states that a regulated body does not need to inform people when they collect personal data if it would prejudice the organisation's public function. The underlying objective behind section 32 is to achieve a balance between privacy and freedom of expression. This is the journalism, literature and art exemption and the courts generally decide on a case by case basis whether this exemption can be utilised. In **Tietosuojavaltuutettu v Satakunnan Markkinapörssi Oy. and Satamedia Oy**[90] the European Court of Justice provided a very broad definition of journalism and said that it extended to new technologies, such as text messages. It did not even matter if the main motive behind the publication is profiteering. Section 33 allows an exemption for research, history and statistics purposes. This exemption can only be used where the relevant data are not processed to make a decision about an individual, nor if the processing is likely to cause damage or substantial distress to another person. Section 34 applies to public records and personal data they contain are partially exempt from the Act's provisions, including subject access and those occasions listed in principle four. Section 35 allows personal data to be disclosed if it is required by an enactment, rule of law or court order.

---

[89] This court replaced the Information Tribunal in January 2010 and was part of a governmental plan to unify numerous tribunals. See Statutory Instrument 2010/22 The Transfer of Tribunal Functions Order 2010.

[90] (2008) Case 73/07.

Personal data is also exempt from the non-disclosure principles if the disclosure is necessary for legal proceedings. The majority of the Act is exempt if the data is processed for a domestic purpose, including personal, household or family affairs as outlined in section 36. This implements Article 3(2) of Directive 95/46/EC and is discussed further in relation to social networking sites and the decision in **Criminal Proceedings against Lindqvist** (the Bodil Lindqvist case)[91] discussed in chapter 9. Section 37 refers to Schedule 7, which lists a number of miscellaneous exemptions (such as the armed forces, judicial appointments, corporate finance, examination marks and self-incrimination), while section 38 provides the Secretary of State with a small discretion to add exemptions or authorise that data be disclosed if it is in the interest of the data subject.

Recent reforms and reform proposals

As the Internet and its applications continue to grow and diversify, it is essential that the data protection legislative regime retains its robustness to ensure that it can ably protect personal information. One such method of strengthening the provisions would be by the addition of a data security breach notification law. This type of law would place obligations on companies to notify when a security breach occurs and the introduction of such a law has been mooted for some time.[92] However, there have been a number of issues that have previously discouraged the introduction of such a law; for instance, an adequate definition of what a data security breach is has historically been very difficult to arrive at. Furthermore the nature of the reporting system and rules on the form of a notification letter and advice given to individuals whose data may be at risk has not been overly clear. There are a number of problems with introducing a law of this type. Key questions remain unanswered; for instance, if an organisation discovers a data security breach, at what stage should they report the breach, or in other words, how big does the breach have to be before it should be reported? Companies are going to be reluctant to report a breach as it could be a PR disaster and could cause a loss of goodwill among its customers, as well as causing the company some considerable financial damage.

In April 2010, the European Union partially addressed this issue and introduced a data breach notification rule for European telecommunications

---

[91] Case C-101/01 [2004] 2 W.L.R. 1385.

[92] See for instance: OUT-LAW.COM Press Release *Why we don't need a security breach notification law in the UK* (19th May 2008). Available at: http://out-law.com/page-9128-theme=print and compare this view with the thoughts contained within the House of Lords Science and Technology Committee Report on Personal Internet Security 10th August 2007, page 54, paragraph 5.56.

firms.[93] This Directive was at the heart of the European Commission's review of the telecommunications sector and made amendments to the provisions relating to spam and cookies and also introduced a data security breach notification law. It inserts into Article 2 of Directive 2002/58/EC a definition of personal data breach as:

> "... a breach of security leading to the accidental or unlawful destruction, loss, alteration, unauthorised disclosure of, or access to, personal data transmitted, stored or otherwise processed in connection with the provision of a publicly available electronic communications service in the Community."

The difficulty with this definition is that a requirement to notify is only placed on telecommunications companies and not to providers of 'information society services'. Therefore banks and other providers of online services are not required to adhere to the provisions and it is only companies that connect users to the Internet that are obliged to comply. The European Commission has suggested that they will consult separately about introducing a wider-ranging breach notification law.[94] The actual workings of the new notification law are inserted into Article 4 of 2002/58/EC and in the event of a personal data breach the electronic communications services shall, without undue delay, notify the competent national authority. In the United Kingdom the competent national authority would be the Information Commissioner. Furthermore, if the breach is likely to adversely affect the privacy of an individual (for instance the breach could result in identity theft, physical harm, significant humiliation or damage to reputation) that individual should also be notified (this notification will need to include the nature of the breach and contact details if an individual wants further information. It should also include advice to the individual about how they can mitigate any potential loss). Controversially, notification to individuals will not be required if the provider can demonstrate to the competent national authority that they already have appropriate technological protection measures in place (which were applied to the data in question). This technological protection must render the data unintelligible to any person who is not authorised to access it. The competent national authority also has the

---

[93] Directive 2009/../EC amending Directive 2002/22.EC on universal service and users' rights relating to electronic communications networks and services, Directive 2002/58/EC concerning the processing of personal data and the protection of privacy in the electronic communications sector and Regulation (EC) No 2006/2004 on cooperation between authorities responsible for the enforcement of consumer protection laws. These changes were adopted by the Commission in September 2009 and they should have been implemented into member states by May 2011.

[94] OUT-LAW.COM *Telcos' data breach notification amendment is passed* (3rd November 2009). Available at: http://www.out-law.com/default.aspx?page=10497. Indeed, an examination of the Declarations suggest that this is an interim measure while the European Commission consults on a broader security breach notification law.

power to compel the service provider to advise individuals of the breach if they have not already done so. A number of issues remain unclear. Whilst a service provider is obliged to notify 'without undue delay' this phrase is not overly clear and despite the definition of a personal data breach it is still not clear at which stage of a breach a service provider is obliged to contact the competent national authority. In any case, the usefulness of this provision is to be doubted considering the narrow range of companies this applies to. The full armoury of a data breach notification law will not be seen until the notification requirements are extended to other online companies and not just telecommunications service providers.

In 2010, the European Commission announced that they will be reviewing the entire data protection legislation. There will be significant changes; one of the major changes is as a result of the introduction of the Lisbon Treaty in December 2009, which brings data protection enforcement within the remit of the Commission and allows the European Court of Justice to hear cases. There is also a range of implementing measures within different member states, meaning that Directive 95/46/EC has been interpreted differently. In preparation for this review, the United Kingdom's Ministry of Justice issued a call for evidence on the current regime in July 2010.[95] This closed in October 2010 and at the time of writing the results are still awaited.

Freedom of Information

The Freedom of Information Act 2000 came into force on 1st January 2005. It has close links with the Data Protection Act, although places particular emphasis on public bodies. Under the Act, a person or organisation may request information from a public authority which has functions in England, Wales or Northern Ireland. The Act confers two statutory rights on applicants in Section 1:

- To be told whether or not the public authority holds that information; and if so,
- To have that information communicated to them.

The Act applies to public bodies, of which there are over 100,000 within the United Kingdom. Schedule 1 of the Act provides an extensive and comprehensive list of who is covered by the Act, including governmental departments, local authorities, the police and the National Health Service. The Ministry of Justice updates this list on a monthly basis. If an organisation falls within the

---

[95] Ministry of Justice *Call for Evidence on the Current Data Protection Legislative Framework* (6th July 2010). Available at: http://www.justice.gov.uk/call-for-evidence-060710.htm.

Public Authority definition, then members of the public are able to contact the organisation requesting information the public body holds. Section 8 of the Act provides that this must be done in writing, with clear details of the sender (including the name and address) and a clear description of the information that is required. A public body has the right to charge a small fee, but must respond to the request for the information within 20 days. Section 14 allows organisations not to comply with requests if they are "vexatious" or on occasions when the same person is continually putting in the same request. Furthermore, Part II of the Act provides a list of exceptions (23 in total), which would legitimately prevent a body from providing the information requested. Such exceptions include defence or security reasons, information that falls within the Data Protection Act, trade secrets, audits and investigations by public bodies.

Enforcement of the Freedom of Information Act is carried out by the Information Commissioner, as with the Data Protection Act.

Concluding thoughts

The Internet is here to stay – both the advantages and disadvantages. The paradox is that although communication becomes easier and the size of the 'world' decreases,[96] the number of situations in which an individual needs to assert and prove his or her identity is increasing. The necessary response of governments is to ensure that a sufficiently rigorous legislative, perceptive and enforcement regime is in place to protect personal information. It seems that the United Kingdom is not currently able to do this with restrictive judicial decisions, coupled with data security disasters and the fallout from these incidents, although increased powers for the Information Commissioner's Office is a useful first step.

Key points:

- Personal information is a key commodity in the 21st century.
- The ease of movement of this personal data is essential to allow services and markets to operate freely.
- A dual concern is that the personal data is not misused and that the privacy of the individual is maintained.

[96] See, for instance Friedman, T *The World is Flat* Farrer, Straus and Giroux Publishing, New York (2005). Friedman argues that there has been three main eras of globalisation, the latter being the introduction of the Internet, which has reduced the size of the world to proportions not seen before.

- The Data Protection Directive 95/46/EC is the key piece of European legislation in the area of protecting personal data. This was implemented into the United Kingdom as the Data Protection Act 1998.
- At the heart of the Act there are eight Data Protection Principles, which in their simplest form act as a guide for good practice when handling personal data.
- These eight principles cover guidelines for *inter alia* the obtaining of the data, ensuring the accuracy of the data, data security and rules for ensuring that personal data is not transferred out of the European Economic Area to a country that does not have an adequate level of protection.
- Definitions of key terms are essential in working out the parameters of the Act. The definition of the term 'personal data' is critical and Durant v Financial Services Authority (2003) is the main authority in providing a two-stage approach to assist in deciding whether or not information held is in fact personal data.
- The Information Commissioner's Office is responsible for enforcing the provisions of the Act. Traditional penalties have extended to Information Notices and Enforcement Notices.
- The Criminal Justice and Immigration Act 2008 has inserted stronger powers for the Information Commissioner into Section 55 of the Data Protection Act. In the event of a deliberate or reckless breach the Information Commissioner can fine organisations up to £500,000 and also has imprisonment of up to two years as a prosecuting option.
- The European Commission is also commencing a complete review of the European data protection legislation.

Further reading:

Books

- Carey, P *Data Protection: A Practical Guide to UK and EU Law* (2009) Oxford University Press, 3rd edition.
- Jay, R & Hamilton, A *Data Protection Law and Practice* (2007) Sweet and Maxwell, 3rd edition.

Articles

- Baker, R K *Offshore IT outsourcing and the 8th Data Protection Principle – legal and regulatory requirements – with reference to financial services* (2005) International Journal of Law and Information Technology, Volume 14, Issue 1, pages 1–27.
- Jagessar, U & Sedgwick, V *When is personal data not "personal data" – The impact of Durant v FSA* Computer Law and Security Report (2005) Volume 21, Issue 6, pages 505–511.

- Turle, M *Durant v FSA – Court of Appeal's radical judgment on the Data Protection Act* Computer Law and Security Report (2004) Volume 20, Number 2, pages 133–136.
- Watts, M *Information, data and personal data – Reflections on Durant v Financial Services Authority* (2006) Computer Law and Security Report, Volume 22, Issue 4, pages 320–325.
- Wong, R *Data Protection Online: Alternative Approaches to Sensitive Data* (2007) Journal of International Commercial Law and Technology, volume 2.
- Zinser, A *The United Kingdom Data Protection Act 1998: International Data Transfer and its legal implications* (2005) International Company and Commercial Law Review, Volume 16, Issue 2, pages 80–87.

Questions for consideration:

7.1. What challenges does the Internet present to protecting the personal information of an individual?

7.2. Give definitions of the following key terms from the Data Protection Act 1998: data subject, data controller, Information Commissioner, processing and relevant filing system.

7.3. How have the courts in the United Kingdom interpreted the term 'personal data'? Why is the definition of this phrase so important?

7.4. In what ways is the United Kingdom's judicial definition of personal data weaker than the original European Union's approach contained within the Data Protection Directive 95/46/EC?

7.5. What are the rights of the data subject? In the event of one of their rights being breached what remedies can they pursue?

7.6. Outline the eight Data Protection Principles and explain their role and importance.

7.7. Out of the eight Data Protection Principles, it is arguable that Principle One is the most important. Why is this the case and how does this principle link into Schedule 2 and Schedule 3 of the Data Protection Act 1998?

7.8. How effective do you consider the powers of the Information Commissioner's Office to be and how far do recent reforms improve their enforcement powers?

7.9. 'The decision in **Durant v Financial Services Authority [2003]** and subsequent case law has led to significantly reduced rights for data subjects. Coupled with the limited protection offered by the Safe Harbour Scheme, it is without doubt that the Data Protection Act 1998 offers a data subject very little protection in relation to their personal data.'

Undertake a critical assessment of this statement.

7.10.   Read the following scenario and answer all the questions that follow:

Reggie Short is a bus driver working for 'London Buses Limited'. Reggie is not happy in his job, as he thinks he does not receive enough pay and so would like to move. He applied for a job with the 'Greater London Bus Company'. He filled in and posted the relevant application form and he obtained an interview, which Reggie thought had gone very well. He was very pleased to hear that he had been offered the job – subject to references.

A reference was requested from 'London Buses Limited', but Reggie was stunned to hear that the job offered had been withdrawn following receipt of the reference.

Fortunately, Reggie's wife Lesley has a close friend who works in the Personnel Department at the 'Greater London Bus Company' and she revealed that there had been considerable correspondence between the two companies. As a result of this considerable correspondence, 'Greater London Bus Company' decided to withdraw the job offer.

Reggie was understandably very angry and contacted the head of personnel at the 'Greater London Bus Company' and demanded to see a copy of the reference and all other information relating to his application

'Greater London Bus Company' is going through a process of updating its personnel department's processes, which will eventually include keeping all applications and interview notes online. However, at present, all application forms and interview notes are clipped together and placed in a box file for the particular month in which the job vacancy was advertised.

(a)   Advise Reggie on the process he should go through to obtain the information he requires.

(b)   Advise 'Greater London Bus Company' whether they are obliged to provide Reggie with the information he requires.

(c)   'Greater London Bus Company' is keen to ensure that their data protection practices are kept up to date and would value your advice on rules that they should be following.

All weblinks mentioned in the text can also be found at:
www.palgrave.com/law/rogers

8 Freedom of Expression and Defamation

> **This chapter will consider:**
>
> - The nature and legal definition of defamation.
> - Specific ways in which the Internet provides a forum for defamation claims and the difficulties in applying defamation rules to the Internet.
> - The differing approaches to defamation claims adopted by the United Kingdom and the United States.
> - The problems relating to successfully prosecuting such a claim (including identity and location), and an analysis of the current levels of damages available.
> - The potential liability of Internet Service Providers and other intermediaries.
> - Reform proposals in this area.

A defamatory statement is one which tends to lower the reputation of a person in the view of right-minded people, or leads the claimant to be shunned or avoided.[1] It is a tort and is therefore a civil wrong. There are two main types of defamation: slander (non-permanent and generally spoken) and libel (permanent and in written form). For a successful action to be brought by a claimant three elements need to be fulfilled. First of all, the statement needs to be defamatory in nature, secondly the statement needs to identify the claimant and thirdly the statement needs to be made (or published) to at least one person other than the claimant.[2] (A person cannot be liable for a defamatory thought, which is not shared with any other person.) Moreover, if the action is for slander the claimant must demonstrate that there has been 'special damage' (for instance, financial – a mere defamatory spoken statement with no significant loss generally does not provide sufficient grounding to

---

[1] See **Sim v Stretch** (1936) 52 TLR 669.

[2] Section 17 of the Defamation Act 1996 states that the statement can be in "words, pictures, visual images, gestures or any other method signifying meaning".

commence a claim for slander). In the United Kingdom, the action must also be commenced within one year of the publication of the article containing the alleged defamatory comment.[3] There is a rich body of case law in this area, which can be researched. The high profile case of **George Galloway MP v Telegraph Group Ltd**[4] is a good example of a libel action. Mr Galloway took the Daily Telegraph newspaper to court over allegations (which surfaced from paperwork found in Iraq after the allied invasion) that he had received payments from Saddam Hussein's Iraqi regime. The statements by the Daily Telegraph were found by Mr Justice Eady to be seriously defamatory and wholly unfounded and Mr Galloway was awarded £150,000 in damages by the High Court. The Daily Telegraph subsequently lost a later appeal (ironically on the same day that Mr Galloway was voted out of the 'Celebrity Big Brother' house).

Defamation actions are at the heart of the inherent conflict within the European Convention on Human Rights, which allows individuals freedom of expression under Article 10, while at the same time acknowledging that this is not a universal right and restrictions can be introduced by the member state as provided within Article 10(2). These restrictions can include the protection of an individual's reputation or rights of others; however these restrictions must be narrowly interpreted.[5] Equally, these restrictions must be prescribed by law and necessary in a democratic society.[6] This conflict between the right of freedom of expression, and ensuring that an individual is not defamed is not unique to the Internet, but the very nature of the Internet intensifies the nature of the problem.[7] In English law, a cause of action arises each time a libel is published, as demonstrated in the case of **Loutchansky v The Times Newspaper Ltd**.[8] In this case The Times newspaper alleged that Mr Loutchansky was linked to international criminal activities. Mr Loutchansky commenced an action based on the publication in hardcopy print, and subsequently started a second action once the article was placed in the online archive system operated by the newspaper. The Times forwarded the defence of qualified privilege saying that the article was in the public interest and had been published honestly and without malice. They also argued that it would set a damaging precedent in terms of restricting freedom of expression if online archive systems were subject to the same defamation rules as hard copy

---

[3] Defamation Act 1996, Section 5.

[4] (2004) EWHC 2786.

[5] **Observer and Guardian v United Kingdom** (1991) 14 EHRR 153.

[6] See: **Sunday Times v United Kingdom (No. 2)** (1992) 14 EHRR 229 and **Wingrove v United Kingdom** (1997) 24 EHRR 1.

[7] For a detailed consideration of this conflict please see Rowland, D *Free Expression and Defamation* (Chapter 5) in *Human Rights in the Digital Age* Routledge Cavendish and Glasshouse Press 2006 (Edited by Mathias Klang and Andrew Murray).

[8] (2002) 1 All ER 652.

publications. They forwarded the contention that the court should adopt the single publication rule, as favoured in other countries such as the United States of America, who introduced the rule in 1948 and offer the rule a great deal of protection.[9] The court was not persuaded by these arguments and found in favour of Mr Loutchansky. The court held that making online archives subject to defamation principles had only a negligible effect on the right of freedom of expression and that an action could indeed be brought for the second publication found within the archives.[10] The defence of qualified privilege could not be relied upon as the newspaper had simply copied the article and placed it in the online archive without any warning that the accuracy of the article was being contested. This action in itself was criticised by the judge as hardly amounting to responsible journalism. The second argument forwarded by the defendant – that there was a notable public interest in publishing the allegations – was also rejected by the court.

After the House of Lords refused permission for The Times to appeal, the newspaper took its case to the European Court of Justice. The decision handed down[11] by the European Court of Justice upheld the decision by the English court. The Times argued again that their use of online archives, and the potential for a new libel action to arise each time they are accessed, was a restriction of their Article 10 right to freedom of expression under the European Convention of Human Rights. The court rejected this argument stating that the newspaper had a duty to ensure responsible journalism. It was irresponsible in the court's view not to place a qualification online that the contents of the article were being challenged. The court held that the restriction of the Article 10 right (by allowing the defamation action to stand) was justified and proportionate as it sought to protect the reputation of others.[12] The disadvantage with this decision however is that publishers who publish information online may continue to err on the side of caution by possibly censoring material to try to avoid defamatory actions. The courts in the United Kingdom are aware of

---

[9] Indeed, at the time of writing a court in California is deciding whether or not a coffee label on a jar, which is reprinted over several years, counts as republishing or is actually a single publication. The issue in **Russell Christoff v Nestle USA Inc.** (2009) 152 Can. App. 4th 1439 concerned image rights and whether a model who appeared on Nestle coffee jar labels could sue Nestle for continuing to use his image for so long without his permission. The judge needed further evidence to decide whether the coffee label was a single publication (meaning that Christoff could not continue his action as he fell outside the limitation period) or whether the coffee label had been republished meaning that he could continue his action.

[10] This case follows a long history of the common law allowing actions to be brought for each libellous publication. See: **Duke of Brunswick v Harmer** (1849) 14 QB 185 and **Berezovsky v Michaels** (2000) 1 WLR 1004.

[11] **Times Newspaper Ltd v United Kingdom** (Applications 3002/03 & 23676/03) [2009] E.M.L.R. 14.

[12] For consideration of this decision see: Mora, P *The compatibility with art.10 ECHR of the continued publication of libel on the Internet: Times Newspapers Ltd (Numbers 1 and 2) v The United Kingdom* (2009) Entertainment Law Review, volume 20, issue 6, pages 226–228.

this potential and have historically handed down judgments rejecting the right of an individual to bring an action for defamation in order to protect free speech in the public interest.[13]

There are a number of other defences available for defamation actions. These are justification or that the comments were true (this is usually a complete defence), fair comment on a matter of public interest, absolute privilege (available for judicial and parliamentary proceedings only, for instance if a member of parliament called the Prime Minister "a liar" during Prime Minister's Question Time; although a probable defamatory statement, an action could not be brought as the MP has a defence through absolute privilege), qualified privilege (as was attempted in the Loutchansky case and also considered in detail in the case of **Reynolds v Times Newspapers Ltd**[14]), innocent dissemination, consent and offer of amends.[15] The last defence is provided in the Defamation Act 1996 within sections 2–4. This requires the author to write a corrective statement, offer an apology and, if relevant, offer compensation. A defence is also found within section 1 of the same Act which provides that if the person was not the author, editor or publisher of the statement, and he took all reasonable care in its publication and he did not know, or have reason to believe, that he caused or contributed to the publication of a defamatory statement, he cannot be found liable. If an author is unsuccessful in relying on one of these defences then a remedy (invariably damages and a requirement that the defendant make some form of corrective apology) will often be awarded to the claimant.

Following this general review of defamation, we turn to the main purpose of this chapter which is to focus specifically upon defamation on the Internet. There have been many defamation actions brought due to comments placed on the Internet – on media such as message boards, blogs, emails[16] and social networking sites, including Facebook and Twitter. The Internet is easy to use and encourages informal communications between individuals; however, the perceived anonymity that is often available online can lull some people into a false sense of security in believing that they can say anything they wish without the threat of being caught. The wide audience on the Internet, coupled with the relative ease of placing material online with less editorial comment make the Internet a hotbed of defamation litigation. The traditional demarcation

---

[13] See, for instance **Derbyshire County Council v Times Newspapers** [1993] AC 534 and **R (on the application of the ProLife Alliance v BBC** [2002] 2 All ER 756.

[14] [2001] 2 AC 127.

[15] For a consideration of the defence of offer of amends see: Henderson, G *Defamation: the offer of amends defence – a lamb in lion's clothing?* (2009) Communications Law, volume 14, issue 2, pages 46–49.

[16] The use of an email in defamation actions is an interesting consideration. A person may not commence an action if an email containing a defamatory statement about him is sent only to him. If that email is sent elsewhere then a defamatory action may arise.

between defamation by libel and by slander is muddied somewhat by the ability of an individual to record their voice (for instance on a podcast or video) and then publish it online, or to place a real-time comment on a bulletin board. Would these be classified as libel or slander? It is likely that this would still come within the heading of libel as they would be in permanent form, but this is not entirely certain.[17] This issue was partially considered in the case of **Smith v ADVFN Plc**[18] where the court maintained the stay on proceedings for 37 libel claims where the comments were likely to found to be fair comment, or vulgar abuse, which was not defamatory. The actions were paused as it was felt that continuation of them would lead to an abuse of process. The comments were placed on bulletin boards and Mr Justice Eady considered that these types of posting were similar to a heated debate in a bar; people add their comments without necessarily reading the whole post and may reply in the heat of the moment. Based on this, his view was this type of posting should be the subject of an action in slander, rather than libel.[19] It is likely though that this issue, along with many other issues relating to defamation and the Internet, will continue to be the subject of legal proceedings.

An obvious cause for concern in this area is the international reach of the Internet and, coupled with jurisdictional problems, this is a difficult area for lawyers. The very nature of the Internet, which allows anyone to be a publisher potentially extends this area of law very widely. There is in fact a large range of potential defendants in an Internet defamation action including authors, editors, Internet Service Providers, the owners of websites, individuals who collate and distribute information and perhaps even search engines. This chapter will consider some of the pertinent issues relating to the Internet and defamation in turn.

Identity

One of the core facets of the Internet is that to a very large degree people can be anonymous, either by hiding behind pseudonyms or using a false name. The Internet Service Providers or website owners do not always carry out identity checks on an individual prior to allowing them to use the site. This means that it can be very difficult to identity an individual who is alleged to have committed some form of wrong. This is an obvious problem when considering defamation as it seems to allow an individual to post a defamatory comment

---

[17] Broadcasting Act 1990, Section 166.
[18] [2008] EWHC 1797 (QB).
[19] Ibid. Paragraphs 13–18. Although curiously in paragraph 108, part of Mr Justice Eady's conclusion was that blogging could form the legitimate basis of a libel claim. Equally, the case of **Godfrey v Demon Internet Limited** (2001) QB 201 (considered below in more detail) suggested that web content should be the basis of a libel claim.

on a blog or a message board, without the law being able to reach them as their identity is hidden. The rights of individuals to retain anonymity while writing offensive or defamatory comments, and the action potentially defamed people may take to rectify the situation was considered by the High Court decision in **Sheffield Wednesday Football Club Limited et al v Neil Hargreaves**.[20] Neil Hargreaves (the defendant) operated and owned a website called www.owlstalk.co.uk. This website hosted a bulletin board where fans of Sheffield Wednesday Football Club could post messages on matters relating to the club. The website was free to use, although prospective users needed to register with a username and password and give themselves a name by which they are known on the site (invariably a pseudonym). The terms and conditions of the website stated that users could not post defamatory or false comments and the website owner was entitled to remove such messages if he deemed it necessary. A number of derogatory comments were posted on the website and Sheffield Wednesday and seven directors of the club felt that 11 comments placed on the website were false, defamatory and made serious allegations about them. Accordingly they sought to commence an action for defamation. The key problem faced by the directors of Sheffield Wednesday was that the identity of the authors who had made the postings was hidden as all the postings were written by individuals who had used a pseudonym. Therefore the club needed to locate a responsible party. The club sought a Norwich Pharmacal order against the website owner, Mr Hargreaves, which in some circumstances allows for hidden identities to be revealed which will allow an action to proceed. This principle was first established in the case of **Norwich Pharmacal v Customs & Excise Commissioners**[21] and was explained by Lord Reid as:

"... if through no fault of his own a person gets mixed up in the tortuous acts of others so as to facilitate their wrongdoing, he may incur no personal liability but he comes under a duty to assist the person who has been wronged by giving him information and disclosing the identity of the wrongdoers ... justice requires that he should co-operate in righting the wrong if he unwittingly facilitated its perpetration."[22]

In other words, if an individual inadvertently assists in a tortuous action of another person that person may be under an obligation to provide the identity of the person who is alleged to have committed the act. This principle was developed in the decision of **Mitsui Limited v Nexen Petroleum UK Limited**[23]

[20] [2007] EWHC 2375 (QB).
[21] [1974] AC 133.
[22] Ibid. Page 175.
[23] [2005] EWHC 625 (Ch).

in which Mr Justice Lightman introduced three conditions that must be satisfied prior to the court granting a Norwich Pharmacal order. Specifically:

(a)   A wrong must have been carried out or arguably carried out by an ultimate wrongdoer;

(b)   There must be a need for an order to enable action to be brought against the ultimate wrongdoer; and

(c)   The person against whom the order is sought must (a) be mixed up in the wrongdoing so as to have facilitated it; and (b) be able or likely to be able to provide the information necessary to enable the ultimate wrongdoer to be sued.

The judge in the Sheffield Wednesday case, Richard Parkes QC, was of the view that the three requirements for a Norwich Pharmacal order had been fulfilled in some of the entries posted on the website. Out of the 11 postings he considered that seven of them were not serious at all. The judge considered that:

> "It seems to me that some of the postings which concern the Claimants border on the trivial, and I do not think that it would be right to make an order for the disclosure of the identities of users who have posted messages which are barely defamatory or little more than abusive or likely to be understood as jokes. That, it seems to me, would be disproportionate and unjustifiably intrusive."[24]

The judge considered the 11 bulletin board postings and held that seven of them consisted of material that could not be classified as defamatory, was simply a joke, or contained just a small amount of personal abuse. However, the four remaining postings were, in the view of Parkes QC, much more serious in nature. Accordingly, the judgment went partly for the claimants, and Mr Hargreaves was asked to reveal the identities of four of the authors who had posted potentially defamatory statements on the bulletin board as the right for the directors to maintain their reputation outweighed the right of the authors to protect their anonymity. Despite the outcome of this case, to date no further action has been taken by either the football club or the directors.

The issue of identity was also considered by the High Court in **Author of a blog v Times Newspapers Limited.**[25] This case concerned a serving policeman who was the author of an anonymous blog. Under the pseudonym 'Night Jack', the police officer commented on his experience at work, including details on criminals and the struggles he faced with police bureaucracy. He also criticised government ministers and policy. The Times newspaper came into the

---

[24]   [2007] EWHC 2375 (QB), paragraph 17.

[25]   [2009] EWHC 1358 (QB).

possession of the name of the anonymous blogger and 'Night Jack' sought an injunction to prevent its disclosure. The blogger argued that his identity should be protected for two reasons. First of all, he contended that The Times had a duty of confidence in respect to the information the newspaper held about his identity, and secondly he argued that he had a right to privacy unless there was a public interest ground for identifying him. Mr Justice Eady rejected both of these arguments. In relation to the duty of confidence, Mr Justice Eady explained that this is only owed in situations where information is provided which is clearly meant to be confidential.[26] The Times discovered the identity of the anonymous blogger through their detective work and were not given the information in confidence. The second forwarded contention was also rejected by the court and the judge was of the view that there was no right to privacy in the publishing of a blog which is available to the public. Even if there was, the public interest in disclosing the identity of the author would outweigh the right to privacy, particularly as he was writing about the shortcomings of a public body – authenticity and accuracy would demand that the author be identified. The judge was of the opinion that it would be perverse for the author of a public blog, who concealed his identity, to expect a right to privacy if his identity were deduced, as blogging is essentially a public activity. Even though the blogger would invariably suffer harm once his identity were released (it is understood that he was disciplined by his police force) this should not be a bar to the disclosing of his identity. A similar position has been taken in the United States of America. The Court of Appeal in the State of California in the case of **Cynthia Moreno v Hanford Sentinel Inc**[27] stated that a right of action to bring a privacy case concerning comments placed on the social networking site MySpace could not be allowed as the site was a public, and not private, forum. The appeal in this case concerned two issues. The first (and most prevalent to the current discussion) was about comments made about her hometown, Coalinga, placed on MySpace by Cythnia Moreno. The comments were very disparaging in nature. Moreno was at university when she wrote the comments, but her family were still based in Coalinga. Moreno removed the comments six days after they were published. However, a head teacher at a school in Coalinga came across the comments and forwarded them on to the editor of a local newspaper and the comments were published in the 'letters to the editor' section. Subsequently, the Moreno family suffered violent reaction and abuse from the local residents, forcing them to leave the area. Due to these events, Moreno filed an application for invasion of privacy and intentional infliction of emotional distress. The court decided that there was no invasion of privacy as Moreno was unable to demonstrate that there was a legally protected privacy interest and a reasonable expectation of

---

[26] **Napier v Pressdram Ltd** [2009] EWCA Civ 443.
[27] (2009) 09 C.D.O.S. 4208.

privacy. It follows that she was also unable to prove that there had been a serious invasion of that interest. Furthermore, by placing her comments on a public website (which included her full name and photograph) she did not behave in a manner consistent with an expectation of privacy. Although rejecting the first ground of appeal, the court stated that the second ground of appeal, relating to emotional distress, should be the subject of a trial by jury.

The role of the Internet Service Provider

The position of an Internet Service Provider (ISP) in defamation actions is of great interest.[28] With international reach, an ISP will have millions of pieces of information, postings or comments go through its service on a daily basis. Depending upon the role of the ISP it may be the subject of a defamation action, although there is a significant range of defences found within both the Defamation Act 1996 and the E-Commerce Regulations 2000[29] that could be relied upon. The default position for an ISP is that it is exempted from liability for defamatory comments placed online, provided they fall within one of the relevant defences.[30] Regulations 17–19 of the E-Commerce Regulations deal with this issue directly. Regulation 17 (which implements Article 12 of the original Directive) states that if an ISP is only a mere conduit for information it will be immune from an action being brought against them. Therefore, immunity will be provided as long as the ISP only transmits the information (in the same way as would a telephone line) and does not initiate, select or modify the information or keep the information for longer than is needed for the transmission. Regulation 18 (which implements Article 13) states that the service provider is not liable when it is caching this information. (Where the service consists of the transmission in a communications network of information provided by a recipient of the service, caching means automatic, intermediate and temporary storage of the information for the sole purpose of making more efficient the onward transmission of the information to other recipients of the service.) Regulation 19 (which implements Article 14) adds further immunity to an ISP, which applies if they are merely hosting the information. In other words, if they are holding the information for viewing purposes and do not have any knowledge of any unlawful activity. Immunity is lost under Regulation 19 when the ISP is made aware and has actual knowledge of unlawful activity. In these circumstances, the ISP is

---

[28] An ISP is defined in Article 2(b) of the E-Commerce Directive 2000/31/EC as "any natural or legal person providing an information society service".

[29] These regulations implemented the E-Commerce Directive 2000/31/EC and they came into force in August 2002.

[30] For a detailed consideration of ISPs and liability please see Sutter, G *Internet Service Providers and Liability* (Chapter 6) in *Human Rights in the Digital Age* Routledge Cavendish and Glasshouse Press 2006 (Edited by Mathias Klang and Andrew Murray).

required to act expeditiously to remove or disable the offending material.[31] This defence for ISPs is also lost if it becomes apparent that they have edited the comments, or have been told of their existence. Furthermore, they may still be liable if they do not take 'reasonable care' as to publication. This is problematic in itself as it tends to encourage ISPs into ignorance. If an ISP does not know what material is contained upon websites within its territory, the E-Commerce Regulations are quite clear in exempting ISPs from liability. This may encourage an ISP to purposively not look in detail at posted material. However, the case of **Godfrey v Demon Internet Limited**[32] demonstrates that the ISP defence is quite limited once an ISP has been warned that a statement that has been published contains potentially defamatory material. In this case, clearly defamatory comments about Dr Godfrey were posted on a website which was hosted by Demon Internet. Dr Godfrey reported these comments to Demon Internet and asked that they be removed. Some weeks later the comments were still available to read online and so Dr Godfrey commenced proceedings against the ISP. Demon Internet argued that they only had a purely passive role in the publication of the comments. This was rejected by the court, which stated that they held a similar position to that of a library or a bookshop and once they had been advised of the defamatory information they had a choice to either to retain the information or to remove it. Therefore, as they knew about the defamatory comments they could not rely on the defence that they only had a passive role. Even though the ISP was not the author of the statements, they were responsible for the site and were thus liable and were required to pay £15,000 in damages.[33] This decision can be contrasted with the case of **Bunt v Tilley and others**[34] in which the ISP was held to have no actual knowledge of the postings and had a merely passive role in facilitating the postings (they were accused only of providing the required connection to the Internet), therefore they could avail themselves of this defence. Mr Justice Eady made an analogy with the postal service, which provides a merely passive role in the transferring of information, and as long as the ISP continues in its passive role it cannot be deemed to be a publisher at common law. The key issue is whether the ISP had any knowing involvement in the alleged defamatory postings.[35] The case of **Kaschke v Gray**[36]

---

[31] The level of actual knowledge required is considered in Regulation 22 of the E-Commerce Regulations. Interestingly, Article 15 of the Directive 2000/31/EC made it clear that member states shall not impose a general obligation on providers, when providing the services covered by Articles 12 to 14, to monitor the information which they transmit or store, nor a general obligation actively to seek facts or circumstances indicating illegal activity.

[32] (2001) QB 201.

[33] The decision in Godfrey was subsequently supported by the decision in **Totalise Plc v Motley Fool Ltd** [2003] 2 All ER 872, but further held that ISPs must hand over the identity of the author of the defamatory comment if requested by the claimant.

[34] [2007] 1 WLR 1243.

[35] Ibid. See paragraphs 9 and 36.

[36] [2010] EWHC 690 (QB).

continued the discussion of how involved the owner of a blog can be in exercising editorial control before they could incur liability under the E-Commerce Regulations. The facts were that a comment was placed on a political blog by John Gray saying that Johanna Kaschke (a political activist) had been arrested for allegedly being linked to a terrorist organisation. Kaschke commenced an action for libel stating that although she had been arrested she had been completely exonerated of terrorist involvement. The owner of the blog, Alex Hilton, sought a summary judgment to dismiss the action, but this was rejected by the court because Hilton could not show that if the action reached the court he would be able to rely on the defence found within regulation 19 of the E-Commerce Regulations (that he was merely hosting the information). This was because although he stored the information there were questions over the extent of his editorial control, which if exercised would have meant that this defence could not be utilised. The court made some interesting points. First of all, chat rooms are information society services (as defined in regulation 2(1) of the E-Commerce Regulations) and chat room owners could rely on the defences found within the E-Commerce Regulations. Secondly, even if they had modified part of their website, they could still rely on the defence for other areas of their website, which they had not modified. However, the reason why the summary judgment to prevent the action was refused was that Hilton exercised some form of editorial control. On the website there were 'recent' and 'recommended' blogs – both of these were listed automatically by either date or votes by users, although on occasions Hilton would 'promote' a blog to a more prominent position if he thought it appropriate. He also removed postings on the grounds of bad language, political provocation or offensiveness. The difficulty with this judgment for the owner of a blog is that it seems that only the most remote or tentative amending of the relevant web pages could lead to the protection from liability being removed. The incentive for a chat room owner to modify their website to ensure respectability is severely curtailed by the threat of an action in defamation, which this case leaves open.[37] The judgment in Kaschke did consider (and can be contrasted with) the slightly earlier case of **Karim v Newsquest Media Group Limited.**[38] This case also concerned an online article purporting to report on a hearing held in the Solicitors Disciplinary Tribunal where Karim had been struck off as a solicitor. The article was entitled: 'Crooked solicitors spent money on a Rolex, loose women and drink' and contained a number of user comments at the end of the article. Karim argued that both the article and a number of the comments were defamatory in nature, and on receipt of Karim's claim, the newsgroup removed the article and the subsequent comments from the website. A similar course of action was taken by

---

[37] For more on this case see: OUT-LAW.COM *High Court ruling serves as a warning against any moderation of user comments* (8th April 2010). Available at: http://www.out-law.com/page-10902.

[38] [2009] EWHC 3205 (QB).

the Newsgroup Media Group in this case to that attempted by Alex Hilton in the Kaschke case, as they made an application for summary judgment to prevent the defamation action from being heard. Their argument was two-fold. First of all, that their article was a fair and accurate reporting of legal proceedings and therefore attracted absolute privilege, and secondly (and more important to the current discussion) that they would have defence under regulation 19 of the E-Commerce Regulations in relation to the user comments. The judge accepted both of these contentions, and in relation to the second point, confirmed that the newsgroup had no actual knowledge of the defamatory nature of the comments until Karim had pointed this out to them. As they did not have knowledge of the comments they were able to rely on the defence provided by Regulation 19. In this case, there was no prospect of Karim being successful in defamation proceedings and so the summary judgment was satisfied.

A publisher's defence is also found within section 1 of the Defamation Act 1996, also known as the secondary publisher's defence. If a person (in this case an ISP) can show that they are not the editor, author or publisher of the state-ment, they took reasonable care in its publication and they did not know or have reason to believe that what they did contributed to the publication of a defamatory statement, they will not be found liable for the statement. To determine whether a publisher took reasonable care, examination is required of section 1(5), which considers the extent of the publisher's responsibility, the nature of the surrounding circumstances and the previous conduct of the publisher.

Yet, in an Internet context, is a search engine a publisher, and thus a poten-tial target for a defamation action? If an individual enters keywords into a search engine, within a matter of seconds the relevant results will be posted, containing a title and a couple of relevant sentences from the site, which may include a copied defamatory statement. A number of sponsored links may also be highlighted by the search engine. (These are where website owners have paid for their website to be emphasised when certain keywords are entered into the search box.) This issue of search engine liability was considered in the case of **Metropolitan International Schools Ltd v Designtechnica Corp (t/a Digital Trends).**[39] The search engine, Google, was sued in the English courts by a training company based in London that offered distance learning courses. One of the available courses was called 'Train2Game'. When this title was entered into the search engine, an American online forum was picked up,

---

[39] [2009] EWHC 1765 (QB). For a case comment see: *Metropolitan International Schools Ltd (t/a SkillsTrain and t/a Train2Game) v Designtechnica Corp (t/a Digital Trends): search engines and publishers (Case Comment)* (2009) Communications Law, volume 14, issue 3, pages 100–101 and James, S & McCormack, L *Closing the floodgates – Google is granted immunity from defamation claims in landmark decision for search engines* (2010) Entertainment Law Review, volume 21, issue 1, pages 29–30.

which was very critical about the courses that were on offer by this training company. The Google search page results picked up the comments posted on this American website and included an alleged defamatory comment in its search results page. The training company sued the search engine for defamation. However, the court was of the view that the search engine was not the publisher of defamatory words, even if libellous words appeared in the search results page. Furthermore, the judge considered that the provisions in the E-Commerce Directive 2000/31/EC relating to exclusion of liability for Internet intermediaries probably covered search engines, although he did point out that both the Department of Trade and Industry[40] and the Law Commission had previously questioned whether this was the case and other European member states had different approaches to this issue.[41] The judge expressed surprise at the limited number of decisions in the courts surrounding this area of law; indeed he noted that at that time there had only been two (Godfrey v Demon and Bunt v Tilley – both discussed above) on the role of Internet intermediaries. The decision in Bunt was more closely aligned to the current case in that Google was merely a facilitator (like telephone lines) and as such was not liable. Clearly this is a very good result for search engines like Google; however the decision is somewhat different to the Bunt decision as search engines do scan webpages and highlight what they perceive to be relevant websites. There is a degree of editorial control, but it would be impossible for search engines to scan the thousands of results that they provide to ensure they are acceptable to the end user and do not contain defamatory content. Equally, there is no human involvement in this editorial operation and so there can be no perceived acquiescence to the comments by search engines, as they are merely a gateway to the resources found online. The judge made reference to the nineteenth century case of **Emmens v Pottle**[42] in which a person passing on a newspaper containing libellous comment could not incur liability unless the person knew that the publication contained defamatory statements. The advantages of the Metropolitan International Schools decision outweigh the disadvantages. If the court had found against Google, a consequence could be that they would need to make their search results pages much more circumspect and vague, with the possible removal of the 'snippets' from the suspected appropriate website to avoid defamation actions. This would make searching for websites and information much more onerous and time-consuming for the individual. Furthermore, it would be impossible for the search engine to remove all references to the defamatory statement as these

---

[40] (As it was known at the time). The majority of the DTI's functions merged into the reformed Department of Business Enterprise and Regulatory Reform (DBERR), which then (in 2009) formed part of the Department of Business, Innovation and Skills (DBIS).

[41] [2009] EWHC 1765 (QB), paragraphs 81–96.

[42] (1885) 16 QBD 354.

comments are often controlled by another individual. The judge did however commend and place considerable reliance on the fact that Google had a 'take down' policy. This means that in a situation where a legitimate complaint has been made about a website, Google takes steps to ensure the offending webpage does not appear on its search results page. The judge was silent however on whether a failure to have such a policy would lead to liability.[43]

The nature of the defence afforded to an ISP is subject to considerable debate. On the one hand it could be argued that ISPs are afforded wide protection, as they need to have actual knowledge of an unlawful activity to be found liable, not merely an idea that a comment may be defamatory. As it is not overly clear what actual knowledge or awareness amounts to (as Regulation 22 only lists a number of items that the court need to have regard to in deciding whether the ISP has actual knowledge), finding an ISP liable may be a complex procedure and it does not seem ideal to wait for case law to provide some direction. On the other hand, it could be argued to be a very narrow defence because once the ISP is informed, it is required to take steps to remove the information. In English law it is unlawful to publish a defamatory statement and so immunity from liability could be lost at a very early stage. The reality is that once an ISP is informed of defamatory statements they are likely to locate the article and remove it, particularly if the comments are about a famous individual or a large business or organisation who has a reputation to protect and money to protect it with. ISPs are a much more attractive party for a person seeking to commence a defamation action than an individual author as they are likely to have significantly more funds than the author. Reviewing the pages is in itself problematic for the ISP as the comment could be in various places in the system and they would need to spend considerable time and resources reviewing the pages and removing the comments. They would also need to review secondary publications, such as hyperlinks to mirror sites, which could contain the same comments. The task of reviewing webpages and removing comments begs the question as to the appropriateness of an ISP censoring information. Their role is as service provider, but also it seems as editor once they are advised of a defamatory comment. ISPs do not have a defence if they considered the comment to be true, privileged or fair comment, which leads us to return to the earlier comment made that ignorance may be a better course of action for the ISP than actively touring the websites within their domain trying to track down unlawful activity. In December 2002, the Law Commission published a substantial report entitled *Defamation and the Internet: A Preliminary Investigation,* in which they reviewed the law to the extent that it applied to the Internet.[44] One of their main contentions was that

---

[43] [2009] EWHC 1765 (QB), paragraphs 48–64.

[44] Law Commission Scoping Study No. 2. Available at: http://www.lawcom.gov.uk/docs/defamation2.pdf.

the law relating to the liability of ISPs for defamatory statements needed to be reviewed. The report argued that as an ISP often has more financial backing, they are a better target for an individual who wishes to bring a claim. A counter argument is that the ability for an ISP to remove a comment, regardless of its truth, could be a restriction on an individual's right to freedom of expression under Article 10 of the European Convention on Human Rights.

The approach taken by the United Kingdom to the liability of ISPs in defamation cases differs from the approach taken by America. Section 230 (c)(1) of the Communications Decency Act 1996 states that the provider or user of an interactive service shall not be treated as the publisher or speaker of any information that was provided by another individual. In other words, in the United States ISPs are given complete immunity from defamation actions. This section is defined very widely. This exclusion of liability approach taken by the United States was prompted by the case of **Stratton Oakmont Inc. v Prodigy Services Company**[45] in which the ISP was held to be liable for defamatory comments that were posted on a bulletin board. The rationale for the liability lay in the fact that they advertised that they were 'family friendly' and had editorial control, including an emergency delete button. This case was seen to be unhelpful in the development of the Internet and led to the enactment of the Communications Decency Act. The case of **Zeran v America Online**[46] is regularly stated as an example of how the Communications Decency Act protects ISPs. The facts were that a false advertisement was placed online offering merchandise arising from the Oklahoma bombings. Mr Zeran received lots of telephone calls and threats. He contacted the ISP and advised them that the advertisement was false and the ISP removed it. However, the advertisement kept reappearing. The court held that the ISP was not liable as ISP immunity was a prerequisite for ensuring the robustness of Internet communication. A number of cases have followed and supported the Zeran decision including **Blumenthal v Drudge and AOL**,[47] **Ben Ezra, Weinstein and Co. v American Online**,[48] **Lunney v Prodigy Services Company**[49] and **Schneider v Amazon.com**.[50] The first example of this liability extending to non-commercial networks was seen in **Batzal v Smith, Cremers and Museum Society Network**.[51] However, judicial support in the United States for the Zeran

---

[45] [1995] WL 323710 (N.Y. Sup. Ct. 1995). This earlier American case can be contrasted with the decision in **Cubby Inc. v Compuserve Inc** (SDNY 1991) 776 F Supp 135 in which the ISP was found not to be liable for defamatory postings as they had no editorial control.

[46] 958 F Supp 1124 (1997), affirmed 129 F 3d 327 (4th Circuit 1997).

[47] 992 F Supp 44. Interestingly, in this case the ISP was granted immunity even though they exercised a degree of editorial control.

[48] (1999) DNM.

[49] 250 A.D. 2d 230. This decision was later upheld by the Supreme Court of New York – see 94 N.Y. 2d 242.

[50] Washington Court of Appeal (17th September 2001) Case No. 46791-3-I 31 P 3d 37.

[51] (26th June 2003) No. 01-56380 DC, No CV-00-09590-SVW.

approach is not universal, as was seen in the Californian Court of Appeal case of **Barrett v Rosenthal**.[52]

User-generated content

The evolving nature of the Internet away from an information forum to a forum that allows users to generate their own content provides opportunity for authors to be the victim of a defamation claim. Wikipedia, which is authored by its readers, has been subject to various defamation and privacy claims.[53] The rise of Twitter, which allows an individual to 'tweet' their thoughts online to a global audience, is a potential minefield of defamatory claims. Twitter has attracted a large number of celebrity authors, including Stephen Fry, Jonathan Ross and Barack Obama and is popular because a posting (of up to 140 characters) can be made in real time. The problem for authors is that these microblogs can easily become subject to a defamation claim as many postings are made in the heat of the moment. Indeed, in March 2009 the Independent Newspaper reported that the singer Courtney Love appeared to ignite the first Twitter defamation action following her tweets against her former fashion designer, which alleged her to be a thief and a user of illegal substances.[54] The courts in the United Kingdom have also upheld an application for an injunction by an individual who had been impersonated on Twitter to compel the other party to identify themselves.[55] Perhaps the most high-profile incident with a defamation action arising from user-generated content (and specifically social networking sites) was in the case of **Applause Store Productions Limited v Raphael**.[56] The facts were that in June 2007 Grant Raphael set up a false profile on Facebook for his former friend, Matthew Firsht. A Facebook group was also set up called 'Has Matthew Firsht lied to you ...?' and a number of other false allegations were made, relating to his sexual preferences and his failure to pay his debts. Firsht discovered the identity of this profile in July 2007 and sought to commence a defamation action. After securing a Norwich

---

[52] 9 Cal Rprtr 3d 142 (2004).

[53] See, for instance **G v Wikipedia Foundation Inc** [2010] E. M. L. R. 14. For other examples of Wikipedia's exposure to defamation proceedings see: George, C & Scerri, J *Web 2.0 and User-Generated Content: legal challenges in the new frontier* (2007) Journal of Information Law and Technology, volume 2, especially paragraph 4.4. Available at: http://www2.warwick.ac.uk/fac/soc/law/elj/jilt/2007_2/george_scerri/.

[54] See Johnson, A & Griggs, I *Love's online spat sparks first Twitter libel suit* (29th March 2009), The Independent. See also, Murray, A *Twittering could harm your wealth* (21st February 2009), The Guardian.

[55] Cran, D & Warren, G *Service by Twitter – the UK courts embrace technology* (2010) Entertainment Law Review, volume 21, issue 2, pages 81–83. One of the more interesting aspects of this case was that the court allowed the injunction to be served via Twitter.

[56] [2008] EWHC 1781 (QB).

Pharmacal order to identify the identity of the author, a successful defamation claim was brought and Firsht was awarded £22,000 in damages. This level of damages was awarded, even though the judge could not be certain how many people had viewed the relevant Facebook pages, but based his view on the number of people who were connected to that particular profile. Conversely, simply because an article is available in an open access website, does not mean that the article has been substantially published.[57] Furthermore, in **Islam Expo Limited v The Spectator (1828) Limited and Stephen Pollard**[58] the court held that in determining whether an article that appears online is defamatory, the court can take into account hyperlinks that appear within the article to assist with the precise meaning of the statement.

Jurisdictional problems

An article or publication placed on the Internet can be read all over the world; equally, reputations cross national borders, meaning that a defamatory comment can be posted from anywhere and reach a worldwide audience. In the past, defamation actions were, generally speaking, purely in the realms of the wealthy, yet with the free flow of information that can be achieved online, any individual can find their reputation tarnished by a comment posted by someone anywhere in the world. The appropriate forum for an individual to bring an action in an international dispute is a complex area[59] and a wide variety of issues need to be examined. First of all, it needs to be considered where the alleged defamatory action took place. This increases in complexity when the approach taken to single or multiple publication actions for the defamation is considered. For instance (and as discussed earlier), English law allows for a new action each time an article is published, while the United States has the single publication rule and an action may only be brought once after the first publication.[60] Whether an article, which appears online, is published, and if so where the claimant could sue, was considered in the Australian case of **Gutnick v Dow Jones and Co. Inc.**[61] An American website alleged that Joseph Gutnick was involved in stock market manipulation and money laundering. This

---

[57] **Brady v Keith Norman** [2008] EWHC 2481 (QB). For comments on this case see: Roy, B *Online libel – open access does not amount to substantial publication* (2009) Entertainment Law Review, volume 20, issue 4, pages 159–161.

[58] [2010] EWHC 2011 (QB).

[59] See Chapter 6 – Jurisdiction and Choice of Law for more detail.

[60] The rationale for this approach almost certainly lies in the protection afforded to the First Amendment right of free speech. See the case of **New York Times v Sullivan** (1964)376 US 254; 11 L Ed 2d 686, which suggested that defamation actions were incompatible with the First Amendment right. In these types of situations in the United States it is deemed appropriate for the defamed party to exercise their freedom of speech to defend themselves.

[61] (2001) VSC 305.

website was viewed by over 500,000 people worldwide, but only 1,700 people in Australia. Even so, the Australian High Court decided that an action for defamation arose once the article was read by a third party and that the state of Victoria was an appropriate jurisdiction as Gutnick was located in that state. At the same time, Gutnick had a reputation to protect in Victoria and he was only suing in respect of the damage caused by the publication in Victoria. Once the location of publication is decided, the appropriate court needs to be located and also the choice of law needs to be determined.[62] The latter is an important point as this could have a bearing on the level of damages to which the claimant is entitled. There is also the issue of enforceability of judgments, as some countries may be unwilling to enforce a judgment given in another jurisdiction. This issue was seen in the case of **Telnikoff v Matusevitch**[63] where the claimant was awarded substantial damages for comments made in a national newspaper. When the claimant tried to enforce the judgment, it was found that the defendant had relocated in entirety to the United States. The claimant tried to enforce the judgment in the District of Columbia but the court chose instead to review the decision in the case and decided that the publication was fair comment.[64] Not only does this decision demonstrate the difficulty in enforcing a foreign judgment, it also shows the favoured approach of the United States in protecting the right to freedom of speech.

The general principle is that an English court will hear an action if the claimant has a sufficient connection to England for their reputation in England to be of concern to them. The interlinking nature of this approach with private international law is uncertain however. In **Shevill v Press Alliance SA**[65] comments were made in a French publication again Shevill, who was an English student working in Paris. The comments alleged that she had been involved in money laundering. The publication had a circulation of nearly a quarter of a million in France, while only selling a few hundred copies in England. The court decided that if an individual was potentially defamed in two European Union countries, then the person had a choice where they could sue: either in the country where the defendant was domiciled or in the country where the harm took place. In the latter option, the claimant would only be able to sue for harm that occurred in that jurisdiction. The difficulties with the apparent uncertainty over relevant jurisdiction leads to increased risks as users and service providers ostensibly need to comply with every legal system in the Internet-connected world, but as has been seen, different jurisdictions have differing approaches to defamation actions. The problem of forum shopping is also apparent, as

---

[62] This Australian case was quoted and followed in the English case of King v Lewis [2005] E. M. L. R. 45.

[63] (1992) 2 AC 343.

[64] (1997) 347 MD 561.

[65] (1995) ECR I-415.

claimants may be willing to try a case in a jurisdiction that is much more claimant-friendly (this is often termed 'libel tourism') to try to obtain higher damages.[66]

An added complexity is noted if an individual seeks to bring an action against an ISP. As discussed, ISPs receive a large degree of immunity from liability. However, in the United Kingdom there are occasions when an ISP may be liable for a defamatory comment. The E-Commerce Directive covers information society service providers and sets the general principle that an ISP is governed by the rules of the country in which they are established, or at the source of their activity.[67] Again it is unclear whether private international law is superseded, retained or reduced in its apparent uncomfortable co-existence with the E-Commerce Directive (as implemented into the United Kingdom by the Electronic Commerce (EC Directive) Regulations).[68] At first glance, the regulations seem to have a considerable effect on civil claims. Regulation 4 states that:

> "any requirement which falls within the coordinated field shall apply to the provision of an information society service by a service provider established in the United Kingdom irrespective of whether that information society service is provided in the United Kingdom or another member state."

A 'co-ordinated field' is defined broadly in Regulation 2 and it appears that defamatory actions are covered. There are a number of exceptions outlined in Regulation 3, including taxation, data protection, unsolicited commercial email, betting and real estate. Further exemptions are found within the Schedule of the regulations. Regulation 4(3) forbids an English court from applying a requirement to an international ISP if it would restrict[69] the freedom to provide information society services to a person in the United Kingdom from that member state. Regulation 5(1) sets out the derogations to this principle. These include the detection and prosecution of crime, public health and public security. The derogation which may be most closely aligned with defamation actions is likely to be public policy to prevent violations of human dignity concerning individual persons. However, these issues simply demonstrate the overall confusion in the applicability of this legislation to ISPs.

---

[66] In **Berezovsky v Michaels** (2001) 1 WLR 1004, Lord Hoffman acknowledged that the case was being brought in the United Kingdom as it was unlikely to succeed if it were taken to the United States. The new Coalition Government is seeking to bring an end to claimants bringing an action in the United Kingdom simply because there is more likelihood of success. See Ministry of Justice *Report of the Libel Working Group* (23rd March 2010). Available at: http://www.justice.gov.uk/publications/docs/libel-working-group-report.pdf and OUT-LAW.COM *Government outlines new libel law plans* (12th July 2010). Available at: http://www.out-law.com/page-11219.

[67] 2000/31/EC, Recital 22.

[68] This confusion is noted particularly within Recital 23.

[69] 'Restrict' is not defined in either the Directive or regulations.

Issues arising from online archives

The benefits of the Internet are well rehearsed, and online archives allow ready access to a multitude of articles and other information originally published months or even years earlier by news groups and other publishers willing to enhance their services (and sometimes income streams). The problem with this facility is two-fold. The first has been discussed above and is the potential for a defamation action to arise each time an online article containing a defamatory comment is accessed. The second is the problems online archives could cause to live legal proceedings. An article written about the criminal record of an individual, which is later archived in an online system, would still be accessible if this same individual subsequently appeared in court for a more recent alleged offence. This opens the possibility of a contempt of court action against the author and/or publisher. The problem of online archives and their effect on live legal proceedings was seen in the Scottish case of **HM Advocate v Beggs**.[70] In this case, William Beggs was charged with murder. During his trial, his defence team found an article online about a previous (quashed) conviction for murder. His defence argued that this amounted to contempt of court as the article commented on issues relevant to a live trial. The court rejected this as there was no evidence that the jury had accessed the article. Regardless of the final decision, this case demonstrates the complexity in this area. The Contempt of Court Act 1981 sets out a strict liability offence when a publication (spoken or written) leads to a substantial risk that the course of justice in live proceedings in question will be seriously impeded or prejudiced.[71] The nature of a 'substantial risk' was considered in the case of **Attorney-General v English**[72] where it was held that there needs to be a serious impeding of justice or prejudice in the hearing. In other words, a remote risk is not sufficient. Furthermore, in **Attorney-General v MGN Ltd**[73] the court provided a list of factors that could be considered in a contempt of court action. These include the likelihood of the publication coming to the attention of the jurors, the number of copies, prominence and circulation area of the publication and the length of time between publication and the trial. This decision was focused on newspapers as opposed to the Internet, although the principles are likely to be the same. The penalties for being found guilty under the Act are a fine and/or a prison sentence of up to two years.[74] Section 3(1) of the Act provides a defence to the charge, specifically that the proceedings were not live at the time of publication, or the author/publisher had no reason to suspect (having taken all

---

70   (2002) SLT 139.
71   Contempt of Court Act 1981, Sections 1 and 2.
72   (1983) 1 AC 116.
73   [1997] 1 All ER 456.
74   Contempt of Court Act, 1981, Section 14.

reasonable care) that the proceedings were active. Section 3(2) also provides a defence for distributors if they do not know (again, having taken all reasonable care) that the material they are distributing contains material that could lead to a contempt of court action. In both cases the task of proving this defence rests on the person who is seeking to rely on it,[75] but it is not clear how far the parties need to go to demonstrate that they have taken reasonable care. A further defence is found within section 5(5), which states that if the publication is part of a wider discussion on public affairs or public interest, and the comment is made in good faith and is merely incidental, a contempt of court action will not arise. The protection given to publications which are deemed to be in the public interest, and the changing nature of that protection, was considered by the Court of Appeal in the case of **Flood v Times Newspapers Limited**.[76] The facts were that in 2006, The Times published an article alleging that Flood (a serving police officer in the Metropolitan Police) was being investigated on suspicion of corruption. That he was being investigated was accurate, but an internal investigation by the police found no case against him. Despite this, The Times retained a copy of the original article on their website. While the judge in this case was of the view that the 'hardcopy' article attracted the defence of qualified privilege, the same could not be said of the online archive copy of the article, which remained online despite the Metropolitan Police writing to them to advise them that no case could be proven. Even though the online article had a warning at the top of the page stating (in red letters) that the contents of the article were the subject of a legal dispute, the court maintained that this did not amount to responsible journalism and the defamatory content was still available and the newspaper could no longer rely on the defence of qualified privilege. This ruling has considerable implications for those who manage online archive systems. It appears that not even a simple disclaimer advising the reader that the contents of the article are disputed is sufficient to avoid a defamation claim, which – following this judgment – can only be achieved by removing the article or at least correcting it to ensure that it is accurate.[77]

The complexities of online archives and live legal proceedings were also seen in the case of **Bedeau v London Borough of Newham**.[78] This case was an appeal from an earlier contempt of court judgment. Bedeau was a radio broadcaster and during an interview he mentioned the name of a child who was involved in Family Division proceedings. After the broadcast he placed the recording on the radio's website for general sale. An injunction was granted to

---

[75] Ibid. Section 3(3).

[76] [2010] EWCA Civ 804.

[77] For a case comment see: King, S *Gary Flood v Times Newspapers Ltd: online archives must be regularly reviewed for defamatory material* (2010) Entertainment Law Review, volume 21, issue 2, pages 79–81.

[78] [2009] EWHC 293 (QB).

remove the recording from sale, but Bedeau was unable to do this as he had got into a dispute with the website manager, who controlled the password to the site. The court partially upheld his appeal, but considered that he was still in contempt of court for failure to remove the recordings from the website.

Online archives are clearly beneficial, yet it is clearly impossible for the owner of such a site to monitor every article and every current legal proceeding to ensure they avoid potential contempt of court action. For companies to close their online archives is not desirable and will also make them less attractive than their international competitors. It is partly for these reasons that an appeal in the Flood case would not be a surprise. A balance needs to be made. In general, a large degree of trust is placed in juries that they will behave appropriately and judges are responsible for providing clear direction to this effect. Although no amount of direction will prevent a 'rogue' juror from undertaking independent research, the potential of this happening should not in itself prevent online archives from providing the valuable service which they do.[79]

Damages and abuse of process

The fact that an article has been published on the Internet and so may have been viewed by a large number of people does not necessarily mean that the level of damages awarded will be higher. Indeed, just because an article is found on the Internet does not mean that it is 'published' or has been read at common law.[80] The key factor is the extent to which the article has been viewed.[81] This principle was highlighted in the case of **John v MGN Ltd**[82] where the court unambiguously stated that the level of damages will not be higher simply because an article is placed online. A key factor will be the number of 'hits' the article has, which in many cases will be technically easier

---

[79] For more on online archives and contempt of court actions see: Johnson, H *Investigating corruption – the article and the archive, and the Reynolds defence in action: Flood v Times Newspapers Ltd* (2009) Communications Law, volume 14, issue 5, pages 157–160.

[80] **Al Amoudi v Brisard** [2006] EWHC 1062 QB. The subsequent pre-trial decision in **Brady v Keith Norman** [2008] EWHC 2481 was consistent with the Al Amoudi judgment and held that an assumption that material placed online has been read should not be made unless there is supporting evidence. This approach follows data protection case law. In **Criminal Proceedings against Lindqvist** [2004] 2 W.L.R. 1384, the European Court of Justice held that the act of simply posting personal data onto a website did not mean that the data had been transferred to a third country.

[81] A fairly high-profile case of damages concerned that of Jeremiah Barber, who posted an indecent image of a child on the Facebook page of Raymond Bryce, along with the suggestion that Mr Bryce was gay and so would like the picture. Mr Bryce was awarded £10,000 in damages, even though the image was online for less than 24 hours, as the judge Mr Justice Tugendhat suggested that hundreds of people in the local area may have seen it. See The Daily Telegraph *Law student wins £10,000 after being branded a paedophile on Facebook* (28th July 2010).

[82] [1996] 2 All ER 35.

to ascertain than a traditional newspaper. Equally, in **Michael Keith-Smith v Tracey Williams**[83] the court awarded damages for defamatory and offensive postings made by Ms Williams against Mr Keith-Smith on an Internet discussion group called 'In the Hole'. She was offered, and rejected, the opportunity to apologise and accordingly the court awarded damages of £10,000, which included both compensatory damages and aggravated damages. Interestingly, Judge MacDuff added that the reason the awarded damages were not higher was due to the fact that the article was not viewed by a wider audience; in fact only a relatively small number of people read the publication.[84] This approach was followed in the case of **Jameel v Dow Jones and Co. Inc.**[85] in which an article was published listing a number of financial donors to the Al Qaeda organisation. The claimant's name was featured on this list and so he commenced a libel action. However, the court took the view that there had been minimal damage as only five people had accessed this article (three of these hits were from his own legal team) and accordingly the case was thrown out for an abuse of process as the cost of bringing the case would fair outweigh any potential damages.[86]

The Jameel decision, particularly the abuse of process element, has been reviewed by a number of later cases. In **Mardas v New York Times Company**[87] an appeal was heard from John Mardas, who was a former associate of the Beatles. An article was written about the death of an Indian guru called Maharishi Mahesh Yogi, who was also linked to the Beatles. The article alleged that Mardas was a conman and trickster and without him the Beatles would have remained together for a longer period of time. At first instance, the court dismissed the case for an abuse of process as the online publication only had 27 hits in the United Kingdom. On appeal, Mr Justice Eady overturned the earlier decision and in turn restricted the scope of the Jameel decision. The view of the court was that it will only be in very rare circumstances that a defamation action will be dismissed for an abuse of process (including that there was no real damage in the United Kingdom). It is not appropriate for the court to play a 'numbers game' and require that a certain number of views are made of the article. Equally, simply because the article referred to an event that occurred forty years previously, this was not a bar to justice. The key consideration for the court was whether a tort had been committed within the United Kingdom jurisdiction and not whether the potential level of damages made

---

[83] [2006] EWHC 860 (QB).

[84] Ibid. Paragraph 24.

[85] [2005] EWCA 75.

[86] For a case comment on the Jameel judgment see: Hooper, D *The importance of the Jameel case* (2007) Entertainment Law Review, volume 18, issue 2, pages 62–64. The need for a threshold of seriousness to be shown by a claimant to be able to commence a defamation action was also noted by Mr Justice Tugendhat in **Thornton v Telegraph Media Group Limited** [2010] EWHC 1414 (QB).

[87] [2008] EWHC 3135 QB.

bringing an action worthwhile.[88] This view was followed by the court in **Haji-Ioannou v Dixon**[89] in which the well-known businessman Sir Stelios Haji-Ioannou sought to commence a defamation action for comments made to a Financial Times journalist by a business with whom he was negotiating. Again the audience of the alleged defamatory comments was tiny, but the court was of the view that Sir Stelios should have the right to bring a defamatory action as he had a reputation in the United Kingdom to protect, the allegations that were made were serious in nature and there was no guarantee that at trial the damages would be minimal. The view of the court was that even if the potential damages were to be less than the cost of bringing an action, this should not be a ground for striking out the application. However, in the more recent case of **Kaschke v Osler**[90] the court dismissed the defamation action because the potential damage to the reputation of the claimant was too small.

The courts appear to be adopting an incremental, case-by-case approach in discerning whether the defamatory article has been published and if an action arises. In **Christopher Carrie v Royd Tolkien**[91] the defendant (Tolkien) made comments on a blog on the website owned and operated by the claimant (Carrie). The website was set up to promote a book, which the claimant had written, where he alleged he suffered abuse at the hands of another member of the Tolkien family. The defendant in this case made a posting on Carrie's blog, containing allegations about the claimant including that he was a fraudster who had previously tried to defraud the Catholic Church. Within five hours the claimant had made an alteration to the posting (by removing an address), but left the posting substantially the same. It remained online for nearly two years. The court took the view that the claimant, by editing the comments, had acquiesced to the posting less than five hours after they had been written, and could have removed or deleted them any time after. The court considered that there was no publication in the time between when the postings were made and when they were edited and so no right of action arose. Finally, in **Budu v BBC**[92] the court rejected Budu's claim for libel in relation to three articles placed on the BBC's website. In broad terms, the articles reported the decision of a local police force to withdraw a job offer to Budu as uncertainty relating to his exact immigration status emerged. The court held that no defamatory meaning could be taken from the articles as any reader would find it almost impossible to discern that the articles referred to the claimant. In any case, the

---

[88] See case comment: Jordan, B *John Alexis Mardas v New York Times Company and John Alexis Mardas v International Herald Tribune SAS* (2009) Entertainment Law Review, volume 20, issue 4, pages 161–163.

[89] [2009] EWHC 178 QB.

[90] [2010] EWHC 1075 (QB).

[91] [2009] EWHC 29 QB. For a comment on this case see: *Libel and consent* (2009) Communications Law, volume 14, issue 1, pages 32–33.

[92] [2010] EWHC 616 (QB).

BBC had placed a Loutchansky 'warning notice' next to the text stating that the accuracy of the article was being challenged.

Reform and conclusions

The Internet has opened up a minefield of potential technological platforms which could form the basis for a defamatory comment to be posted. The courts appear to be taking an incremental approach to the liability of intermediaries, including search engines and ISPs, interpretation of the relevant jurisdiction and also the appropriateness of commencing an action. Various reforms in this area have been mooted. The introduction of a take-down procedure, mentioned above and in the Metropolitan International Schools case (which if followed could make intermediaries immune from prosecution) would remove the complex landscape of what amounts to actual knowledge of an unlawful action. This would involve an intermediary taking steps to block a website or an article once they received notice that it contained potentially defamatory comments. Questions remain unanswered, such as what constitutes notice, how specific the notice has to be and how much time the intermediary will have to act to block the article. The Liberal Democrat peer Lord Lester sought to answer some of these questions in early 2010 when he forwarded his proposal for a new libel law. Under his proposals, contained with the Libel Bill[93], an ISP would have (arguably, quite a lengthy) 14 days within which they would need to remove a defamatory publication after they had received notice. The bill also proposes that an online article should only be actionable on its first publication. Even though the Liberal Democrats are part of the Coalition Government, there is no guarantee that this will be enacted, despite both the Conservatives and the Liberal Democrats pledging to reform libel laws in the run-up to the 2010 General Election. However, this proposal does not answer the question about the appropriateness of an intermediary acting as a censor for information that may in fact be true and accurate.

A second reform idea within the United Kingdom is the adoption of the single publication rule, as followed in the United States of America.[94] This would remove the potential for an action to commence many years after the original publication of the article. However, the approach taken by the United Kingdom and the United States in terms of freedom of expression differ. While, generally speaking, the United Kingdom tends to favour the right to privacy over freedom of expression, America take the opposite approach. Introducing the single publication rule would necessitate a major sea-change in the direction of the law in balancing freedom of expression rights with privacy rights.

---

[93] Available at: http://www.out-law.com/page-11083.
[94] Firth v State of New York (2002) NY int 88.

Furthermore, problems do exist with the single publication rule as it is possible that an individual who is defamed by an article may not discover its existence until many years after publication. To prevent access to justice because an individual was ignorant of a publication appears a little perverse, particularly if that individual may still have a considerable reputation that needs to be protected. Nevertheless, the courts will continue adopting their incremental strategy in discerning the appropriateness of commencing a defamation action within the parameters of the existing rules. In 2009, the Ministry of Justice released a consultation paper on Internet libel, with a particular consideration on whether the United Kingdom should adopt a publication rule more in line with the United States of America.[95] The consultation paper invited interested parties to forward their views on whether a single publication rule should be introduced. A proposal to alter the rules in relation to online archives was also forwarded, which would retain the defence of qualified privilege in circumstances, unless the publisher had failed to alter the article after they had been notified of the harmful material. In all, 34 responses were received and the response by the Ministry of Justice was published in March 2010, with a majority (55 per cent) of the respondents favouring a shift to the single publication rule, while 29 per cent wanted the multiple publication rule maintained.[96] Reform is likely and is being championed by many in Fleet Street, although at the time of writing, no substantial proposal for altering the law in the area has been forthcoming.

Key points:

- A defamatory statement is one that lowers the reputation of a person in the view of right-minded people, or leads the claimant to be shunned or avoided.
- For an action to arise, the statement must have been made to someone other than the claimant. Furthermore, special damage must be shown if the claimant wishes to commence an action for slander.
- The Internet provides a wealth of new opportunities for defamatory statements to be made, including blogs, message boards, email and podcasts. It is presumed that comments placed online would be subject to an action in libel, although this is not certain, as seen in **Smith v ADVFN (2008)**.

---

[95] Ministry of Justice *Defamation and the Internet: the multiple publication rule* CP20/09 (September 2009). Available at: http://www.justice.gov.uk/consultations/docs/defamation-consultation-paper.pdf.

[96] Ministry of Justice Response *Defamation and the internet: the multiple publication rule* CP(R) 20/09 (23rd March 2010). Available at: http://www.justice.gov.uk/consultations/docs/defamation-internet-response-web.pdf.

- This problem is compounded by the ease by which individuals can hide their true identity with a pseudonym (**Sheffield Wednesday Football Club v Neil Hargreaves (2007)**) and the international reach of the Internet.
- In the United Kingdom, an action for defamation can arise each time an article is published (**Loutchansky v Times Newspapers Ltd (2002)**). This approach differs to that in the United States, where a defamation action may only arise from the original publication.
- Internet Service Providers are given immunity from defamation actions provided their role in the publishing comes within one of the defences provided by the E-Commerce Directive 2000/31/EC in regulations 17, 18 and 19 or the Defamation Act 1996.
- The current approach of the United Kingdom courts to search engine liability is that they should not be liable for defamatory statements (**Metropolitan International Schools Ltd v Google UK Ltd (2009)**).
- As the Internet contains vast amounts of information there is the potential that some articles could refer to live legal proceedings, which may lead to a contempt of court action (**Bedeau v London Borough of Newham (2009)**).
- The courts in the United Kingdom appear to be taking an incremental approach to deciding whether an article which appears online has actually been published (consider **John v MGN Ltd (1996)**, **Jameel v Dow Jones and Co. Inc (2005)** and **Mardas v New York Times Company (2008)**).
- Remedies for proven defamatory statements can include damages (**Michael Keith-Smith v Tracey Williams (2006)**) and invariably the requirement to publish an apology and/or correction.
- Future reforms could include a reconsideration of the single publication rule within the United Kingdom and developing a notice and take-down rule, which would place greater onus on the ISP.

Further reading:

- Armstrong, N *Blog and be damned?* (2008) New Law Journal, volume 158, issue 7321, page 387.
- Balin, R, Handman, L and Reid, E *Libel tourism and the Duke's manservant – an American perspective* (2009) European Human Rights Law Review, issue 3, pages 303–331.
- Deturbide, M *Liability of Internet Service Providers for Defamation in the US and Britain: Same Competing Interests, Different Reponses* (2000) Journal of Information Law and Technology, volume 3.
- Deveci, H *Usenet defamation: FE/HE liability* (2005) Computer and Telecommunications Law Review, volume 11, issue 5, pages 137–143.
- Harper, J *Against ISP Liability: Do ISPs have a duty to protect the world?* (Spring 2005) Telecommunications and Technology, pages 30–33.

- Karniel, Y *A new proposal for the definition of defamation in cyberspace* (2009) Communications Law, volume 13, issue 2, pages 38–46.
- Mullis, A & Scott, A *Something rotten in the state of English libel law? A rejoinder to the clamour for reform of defamation* (2009) Communications Law, volume 14, issue 6, pages 173–183.
- Tumbridge, J *Defamation – the dilemma for bloggers and their commentators* (2009) European Intellectual Property Review, volume 31, issue 10, pages 505–507.

Questions for consideration:

8.1.   What is defamation?

8.2.   What is the difference between libel and slander? Is there a clear application of how these two 'traditional' forms of defamation extend to the Internet?

8.3.   What defences are there to a defamation action?

8.4.   What reasons are there for the belief that the Internet provides fertile ground for claimants to bring defamation actions?

8.5.   Explain the single publication rule and the different approaches to this rule taken by the United Kingdom and the United States of America.

8.6.   What defences are available to an English Internet Service Provider if a defamatory statement is found on a website under its control? Does your answer differ in any way if the Internet Service Provider is located and established in New York?

8.7.   How far should Internet Service Providers be responsible for defamatory statements that are placed on pages within their control?

8.8.   To what extent do the courts in the United Kingdom adopt the approach that once a defamatory statement is posted online an action can automatically arise?

8.9.   Gaynor operates a website, which allows for people who are fans of cookery television programmes to leave messages on a message board about the recipes used and also allows members to offer one another assistance with cookery dilemmas. All members are required to sign up to the site, providing basic details about themselves, and have to agree to the terms and conditions of the website, which amongst other things requires users not to post defamatory comments on the site.

A number of users however have begun posting comments on the website about the presenters of these television programmes. Three comments in particular, which are all aimed at the chefs stated: "Chef A couldn't find an egg in a battery farm", "Chef B is a lazy, incompetent who clearly slept his way through cookery school, and probably with most of the teachers there" and "Chef C doesn't know the difference between a hand-whisk and the card game whist".

All of these postings were made by people using a pseudonym and accordingly it is not clear who wrote them. It is also uncertain whether the Internet Service Provider is aware of the comments. The chefs who are referred to in the postings are very upset and are seeking to commence a defamation order against Gaynor and the authors.

Consider the available courses of action and any potential remedies.

8.10.   'It is without doubt that the landscape for commencing defamation actions has altered dramatically with the developments introduced by the Internet and associated technologies. It is also clear that the law within the United Kingdom is currently robust and responsive enough to be able to keep up with the challenges the Internet has introduced to the arena of these defamation actions. Accordingly reform in this area is not required.'

Using case law, legislation and academic comment undertake a critical examination of the truth of above statement.

All weblinks mentioned in the text can also be found at
http://www.palgrave.com/law/rogers

9 Web 2.0 and Social Networking

This chapter will consider:

- The concepts in this area, including the nature of social networking sites and other Web 2.0 developments.
- The nature, role and purpose of social networking sites.
- The dangers posed to children through their use of social networking sites, particularly through grooming and the potential misuse of their data.
- Pertinent legal issues relating to social networking sites, particularly those concerning children, employment and data protection.

The Internet has seen a rapid development in user interaction in recent years. Websites offering the user the ability to upload videos, record opinions through blogs, wikis or Twitter and dynamically communicate with individuals have radically altered Internet usage. 'Traditional' Internet usage (termed Web 1.0) involved static websites, which allowed individuals to search different websites for information (often with the assistance of a search engine) and download the required content. This model has been replaced by a much more interactive, dynamic and user-driven approach, which allows people to chat, gamble, discuss, create, search, message, upload, download, blog and communicate.[1] Social networking sites and virtual worlds are at the forefront of this development as users are no longer simply engaging with the Internet in a passive manner, but through a huge range of media and through a tranche of different interfaces, including personal computers, mobile phones and game consoles.

---

[1] Indeed, a report by the BBC in May 2010, suggested that the activity of Instant Messaging (which lets users sends messages in real time), has significantly reduced in popularity from 14 per cent of the average time spent online per user in 2007 to 5 per cent in 2010. Part of the reason for this was the development of social networking sites that allowed users to engage in broader activities than simply Instant Messaging. See BBC News Magazine *The decline of instant messaging* (24th May 2010). Available at: http://news.bbc.co.uk/go/pr/fr/-/1/hi/magazine/8698174.stm.

Social networking sites

Social networking sites have seen exponential growth in recent years. Audience growth in sites such as Facebook[2], MySpace, Bebo, LinkedIn and Flixster has been massive, due predominately to their appeal to a range of different interest groups, including students, film experts, entrepreneurs and music fans. Reports suggested that in June 2010, one in six webpages viewed by users in the United Kingdom were on Facebook.[3] Although the functionality of each of the different social networking sites does differ, in general users can engage in an extensive range of activities. Users can create their own content, including a profile (containing some personal information) and share it with the vast audience which has also joined the site. There is ample opportunity to communicate with friends and contacts around the world, while retaining a degree of privacy by allowing only those 'accepted' as 'friends' to see your complete profile. Events can be recorded and third parties can be 'tagged', or named, in any photographs or videos that are uploaded. News can be shared, arrangements can be made and online games and quizzes can be played. Individuals can also join an interest group and share information on their interest. Social networking sites are sociologically complex and they do not conform to the traditional boundaries of time. The work and private life distinction is becoming increasing blurred, as added 'friends' could include family, friends, work colleagues, or even someone that you have never met before, and a sense of worth arises from either the number of 'friends' a social networking site user has or the number of famous people who have accepted a 'friend request'. Communicating any information on one of these sites means that the information is potentially available to any user around the world and the range of potential users is as wide as the demographics of the planet itself; there seems to be no demarcation in membership as both old and young, rich and poor have – to a large degree – an equality of online opportunity. Social networking sites are becoming a new organising system as dates, meetings, arrangements and updates can all be orchestrated through one of these sites.

The business model of each of these sites seems to be expert in its simplicity. Individuals can sign up to a site, and in doing so will provide some personal information (including name, email address, location, date of birth and perhaps even a photograph). Once the users become members they then have

---

[2] As an example, Facebook was established in 2004 by Mark Zuckerburg, a student at Harvard University. Initially it was designed to allow Harvard students to communicate with one another, but within a very short period of time students from other colleges in the area were demanding to be added to the Facebook network. In September 2006, Facebook was opened up to the international population.

[3] Clark, J *Facebook hits one in six UK page views* (10th August 2010) ZDNet News. Available at: http://www.zdnet.co.uk/news/workspace-it/2010/08/10/facebook-hits-one-in-six-uk-page-views-40089784/.

the opportunity, or even the responsibility, to invite other members to become contacts, or even invite non-members to become members so they can be added as a contact. These members can all communicate with one another as well as engaging with applications, such as IQ tests or a poker game, which are available on the website. One of the key characteristics of Web 2.0 is that it is user-driven and that websites are in competition with one another to achieve the largest number of hits, or visits, to ensure the optimum return from marketing and advertising revenue. Editorial control has diminished in importance and any user can post a video, opinion or account of an event which may be seen as factual. Web 2.0 applications depend on people; the most successful and long-standing applications are the most dynamic and appeal to a large number of people ensuring their longevity – the so-called pull of the masses.[4] Once a group of people are in contact with one another they can then share ideas, news, thoughts and opinions and while doing so will invariably provide information about their likes and dislikes, various preferences relating to a range of topics from food to music to fashion, as well as engaging in more social pursuits. As engagement with social networking sites is free at the point of entry, it is difficult to see how they are so profitable – indeed on the face of it there is no apparent profitability. Yet Microsoft still spent $240m in 2007 for a 1.6 per cent share in Facebook. The answer to this seems to lie in the advertising capability. Over time the social networking site is able to build up a profile of the user (including likes, habits, hobbies and other activities) and the people they communicate with and will be able to target advertising to that particular individual.[5]

Unsurprisingly, the advantages of social networking sites do need to be balanced with the perceived disadvantages, of which there are several. On a general level there are the instances of identity theft as criminals may be able to build up a profile of a user and be able to impersonate them or potentially even obtain goods, services or credit in their name. It would not require too much detective work for a criminal to ascertain the answers to key security questions, such as a date of birth or mother's maiden name. Equally, it is possible to be able to pass yourself off as another individual as there are very few, if any, adequate verification applications in place beyond this initial registration, meaning that there are no checks to see if the person is who they say they are.[6] A number of defamation actions have arisen due to social networking sites and there are privacy concerns.[7] There is a broad range of data protection issues

---

[4] Andrew Keen refers to these ideas as "digital Darwinism" in his excellent book *The Cult of the Amateur: How Today's Internet is Killing our Culture and Assaulting our Economy* Nicholas Brealey Publishing (2007).

[5] See Appleyard, B *Beware: Facebook's Dr Evil wants to be your closest friend* (2nd May 2010), The Sunday Times, News Review, page 5.

[6] Barnett, D *United Kingdom: Minors: online age verification* (2008) E-Commerce Law and Policy, volume 10, issue 6.

[7] See chapter 8 on defamation for more details.

with these sites and at first glance it is not clear how far and in what ways the Data Protection Act 1998 and other similar legislation applies to this context. For instance, who is responsible for the management of the processing? It may be the user or the social networking site. Privacy concerns intensify when users seek to delete their profiles, as total deletion of the web pages is the source of some considerable controversy.[8] There are two problem areas relating to social networking sites. First of all, the use of these sites by those under the age of 18 years old is contentious and full of legal implications. Secondly, the use of social networking sites by employees of a company, either during the working day or in their own time, but clearly indicating who their employer is. This chapter will continue to consider the legal implications of social networking sites in these two areas.

Use by minors

The use of social networking sites by minors is surrounded with legal implications.[9] Many of the sites are targeted at teenagers and so it is little surprise that individuals in the age range of 14–18 years old form the main user group. Social networking sites need to secure a very delicate balance between ensuring that their site is user-friendly, engaging and welcoming to the teen-age groups, while ensuring that they safeguard their reputation by providing adequate security and privacy standards.[10] The young person in the twenty-first century needs to be Internet-savvy and use of sites such as Facebook is a necessary social utility, encouraged by a strong inducement to register from within their peer group. In many cases, young people have a greater technical

---

[8] BBC News *Facebook changes privacy policy* 27th August 2009. Available at: http://news. bbc.co.uk/1/hi/technology/8225338.stm and Rushe, D *Facebook and a question of trust* (23rd May 2010) The Sunday Times, Business Section, page 10.

[9] In 2008, the Home Office Task Force on Child Protection on the Internet published a comprehensive document entitled *Good practice guidance for the providers of social networking and other user interactive services*. The document (available at: http://www.ifap.ru/library/book293.pdf) details how social networking services have developed and the problems that they have introduced and makes a series of recommendations for both users and parents on good practice, including that parents take an active involvement in monitoring the engagement of their child on Internet services and users should take greater care over safeguarding their privacy.

[10] The European Court of Human Rights has held that Article 8 of the European Convention on Human Rights also imposes positive obligations upon the state and individuals when seeking to protect the privacy of an individual. In the case of **KU v Finland** (2872/02)) (2009) 48 E.H.R.R. 52, an unknown person placed an advertisement about a 12 year old boy ('K') on an internet dating site stating that he was seeking a homosexual relationship. The service provider stated that they were bound by confidentiality when the police asked who the author of the advertisement was. On appeal to the European Court of Human Rights, the court held that although Article 8 existed to protect individuals from interference by public authorities, it also placed a positive obligation on the state to ensure that privacy could be maintained between individuals and a derogation in this case to allow 'K' to protect his privacy was permitted.

and social competence than their parents or guardians and it is this issue that causes social networking sites some problems. Terms and conditions of use often include provisions outlining that those under 18 are not permitted to sign up without parental consent (or, in some case, children below a certain age may not be able to sign up at all). However, it is difficult in the extreme to verify these conditions, particularly when a site has millions of users from a range of different countries. Verification of either age or parental consent is very difficult to definitively obtain and mechanisms such as asking a person under 18 to 'tick a box' to demonstrate that their parents have consented to their use of the site can be easily circumvented by the minor and it is very difficult for the social networking site to prove otherwise. Some technical capabilities to verify age do exist, such as installing cookies which prevent the inputting of false information, various parental monitoring packages and systems that monitor network usage to highlight language and interests akin to that of a minor under the age of thirteen. While a minor may be socially and technically competent the same may not be the case with their legal competency. The law in the United Kingdom stipulates that those under the age of 18 may avoid contracts.[11] As those in the 14–18 age group are the main users, it may be that the terms and conditions to which these users are 'signing up' to are invalid for their purposes. To date, this is uncertain. However, websites do need to ensure that they take privacy and security settings seriously and outline the options in a teenage-friendly manner. Other dilemmas that exist for social networking sites which engage with minors are wide-ranging. The potential for advertisements and other publicity advocating self-harm, eating disorders, unhelpful content and other dangerous activities to reach adolescents is obvious.[12] Equally obvious is that the openness of these sites to all people provides a forum for adult abusers of children to contact and try to build a relationship with a minor. Paedophiles are able to take advantage of the anonymity available and the lack of consistent monitoring to communicate with children – so-called grooming.[13] This is an offence under the Sexual Offences Act 2003, which states that a person over the age of 18 commits an

---

[11] Minors' Contracts Act 1987.

[12] A disturbing case was reported in June 2010, where 18 year old Salum Kombo was fatally stabbed in East London after he had allegedly traded insults on Facebook with his eventual killer, who was aged 16. A conviction for murder was upheld and the perpetrator (who could not be named for legal reasons) was detained for 14 years. See: BBC News *Boy detained for Facebook insult murder in London* (22nd June 2010). Available at: http://news.bbc.co.uk/1/hi/england/london/10372678.stm.

[13] Facebook and the United Kingdom's Child Exploitation and Online Protection Centre (CEOP) reached a compromise in July 2010 to allow an application to be added to the Facebook pages of those between the ages of 13–18, which will allow users to be able to click on a link, which will direct them to CEOPs advice and reporting centre. The aim behind the initiative is to make use of Facebook safer for those under the age of 18. For more on this story see the CEOPs Press Release *Facebook and CEOP join forces to deliver internet safety to young internet users* (12th July 2010). Available at: http://www.ceop.police.uk/mediacentre/pressreleases/2010/ceop_12072010fb.asp.

offence if (having met or communicated with a person under the age of 16 on at least two earlier occasions) they intentionally meet, or travel with the intention of meeting the person under the age of 16, with the intention of committing an offence against the minor. The potential offences are listed in Schedule 3 of the Act and include rape, intercourse with a girl under 16, indecent assault and incest. The maximum available sentence available for grooming is ten years' imprisonment.[14] The first case where an adult male was found guilty of grooming a girl under the age of 16 was **R v Patrick Steven Green**.[15] In this case, 33 year old Mr Green made contact with a 12 year old girl through an Internet chat room. This communication soon developed into emails and telephone conversations. This grooming led to the girl physically meeting Green and later being sexually assaulted. In October 2000 he was sentenced to five years' imprisonment, which was reduced to two and a half years on appeal. The case of **R v Mansfield**[16] was a further case based on section 15 of the Sexual Offences Act. The facts were that the defendant (a 42 year old man) posed as a 17 year old boy in an Internet chat room. He initiated communication with a 13 year old girl. Despite her mother finding sexually explicit messages on her mobile telephone and contacting the defendant to warn him off (although he was able to pass himself off as a 17 year old to the victim's mother), he continued this communication and the defendant and the victim met on two occasions and they engaged in sexual activity. The court held that even though the victim was compliant and not inexperienced, the law was there to protect young children and so Mansfield was sentenced to three years and nine months' imprisonment. The principles in the Mansfield case were applied in **R v Mohammed (Raza)**,[17] which had a very similar set of facts, although the 13 year old girl in the latter case had significant learning difficulties and behavioural problems. Accordingly a sentence of three years and six months was not held to be, on appeal, excessive, but demonstrated that the law was in place to protect children from older men who took advantage of their vulnerability. The approach taken in the last two cases can be contrasted somewhat with the decisions in **R v Barnett (Graham)**[18] and **R v Cortillo (Luis)**.[19] This Barnett case concerned a 46 year old man who posed as a 17 year old in a chat room aimed at teenagers. He built up a relationship with a girl who said she was 12 years old, but was in fact an undercover investigative newspaper journalist. Barnett sent a number of sexually explicit messages and met whom he thought to be the 12 year old girl (but was in fact a young-looking colleague of the journalist). The grooming continued until the newspaper

---

14 Sexual Offences Act 2003, Section 15.
15 [2001] EWCA Crim 642.
16 [2005] EWCA Crim 927.
17 [2006] EWCA Crim 1107.
18 [2007] EWCA Crim 1625.
19 [2009] EWCA Crim 216.

exposed him. His sentence (originally 30 months) was reduced on appeal to 18 months as there was no child involved and the defendant had experienced humiliation arising from his national exposure. A similar set of facts were present in the Cortillo case, where a retired police officer posed as a 12 year old girl in an Internet chat room, and the defendant initiated communication with her. As in the Barnett case, Cortillo sent a number of sexually explicit messages including that he wanted to have sexual intercourse with the girl. He was subsequently arrested and sentenced to ten years, which was reduced to 18 months on appeal. It seems a tad perverse that a sentence should be reduced (in part) if the defendant was not actually communicating with a minor. In both the Mansfield and Mohammed case, the judges expressly stated that the law was to protect children from adults seeking to take advantage. It is suggested that the impossibility of an offence against a child taking place (by virtue of the communication being with another adult) should have little or no bearing on the sentence imposed by the court. In other areas of criminal law, for instance attempted drug smuggling[20] or causing or inciting a child under 13 to engage in sexual activity[21], the impossibility of the offence being carried out does not negate liability. It needs to be queried why sentencing was reduced in the Barnett and Cortillo cases. The issue of sentencing was also considered by the Court of Appeal in **R v Geoffrey David Dennis**.[22] In this case, the appellant pleaded guilty to two offences following sexual grooming. He had contacted a 14 year old girl called 'Helen' (who unbeknown to him was a specially trained police officer who had created the profile) and asked her a range of sexually explicit questions. They arranged to meet, and on his arrival at the meeting place he was arrested. His appeal was based on the sentence he received and he argued that a custodial sentence was inappropriate as he did not pose a risk to public protection, as his behaviour was out of character. The appeal was allowed based on completion of sexual offender treatment and probation reports. It is important to note that the grooming of children is not always of a sexual nature, as there are suggestions that children are being groomed by terrorist organisations.

Grooming is not the only potentially criminal action which can affect children engaged in these websites. Cyber-bullying can also affect children. This is where an individual (or group of people) deliberately sets out to bully, tease or abuse another person online. This could be achieved through intimidation, impersonation, posting images of bullying incidents, stealing a password to take over a website or through simple exclusion.[23] Due to the significantly

---

[20] **R v Shivpuri (Pyare)** [1987] AC 1.
[21] **R v Jones (Ian Anthony)** [2007] EWCA Crim 1118.
[22] [2008] EWCA Crim 2954.
[23] The problem of online abuse, harassment or bullying is not contained to minors and often 'high profile' celebrities are the victims of Internet abuse. In September 2009, the boxer Amir Kahn and his promoter Frank Warren threatened legal action to compel Facebook to remove abuse and rascist

broader reach of the Internet, the available audience is much wider and there is no real hiding place from the bullying, as perhaps there could be in physical bullying. There have been couple of high-profile and tragic examples of cyber-bullying in the United States of America. In October 2006, 14 year old Megan Meier hanged herself following online bullying. She had suffered from self-esteem problems as a child and during 2006 she built up a relationship with a 16 year old boy called 'Josh Evans' on the social networking site MySpace. Although this started off very positively, the messages she was receiving from Josh turned nasty and suggested that she was fat, ugly and had no friends.[24] These messages continued for a while and despite her parent's best efforts to remove her from the site, Megan tragically hanged herself from her wardrobe. On investigation the police found that the profile of Josh Evans had been deleted and the individual did not actually exist. It was discovered later that the person responsible for setting up the profile and sending the messages was a friend that Megan had fallen out with. This girl was assisted by her mother Lori Drew, who was indicted in the United States in 2008 for three offences under the Computer Fraud and Abuse Act,[25] which is an offence barring people from accessing a computer without authorisation and is usually used against hackers. This offence has a maximum of five years, although no criminal action in relation to the death of Megan Meier was brought.[26] Another tragic story was that of Ryan Patrick Halligan, who after struggling with being bullied online built up a relationship with another individual who was depressed. This other person advised Ryan that the only worthwhile thing he could do was to end his life. Ryan hanged himself shortly after this conversation.[27] These two examples demonstrate the worst consequences of cyber-bullying.[28] Coupled with websites that advocate personal destructive behaviours (such as self-harm, drug misuse and suicide) there are a variety of potentially dangerous websites readily accessible to young people.

With these dangers in mind, the European Commission published in February 2009 a document entitled 'Safer Social Networking Principles for the EU'.[29] This document was authored by the European Commission with the

---

comments about the pair of them. See Jamieson, A *Amir Khan and Frank Warren launch legal bid to force Facebook to remove 'racist' content* (10th September 2010), The Daily Telegraph.

[24] For a fuller account of this tragic story, see: The Megan Meier Foundation website: http://www.meganmeierfoundation.org/.

[25] 18 USC 1030(a)(2)(c).

[26] See Case Comment *United States: Criminal Law – Computer Misuse* (2009) Computer and Telecommunications Law Review, Volume 15, Issue 3, N71 and *United States: Criminal Law – Computer Crime* (2008) Computer and Telecommunications Law Review, Volume 14, Issue 7, N203.

[27] See *Ryan's Story* available at: http://www.ryanpatrickhalligan.org/.

[28] Further discussion on this topic can be located in chapter 11 on cyber-harassment and online pornography.

[29] Available at: http://ec.europa.eu/information_society/activities/social_networking/docs/sn_principles.pdf.

assistance of a large number of social network providers, as well as non-governmental organisations and researchers. The document provides seven good practice recommendations with the aim of enhancing the safety of children online. The principles are not legally binding, but provide a benchmark against which providers can measure themselves against. The seven principles are:

1. To raise awareness of safety education messages and acceptable use policies, and present them in a clear and age-appropriate manner.
2. To work towards ensuring that services are age-appropriate for the intended audience.
3. To empower users through tools and technology.
4. To provide a user-friendly mechanism to report inappropriate content or conduct.
5. To expeditiously respond to reports of inappropriate content or conduct.
6. To encourage users to employ a safe approach to personal information and privacy.
7. To assess the means to review illegal or prohibited conduct or content.

The document provides more detail on how these principles are to be achieved, including the provision of a 'report abuse' button, ensuring that the privacy settings are always prominent and accessible and having the privacy default for those under the age of 18 set at 'private' and preventing those under the age of 13 from using the service. In Annex II of the document, a self-declaration form is included where social network providers can declare the extent to which they are complying with the principles. These principles are clearly a useful addition to other bodies that are in existence to protect children online. One such body is the Internet Watch Foundation (IWF)[30], which was established in 1996. This is a non-governmental body, funded by the European Union and by those in the online industry. It provides a hotline which allows people to report websites and Internet content that is potentially illegal. In partnership with the police and other law enforcement agencies the IWF will then inform all British Internet Service Providers once they locate illegal content, thereby depriving those providers of the legal excuse that they were unaware of the relevant material. The police will then be entitled to take action against any ISP which does not remove any material the IWF has requested them to remove. A second body set up to tackle online abuse of children is the Child Exploitation and Online Protection Centre.[31] This organisation seeks to assist the police and other law enforcement agencies in tracking down and bringing perpetrators of online child abuse to justice. They place a high emphasis on intelligence to ensure that the information they hold is current

---

[30] See: http://www.iwf.org.uk.
[31] See: http://www.ceop.gov.uk.

and work towards understanding the criminological reasons behind the actions of the offenders to try to eradicate the problem.

A number of other difficulties arise with the use of social networking sites by minors. Some sites allow users to 'tag' photographs which are placed online. In other words, to name people who are captured by a photographer and also to place a comment about them or the event. Both members and non-members can be 'tagged' and users can cross reference to pages belonging to another user, perhaps without their knowledge. The Data Protection Act 1998 is clearly relevant, although the extent to which this is the case is not definitively clear. Although data is being processed, the Act is silent as to age. Put another way, it is not clear whether a minor can legally consent to their data being processed. What is clear however is that social networking sites need to be particularly careful if they target and collect information from children. In 2007, the Information Commissioner published a Good Practice Note entitled 'Collecting personal information using websites'.[32] Part of this guidance was aimed at websites collecting information from children. The view of the Information Commissioner is that stronger safeguards should be in place to ensure that children are subject to fair processing. The guidance includes requirements that privacy notices be written and displayed in a way which is appropriate to a child's understanding, and that parental consent should be obtained if a website is collecting or displaying a child's personal information or intends to transfer the data to a third party (although, as discussed, verification of this consent is difficult to obtain). In these circumstances, the suggestion is that if verifying consent would be a disproportionate exercise for the website to undertake, the activity requiring the personal data should not be undertaken. Further, the Information Commissioner is of the view that information about third parties should not be collected from children and that competitions that require a child to divulge personal information should not be run.

Use by employees

The use of social networking sites by employees is a potential legal minefield.[33] There is the simplistic problem of employees wasting time online, instead of

---

[32] Information Commissioner's Office Good Practice Note *Collecting personal information using websites* (June 2007) Available at: http://www.ico.gov.uk/upload/documents/library/data_protection/practical_application/collecting_personal_information_from_websites_v1.0.pdf.

[33] Although this element of the chapter focuses upon the use of social networking sites by employees, it needs to be noted that problems in this area are not restrained to employer–employee relationships. A further example of the difficulties in this area was noted in 2008, where a juror listening to a sexual assault case posted comments on Facebook asking her friends to comment on whether they thought that the defendant was guilty. The juror was dismissed from the case. See: *Juror shares trial details on Facebook* (24th November 2008), The Guardian.

focusing on their work. Further problems exist as social networking sites are fertile ground for intellectual property or confidentiality leaks, data security breaches, harassment or bullying among staff and even damage to a company's reputation. The latter issue has seen a number of high-profile examples of employees having their contract of employment terminated for airing grievances online. Towards the end of 2008, Virgin Atlantic dismissed 13 cabin crew employees who had made disparaging comments about the safety and condition of the aeroplanes and insulted customers on the social networking site Facebook.[34] Similar disciplinary problems have been experienced by companies such as Argos and British Airways and public bodies such as the Metropolitan Police. In February 2010, Vodafone had to apologise to thousands of their customers on Twitter after one of their customer service representatives posted an obscene message on the blogging service. Vodafone uses Twitter to deal with customer complaints and one of its employees posted a comment that led to over 8,000 customers contacting the company asking whether they had been hacked into. The employee was suspended from their post.[35] However, social networking sites do have advantages within companies, and there is a split between companies that try to curtail the usage of social networking sites due to some or all of the problems mentioned above and those companies that fully embrace the applications, seeing their potential for marketing, internal communication and human resource management within the organisation. As more and more friendships are built up online, social networking sites are seen as a natural method to make acquaintances and build friendships; it is a medium to which an increasing number of people are becoming accustomed. Accordingly, by embracing the technology, relationships among staff within the firm could be strengthened by allowing liberal usage, within certain parameters. Many companies find themselves in a dilemma by wanting to protect the integrity and reputation of the company, while at the same time seeking to utilise the advantages provided by Web 2.0. Ensuring that an adequate policy regarding Internet usage is in place is a necessary first step. This policy should include whether employees are permitted to use these sites during working hours (including statutory rest periods) or whether such use is banned; if use is permitted, whether there are any restrictions in place as to what can be accessed or downloaded; whether any monitoring of Internet use is in place; whether a corporate email address can be used on a private personal profile; and also the penalties available to the employer if the policy is breached. This policy should be advertised on a staff intranet and other avenues of communication to ensure that it is known about by all employees.

---

[34] OUT-LAW.COM news release *Virgin Atlantic sacks 13 over Facebook comments* 4th November 2008. Available at: http://www.out-law.com/default.aspx?page=9554.

[35] Wray, R *Vodafone suspends employee after obscene tweet* 5th February 2010, The Guardian.

The implemented policy should complement a range of legislation that is applicable to this context. The Data Protection Act 1998 is of obvious relevance as the Act concerns the protecting of personal data, while the Human Rights Act 1998 is also of significance in this area in relation to the freedom of expression/right to a private life debate. In some circumstances, employers have the right to monitor Internet and email usage of employees, subject to the provisions in the Regulation of Investigatory Powers Act 2000 and also the Law Business Practice Regulations 2000.

Employee usage and monitoring

Employers may have a range of reasons for wanting to monitor the online activities of their employees.[36] They may wish to ensure that the company or organisation's brand and reputation is protected by ensuring that no defamatory, inaccurate, price-sensitive or secret commercial information is released, either inadvertently or intentionally. Employers may also consider monitoring to be necessary to safeguard the security and privacy of the computer network and also to try to avoid vicarious liability claims. The vicarious liability of an employer for employees engaged in online activity was an issue for the Employment Appeal Tribunal in **Moonsar v Fiveways Express Transport Ltd**.[37] In this case, the appellant appealed against an earlier judgment, which did not uphold her allegation of sex discrimination. The complaint of sex discrimination arose from events during evening shifts, where her male colleagues downloaded pornography on to a computer while the appellant was in the room. The Employment Appeal Tribunal reversed the earlier decision saying that even though the appellant had not complained at the time, the employer was still vicariously liable for the acts of the male employees and the allegation of sex discrimination was proven. The starting point for examining whether employee monitoring is permitted is the Regulation of Investigatory Powers Act 2000, which replaced the Interception of Communications Act 1985 and was introduced to provide a legislative landscape for intercepting communications and providing a framework for legitimate surveillance. Section 1 of the 2000 Act sets out the offence of intentionally and without lawful authority intercepting a communication transmitted by means of a public telecommunications system. The application of this Act extends to interference with a telecommunications system to make the contents available to someone other than the sender or recipient during transmission and also

---

[36] According to a report in 2008, nearly two-thirds of employers monitor the online activities of their staff, rising to 86 per cent in local government and 88 per cent in the police. See: Carvel, J *Most employers restrict staff time on internet, says survey* (2nd December 2008), The Guardian.

[37] [2005] I.R.L.R. 9.

applies to the recording of a transmission to be read or viewed at a later time. The offence carries an available sentence of two years.[38] Section 2 of the Act explains that a person is intercepting a communication if they are modifying or interfering with the system or its operation or monitoring the transmission made by means of the system. Various exceptions to the default position are found further on into part one of the Act. Section 3 deals with lawful interception without an interception warrant, while section 4 addresses the power to provide for lawful interception. Accordingly, the ability for an employer to monitor the Internet use of an employee is legitimate if they hold a reasonable belief that both the sender and recipient have consented.[39] A second option for a business to be able to legitimately monitor Internet usage is found within the Telecommunications (Lawful Business Practice) (Interception of Communications) Regulations 2000. These regulations state that businesses may monitor and record communications to establish the existence of facts to ascertain compliance with regulatory or self-regulatory practices or procedures or to ascertain or demonstrate standards which are or ought to be achieved: in the interests of national security; to prevent or detect crime; to investigate or detect unauthorised use of telecommunications systems or to secure, or as an inherent part of, effective system operation. The interception must be solely for the monitoring or recording of communications relevant to the business and it is essential that employers make all reasonable efforts to inform their staff that the monitoring is about to be carried out. It should be sufficient to include an email/Internet statement with such a clause or include a section in the contract of employment highlighting that monitoring may take place.[40] Interestingly the business is only required to make all reasonable efforts to inform the employees of the interception and there is no requirement that the employees consent to the monitoring. Businesses may also monitor but may not record received communications to determine whether they are business or personal communications and communications made to anonymous telephone helplines.[41] Accordingly, if an employer wishes to monitor their employees there are two available routes to ensure that the action is legally carried out. First of all, by a reasonable belief that the sender and the recipient have consented to the monitoring, and secondly under the Law Business Practice Regulations.

Implications for employee monitoring also arise from the Data Protection Act 1998. It is clear that from the wide definition of processing contained within the Act, the act of monitoring would be included.[42] It is likely that a large

---

[38] Section 1(7).
[39] Section 3(1).
[40] Lawful Business Practice Regulations, regulation 3(2).
[41] Lawful Business Practice Regulations, regulation 3(1).
[42] Data Protection Act 1998, Section 1(1).

proportion of the data processed would be classified as personal data. Accordingly, as an organisation that processes personal data it would need to register with the Information Commissioner. By virtue of registering with the Information Commissioner and aligning itself with the provisions of the Data Protection Act, the organisation would need to follow the eight Data Protection Principles, which are located in Schedule 1 of the Act. In abbreviated form these principles are that data must be processed fairly and lawfully; data should be processed for limited purposes; the data held should be adequate, relevant and not excessive; data should be accurate and kept up to date; data should not be kept for longer than necessary; it should be processed in accordance with the data subject's rights; data should be kept secure using technical and organisational methods and finally the data should not be transferred to a country outside of the European Economic Area that does not have an adequate level of protection.[43] Arguably the key principle which relates to the monitoring of employees is principle one, which states that data must be processed fairly and lawfully. The processing is fair if a condition from Schedule 2 or Schedule 3 (if sensitive personal data is being monitored) is met. The consent of the data subject is the main ground for ensuring that data is fairly and lawfully processed, however this would impose an additional requirement for the employer over the Telecommunications (Lawful Business Practice) (Interception of Communications) Regulations 2000, which simply requires the employees to be notified of the monitoring. Other conditions for permitted processing that could be of relevance in this context include the third principle, which is that the processing is necessary for the data controller to ensure that they are complying with any legal obligations and the sixth condition, which allows processing that is necessary for the legitimate interests of the data controller. It is probable that ensuring that employees are working effectively and are not damaging the reputation of the business in any way could be held to be a legitimate interest. Furthermore, if the processing does cover sensitive personal data, the Schedule 3 condition that would be most relevant to ensure that the data is being processed fairly and lawfully is the second principle, which states that processing sensitive personal data is legitimate for the purposes of exercising or performing any right or obligation imposed on the data controller in connection with employment. It seems that the Data Protection Act does not outlaw monitoring, although does provide parameters in which it should operate. Employees should be advised of the monitoring (there are very few occasions where covert monitoring would be permitted) and employers should also consider any adverse impact on the workers caused by the monitoring. If an adverse impact is noted, it is the responsibility of the employer to justify this impact. Additionally, any personal information which is collected during a

---

[43] For more detail on these eight Data Protection Principles, please see chapter 7 on Data Protection.

monitoring exercise should not be used by the employer unless it reveals criminal behaviour or gross misconduct, which a reasonable employer could not ignore. There have been a couple of cases within the United Kingdom, which have reached the European Court of Human Rights in relation to employee monitoring. In **Halford v United Kingdom**[44] Halford became Assistant Chief Constable for Merseyside Police in 1983. She subsequently made numerous attempts for promotion which were always refused, eventually leading to her commencing a sex discrimination action against her employers, as Halford was of the view that her rebuttals at promotion were due to her gender. After winning her case, Halford brought a subsequent action against the government and her employers under Article 8 of the European Convention on Human Rights, which states that everyone has the right to respect for his private and family life, his home and his correspondence. Halford alleged that during the earlier case she had been the victim of telephone tapping by her employer, who had tried to obtain information about her which could harm her case. The European Court of Human Rights upheld Halford's complaint and held that even though the majority of the telephone monitoring was through her work telephone, several of these calls were of a personal or private nature meaning that her Article 8 right had been violated. This case does not however prevent employers from monitoring the activities of their employees and was decided on a narrow set of facts. Although Halford was not advised of the monitoring, she was told that she could use the work telephone to further her earlier sex discrimination case.[45] The issue relating to work place monitoring was developed in the case of **Copland v United Kingdom**.[46] In this case, the complainant was employed in a college of further education and she complained that she was being subjected to monitoring of her telephone, email and Internet usage at work. The monitoring of the telephone calls was carried out by the employer to ensure that too many personal calls were not being made, while email addresses were being monitored, along with the time they were sent and websites were also being monitored to see the actual website visited, the time and the date. No monitoring policy existed within the college and Copland alleged that there had been a breach of her Article 8 right under the European Convention of Human Rights. The European Court of Human Rights upheld the decision in Halford and held that telephone calls – even if made from a work telephone – were still to be afforded protection under Article 8. The same principle was applied for emails and Internet usage. As there was no policy in force and Copland did not know

---

[44] (1997) 24 E.H.R.R. 523.

[45] For a case comment see: *Employee's privacy breached by employer's monitoring* (24th April 2007), The Times. Available at: http://business.timesonline.co.uk/tol/business/law/reports/article1695516.ece.

[46] (62617/00) (2007) 45 E.H.R.R. 37.

that she was being monitored it was held that there was a breach of Article 8 in this circumstance.[47]

A secondary issue with employees utilising social networking services is the ownership of the contacts obtained. A standard contract of employment states that discoveries, business secrets and methods, intellectual property rights and confidential information remain the property of the employer. Whether this extends to contacts obtained through a social networking site was part of the issue considered in the pre-action disclosure application in **Hays Specialist Recruitment Limited v Mark Ions**.[48] The facts were that for over six years Mark Ions was employed as a management consultant by Hays Recruitment Agency. After his employment came to an end he set up his own employment agency, Exclusive Human Resources Limited, which was a competitor to Hays. During his notice period (where he was not allowed to work for the firm) Hays noticed that Ions invited a number of clients by email to join his personal 'LinkedIn' professional network during this time. Hays actively encouraged its employees to use this website as it was seen to be a useful tool in engaging with potential clients. The allegation by Hays was that Ions added contacts obtained during his employment to his own LinkedIn account for his use after he had established his new company. Hays sought disclosure of all clients he had obtained during his new business. Ions presented an interesting argument by saying that it was not his inviting people to become his contacts that resulted in their information becoming available to him on LinkedIn, but their acceptance. The court rejected this argument saying the email address of the contact in itself was confidential and decided that disclosure should be limited to business contacts Ions had obtained during his employment with Hays (including emails sent or received through his LinkedIn account) and also any documentation demonstrating his use of the LinkedIn contacts in his new business. Although this was a pre-trial hearing, it provides an interesting insight into the view of the courts when considering social networking site usage that blurs the private and personal with employment and also provides guidance to employers who encourage their employees to make use of social networking websites.

Broader data protection implications

In all social networking usage, data protection implications remain a constant thread. Yet, the extent to which, and in what circumstance, the Data Protection Act applies and the rules relating to the publication of personal data by an individual on a website are not very clear. Issues as to the applicability of

---

[47] For a case comment see: *Telephone, email and internet monitoring* (2007) Communications Law, volume 12, issue 3, pages 102–103.
[48] [2008] EWHC 745 (Ch).

the Act and other surrounding legislation are unclear, particularly with many websites established outside of the European Community. Furthermore, notwithstanding this issue (and presuming that the Data Protection Act is relevant to social networking sites) the technical competency of the Act is unclear. For example, should the data controller be the social networking site or the person who places their profile on to the system? Under the Act, the data controller is the person who is responsible for determining the purposes and manner in which the data is processed. He has additional responsibility for notifying the Information Commissioner that personal data is being processed and the reasons for its processing. In a social networking context, whether the website is the data controller or the user is the data controller is a matter of conjecture.[49] Other concerns surround the use of cookies and targeted advertising.

In 2009, the Article 29 Working Party published an opinion on online social networking.[50] The Article 29 Working Party was established under Article 29 of the Data Protection Directive 95/46/EC and acts as an independent European advisory body on privacy and data protection. The working party is composed of representatives from each of the member states' regulatory bodies and was established to provide opinion and assessment on measures to safeguard rights and freedoms.[51] The opinion provided by the Article 29 Working Party is an opinion and has no binding authority, although it states that the Data Protection Directive 95/46/EC does apply to social networking sites, even if the headquarters of the provider are outside of the European Community. Their contention is based on the fact that equipment used for direct marketing purposes (such as cookies) are located in the European Community meaning that the Directive obtains jurisdiction. They also refer to an earlier opinion they made in 2008 on data protection issues relating to search engines which stated that establishment and use of equipment are the key factors in ascertaining applicability.[52] By using equipment located within the European Community, the Data Protection Directive applies when personal data is being processed. The working party's opinion on social networking also states that the Privacy and Electronic Communications Directive 2002/58/EC is applicable, as is the Data Retention Directive 2006/24/EC, if they offer additional services, which fall within the definition of electronic communication services found in Article 2(c) of the Framework Directive 2002/21/EC.

---

[49] See Wong, R *Social networking: a conceptual analysis of a data controller* (2009) Communications Law, volume 14, issue 5, pages 142–149.

[50] Article 29 Data Protection Working Party *Opinion 5/2009 on online social networking* (June 2009) 01189/09/EN WP 163. Available at: http://ec.europa.eu/justice/policies/privacy/docs/wpdocs/2009/wp163_en.pdf.

[51] See Directive 95/46/EC, Article 30 for a comprehensive list of functions.

[52] Article 29 Data Protection Working Party *Opinion 1/2008 on data protection issues relating to search engines* (April 2008) 00737/EN WP 148. Available at: http://ec.europa.eu/justice/policies/privacy/docs/wpdocs/2009/wp163_en.pdf.

The working group also considered the identity of the data controller in the social networking context. Their view was that the social networking providers should be classified as the data controllers as they provide the means for the data to be processed and also have a user-management role. They are further responsible for registration and deletion of accounts, they allow third parties to introduce tools and other applications to enable users to engage in a variety of different ways and they also determine (or use) the data collected for marketing purposes, including by potentially providing the information to third parties. As a data controller, they would need to follow the relevant data protection legislation, including adherence to the eight Data Protection Principles. Equally, those who provide applications for users to engage with may be considered to be data controllers (in addition to the social networking site itself), if those applications are in addition to those already available on the site. The issue of whether a user could be classified as a data controller was also discussed and the conclusion of the working party was that the majority of users should not be classified as data controllers. The rationale provided for this is that Article 3(2) of Directive 95/46/EC states that the Directive is of no relevance to people who are engaging in a purely personal or household activity – the so-called household exemption. The difficulty with this view is that it offers a very restrictive view of the use of social networking sites and this leads to a possible conflict with the European Court of Justice's decision in **Criminal Proceedings against Lindqvist** (the Bodil Lindqvist case).[53] The presumption by the working party in saying that the household exemption is applicable to users is that users are only operating in a personal sphere; however there is occasionally a blurring between private use and use to provide a service. In circumstances where the user does provide a service or is acting on behalf of a company, then they may become a data controller, but arguably it is not clear when a user goes beyond the pursuing of a purely personal activity and therefore comes within the remit of the legislation. It is submitted that, were this element of the opinion to be adopted, it would be a fertile ground for litigation. The Bodil Lindqvist case is an example of the difficulties in this area. In 1998 Mrs Lindqvist, a church volunteer in Sweden, set up a website with information about herself, her husband and other members of the parish. The aim of the site was to assist parishioners in finding out the information they needed. Along with names, she included reference to their jobs and hobbies, and occasionally the family circumstances. The information also included telephone numbers and other personal information and in one circumstance referred to the injured foot of one of her colleagues, meaning that this person could not work full-time. Mrs Lindqvist had not told or obtained the consent of her colleagues who were mentioned on the site, for permission to process their

---

[53] Case C-101/01 [2004] 2 W.L.R. 1385.

data in this way. Further, the Datainspektion (the Swedish data protection regulator – an equivalent body to the United Kingdom's Information Commissioner) had not been notified of the processing. Even though the website was removed swiftly after Mrs Lindqvist discovered that some of her colleagues were unhappy with the creation of the website, she was prosecuted for setting it up, was found guilty of processing data (including sensitive data) by automated means without notifying the relevant body and for transferring data out of the European Economic Area. Mrs Lindqvist was fined. She appealed and her case was referred to the European Court of Justice. They considered seven different questions, including whether the mention of a name and telephone number on an Internet home page comes within Directive 95/46/EC, whether placing information on a website automatically means that the data has been transferred to a third country and also, importantly for the current discussion, whether loading such information on to a website is exempt from the provisions of the Data Protection Directive by virtue of falling within one of the exemptions in Article 3(2). The European Court of Justice held that the 'household exemption' found within Article 3(2) only extends to the private or family life of the individual. The judgment referred to Recital 12, which gives examples of personal or domestic use, including correspondence and keeping a record of addresses, and therefore placing all the information online as Mrs Lindqvist did meant that her activities fell within the provisions of the Data Protection Directive.

This decision seems to leave the position of a user of a social networking site in a degree of limbo. The working party states that the 'household exemption' is a valid exemption for the majority of users, meaning that they will not be regulated by the relevant data protection legislation (including the need to notify). However, the decision in Bodil Lindqvist provides a very narrow interpretation of this exemption. A user of a social network site can refer to a person's name, age, address, picture, place of work, hobbies and interests and well as their whereabouts at any given time. Arguably these details extend beyond simple domestic or personal usage, which could mean that the user could find themselves within the remit of the legislation. This element of the working party's decision is potentially very dangerous and full of litigious intent. If a user is offering a product or service, or using the site for a commercial, charitable or political platform, the working party argues the user should notify the regulator that they are processing personal data. Equally, a user should also notify the regulator if they have a very large body of friends (although provides no indication on the size of the contact list). Yet the line between personal or household and other uses remains very uncertain and is likely to remain so until litigation provides a way forward.

The working party also offered an opinion on the required privacy and security levels. Throughout the document the working party advises that social networking sites should provide their identity and also outline the purposes for the processing of data (which may include direct marketing, sharing with third parties and also how they handle sensitive personal data). Recommendations include that adequate information regarding privacy risks should be made available to users and these same users should also be advised of the potential for infringing the rights of a third party by uploading their content (e.g. personal details or a photograph) and in these circumstances the consent of the third party should be obtained. Guidance is also provided on the use of sensitive personal data. Sensitive personal data is defined in section 2 of the Data Protection Act and includes racial or ethnic origin, political opinions, religious beliefs, any membership of a trade union, physical or mental health, sexual life, details on the commission of any offence or alleged offence and any court proceedings. If sensitive personal data is to be processed, a condition listed in Schedule 3 needs to be met. The main condition is that of explicit consent. The working party considers that if sensitive personal data about a third party is included by another user, then that user would need the explicit consent of the third party, unless the third party volunteered the information at an earlier occasion. Yet, the difficulty with this is the form the sensitive personal data takes. While typing in the medical condition or details of any offence they have committed would count as disclosing sensitive personal data, the situation is less clear with photographs. In many cases photographs may be able to provide details of ethnicity, could highlight a physical medical problem and may provide some details on political or religious beliefs. Finally, the working party considered the rights of non-members and took the view that social networking sites cannot build up a profile of non-members based on the comments that are made by members of the site.

The Article 29 Working Party's opinion on social networking sites has covered a wide variety of issues pertinent to data protection legislation. The document is purely opinion at this time and has no binding precedent, which will only be forthcoming through litigation or legislation. It is encouraging to note how they anticipate social networking sites to comply with the Data Protection Directive, although it is contended that the view they have reached (particularly in relation to the identity of the data controller – including that users could indeed become data controllers) is fraught with difficultly.

The future

Crystal ball gazing is a very inaccurate science. Seeking to chart exactly how the Internet will develop is shrouded in uncertainty and complexity, as many of the applications are driven by the users themselves. The evolution of Facebook and Twitter are examples of this and the ease of accessibility through wifi systems and mobile devices enhances their development and evolution. Cloud computing is a relatively new concept that allows users to store data online and then retrieve it anywhere in the world. Again, Facebook is a model that employs cloud computing, although an increasing number of businesses are looking to utilise cloud computing as a method of reducing costs and increasing efficiency.[54] There are a number of difficult legal questions relating to cloud computing, including data protection implications and security, which at this stage have not been answered.[55] The increase in interest in virtual worlds and the desire for people to engage in virtual communities also brings with it a range of legal issues. The boundaries between the real and virtual world are likely to become blurred as interest in virtual worlds increases.[56] Yet, it is clear that users will continue to seek to take advantage of the Internet. The communication and commercial advantages are too great a pull and users will continue to seek speedier, cheaper and more diverse applications. Many applications provide services which are free at the point of entry and users are keen to take advantage of them. The reason for the free use is largely due to the advertising revenue involved. Personal information makes up a large part of the 'currency' of the Internet. A large number of users are willing to trade their personal details to receive these 'free' services. With this information, advertising companies are able to target their advertisements with more precision. As long as this remains a financially viable business model, services will remain – on the whole – free, although this is tempered by the concern in some quarters of a surveillance state, where organisations know too much about individuals. One suggestion of the future is the evolution of Web 2.0 to Web 3.0. While Web 2.0 increased the range of applications, it is suggested that Web 3.0 will be able to offer a much more personalised service to the user, by understanding their character and then offering directly the types of services that the user needs. There are a range of different definitions of Web 3.0, although it is suggested that individuals will be able to filter complex searches to a much higher degree than currently. If this is a correct prediction for the future, a new range of legal questions will require to be answered.

Key points:

- Web 2.0 allows users to engage with Internet systems dynamically and post comments, upload material and respond to the material of others in

---

[54] See: Taylor, M & Matteucci, M *Cloud Computing* Computer and Telecommunications Law Review (2010), volume 16, issue 2, pages 57–59.

[55] See the speech given by Peter Hustinx, the European Data Protection Supervisor at the 3rd European Cyber Security Awareness Day (13th April 2010) entitled *Data Protection and Cloud Computing under EU Law*. Available at: http://www.edps.europa.eu/EDPSWEB/edps/site/mySite/SA2010.

[56] Taylor, M & Matteucci, M *Virtual Worlds* (2009) Computer and Telecommunications Law Review, volume 15, issue 5, pages 124–127.

a variety of media, with social networking sites being one of the most popular.

- There are a number of inherent dangers in such responsive communicative systems, most notably to children, who could find themselves exposed to harmful material through their online engagement.
- One such example of the dangers children can face through social networking sites is that of grooming, where an adult will locate a child or young person through a chat facility with the aim of trying to meet up with the young person.
- The relevant law in relation to grooming is section 15 of the Sexual Offences Act 2003, which makes it an offence (having met or communicated with a person under the age of 16 on at least two earlier occasions) to intentionally meet, or travel with the intention of meeting the person under the age of 16, with the intention of committing an offence against the minor.
- The monitoring of an employee's online activities is permissible, although subject to a range of rules covered in a variety of legislation, including the Human Rights Act 1998, the Data Protection Act 1998, the Regulation of Investigatory Powers Act 2000 and the Telecommunications (Lawful Business Practice) (Interception of Communications) Regulations 2000.
- The decisions by the European Court of Human Rights in Halford and Copland extend the provisions of Article 8 of the European Convention of Human Rights to work place communications.
- The applicability of the Data Protection Directive to social networking sites is an area full of opinion, with relatively little fact.
- It is uncertain whether the user of the system or whether the social networking sites should be classified as the data controller. This is important as the data controller has a range of responsibilities including notifying the Information Commissioner.
- Issues relating to consent, the 'tagging' of an individual in a photograph, the processing of sensitive personal data and deletion policies are other areas where the applicability of the legislation to social networking sites is uncertain.
- The Article 29 Working Party has issued an opinion of the applicability of the legislation to social networking sites.

Further reading:

- Anderson, H *A privacy wake-up call for social networking sites?* (2009) Entertainment Law Review, volume 20, issue 7, pages 245–248.
- Gillespie, A A *Indecent images, grooming and the law* (May 2006) Criminal Law Review, pages 412–421.

- Gillespie, A A *Regulation of internet surveillance* (2009) European Human Rights Law Review, issue 4, pages 552–565.
- Graham, N & Anderson, H *Are individuals waking up to the privacy implications of social networking sites?* (2010) European Intellectual Property Review, volume 32, issue 3, pages 99–103.
- Mann, B L *Social networking websites – a concatenation of impersonation, denigration, sexual aggressive solicitation, cyber-bullying or happy slapping videos* (2009) International Journal of Law and Information Technology, volume 17, issue 3, pages 252–267.
- McLaughlin, S *Online sexual grooming of children and the law* (2009) Communications Law, volume 14, issue 1, pages 8–19.
- Miles, J *Distributing user-generated content: risks and rewards* (2007) Entertainment Law Review, Volume 18, Issue 1, pages 28–30.
- Oliver, H *Email and Internet monitoring in the workplace: information privacy and contracting out* (2002) Industrial Law Journal, volume 31, issue 4 pages 321–352.
- Reid, A S *Online protection of the child within Europe* (2009) International Review of Law, Computers and Technology, Volume 23, Issue 2, pages 217–230.
- Schifreen, R *The Internet: Where did IT all go wrong?* (August 2008), Script-Ed, volume 5, issue 2, pages 419–427.
- Sithigh, D M *Law in the Last Mile: Sharing Internet Access Through WiFi* (August 2009) ScriptEd, volume 6, issue 2, pages 355–376.

Questions for consideration:

9.1. Outline the key changes in Internet usage from Web 1.0 to Web 2.0.

9.2. What challenges are presented to the law enforcement agencies by Web 2.0?

9.3. One of the real dangers to young people engaging in social networking sites and chat rooms is that of grooming. Outline the response of the legislation in the United Kingdom to this problem.

9.4. Undertake a critical assessment of whether the applicability of the Data Protection Act 1998 to social networking sites is sufficiently clear and precise, and protects the personal data of users from being misused.

9.5. One of the key facets of the data protection legislation is that a data subject is able to consent to the processing of their personal data. In relation to social networking sites, how does this work in reality, particularly when the user is under the age of 18?

9.6. From the point of view of an employer, list some of the advantages and disadvantages of allowing employees to engage in social networking sites.

9.7.   In what circumstances is an employer permitted to monitor the online activities of one of their employees?

9.8.   Critically assess the effectiveness of the legislation in place, which allows employers to monitor the online activities of employees and whether adequate safeguards in terms of privacy are in place for the employee.

9.9.   'In 2009, the Article 29 Working Party published an opinion on online social networking. It stated that the Data Protection Directive 95/46/EC did indeed apply to social networking sites, yet despite a large degree of opinion contained within their document there is still a significant amount of conjecture as to how the Directive applies.'
Undertake a critical evaluation of this view.

9.10.   Helen is the managing director of a small company advertising lesser-known musical artists on the Internet though a (fictional) website called www.lesserknownartist.com. The business model is simple. Her company obtains income from each musician listed on her website that is visited by a person through a hyperlink on www.lesserknown artist.com. The company also obtains a small percentage of any merchandise that is sold during these visits. By ensuring that her website features prominently on search engine results pages, she can increase her company's income through 'hits' on the advertised websites.

Helen has built the company up to be very successful and each month it makes a very healthy financial profit. She has a very strong work ethic, which was drummed into her from her youth and Helen believes that all of her staff should have the same approach to work. To this end, Helen believes that the office computers, which are all connected to the Internet, should only be used for work purposes and that her three employees should not use the work computers for personal use. Helen is concerned that her employees are using the computers for personal use and therefore decides to monitor the usage of the work computers. Helen introduces a system that monitors websites that are visited by her employees during working hours. Helen reads the monitoring reports and places them in her employee folders, which contain personal information and bank details. She regularly leaves these folders on her desk, where anyone could access them.
Advise Helen on the legality of the monitoring activity.

All weblinks mentioned in the text can also be found at
http://www.palgrave.com/law/rogers

10 Internet and Other Computer-related Offences

This chapter will consider:

- An analysis of the concept of Internet crime and the types of offences which could come within this heading.
- The difficulties in detecting and prosecuting these crimes.
- The assistance provided by the Fraud Act 2006 and the Computer Misuse Act 1990 (as amended by the Police and Justice Act 2006) in defeating Internet crime.
- The strategy introduced by the government in 2009 to provide safeguards against online criminality.

The Internet has had many tremendous successes: commerce and communication are two areas positively transformed by the rise of the World Wide Web. Yet, coupled with these clear advantages is the ability for people to use the Internet for a whole range of immoral, unethical or even criminal acts. Although the Internet could be termed as a new playground for criminals, it is contended that there is a range of legislation in place within the United Kingdom which is set up to tackle these crimes and this chapter will consider this legislation, particularly the Fraud Act 2006 and the Computer Misuse Act 1990. This chapter will commence with consideration of some of the problems surrounding the detecting and prosecuting of Internet crime.

Some difficulties surrounding Internet crime

The initial difficulty presented is to define the parameters within which Internet crime can be placed. One part of the problem is the different generic terms which are used in the categorisation of these offences. Computer fraud is perhaps one of the more traditional terms employed for criminal acts which are carried out by used of a computer.[1] The development of the Internet led to the introduction of the term 'Internet crime' or 'Internet fraud', while more recently 'cybercrime' or ' e-crime' have become prevalent in discussing this type of offence. The relative inter-changeability of these terms is perhaps a moot point, but the crimes that they are suggested to cover include fraud (including phishing, credit card fraud, bank account fraud and viruses), hacking (including unlawful access and modification and attacking the integrity of computer systems, for instance through a Denial of Service attack) and illegal content (which could include online harassment and dissemination of indecent images of children). Placing offences committed by the means of technology within a specific heading is not an approach which the legislature has adopted, due in part to uncertainty as to what would be required for an offence to fall within any given heading.[2] Questions such as whether a computer needs to be used, what – or who – needs to be affected and what type of technology, if any, needs to be used have not been satisfactorily answered. To a large degree the response of the law to Internet crime has been reactionary instead of visionary in nature (the Computer Misuse Act 1990, which shall be considered later, is a case in point and was introduced after a high-profile 'hacking' incident where the alleged perpetrators were found not to have committed an offence) and legislation and its interpretation by the judiciary reacts to the latest method employed by the criminal in seeking to achieve their nefarious ends. This response is caused by an incomplete appreciation of what an Internet crime is.

Ascertaining the precise level of fraudulent activity online is notoriously difficult to achieve. Coupled with this and the need to define what an Internet crime is, there is a difficulty in ensuring that the perception of Internet crime is that it is criminal in nature.[3] There are two branches to this particular problem: first of all there needs to be a general societal recognition that online criminality is illegal and not merely a 'computer buff' demonstrating his or her technical prowess and intelligence by being able to manipulate a machine to achieve an illegal result. In other words, that computer crime is indeed 'real crime'. Secondly the seriousness with which it is treated by the criminal justice system and organisations needs to be addressed. Various headlines are produced

---

[1] Although there is no definition in statute, common law has defined the term 'computer' very widely.

[2] See Moitra, S D *Developing Policies for Cybercrime* (2005) European Journal of Crime, Criminal Law and Criminal Justice, Volume 13, Issue 3, pages 435–464. This article argues that cyber laws are being developed incrementally in response to individual cases, media outcry and statistics, which are very difficult to verify.

[3] See: Wilson, S *'Collaring' the Crime and the Criminal?: 'Jury Psychology' and Some Criminological Perspectives on Fraud and the Criminal Law* (2006) Journal of Criminal Law, Volume 70, Issue 1, pages 1–26.

advocating the need for a greater focus on dealing with Internet crime. Whilst these headlines may often point to a lack of training and education for those in the criminal justice system (perhaps arguing that the police force do not have adequate training and the judiciary do not understand the nuances of the technology), organisations also need to treat information security breaches with more seriousness. If an organisation is the victim of a security breach caused by a weakness in their technology, there is likely to be a reticence to report this breach as the organisation would not want to risk damaging its customer goodwill. A security breach has the potential to be a major public-relations risk and also has the potential to damage the internal workings of the organisation if it does not have sufficient contingency plans in place. However, in mitigation it is not always clear at what stage an Internet crime should be reported. Is a simple spam or phishing email sufficient for a report? Arguably legislation, notably the Fraud Act 2006, states that a phishing email in itself is a criminal offence. Does an account need to be hacked into? Does information or money have to be stolen? The point is that it is not apparent at what stage a report should be made, or at which point the law enforcement agencies will – or should – take a report seriously. It is difficult to comprehend any police offi-cer taking the reporting of a random phishing email seriously. This is under-standable, but even in the event of a serious offence (however that may be defined) a range of evidential problems exist. Gathering electronic evidence is problematic as it can be deleted, destroyed or modified with relative ease. Computers can hold vast amounts of information, which means they can take a very long time to search. Equally, the digital information that is held by computers is susceptible to malicious attacks and is often only protected by passwords or a form of encryption. Generally speaking, criminal courts are still catching up with the intricacies of computer evidence and there is often an underestimation of the technical complexity of cases that involve computer evidence. Furthermore, procedurally the mishandling of computer evidence quite frequently leads to prosecutions having to be abandoned. The technol-ogy involved can add to the difficulties. Criminals can hide behind the technol-ogy at a basic level by concealing their identity and police technology may not be up to the same standard. The more technically sophisticated a criminal is, the harder they are to trace. For instance, a person's location can be traced from their mobile phone, but a technology-savvy individual could send misleading signals, while a criminal may be able to conceal their behaviour by using a range of different types of technology and routing their activities through different jurisdictions. This chapter will continue by examining the legislation enacted to deal with arguably the main types of Internet crime: securing unauthorised access to a computer system and, first of all, online fraud.

The Fraud Act 2006 in general

After a lengthy conception, the Fraud Act 2006 received Royal Assent on 8th November 2006 and came into force in England, Wales and Northern Ireland on 15th January 2007.[4] The Act introduced a general fraud offence under Section 1, and outlined the three ways in which the offence can be committed:

Section 2 – by false representation;
Section 3 – by failure to disclose information;
Section 4 – by an abuse of position.

The introduction of a general offence of fraud, with three methods of committing it, is intended to provide a substantial scope to ensure that technologically focused crime can be targeted by this provision. This covers 'newer' offences such as phishing and spoofing and provides a sentence of up to ten years' imprisonment,[5] which is the same as the old deception offences found within the Theft Acts and also for the common law offence of conspiracy to defraud. There are further new offences included in the Act, such as possessing articles for use in frauds,[6] making and supplying articles for the use in frauds[7] and obtaining services dishonestly.[8]

The background to the Act

The key reason for the introduction of the Fraud Act was the history of complexity and uncertainty concerning offences involving deception and their relevance to computers.[9] Demonstrating that an act was carried out deceptively was a critical requirement in proving that one of these offences had been committed. This became difficult with the development of computers as case law determined that the implication within the statutory words was that the deception must be played upon a human mind and not a computer – a machine cannot be deceived. This clear principle of law was noted in the case

---

[4] The Act does not extend to Scotland, which the exception of Section 10(1).

[5] Fraud Act 2006, Section 1(3)(b).

[6] Ibid. Section 6. See **R v Oliver Omotago Mafe** [2009] EWCA Crim 2752 for an example of the application of this section.

[7] Ibid. Section 7. See **R v Huang (Jian)** [2010] EWCA 375 for an example of the application of this section.

[8] Ibid. Section 11.

[9] These deception offences included: Section 1(1) Theft Act 1978 (dishonestly obtaining services from another by deception), Section 15(1) Theft Act 1968 (dishonestly obtaining property belonging to another by deception), Section 2 Theft Act 1968 (evading liability by deception) and Section 15A Theft (amendment) Act 1995 (dishonestly obtaining a money transfer for himself or another by deception).

of **DPP v Ray** where Lord Morris stated: *"For deception to take place there must be some person or persons who will have been deceived."*[10] Indeed, this principle stretches back as far as the early twentieth century in the case of **Re London and Global Finance Corporation Ltd.**[11] The requirement that deception needs to be played on a human mind presented a considerable obstacle to the successful prosecution of an individual where a computer was involved. Accordingly, these provisions were of very little assistance when they were attempted to be applied to Internet crimes.[12] There were also a range of inter-pretative difficulties in applying these deception offences. These difficulties were highlighted by both the judiciary and academics.[13] The nature of these difficulties was that the sections were technically specific, meaning that their applicability was always uncertain. In 2002, the Law Commission published a report entitled 'Fraud'[14] and commented that wider problems could arise due to the potential number of statutory provisions which could be used in fraud trials. The judicial minefield it caused – most notably with technical arguments – led to occasional swift responses to plug loopholes.[15] The Law Commission argued that the range of statutory provisions that could be employed in fraud trials was overlapping and over particularised in that it sought to be specific for a range of crimes, yet the consequence was that there was a mass of poten-tially relevant legislation without a coherent path through it. This meant that defendants could be found not guilty if their specific act did not meet the exact requirements of the statute. The report commented that as fraud continues to evolve it is impossible to define each specific occasion where it occurs; indeed if this were to happen legislation would soon find itself jammed with a plethora

---

[10] [1974] AC 370.

[11] [1903] 1 Ch. 728.

[12] The decision of **Renault UK Limited v Fleetpro Technical Services** [2007] EWHC 2541 (QB) needs to be considered at this point. In this case, Fleetpro operated a scheme where pilots who worked for British Airways and their immediate families could sign up to obtain discounts for new Renault cars. The orders were placed with Fleetpro, who would then forward the orders on to Renault who would build the cars. The deception was that the sole director and owner of Fleetpro had made 217 orders for these cars, but out of these orders only three were for people who were eligible for the scheme. The others were sold through a website to other Internet suppliers. The judge was of the opinion that there was no objection to a misrepresentation being made to a machine acting on behalf of a claimant. However, as Renault could not demonstrate any loss the judge found against them. See case comment: Morgan, G *Lying on the web: is misrepresentation made to a machine equivalent and actionable as if made to another person?* (2008) Computer and Telecommunications Law Review, volume 14, issue 4, pages 92–93, who argues that this common sense approach is to be welcomed. See also: OUT-LAW.COM News *Telling lies to a computer is still lying, rules High Court* (23rd November 2007). Available at: http://www.out-law.com/default.aspx?page=8660.

[13] See **Brian Royal (1971)** 56 Cr.App.R 131 – particularly the judgment of Edmund-Davies ʟ at page 136 and also David Omerod's excellent article *The Fraud Act 2006 – Criminalising Lying* (2007) Criminal Law Review, pages 193–219.

[14] The Law Commission Report No. 276/CM 5560 *Fraud* July 2002. Available at: http://www.lawcom.gov.uk/lc reports.htm#2002. This report also included a draft Bill (pages 95–106), which formed the basis of the subsequent Bill brought forward by the government in 2004.

[15] See the discussion on R v Preddy [1996] AC 815 and Section 15A Theft Act 1968 below.

of fraudulent offences, while the creativity of man would still find new ways of circumventing the law.[16]

The inadequacy of the law in capturing all fraudulent behaviour was seen in the case of **R v Preddy**.[17] This is a good example of how the courts tried to apply the exact requirements of the statute (specifically Section 15 of the Theft Act 1968[18]) to the alleged fraudulent act. In this case, Mr Preddy made a series of loan applications to different building societies. On each occasion he knowingly deceived the building societies by providing false information. At first instance, he was convicted of this offence, however on appeal the House of Lords found in Mr Preddy's favour. Their reasoning centred on the phrase 'property belonging to another' and they ruled that the loans were not strictly property belonging to another as required under section 15 of the Theft Act. The House of Lords (with Lord Goff making the leading judgment) took the strict view that an amount in a bank account is a *chose in action* and not strictly a property right. A chose in action provides a person with a right to sue the bank for the amount of money in their account. The transfer from the lender's bank account to Mr Preddy's bank account did not lead to a situation where property belonging to another was obtained, but a situation where the right to the chose in action had altered. In other words Mr Preddy obtained a chose in action to the amount of money that he had deceptively obtained, but he did not own the property rights in it. Therefore, according to the House of Lords, Mr Preddy did not obtain property belonging to another, which was a key requirement of Section 15 Theft Act 1968, he had simply deceptively transferred a chose in action.[19] There were a number of problems with this decision. First of all, it demonstrated that if anyone engineered a money transfer they could escape conviction on the legal technicality that the attaining of a chose in action could not be held to be obtaining 'property belonging to another'. The argument was that when there was an electronic transfer from one account to another, the first amount is extinguished and then a new amount is sent to the new account. It is not the same 'property' and is therefore new 'property'. This loophole was closed very quickly with the addition of section 15A of the Theft Act 1968.[20] It is noticeable however that the element of

---

[16] See: The Law Commission Report No. 276/CM 5560 *Fraud* July 2002. Available at: http://www.lawcom.gov.uk/lc_reports.htm#2002, particularly paragraphs 3.10–3.20.

[17] [1996] AC 815.

[18] Section 15 (1) Theft Act 1968: "A person who by any deception dishonestly obtains property belonging to another, with the intention of permanently depriving the other of it, shall on conviction be liable to imprisonment for a term not exceeding 10 years."

[19] Preddy was not the only case that was faced with this problem. Other cases include: **R v Duru** [1974] 1 WLR 2, **R v Halai** [1983] Crim LR 624, **R v King** [1992] 1 QB 20, **R v Manjdadria** [1993] 73, **R v Mitchell** [1993] Crim LR 788 and **R v Mensah Lartey and Relevy** [1996] Crim LR 203, all of which required precise interpretation of the complex statutory provision.

[20] Section 15A Theft Act (inserted by Theft (Amendment) Act 1996) reads: "A person is guilty of an offence if by any deception he dishonestly obtains a money transfer for himself or another".

deception was still present meaning that the deception problems in relation to computers were still in existence. Although the amendment plugged this particular loophole, the problem with plugging loopholes when they appear is that the law is continually playing 'catch-up' with criminality.[21]

In May 2004, the Home Office released a consultation entitled *Fraud Law Reforms*.[22] The foundation of the final Fraud Act (specifically fraud by false representation, failure to disclose information and abuse of position) was seen within this consultation, as was a consideration of the common law conspiracy to defraud offence. The difficulty with the offence of conspiracy to defraud is that the definition of 'defraud' is very wide – indeed it was wider than the legislative provision pre-Fraud Act 2006, as was seen in the case of **Scott v Commissioner of Police of the Metropolis**.[23] In this case, the House of Lords held that there was no requirement for deception to be present in the offence of conspiracy to defraud. The common law offence of conspiracy to defraud runs alongside the statutory conspiracy offence found within Section 1 of the Criminal Law Act 1977.[24] The advantage of the statutory conspiracy to defraud offence is that it can be used to target those who plan or commit acts outside of the United Kingdom, as Section 5 of the Criminal Justice (Terrorism and Conspiracy) Act 1998 has inserted Section 1A into the Criminal Law Act 1977, which extends the jurisdictional reach of the offence, subject to the conduct taking place in a territory outside of the United Kingdom, that the conduct in question was also an offence in that other territory and that a party to the agreement did anything in relation to the agreement in England or Wales. The apparent breadth of the offences, coupled with there being no need for deception to be present had the quirky effect of making an offence a crime if committed by two people, but the act lawful if carried out by an individual. Accordingly, the Home Office consultation sought to repeal all the existing legislation and also the common law offence of conspiracy to defraud in order to tidy up the mass of legislation in this area. The responses to this consultation were published towards the end of 2004, with the vast majority of responses in favour of the general approach to tackling fraud by statute, but critical of the removal of the conspiracy to defraud offence. Accordingly, the latter offence remained and at the time of writing is still in existence.

---

[21] See **Re Holmes** [2005] 1 All ER 490. In this case the defendant was found guilty of an offence under Section 15A Theft Act, although in concluding the judge expressed frustration at the unnecessary technicality of the English law of theft and fraud, particularly in relation to money transfers.

[22] For the full range of papers in this consultation exercise see: http://webarchive. nationalarchives.gov.uk/20100418065544/http://www.homeoffice.gov.uk/documents/cons-fraud-law-reform/index.html.

[23] [1975] AC 819.

[24] For an example of conspiracy offences in action see: **R v Bakker** [2001] EWCA Crim 2354 and **R v Daniel Levi & Others** (2005), Preston Crown Court, reported in E-Commerce Law Reports, volume 5, number 5, pages 10–11.

Academic, legislative and judicial criticism aside, there were wider reasons for the introduction of new legislation. It is without doubt that, in recent years, technology-based crimes have been on the increase. The government-backed *Get Safe Online Report*[25] (most recently published in November 2010) suggested that 19% of people surveyed had been the victim of identity fraud and, according to the National Fraud Authority, the average cost in the United Kingdom of dealing with the detection, prosecution and compensation of online fraud was £30.5 billion. Additionally, 23% of people surveyed said that they had been the victim of a phishing attack. More alarmingly, in June 2010 the United Kingdom's Serious Organised Crime Agency reported that these crimes were costing around £3.5bn per year and fractionally more people (11 per cent) had been the victim of online fraud.[26] Yet, accurate information relating to online fraudulent activity and identity theft is very difficult to obtain with any confidence and figures need to be treated with a considerable degree of caution. First of all, there is a presumption that all Internet crimes are reported by individuals and by businesses. As considered earlier in this chapter, this is unlikely. A business which has suffered a minor breach of its online security is likely to be unwilling to report this security breach for fear of losing customer goodwill due to the bad publicity which could follow. But what constitutes a minor breach? A virus sent via email is commonplace and is not going to lead to the recipient walking down to the police station to report an offence. Any attempt to provide specific statistics on the relative increase (or decrease) in technology-based fraud is fraught with difficulty and almost impossible to achieve. What can be stated with some certainty is that the opportunity to engage in crime over the Internet or by alternative electronic methods is growing, as is the ingenuity of perpetrators to stretch boundaries. In part, these issues return to the discussion at the beginning of the chapter on the exact parameters of Internet crime, but whatever scale is used to measure the types and seriousness of these crimes, it is apparent that such offences are on the increase and it is partially this continual increase and expansion in this type of criminal activity that led to the government needing to modernise and simplify the law relating to fraud.

The Fraud Act 2006

The Fraud Act 2006 is an attempt to introduce flexibility within the legislation by providing a broad net where a number of 'fraud' offences can be caught.

---

[25] Available at: http://www.getsafeonline.org/nqcontent.cfm?a_id=1517.

[26] See: Ashford, W *UK Internet users need to be more vigilant as online fraud hits £3.5bn, says VeriSign* (1st June 2010). Available at: http://www.computerweekly.com/Articles/2010/06/01/241410/UK-internet-users-need-to-be-more-vigilant-as-online-fraud-hits-1633.5bn-says.htm.

The deception offences in sections 15, 15A, 16 and 20(2) of the Theft Act 1968 (respectively: obtaining property by deception, obtaining a money transfer by deception, obtaining a pecuniary advantage by deception and procuring the execution of a valuable security by deception) and sections 1 and 2 of the Theft Act 1978 (respectively: obtaining services by deception and evasion of liability by deception) were repealed.[27] A general offence of fraud is set out in Section 1 (with a maximum sentence of ten years' imprisonment). There is no specific definition of fraud within the statue, but sections 2, 3 and 4 (false representation, failure to disclose information and abuse of position respectively) provide the mechanisms by which the offence can be committed. It is likely that Section 2 (fraud by false representation) will be the most widely used section, particularly in respect of online criminal behaviour. An example is the case of **R v Olufunsho Suleman**[28] where the defendant was convicted of a Section 2 offence and imprisoned for three years after he obtained documents (such as fictitious driving licenses, utility bills and tenancy agreements) and then successfully applied for credit cards in these fictitious names, fraudulently gaining around £100,000.

Section 2 makes it an offence to commit fraud by false representation. This requires the defendant to have dishonestly made a false representation[29] with the intention of making a gain or causing a loss (or risk of a loss) for himself or another.[30] The immediate advantage of this section in its applicability to the Internet is that there is a shift in focus away from deception and the accompanying 'deception problems' towards the concept of dishonesty. Dishonesty is the key *mens rea* element for proving liability within this part of the Act, although the definition of dishonesty, which was established by Lord Lane in the decision of **R v Ghosh**[31] by the creation of a two-stage test, is not without its own controversy. The two-stage test is broken down into two questions. The first question is whether the behaviour of the defendant was dishonest by the standards of reasonable and honest people. If the behaviour was held to be dishonest by this standard the second question can then be asked, which is whether the defendant himself was aware that what he was doing by those standards was dishonest. If both of these two questions can be answered affirmatively, the jury is able to find that the defendant acted dishonesty. The reliance on dishonesty is a major alteration to the law in this area, particularly as it widens the scope of the fraud legislation as there is no exclusive 'human mind' requirement as there was with deception. However, there is a difficulty with the definition of dishonesty in that the test outlined by Lord Lane does

---

27 The full list of repeals and amendments is found in Schedule 1 of the Fraud Act 2006.
28 [2009] EWCA Crim 1138.
29 This representation can be expressed or implied (Section 2(4)).
30 Fraud Act 2006, Section 2(1).
31 (1982) QB 1053.

presume that there is a standard degree of honesty (or dishonesty) in the minds of reasonable and honest people. This clearly is not the case. A simple example of a shopkeeper providing you change from a £20 note, when you only handed over a £10 note in the first instance will demonstrate a range of answers when asking whether or not you would return the difference. An additional qualification is whether the answer would differ if you were in a major supermarket or a small local shop. Standards of honesty will vary between ages, cultures and situations. A second problem with dishonesty is that it may allow juries to stray into the murky arena of considering whether behaviour is immoral rather than illegal and could leave the Fraud Act available for actions which juries disapprove of instead of criminalising illegal acts.

A second consideration within Section 2 is the definition of 'gain' and 'loss'. Gain and loss are widely defined in Section 5. 'Gain' (which covers money and other property, including intangible property such as intellectual property rights) includes a gain by keeping what one has, as well as a gain by getting what one does not have,[32] while 'loss' includes a loss by not getting what one might get, as well as a loss by parting with what one has.[33] Both the gain and loss can be permanent or temporary in nature.[34] Interestingly though, the Fraud Act removes the need for a gain to be *obtained* or loss to be *made*. The wording in Section 2(1) states that the defendant only needs to intend to make a gain or a loss. There is no requirement to achieve the intention and to have gained something or caused a loss to another. Under the old sections of the Theft Acts (which are now repealed) there had to be the *obtaining* of a money transfer, or property, or a service, as a result of a deception. The defendant had to gain, or the victim had to lose control or ownership of property. Without the gain or loss, a possible charge of an attempted crime could result, as long as the defendant had gone beyond a 'more than merely preparatory act' towards the commission of the full offence,[35] and subject to the *mens rea* of intention to commit the particular *actus reus*. Indeed, it can be seen that this *modus operandi* does away with the need for a victim altogether, and even if there is a 'victim' there is no requirement for the victim to even believe the false representation made, as it simply needs to be made. The net result of this is that the Fraud Act has changed the nature of fraud from a result crime to that of a conduct crime as it focuses solely on the conduct of the defendant. It is no longer the obtaining of a gain or the causing of a loss which is fraudulent, but it is the intention to do so.

---

[32] Fraud Act 2006, Section 5(3).
[33] Ibid. Section 5(4).
[34] Ibid. Section 5(2)(b).
[35] Criminal Attempts Act 1981 section 1(1). The definition of 'more than merely preparatory' in this context was a regular point for discussion in the courts. See, for instance, **R v Jones (Kenneth Henry)** [1990] 1 WLR 1057, **R v Geddes (Gary William)** [1996] Crim LR 894 and **R v Tosti (Andre)** [1997] Crim LR 746. For more on this area see: Clarkson, C M V *Attempt: the conduct requirement* (2009) Oxford Journal of Legal Studies, volume 29, issue 1, pages 25–41.

Section 2(2) considers the nature of the false representation and states that a statement is false if it is untrue or misleading and the person making the representation knows that it is untrue or misleading.[36] The level of knowledge required is one of the more uncertain aspects of this legislation. Although there is the element that the representation 'might be' untrue or misleading[37] it is not certain whether this will extend to wilful blindness, or if a person making the representation does not find out for certain whether or not a statement is true. It is possible that the Fraud Act will cover an online supplier of designer clothes when he knows that the clothes that he is selling may not be designer and a supplier who knows that the clothes are indeed forgeries and a supplier who may not know one way or the other. The maxim of caveat emptor or 'let the buyer beware' itself seems to have developed a caveat – the buyer does need to be wary, but even if they are not and a false representation is made to them (whether or not the seller knew this) they could have an action within this Act.

It is likely that Section 2 will be the most widely used section in tackling Internet crimes. Due to its wide scope and the fact that liability can be found at an early stage, due to the nature of fraud being a conduct, as opposed to a result crime, this Act could cover activities such as phishing and spamming. Indeed arguably, the very nature of the Act means that a defendant could be liable for creating an email on their home computer without in fact sending it as the false representation is made, the defendant knows that the representation is false and there is an intention to make a gain or cause a loss. Section 2(5) states that a representation has been made if it is submitted in any form to any system or device that is designed to receive, convey or respond to communications. Therefore, the mere creation of a phishing email on a computer may be sufficient for a person to be successfully charged for a Section 2 offence.

Government policy: current and future trends

In June 2009, the United Kingdom Government published two important documents on the future of the Internet. The first, and more substantial, was the *Digital Britain Report*.[38] This 230-page report arose from a joint project between the Department for Business, Innovation and Skills and the Department for Culture, Media and Sport and was chaired by Lord Stephen Carter. It set out how the government intended to support the growth in digital services and

---

[36] Fraud Act 2006, Section 2(2)(i) & (ii).
[37] Ibid. Section 2(2)(b).
[38] Department for Business, Innovation and Skills *Digital Britain: Final Report* (June 2009). Available at: http://www.culture.gov.uk/what_we_do/broadcasting/6216.aspx.

improve public service content. At its heart was the desire to tackle online piracy and introduced a Digital Economy Bill, which sought to make the United Kingdom a world leader in digital and creative industries. It covers four main themes. First, creative industries in a digital world; second, digital safety; third, public services broadcasting; and finally, strengthening the communications infrastructure. The bill set out to deal with online copyright infringement while allowing people to licence their work and allowing consumers to access the material with a greater degree of ease. Some of the powers included within the Bill were the ability for households to be disconnected from the Internet if they faced allegations of illegal file-sharing and also for British Internet Service Providers to be able to block websites that were accused of copyright infringement. It also sought to change the video game classification system to ensure that children did not have access to games that they should not see.[39] In April 2010, the then UK Prime Minister, Gordon Brown, announced that a general election would be held on 6th May 2010. During these periods, the workings of Parliament alter and there are lots of 'behind the scenes' negotiations over which bills should be 'rushed through' into law, and which should be rejected. This period is known as the 'wash up' – the period after an election has been called, but before Parliament has been dissolved. A five hour debate was held in the House of Commons on 7th April 2010 and the Bill was controversially passed with a majority of 142 votes.[40] No further amendments were made by the House of Lords and so the Digital Economy Act came into force.

The second report was the *Cyber Security Strategy of the United Kingdom*.[41] This was a significantly smaller report at just over 20 pages, but set out the strategy the UK government would be taking to ensure that the Internet can be used safely. Again, this report set out the importance of cyberspace, while emphasising that as our reliance on the Internet grows it is essential that the security of cyberspace is continually strengthened and maintained. The report set out plans for a coherent approach to ensuring the safety of Internet users and systems and called for a joined-up approach with government, public bodies, cross-sectoral organisations, international partners and the general

---

[39] For more details on the background to the report and the Bill's proposals see: http://www.culture.gov.uk/what_we_do/broadcasting/5631.aspx.

[40] See Hansard: http://www.publications.parliament.uk/pa/cm200910/cmhansrd/chan67.pdf from pages 836–936 and BBC News *Anger about digital 'stitch up'* 8th April 2010 available at: http://news.bbc.co.uk/1/hi/uk_politics/election_2010/8608478.stm, and OUT-LAW.COM Opinion *The legislative farce of the Digital Economy Bill* 7th April 2010 available at: http://out-law.com/page-10900. The rushed nature of the debate and the passing of the Digital Economy Bill was highly controversial – indeed one blogger commented that during the debate in parliament, nearly 25,000 tweets were posted on the subject. See: http://debillitated.heroku.com.

[41] The Cabinet Office *Cyber Security Strategy of the United Kingdom: Safety, Security and Resilience in Cyber Space* (June 2009). Available at: http://www.official-documents.gov.uk/document/cm76/7642/7642.pdf.

public working together to safeguard the Internet for its users. At the outset, the vision was set out as:

"Citizens, business and government can enjoy the full benefits of a safe, secure and resilient cyber space: working together, at home and overseas, to understand and address the risks, to reduce the benefits to criminals and terrorists, and to seize opportunities in cyber space to enhance the United Kingdom's overall security and resilience."[42]

The report stated that this vision would be realised through a number of strategic objectives. First of all, by reducing the heightened security risks caused by use of the Internet, including reducing the level of security threat and the impact if there was an attack and also the United Kingdom's vulnerability to such an attack. Secondly, by exploiting the opportunities that are provided by cyberspace; and thirdly, by improving knowledge, capabilities and decision-making abilities. The report then set out how these objectives were to be achieved. The key proposal was for the establishment of an Office of Cyber Security (OSC). This was established in September 2009 and came into effect in March 2010. This body aims to provide leadership within the Cabinet Office to ensure the objectives of the cyber security strategy are achieved. To assist in this aim, a Cyber Security Operations Centre (CSOC) was established and this organisation assists the OSC by monitoring the health of cyber security within the United Kingdom and providing businesses with advice on the risks and opportunities afforded by the Internet. The objectives were also to be achieved by establishing cross-government agreement for the priorities and liaising with all relevant stakeholders. The report does not go into fine detail about how the government will achieve its objectives, citing security reasons. However, the report did highlight that the OCS would work to ensure that there are safe, secure and resilient systems in place; consideration of policy, doctrine, legal and regulatory issues would be a key responsibility along with trying to achieve a culture change in cyber security awareness through skills and education. The OSC would also work on researching and developing technical capabilities and would consider how the United Kingdom could fully exploit the benefits of cyberspace. Finally, the OSC would be required to work on a national and international level, ensuring that the government is aware of its roles and responsibilities, and liaising with international partners and other stakeholders.

The relative success of this cyberspace strategy is invariably dependant upon the funding that is provided. The report was reticent about how the OSC and CSOC would be funded and sufficient finance needs to be in place to ensure that the strategy is achieved. The question of sufficient funding must be in

---

[42] Ibid. Page 3.

doubt in view of the Coalition Government's severe Comprehensive Spending Review (published on 20th October 2010), though the Strategic Defence and Security Review published on the 19th October 2010 did lay considerable stress on the United Kingdom's stance on cyber attack.

Unauthorised access and acts (hacking)

The credibility and integrity of computer systems in terms of security is of paramount importance if a company seeks to retain the goodwill of its clients and customers. The bad publicity arising from an external security breach can be very damaging, meaning that internal security systems and business continuity arrangements need to be in place. If a person gains unauthorised access to a system it could lead to further criminal activities, such as theft (of property or ideas), fraud and blackmail. The legislation needs to be flexible enough to counter the dangers posed by individuals who attempt to hack into computer systems, while not being overly restrictive. Although a present danger in the Internet world, hacking as a crime is still relatively recent. As recently as 1988, the House of Lords was handing down judgments which appeared to permit individuals to hack into computer systems to which they did not have the authority or the access to enter. The case of **R v Gold and Schifreen**[43] led to uncertainty over whether hacking was an offence or simply juvenile behaviour. It was the first case on hacking to reach the appellant courts and had a significant effect on altering the law's response to the activity. In this case, Gold and Schifreen were able to access a new Prestel computer system operated by British Telecommunications by means of a dishonest trick[44] allowing them to obtain the username and password. Once access had been gained they looked around the system, including at the personal message box of the Duke of Edinburgh. They were tried and found guilty of forgery under Section 1 of the Forgery and Counterfeiting Act 1981 as Southwark Crown Court ruled that the inputting of the username and password led to the creation of a forged instrument, which was a prerequisite for a successful prosecution under the section. Gold was fined £600, while Schifreen was fined £750. The Court of Appeal and House of Lords disagreed with the first instance decision and held that no offence had taken place as they had not created a 'false instrument' since the password had not been 'recorded or stored' as was required by Section 8 of the Act – it had only been used momentarily to allow access to the system.

---

[43] [1988] 2 WLR 984.

[44] The trick by modern day standards was basic and simply required the accused looking over the shoulder of a technician while they entered their username and password and memorising the details. This behaviour has subsequently been termed as 'shoulder surfing'. In any event, the username (22222222) and password (1234) were easy to remember.

Equally, the password that they entered could not be said to be false as it was the correct password that allowed them free access to the system. The difficulty with this decision, which received considerable attention, was that it gave the impression that hackers were above the law and was a real example that the legislation at the time was not robust enough to deal with the technological problems posed by computers. The threats posed by hacking are real and in some circumstances can lead to extreme difficultly and further criminal offences being committed. Therefore, Michael Colvin MP put forward a Private Member's Bill seeking to make unauthorised access and the committing of further criminal actions once unauthorised access had been achieved an offence. This received governmental support and in 1990 the Computer Misuse Act came into force. Although some amendments have been introduced over the last two decades, notably by the Police and Justice Act 2006, the Act has retained the majority of its original wording.

Computer Misuse Act 1990

The Computer Misuse Act sets out three main offences. The Section 1 offence is the basic hacking offence and makes it illegal to intentionally seek to secure unauthorised access to programmes or data on a computer. Section 2 is an extension of the basic hacking offence and makes it an offence to intentionally seek unauthorised access with a view to facilitating the commission of a further offence. Finally, Section 3 makes it an offence for a person to commit any unauthorised act in relation to a computer.[45] Section 3A was added subsequently and made it an offence to make, supply or obtain articles for use in an offence under sections 1, 2 or 3.

Section 1

The basic hacking offence is set out in Section 1. Prior to this, no provision existed to legislate against unauthorised access to data held on a computer system. Under this section (which was amended by Section 35 of the Police and Justice Act 2006), a person is guilty of an offence if he causes a computer to perform any function with intent to secure access to any program or data held in any computer, or enable such access to be secured, and the access he intends to secure, or enable to be secured is unauthorised and that he knows at the time when he caused the computer to perform a function that his access is unauthorised. This offence can be broken down into its constituent elements. First of all, a person needs to cause a computer to perform a function. This

---

[45] These sections were amended by the Police and Justice Act 2006.

means that the accused must interact with the computer. Simply reading information left on a monitor is not sufficient. The accused must interact with a
computer to the extent that it responds to his instructions and so will include
actions such as using the computer, altering or copying data, moving files or
documents and typing. In **Ellis v DPP (No. 1)**[46] the defendant was a former
student at the University of Newcastle. He used computers which had been left
logged on by other users, despite having previously been told that he was only
able to use open access computers. He appealed against his conviction under
Section 1, but it was dismissed by the court as they had found that Ellis had
indeed used the computers and the Act was sufficiently broad enough to cover
his actions. The second element for a person to be found guilty of a Section 1
offence is that the accused needs to intend to secure unauthorised access.
Section 1(2) is clear in outlining that the intent a person has in committing an
offence under this section does not need to be targeted against any particular
program or data on a computer. Furthermore, it does not need to be shown
that there was a second computer involved in the obtaining of the unauthorised access. In the **Attorney-General's Reference (No. 1 of 1991)**[47] the
accused was an employee who entered discount codes into the shop computer
to allow him to obtain significant discounts on goods he was purchasing. At
first instance, it was found that he did not have a case to answer as he successfully argued that he did not use one computer to secure unauthorised access
to another. On appeal by the Attorney-General, the decision was reversed. The
rationale provided by the Court of Appeal was that although hackers are generally thought of as being 'outsiders' it was necessary to ensure that the reach of
the legislation extended to hackers who operated as 'insiders' within an organisation. In looking at Section 1(1)(a), the court was of the view that the ordinary meaning should be given to the phrase '... intent to secure access to any
program or data' and there was no justification for inserting the word 'other'
between 'any' and 'program'. The third (and final) element is that at the time
of causing the computer to perform a function the person knew that the access
was unauthorised. Section 17 of the Act provides some assistance with this as
it contains the core definitions. Interesting key words such as 'computer',
'program' or 'data' are not defined, although Section 17(5) does provide a
definition for unauthorised access. Access is unauthorised if the accused is not
entitled to control access of the kind in question to the program or data and
he does not have the consent to access the program or data from the person
who is so entitled. The intention for this offence is therefore knowledge that
the access that the accused secures is unauthorised. This is fairly clear if the
hacker is from outside an organisation, but is less clear in circumstances where
the person who has secured the access is an insider, for instance the employee

---

[46] [2001] EWHC Admin 362.
[47] [1992] 3 WLR 432.

of a business. As a starting point, the courts have held in an employment context that a person is guilty of gross misconduct if they use another person's username and password to access information which they were not entitled to view.[48] Two cases towards the end of the 1990s considered this issue in more detail. The case of **DPP v Bignall**[49] concerned a husband and wife who were serving police officers. They used the Police National Computer for personal purposes in looking into the ownership of cars by Mrs Bignall's ex-husband. Although they were authorised to access the police computer for official purposes, they had accessed the system for unauthorised purposes. Somewhat controversially, the court held that the accused had not committed an offence as Mr and Mrs Bignall were authorised to access the system and it did not matter what type of data they were looking for. The view of the court was that the purpose of the Computer Misuse Act was to protect the integrity of computer systems, rather than the information stored on computer systems.[50] This case was reconsidered in **R v Bow Street Magistrates Court, ex parte Allison (No. 2)**[51] in which the defendant was the employee of a credit card company. She was able to access the credit card accounts of all the company's customers, but was only allowed to access the credit card accounts of customers that had been assigned to her. She provided customer account details to Allison, who was later charged with conspiracy to secure unauthorised access to the company's computer system with intent to commit theft and forgery. The United States government wanted Allison extradited, although at first instance the Divisional Court refused the extradition request saying that the Computer Misuse Act only extended to external hackers and not those who did actually have authorised access. As there had been no offence, there was no conspiracy. The House of Lords disagreed with this decision and held that the Computer Misuse Act was not concerned so much about the access to kinds of data, but whether the individual had authority to access that kind of data. In other words, notwithstanding the fact that they had access to data, the question the court needs to ask is whether the defendant had authorisation to view the data that was accessed. The definition of authorised access in Section 17(5), and in particular the reference to 'entitled to control' had, in the opinion of the House of Lords, been incorrectly defined in Bignall. The entitlement to control relates to the specific data that has been accessed, as opposed to the access to the computer system itself. The House of Lords stated that simply because an individual has access to one type of data, it does

---

[48] **Denco Limited v Joinson** [1992] 1 All ER 463.

[49] [1998] 1 Cr. App. R. 1161.

[50] For a critique of this decision see: Smith, J C *Police officers securing access to Police National Computer for non-police purposes* (January 1998) Criminal Law Review, pages 53–54.

[51] [1999] 3 WLR 620. For a critique of this case see: *Misuse of computer – unauthorised access to computer program or date – meaning of unauthorised* (December 1999) Criminal Law Review, pages 970–972.

not follow that they automatically have authorisation to access all the types of data on the system. Although the Allison decision distinguished Bignall, it did not expressly overrule it, so technically both decisions are still good law, although in all likelihood if a similar situation were to reach the courts it is probable that the Allison decision will be followed. The decision in Allison seems to support the convictions (in earlier, unreported cases) of individuals who had accessed data which they did not have authorisation to access. For example, in **R v Bonnett**[52] a police officer had accessed information from the Police National Computer to discover who owned a particular car. He did this because he wanted to make an offer to buy the registration number of the car (which was BON1T).

Following amendments introduced by the Police and Justice Act, a person who is guilty of an offence under this section can be tried either in the Magistrates Court or the Crown Court and the maximum sentence is two years' imprisonment and a fine not exceeding the statutory maximum.[53] Under section 11(2) proceedings must be brought within six months from the date on which sufficient evidence to warrant proceedings is present and, following Section 11(3), not longer than three years after the commission of the offence.[54]

Section 2

The Section 2 offence builds upon the basic hacking offence of Section 1 and states that a person is guilty of an offence if they secure unauthorised access and so commit a Section 1 offence, with an intent to commit a further offence or to facilitate the commission of a further offence (whether by himself or another person). According to Section 2(1)(b), the further offence can be committed by the person hacking into the system, or by another person entirely. In **R v Delaware**[55] the Court of Appeal upheld the verdict of the lower court, although reduced the sentence from eight months imprisonment to four months. The facts were that the defendant was employed in a bank and an acquaintance asked him for the bank details relating to certain people. The acquaintance then intended to impersonate the account holders and transfer money out of the accounts. This case not only shows that the further offence

---

[52] Unreported, Newcastle under Lyme Magistrates' Court, 3rd November 1995.

[53] The Act does not provide defences, although see Charlesworth, A *Addiction and Hacking* (1993) New Law Journal, volume 143, page 540. This article considers the strange case of Paul Bedworth (see The Times, March 18th 1993, page 3), who was a student at the University of Edinburgh. He was acquitted of charges of conspiracy under the Computer Misuse Act on the ground that he was addicted to computers and hacking.

[54] **Burwell v DPP** [2009] EWHC 1069 (Admin). For a comment on this case see: Ormerod, D *Burwell v Director of Public Prosecutions: time limit for prosecution – computer misuse* (2009) Criminal Law Review, issue 12, pages 897–899.

[55] [2003] EWCA Crim 424.

can be committed by a different person, but also that the offence can take place at a later time from when the system was initially hacked into. This later point is confirmed in Section 2(3). The rationale behind the Section 2 offence is that it applies at an earlier stage than the law on attempt. It was not clear whether the entering of a password a number of times with a view to accessing a system to commit a further offence was 'more than preparatory' and therefore the Section 2 offence bites at an earlier stage as the further offence does not even need to be committed. (Indeed Section 2(4) states that even if the further offence is impossible, for instance trying to blackmail a person who is dead or trying to steal money from an account that is empty, a person could still be found guilty of a Section 2 offence[56] – the intention is the important aspect.) This offence is a step up from simply snooping around in a another person's computer system and requires that the further offence is one that has a penalty fixed by law or is an arrestable offence with a sentence of five years or more.[57] Note that to be successful in conviction the prosecution does not need to be precise in specifying what the further offence is. In **R v Governor of Brixton Prison ex parte Levin**[58] the House of Lords affirmed the earlier court's decision by allowing Levin's extradition to the United States to go ahead, even though the offence the United States wanted to prosecute him for did not have an obvious parallel within the United Kingdom, although the conduct of Levin meant he could be tried in the United Kingdom for over sixty offences. As long as the prosecution can show the type of further offence that has been committed, that will be enough for the accused to come within Section 2 and the offence can be proved. Finally, it must also be noted that Section 12 states that a person who is tried on indictment (in the Crown Court) for a Section 2 (or Section 3 – see below) offence can, if found not guilty, be convicted in the alternative by the jury of the Section 1 offence (if, of course, the facts support such a finding). Section 2(5) (as amended by the Police and Justice Act 2006) outlines the maximum sentence of five years' imprisonment or a fine, or both, if a person is found guilty of a Section 2 offence.

Section 3

Prior to the enactment of the Computer Misuse Act, situations which involved the damage or erasure of computer programs or data were often dealt with under the Criminal Damage Act 1971. Under this Act it is an offence under Section 1 to destroy or damage any property belonging to another and a guilty

---

[56] This principle is similar to that found in the case of **R v Shivpuri** [1987] AC 1 where the defendant believed he was transporting heroin. In fact he was not, although he was still found guilty as the intention was present.

[57] Section 2(2).

[58] [1997] 3 WLR 117.

verdict could lead to a maximum sentence of ten years' imprisonment. One of the issues the courts had to deal with was whether intangible property could, in law, be 'damaged'. In **Cox v Riley**[59] the defendant deliberately erased a computer program from a plastic circuit card that operated a computerised saw. The erasure of this program meant that the saw was inoperable. He was convicted and appealed arguing that as a computer program was not tangible property it could not be damaged. This argument was rejected by the court, which held that the card itself had been damaged and no longer worked, meaning that property had been damaged. The decision in Cox v Riley was relied upon by the Court of Appeal in **R v Whiteley (Nicholas Alan)**[60] in which the defendant hacked into an academic computer to amend and delete data held on discs. Neither the computer nor the discs were damaged, but the information contained on them had been altered. He was convicted under the Criminal Damage Act, but appealed arguing that there had been no damage to any tangible property and he had only altered some particles on a disc. The Court of Appeal dismissed his appeal stating that although the property itself needs to be tangible, the damage does not need to be. In this case the workings of the discs had been impaired. The Whiteley case was heard after the Computer Misuse Act had come into force, but the timing of the offence meant that it had to be heard under the Criminal Damage Act.[61]

The Section 3 offence found within the Computer Misuse Act received the most amendment by Section 36 of the Police and Justice Act 2006. Previously, a person was guilty of an offence if they committed any act that led to the unauthorised modification of the contents of a computer, and at the time of the act they had the requisite intent and knowledge. Modification included the altering or erasing of data held in any content or adding any data to the content. Post-amendment, it is now an offence to commit any unauthorised act in relation to a computer, and at the time of the act the accused knew that the act was unauthorised. This is a much wider offence and it can be carried out intentionally or recklessly.[62] Section 3(2) requires an intention to impair the operation of any computer, to prevent or hinder access to any program or data held in any computer, to impair the operation of any such program or the reliability of any such data or to enable any of the aforementioned actions to be done. The impairment of the reliability of the data was the issue in the case of

---

[59] (1986) 83 Cr. App. R. 54.

[60] (1991) 93 Cr. App. R. 25.

[61] For more on the decision in Whiteley see: *Tampering with computer software – whether "tangible" property – whether "damage" caused* (June 1991) Criminal Law Review, pages 436–437 and *Impairing value of disc amounts to criminal damage* (1991) Justice of the Peace and Local Government Law, volume 155, issue 10, pages 145–146.

[62] The current test for recklessness within the United Kingdom is a subjective test as held in the case of **R v Cunningham (Roy)** [1957]2 QB 396.

Yarimaka v Governor of Brixton Prison[63] heard under the 'old' Section 3 offence. In this case, the defendants appealed against their proposed extradition to the United States to face charges of blackmail and conspiracy to gain unauthorised access to a computer and to cause unauthorised modification of computer material. They had set up a meeting in London with the representative of a financial news information provider based in New York. Yarimaka and Zezev had worked out the weaknesses of the website belonging to the American news provider and demanded that if they were not paid money, they would expose these deficiencies to the company's clients. This would inevitably result in a loss in confidence of the company's system. In their appeal against extradition they argued that they could not be found guilty of unauthorised modification because the aim of this section of the Act was to prevent modification to data held within a computer. They argued that by inputting inaccurate data into the American Company's computer they could not be found guilty of unauthorised modification because the data that appeared within the computer system was exactly that which they had fed into the computer. In other words, as long as the information that had been fed into the computer was still accurate (even if untrue) they had not impaired the operation of any computer. This argument was rejected by the court, which held that they had accessed the company's computer and fed inaccurate data into it, therefore the reliability of the computer system had been impaired.[64] Section 3(3) states that the offence will still be relevant if any of these actions are carried out recklessly and whether the act is carried out intentionally or recklessly. Section 3(4) states that it does not need to be aimed at any specific program, data or computer. A person found guilty of this offence is liable, according to Section 3(6), to a maximum sentence on indictment of ten years' imprisonment or a fine, or both. There have been a number of successful prosecutions under this section. In **R v Rymer**[65] a nurse amended the computer records of patients relating to prescriptions and treatment and was found guilty of a Section 3 offence. Equally, in **R v Spielman**[66] the defendant was found guilty under a Section 3 offence for deleting employee emails. Finally, in **R v Whitaker**[67] a typesetter tampered with a computer owned by a client, installing a security package which could only be disarmed by the use of a password. He withheld the password from the client, which in turn denied the client access to the computer for several days with resultant losses to the client which were estimated at

---

[63] [2002] EWHC 589 (Admin) (In some contexts, this case is also known as Zezev v United States).

[64] For more on this case, see: Smith, J C & Tausz, D *Computer misuse: whether sending an email which did not come from the purported source affected the reliability of data* (August 2002) Criminal Law Review, pages 648–650 and Calleja, R & Rees, P *Computer Crime* (2002) International Journal of Electronic Commerce Law & Practice, volume 2, issue 2, pages 65–67.

[65] Unreported, December 1993, Liverpool Crown Court.

[66] Unreported, March 1995, Bow Street Magistrates Court.

[67] Unreported, 1993, Scunthorpe Magistrates Court.

some £36,000. The defendant claimed the reason why he had done this was because the client owed him £2,000 in fees. Whitaker was convicted under Section 3 and he was given a two-year conditional discharge and a fine of £1,650.[68]

One of the criticisms of the old Section 3 offence was that it was not clear whether it extended to Denial of Service attacks. A Denial of Service attack is where a person deluges another person's computer system to the extent that it is no longer able to function. An example is the repeated sending of thousands of emails leading to the recipient's inbox becoming clogged up meaning that it cannot send or receive any more emails. The difficulty comes in trying to establish that such modifications were *unauthorised*, given the open invitations to visit such websites and to send emails to inboxes. The amendments were working their way through Parliament at the same time that the case of **DPP v David Lennon** was heard.[69] The facts were that the defendant 'mail-bombed' his previous employer's email account and set up a system that sent around half a million emails to the former employer's inbox. He was found not guilty in the Youth Court of an offence under Section 3 as the judge considered that an inbox is set up to receive emails and the section was enacted to deal with the sending of malicious material, such as viruses. As the inbox had accepted the emails, it had accepted the modification and therefore Lennon had no case to answer. This decision was overturned on appeal in the Divisional Court and the judge stated that while an inbox is set up to receive emails, the consent to receive emails was not without limits. In this case, as the emails were not for communication, but to impair the operation of the computer system, the implied consent for an inbox to receive emails could be reasonably be assumed to have been revoked. The judge drew an analogy with the implied consent given to a visitor by a householder to walk up their garden path, but not to have his letter box choked with rubbish. Although Lennon showed that Section 3 could be used to tackle Denial of Service attacks, it also leaves open the possibility that a spammer could be tried under the same section, which in some circumstances may be more effective than the provisions in the Privacy and Electronic Communications (EC Directive) Regulations.[70]

The Police and Justice Act 2006 also inserts Section 3A into the Computer Misuse Act. Section 3A sets out the offence of making, supplying or obtaining articles for use in offences under sections 1 or 3. This was introduced partly as

---

[68] For more details on this case and other similar cases see: Waldon, I *Update on the Computer Misuse Act 1990* (1994) Journal of Business Law, September issue, pages 522–527.

[69] [2006] EWHC 1201 (Admin). For commentary on this decision see: Worthy, J & Fanning, M *Computer Misuse Act: new tools to tackle DoS attacks* (2007) E-Commerce Law & Policy, volume 9, issue 1, pages 5–7 and Kon, G & Church, P *A denial of service but not a denial of justice* (2006) Computer Law and Security Report, volume 22, issue 5, pages 416–417.

[70] See Chapter 5.

an initial response to the uncertainty over whether Denial of Service attacks were covered by the legislation. Under Section 3A(1), a person is guilty of an offence if he makes, adapts, supplies or offers any article intending it to be used to commit, or to assist in the commission of, an offence under either sections 1 or 3. Section 3A(2) makes it clear that a person may still be found guilty of an offence if they supply an article which they believe is likely to be used in a further offence. The maximum available sentence on indictment is two years' imprisonment, or a fine, or both.

Jurisdiction

For each of the above offences, the jurisdiction of the English courts needs to be identified. This can be difficult as the Internet allows criminals to operate cross-border.[71] In relation to a Section 1 or 3 offence, the prosecution need to show that there is a 'significant link' with the domestic jurisdiction in order to show that the offence has been committed. Section 5(2) defines a significant link for the purposes of Section 1 as the accused being in the domestic jurisdiction[72] at the time that he caused a computer to perform a function, or that the computer that the accused person used to obtain unauthorised access was based in the domestic jurisdiction at that time. The definition of 'significant link' for the purposes of Section 3 is found in Section 5(3) as the accused being in the domestic jurisdiction when he carried out the unauthorised act, or the unauthorised act being done in relation to a computer based in the domestic jurisdiction. A Section 2 offence is not as straightforward. Under sections 4(4) and 8(1), if the accused operates from within the domestic jurisdiction, intending to commit or facilitate a further offence in a different country, those intended actions must involve the commission of an offence under the law of that other country. This is known as the principle of 'double criminality'.

An approach to the complexities of jurisdiction was introduced by the

---

[71] Although decided at a time before the Internet was commonplace and the Computer Misuse Act was in force, the decision in **R v Thompson (Michael)** [1984] 1 WLR 962 is a good example of how the United Kingdom courts have dealt with the issue of jurisdiction. In this case, Thompson was a computer operator who worked for a bank in Kuwait. He opened a number of savings accounts in his own name and he then programmed the bank's computer to take money from accounts belonging to other customers and credit his account with the same amount. He then returned to England and wrote to the Kuwaiti bank asking for them to transfer the money from the accounts that he had set up in his name in Kuwait to his accounts held in England. Thompson was subsequently convicted of obtaining property by deception under section 15 of the Theft Act 1968. He appealed, arguing that the court in the United Kingdom had no jurisdiction as the offences were committed in Kuwait. The Court of Appeal disagreed and held that there was adequate jurisdiction as Thompson had written to the Kuwaiti banks from England.

[72] Section 4(6) states that the domestic jurisdiction extends to England, Wales, Scotland or Northern Ireland.

Council of Europe in 2006. The Convention of Cybercrime[73] is the first international treaty which attempts to tackle Internet and computer crime through harmonising national laws and enhancing co-operation between countries. It seeks to achieve a common criminal policy to protect society against cybercrime. A large number of offences are listed in the Convention and a number of countries outside of the European Union have signed up to it, including Canada, Japan and the United States of America. The issue of jurisdiction and particularly the right of a second country to demand the extradition of a United Kingdom citizen has been played out in the media during the past decade with the case of Gary McKinnon. Mr McKinnon was a computer enthusiast who, by using his home computer, was able to hack into computer systems operated by the American government. The United States called his actions the biggest military computer hack of all time and alleged that after he had secured access he caused substantial damage. This was refuted by Mr McKinnon who argued that he was simply looking for, amongst other things, evidence of UFOs and technologies which could be of use to the general public. At the time of writing, the arguments for and against his extradition are being passed between the High Court, the Home Secretary and the European Court of Justice, with little hope of an immediate end to the saga, although the new Home Secretary has recently adjourned the hearing for his extradition.[74]

Key points:

- There are a number of problems in defining what an Internet crime is and statistics highlighting the scale of the problem are notoriously difficult to verify.
- Prior to the introduction of the Fraud Act 2006, the statutes that could be used for computer fraud were difficult to apply as many of them required 'deception' to be proven.
- The difficulty was that a computer could not be deceived, as was stated in **DPP v Ray.**
- The Fraud Act sets out a general offence of fraud in Section 1.
- A person can be found guilty of a Section 1 offence in three ways: Section 2 – by false representation, Section 3 – by failure to disclose information and Section 4 – by an abuse of position.

---

[73] Available at: http://conventions.coe.int/treaty/en/treaties/html/189.htm.
[74] See **R (on the application of McKinnon) v Secretary of State for Home Affairs [2009] EWHC 2021 (Admin)** and for more details of the events leading to the demands for his extradition and the surrounding publicity see: BBC Website *How Gary Mckinnon became a cause celebre* (4th August 2009). Available at: http://news.bbc.co.uk/1/hi/magazine/8181100.stm and *Ministers agree Gary McKinnon hacker case adjournment* (20th May 2010). Available at: http://news.bbc.co.uk/1/hi/uk/8694210.stm.

- The Fraud Act was introduced explicitly to deal with the problem of phishing and the *mens rea* requirement for deception has been replaced by dishonesty as defined in **R v Ghosh (1982)**.
- The Computer Misuse Act 1990 was introduced after the case of **R v Gold and Schifreen**, which seemed to suggest that hacking was above the law.
- The 1990 Act has subsequently been amended by the Police and Justice Act 2006.
- There are three main offences in the 1990 Act. Section 1 is the basic hacking offence, Section 2 is the basic hacking offence with the intention of committing a further offence, while Section 3 makes it an offence to do any unauthorised act in relation to a computer with intent (or with recklessness) to impair the operation of a computer.
- Section 3A (inserted by the Police and Justice Act 2006) makes it an offence to make, supply or obtain articles for use in an offence under either sections 1 or 3, while Section 5 deals with jurisdiction.

Further reading:

- Arnell, P & Reid, A *Hackers beware: the cautionary story of Gary McKinnon* (2009) Information and Communications Technology Law, volume 18, issue 1, pages 1–12.
- Bainbridge, D *Criminal law tackles computer fraud and misuse* (2007) Computer Law and Security Report, volume 23, issue 3, pages 276–281.
- Brenner, S W *Cybercrime Metrics: Old Wine, New Bottles?* (2004) Virginia Journal of Law and Technology, volume 9, number 13, pages 1–52.
- Fafinski, S *Computer misuse: the implications of the Police and Justice Act 2006* (2008) Journal of Criminal Law, volume 72, issue 1, pages 53–66.
- Johnson, M & Rogers, K M *The Fraud Act 2006: the e-crime prosecutor's champion or the creator of a new inchoate offence?* (2007) International Review of Law, Computers and Technology, volume 21, issue 3, pages 295–304.
- MacEwan, N *The Computer Misuse Act 1990: lessons from its past and predictions for its future* (2008) Criminal Law Review, issue 12, pages 955–967.
- Nehaluddin, A *Hackers' criminal behaviour and laws relating to hacking* (2009) Computer and Telecommunications Law Review, volume 15, issue 7, pages 159–165.
- Wasik, M *Computer misuse and misconduct in public office* (2008) International Review of Law, Computers and Technology, volume 22, issues 1/2, pages 135–143.
- Worthy, J & Fanning, M *Denial-of-service: plugging the legal loopholes?* (2007) Computer Law and Security Report, volume 23, issue 2, pages 194–198.

Questions for consideration:

10.1.   What are some of the difficulties in explaining what an Internet crime is?

10.2.   Why would a business be reticent to report a security breach?

10.3.   Prior to the Fraud Act 2006, what difficulties were there in using statutory provisions to prosecute an Internet crime?

10.4.   Outline the scope and workings of Section 2 of the Fraud Act 2006. How effective will this provision be in the tackling of Internet crime?

10.5.   Outline the main offence in the Computer Misuse Act 1990 (as amended by the Police and Justice Act 2006).

10.6.   How is jurisdiction decided in the Computer Misuse Act 1990 in relation to the offences contained in sections 1, 2 and 3?

10.7.   'It seems to be that if someone commits fraud by using their brain to defeat a computer system it is something to be applauded and not really a serious crime. However, this form of crime causes great anxiety in the commercial world and is considered by the authorities to be very serious.'
   Critically examine the ways in which the criminal law has sought to combat the problem of 'computer fraud' before the advent of the Fraud Act 2006.

10.8.   "The Fraud Act provides for a general offence of fraud with three ways of committing it, which are by false representation, by failing to disclose information and by abuse of position. It creates new offences of obtaining services dishonestly and of possessing, making and supplying articles for use in frauds." Explanatory notes to the Fraud Act 2006.
   Undertake a critical evaluation of how successful the Fraud Act 2006 will be in tackling Internet crime.

10.9.   Helen works in the payroll department of PocketLining Plc, which is a company based in Birmingham specialising in providing financial advice. There are over 25,000 employees working within the company and Helen is responsible for the processing of the monthly payroll run. Helen has come up with a scheme whereby she will transfer a small amount of money from each employee and redirect it into her own pay-packet. Once the money has cleared in her own bank account and before her activities are discovered she intends to flee the country for New Zealand, where she will live out the rest of her life on the money that she redirected.

On the day that Helen intended to put her plan into action, she went into work as normal and entered her office. She turned on her computer and entered her password, which gave her access to PocketLining Plc's payroll system. She then set up the system to transfer £50 from each of the employee's pay-packet into her own.

The payroll was due to be run the following day, however Helen did not appreciate that all changes to payroll at this late stage could only be carried out with the Chief Executive providing an additional username and password. This was a further security measure, which the company had available for many years, although as it had never needed to be used and Helen was unaware of it. Helen's activities were noticed and the police were called and she is currently being held by the police.

Dan is also an employee at PocketLining Plc. One evening he was reading a blog online and the author made a comment suggesting that PocketLining Plc was involved in selling weapons overseas and in some cases these weapons were falling into the hands of regimes that oppressed their own people. Dan decided that he would investigate whether this was true by trying to access the company's system where they hold their confidential information.

In order to put this plan into operation, Dan went into work early and went to the desk of a senior colleague, who he knew kept their various usernames and passwords in a small book in the top of a filing cabinet. He took down the relevant details and then returned to his desk and began to enter the details which would possibly lead him to the confidential information he was searching for. However within a few minutes a senior employee noticed what Dan was doing and called the police. Dan is also being held in police custody.

With which offence(s) would Helen and Dan each be most appropriately charged? Evaluate the likelihood of a successful prosecution for the offence(s).

10.10.   For many years, Andrew has worked for a bank in Berlin. In early 2006 he resigned his position and moved back to England. However, in the months leading up to his final day, Andrew identified a number of bank accounts which had been unused for more than six years. Once he had identified these accounts he came up with a plan to transfer money from these accounts into an account he had set up. The plan involved the creation of a computer programme that would transfer the money, after Andrew had left the bank and was back in England.

After Andrew returned to London, he effected a further bank transfer from the account he had set up in Berlin to an account he had set up in the United Kingdom. The money was successfully transferred. However, a number of people in Berlin had since contacted the bank to complain about movement of funds from their account. This led to Andrew's activities being discovered.

With which offence(s) could Andrew be charged and how likely is a successful prosecution? To what extent would your answer change if this happened in early 2008?

All weblinks mentioned in the text can also be found at:
http://www.palgrave.com/rogers

11 Cyber-Harassment and Online Pornography

This chapter will consider:

- How the Internet has exacerbated the problems of bullying, harassment, pornography and other indecent material.
- The legislation dealing with extreme and obscene pornography will be considered, along with the legislation that deals with indecent images of children.
- Analysis of the recently introduced Criminal Justice and Immigration Act and how it introduces a new offence into the Protection of Children Act 1978 relating to virtual indecent images of children.
- Newer offences relating to extreme pornography, 'virtual' indecent images of children and the broader offence contained within the Coroners and Justice Act 2009.
- The main pieces of legislation which deal with the contemporary issue of online harassment including the Protection from Harassment Act 1997.

The very nature of the Internet facilitates different forms of bullying and the distribution of indecent material. The wealth of interactive chat rooms, blogs, social networking sites and methods of communication allow this behaviour to be introduced into a new arena. Issues such as bullying, harassment and dissemination of indecent material are certainly not new, or even exclusive, to the Internet world, although the ease with which this behaviour can be perpetrated not only removes the hiding places that may have existed in the 'physical' realm, but also causes law-makers a problem as they try to ascertain the applicability of traditional offences to the medium of the Internet. There is a variety of problems when it comes to tackling cyber-harassment or online indecent images. Jurisdiction and enforcement have been discussed elsewhere, but there is also a divergence of views on what is acceptable behaviour. This chapter will consider these two interlinking areas. First of all, it will consider online indecent images – both those of children and also images that may be deemed to be extreme or obscene. The chapter will then consider the issue of cyber-harassment and the legislation that is in place to deal with this problem.

Online indecent or illegal images and content

The ease of accessing and downloading material from the Internet presents a range of problems. Parents and guardians are faced with a dilemma between allowing their child the opportunity to explore the riches of the Internet, and feeling naturally concerned about the material that they could come into contact with. Businesses need to ensure that employees are not using work systems for accessing illegal or inappropriate material, while law enforcement agencies are presented with a range of problems relating to the detection of purveyors of illegal content and also bringing a successful prosecution against them. The safety and well-being of the victim are also of paramount concern, although this is outside the immediate remit of this chapter. Indecent images are a staple diet for the Internet today, as are websites advocating illegal or extreme behaviour such as anorexia and other eating disorders, racism[1], terrorism and even suicide. It is often easier for a person to obtain pornographic material online than it is from a local shop, and in many cases the parent may be completely oblivious to the viewing habits of their child, or the business may not be aware how their networks are being used by their employees. The ability for anyone to download indecent, or even illegal material is made easier (and less risky from the point of view of detection) by the multitude of methods by which one can conceal one's identity by, for instance, using a pseudonym or false credit card details. However, the importance of accessibility issues pale into the background when put up against the proliferation of online indecent images of children. The alleged increase and wide accessibility of images depicting abuse of children is one of the moral panics of our age. The vilification of perpetrators by the press and often by local people indicates the high level of feelings which surround these crimes, yet websites containing this material continue to increase.[2]

There is a range of legislation in the United Kingdom which seeks to legislate against obscene or extreme pornography and indecent images of children. These include the Obscene Publications Act 1959 and the Criminal Justice and Immigration Act 2008 and, with more focus on indecent images of children, the Protection of Children Act 1978 (as amended) and the Coroners and Justice Act 2009. Each will now be considered and analysed in turn, along with groups

---

[1] See for instance: **R v Simon Guy Shepherd and Stephen Whittle** [2010] EWCA Crim 65.

[2] Although accurate date is hard to come by there are approximately 4.2m websites containing pornography (100,000 containing indecent images of children) *Internet Filter Review, 2006*. Around 2,755 websites in the English language contain indecent images of children *Internet Watch Foundation Annual and Charity Report, 2007*. Available at: http://www.iwf.org.uk/accountability/annual-reports/2007-annual-report.

such as the Internet Watch Foundation, which seek to assist the law enforce-ment agencies in reducing these websites.

Obscene Publications Act 1959

Section 2 of the Obscene Publications Act 1959 makes it an offence to publish (or to hold with a view to publishing) an obscene article. It does not matter if the person making the publication intends to make a gain or not. A prosecu-tion under this Act must be commenced within two years of the commission of the offence.[3] The maximum available sentence for this offence is a fine or up to three years' imprisonment, or both.[4] The definition of 'obscene' is found within Section 1 and it requires that the article, if taken as a whole, tends to deprave or corrupt persons who are likely to read, see or hear the matter contained within it. The courts have adopted as wide an approach as possible in defining the term 'article'.[5] The 'deprave and corrupt' test is notoriously difficult to prove as whether an article depraves or corrupts depends very much on the context, including the social or religious background. The general approach of case law – in line with Section 1(1) – is to consider whether it would deprave or corrupt the types of persons who may come into contact with the material. The effect of this approach, however, is that whether an arti-cle is obscene is decided upon a case-by-case basis, by looking at the view of a significant element of the audience. A flexible definition of obscenity is posi-tive as there is clearly no uniform level within society at which an article becomes 'obscene' and therefore juries can respond to the changing moral landscape of society, but the difficulty in applying these rules to the Internet is that it is often not easy to ascertain precisely the types of people who have been accessing the material. In **R v Perrin (Stephane Laurent)**,[6] the defendant was a director of a website based in the United States which contained adult material that was available both as free-to-view (including a trailer advertising the website) and by subscription. Users who subscribed to receive the material were required to provide their name, address and credit card details. The court drew a distinction between the free-to-view material and the subscription material and held that as the free-to-view material could be accessed by a wider range of people, including (potentially) children, the defendant was found liable for these pages, but not for the subscription-only pages, which were only viewable to users with accurate credit card details.

---

[3] Obscene Publications Act 1959, Section 2(3).
[4] Obscene Publications Act 1959, Section 2(1)(b).
[5] For instance, in **Attorney General's Reference (No. 5 of 1980)** [1981] 1 WLR 88 the Court of Appeal held that a video cassette was an article as defined in section 1(2) of the Obscene Publications Act 1959.
[6] [2002] EWCA Crim 747.

The clarification that the Obscene Publications Act extends to computer generated images was provided by Section 168(1) and Schedule 9, paragraph 3 of the Criminal Justice and Public Order Act 1994 so that the definition of an article was to include electronically stored data and that publication would include transmission of that data.[7] The definition of publication found within Section 1(3)(a) covers a wide range of actions, and includes: to distribute, circulate, sell, let on hire, give, or lend it, or to offer it for sale or hire it out. The case of **R v Fellows, R v Arnold**[8] concerned an appeal over whether images held on a computer screen were photographs, as outlined in Section 1(1) of the Protection of Children Act 1978, and secondly (and more importantly for our current discussion), even if they were photographs, whether or not they were being 'shown' or 'distributed' as the database was stored on a university computer and providing access to view the material (via a username and password) was merely passive conduct. As there was no active conduct the photographs could not have been published. The court did accept that active conduct is required to come within this heading, however it dismissed the appeal arguing that the term 'to show' should be given its ordinary meaning and that providing access to an online archive of indecent images amounted to showing. Furthermore, the behaviour of communicating with people and providing them with the required access details to the archive amounted to active conduct. The court was silent, however, on whether the materials had in fact been distributed. Subsequent case law has continued this broad approach to the terms in the legislation and the broadening of the term 'publisher' is another example of the courts trying to ensure that the Act is as encompassing as possible. In **R v Waddon**[9] a defendant was based in the United Kingdom and uploaded obscene material on to a web server based in the United States. The Court of Appeal held that as a police officer was able to access and download the material from the United Kingdom, the defendant had 'published' it within the United Kingdom. The view of the judge was that as the sending and the receiving of the information was within the domestic jurisdiction it did not matter that the material left the jurisdiction between these two times. The court also stated that there can be more than one publication at any one time as an article could be published on its uploading onto a server and also its subsequent downloading; it does not matter whether the material originated in the United Kingdom or not, publication can be determined by uploading or downloading. This was confirmed in the case of **R v Perrin (Stephane Laurent)**,[10] which held that an article is published when it is accessed in the United Kingdom, even though (as in this case) the obscene material (which

---

7 Inserted into the Obscene Publications Act 159, Section 1(3)(b).
8 [1997] 1 Cr. App. R. 244.
9 [2000] All ER (D) 502 CA (Criminal Division).
10 [2002] EWCA Crim 747.

was a sexually obscene website that could be viewed by anyone) was prepared and uploaded in a different jurisdiction. The court does not need to show that the major steps to publication took place within this jurisdiction, there simply needs to be transmission or access. Although the broad approach is generally welcomed, it is clearly not a panacea for removing all obscene material from the Internet. Simply because the material can be accessed within the United Kingdom does not mean that the originator of the material will be within the reach of the courts, as they may reside outside the United Kingdom's jurisdictional territory. Evidence suggests that the vast majority of obscene material accessed within the United Kingdom originates overseas. There has also been criticism of the broad approach as it makes material created in an external jurisdiction potentially subject to the law of the United Kingdom.[11]

Section 2(5) provides the defences against prosecution. A person may not be convicted under the Act if they did not examine the article and no had no reasonable cause to expect that its publication would be an offence under the statute. Accordingly, actual knowledge of unlawful action is required in order to commence an action. There is also a public good defence to ensure that works of literature, art, science or learning, or other object of general concern are not penalised.[12]

Criminal Justice and Immigration Act 2008

In August 2005, the Home Office and Scottish Executive produced a joint consultation paper on the possession of extreme pornographic material.[13] There were a number of reasons for this consultation. First of all, the Home Office considered that the growing trend of extreme pornographic images online was not positive for society as a whole and legislation should be introduced to make such images illegal. Furthermore, the images themselves often depicted criminal activity and, coupled with the ease of accessibility, the need for legislation was increased. While the Obscene Publications Act legislated against the publication of obscene articles, it was of little use when seeking to prosecute people who had held on to the images without publishing them or people who had no intention to publish or sell the images. It was equally ineffective against those who operated in different jurisdictions. The consultation paper advocated the introduction of a possession offence, meaning that an offence could be committed by merely possessing the material. The government issued its

---

[11] Hirst, M *Cyberobscenity and the Ambit of English Criminal Law* (2002) 13 Computers and Law 25.

[12] Obscene Publications Act 1959, Section 4(1). Section 4(2) allows expert evidence to be admitted to establish the artistic, literary or scientific merits of the object.

[13] *Consultation on the possession of extreme pornographic material* (Home Office, August 2005). Available at: http://news.bbc.co.uk/1/shared/bsp/hi/pdfs/30_08_05_porn_doc.pdf.

response to the consultation in August 2006 after receiving 397 responses[14] and the proposals now contained in Section 63 of the Criminal Justice and Immigration Act 2008, which legislates against the possession of extreme pornographic images[15], were put forward. It is a free-standing provision and is not inserted into other legislation as are some of the other provisions in the Act. The Home Office was of the view that the free-standing section would provide greater flexibility. Section 63(3) states that an image is pornographic if it can reasonably be presumed that the principal purpose behind the creation of the image was sexual arousal. The definition of 'extreme image' is an image that is grossly offensive, disgusting or otherwise of an obscene character. An image will also be held to be extreme if its subject matter is listed within section 63(7), including:

(a)   an act which threatens a person's life;
(b)   an act which results, or is likely to result, in serious injury to a person's anus, breasts or genitals;
(c)   an act which involves sexual interference with a human corpse, or
(d)   a person performing an act of intercourse or oral sex with an animal (whether dead or alive).

Furthermore, the Section requires that a reasonable person looking at the image would think that any such person or animal was real. Section 63(8) states that the image can be created by any means, which ensures that digital and computer generated images are covered by this provision. Section 65 provides the general defences that may be relied upon by person charged with an offence under Section 63. The defences include:

(a)   that the person had a legitimate reason for being in possession of the image concerned;
(b)   that the person had not seen the image concerned and did not know, nor had any cause to suspect, it to be an extreme pornographic image;
(c)   that the person –
      (i)   was sent the image concerned without any prior request having been made by or on behalf of the person, and
      (ii)   did not keep it for an unreasonable time.

---

[14] Ibid.

[15] Criminal Justice and Immigration Act 2008, Section 63(1). For further general information on these provisions see the Ministry of Justice's Information Note *Further information on the new offence of Possession of Extreme Pornographic Images* (November 2008). Available at: http://www.justice.gov.uk/publications/criminal-extreme-offence.htm.

If a person does not prove one of these defences and is found guilty of an offence under Section 63, they are liable to imprisonment for a maximum of three years, or a fine, or both.[16]

Protection of Children Act 1978

The main piece of legislation which seeks to legislate against indecent images of children is the Protection of Children Act 1978. The aim of this Act is to prevent the exploitation of children through making indecent photographs of them. In determining whether a photograph is indecent an objective test is used as highlighted in the case of **Kosmos v DPP**.[17] The Act further seeks to penalise individuals who distribute, show or advertise such material. Section 1(1) of the Act sets out four main offences:

(a)   It is an offence to take (or permit to be taken) or make any indecent photograph of a child;
(b)   It is an offence to distribute or show any such photograph;
(c)   It is an offence to be in possession of any such indecent photograph with a view to them being shown or distributed by either the holder or another party; and
(d)   It is an offence to publish any advertisement that is likely to be understood as conveying that the advertiser distributes or shows such indecent photographs, or intends to do so.

The maximum sentence provided by the Act is ten years' imprisonment.[18] The clear addition to this area of law by the Protection of Children Act is that simple possession of such indecent material is now an offence.[19] One of the disadvantages of the Obscene Publications Act (discussed above) is that the indecent material needed to be distributed. Under the Protection of Children Act this (although criminalised) is no longer required as a pre-requisite to

---

[16] For more analysis of this section see: Attwood, F & Smith, C *Extreme concern: regulating "dangerous pictures" in the United Kingdom* (2010) Journal of Law and Society, volume 37, issue 1, pages 171–188, McGlyn, C & Rackley, E *Criminalising extreme pornography: a lost opportunity* (2009) Criminal Law Review, pages 245–260 and Murray, A *The Reclassification of Extreme Pornographic Images* (2009) Modern Law Review, volume 72, issue 1, pages 73–90.

[17] [1975] Crim L. R. 345. This principle was confirmed in the case of **R v O'Carroll (Thomas Victor)** [2003] EWCA Crim 2338 where the defendant was refused leave to appeal against a conviction for possessing indecent photographs of children. He argued that as the concept of 'indecent' material was too vague a person would be unable to ascertain what the parameters of the law were to ensure that his activities were legitimate. This was rejected by the court who said that their role is to examine the image, as opposed to the motive or objective of the person taking the photograph.

[18] Section 6(2). This was increased from three years by the Criminal Justice and Courts Services Act 2000, Section 41(1).

[19] Inserted by Criminal Justice Act 1988, Section 160(5).

finding criminal activity. Further, it was found that the definition of a 'photograph' within section 7(2) was becoming dated[20] and so the Criminal Justice and Public Order Act 1994 inserted section 7(4) into the Protection of Children Act to include both the negative as well as the positive version of the image and also extended the definition to include data stored on a computer disc or by other electronic means which is capable of conversion into a photograph. It also responded to the evolving nature of technology to include 'pseudo-photographs' in all the above offences.[21] A pseudo-photograph is a photograph which shows an image, whether made by computer graphics or otherwise, which appears to be a photograph. This could also include a collage made by other sources depicting an indecent image of a child. For the purposes of this legislation a child is termed as being under the age of 18.[22]

One of the difficulties faced by the judiciary was highlighted in the decision in **Atkins and Goodland v DPP**.[23] In this case the court had to consider two main issues. First of all, whether the storing of indecent images of children on a computer system amounted to possession and secondly whether the downloading of these images constituted the 'making' of a photograph, which is an offence under Section 1 of the Act. The facts were that Atkins had unknowingly downloaded indecent images on to his computer, while Goodland appealed against his conviction of possession of an indecent pseudo-photograph under Section 160 Criminal Justice Act 1988, which was two photographs taped together with a naked woman super-imposed over the body of a child. The Divisional Court held that in order for a person to be in possession of an indecent photograph they need to possess it knowingly. Inadvertent possession is not sufficient. Equally, the inadvertent saving of the image on to a particular area of the computer was not sufficient for an individual to be found guilty of 'making' an image. Therefore, if on the balance of probabilities a defendant can show they did not know, or did not have reason to know that they were in possession of an indecent image of a child they must be found not guilty. In reaching this decision, the court applied the Court of Appeal decision in **R v Bowden (Jonathan)**.[24] In this case, the defendant appealed against his sentence and his conviction for the making of indecent images of children. Bowden had downloaded the material from the Internet, some of which he printed and some of which he saved on to a disc. He argued

---

[20] It merely included an indecent film, a copy of an indecent photograph or film, and an indecent photograph comprised in a film.

[21] Criminal Justice and Public Order Act 1994, Section 84(2).

[22] Section 7(6) of the Protection of Children Act was amended by the Sexual Offences Act 2003, Section 45. There are a number of defences to prosecution if the subject is 16 or 17 years old, specifically if they are married or were living together as partners in an enduring family relationship. It is a further defence if the defendant can prove it was necessary to make the photograph for the prevention, detection or investigation of a crime.

[23] [2000] 1 WLR 1427.

[24] [2000] 2 All ER 418.

that this behaviour amounted to the possession of indecent material, but not making. The court disagreed with this argument and held that the phrase 'to make' should be given its standard meaning. Therefore the storage of images on discs was held to be an activity 'making' such indecent images. The court stressed that the Act intended to reduce the amount of indecent images and was not simply focused on the original perpetrators, but also extended to users further down the line. The difficulty with this approach is that it places the these two types of offenders under the same heading: an individual who takes photographs of a child while sexually abusing them is in the same category as an individual who further down the line accesses these photographs and downloads them on to their personal computer.[25] The decisions in Atkins and Goodland and Bowden were followed by the Court of Appeal in the decision of **R v Smith and Jayson**.[26] This was a joint appeal against conviction by Smith (who had opened an email with an attachment that contained an indecent image of a young girl), and Jayson (who downloaded indecent images of children from the Internet). Smith had argued that his opening of the unsolicited email was an unintentional act and could not fall within the provisions of Section 1 of the Protection of Children Act, while Jayson argued that the mere downloading was not an offence, particularly as he had no intention to retrieve the material at a later date. The court rejected both of the appeals and confirmed that the 'making' of an image should be intentional, with knowledge that the image contained, or was likely to contain, an indecent image. The court's view was that Smith should have known what the email attachment contained and therefore upheld his conviction. The court also reiterated the decision in Bowden in relation to Jayson's appeal and stated that the downloading of indecent images from the Internet does constitute making an indecent image. The lack of intention to retrieve the material at a later date is irrelevant. Shortly after the decision in Smith and Jayson, the Court of Appeal established a scale in **R v Oliver**[27] which provided five levels of indecency to assist with sentencing. The five levels identified by the court in ascending order of seriousness were: (1) images depicting erotic posing with no sexual activity; (2) sexual activity between children, or solo masturbation by a child; (3) non penetrative sexual activity between adults and children; (4) penetrative sexual activity between children and adults, and (5) sadism or bestiality.

The issue of possession and the complexities in relation to computers was considered in the case of **R v Porter (Ross Warwick)**.[28] The issue in this case was the defendant appealing against his conviction for possessing indecent

---

[25] For more on this issue see: Akdeniz, Y *Possession and dispossession: a critical assessment of defences in possession of indecent photographs of children cases* (April 2007) Criminal Law Review, pages 274–288.

[26] [2002] EWCA Crim 683.

[27] [2002] EWCA Crim 2766.

[28] [2006] EWCA Crim 560.

images of children on his computer. The police had confiscated all of his computers and had found indecent images. However some of the images had been deleted and removed to the recycle bin. Although thumbnail images were still available, specialist software was required to recreate the images back to their full size. Therefore, while the owner of the computer may have placed the images out of their reach, a computer expert with access to the necessary software would be able to access them. The defendant did not have access to this specialist software and so argued that he no longer had the images in his possession. The court held that in the situation of a person who has deleted images on his computer system, which they are unable to access, then the individual would not be in possession of the image. The answer to this question would however be left up to the jury to decide whether the images were in fact outside of the possession of the individual. In this case, Porter was successful in arguing that the images were no longer in his possession. The decision in Porter was followed by the Court of Appeal in **R v Rowe (Christopher)**.[29] This case concerned the appeal of the defendant against his conviction of possessing indecent images of children. The police had previously searched the house belonging to his parents and had found 20 discs containing deleted indecent images of children. At his trial it was agreed that in order for the defendant to access the files he would need specialist software, which he did not appear to possess. The Court of Appeal held that as the jury had not been directed to consider that the images had been deleted the conviction was unsafe and was quashed. A further complexity of proving possession of indecent images of children was seen in the case of **R v Harrison (Neil John)**.[30] The defendant was a regular user of pornographic websites. He became aware of illegal images appearing on these websites through a pop-up which would download itself on to his computer hard drive and would advise him of the existence of such an image on the websites that he frequently visited. Harrison argued that he should not be liable for the automatic appearance of illegal pornographic images on his computer system by virtue of visiting sites that contained lawful pornographic images. In any case he contended that he was not actually making the images as it was the website creator that caused the images to appear and not himself as the end user. The court rejected this argument immediately and held that he should have known that images may be automatically stored on his computer. The court also applied the decisions in Bowden and Atkins and Goodland which held that it was the user who made the image on their computer and not a website designer or other third party.

---

[29] [2008] EWCA Crim 2712.
[30] [2007] EWCA Crim 2976.

Virtual indecent images of children

As well as legislating against extreme pornography (as discussed above) a second element was introduced by the Criminal Justice and Immigration Act which related to virtual indecent images of children. The difficulty with the legislation up to this point was that although it was clear that it covered photographs (and derivatives thereof, as the legislation had been amended) it was not clear whether it extended to cover virtual images, such as those which could appear in a virtual world. On 22nd June 2007 the response period to the Home Office Consultation Paper on the Possession of Non-Photographic Visual Depictions of Child Sexual Abuse[31] closed. This consultation paper was introduced as it was recognised that there was a potential gap within the law, which meant that virtual indecent images of children may not have been covered by the existing legislation. The paper sought views on three prospective ways of dealing with the 'problem' of disturbing sexual images that are created without using actual children – described in the paper as "*Cartoons, drawings, computer generated images (CGIs) and other non-photographic representations.*"[32] There were three initial proposals within the consultation: to extend the current position in the Protection of Children Act 1978, to enact a further offence of possession of indecent images of children, or to leave the law in the state it was in. The consultation paper was clear that there was a gap in law and pointed to examples where the police were unable to prosecute as the accused was only in possession of drawings and cartoons featuring indecent images of children – there was no illegal photograph (or pseudo-photograph) in existence, the images were merely taken from the imagination of the accused. Further, the consultation paper pointed to the increase in websites featuring animated images depicting child sexual abuse, and although most of the images were hosted beyond the United Kingdom's jurisdiction, it was apparent that there was a gap in the United Kingdom's legislative armoury to deal with this offence.[33] Section 69(3) of the Criminal Justice and Immigration Act was therefore introduced to extend the definitional reach of a photograph contained within section 7(4) of the Protection of Children Act, and inserted part 4A: to include a tracing or other image, whether made by electronic or other means (of whatever nature), which is not itself a photograph or pseudo-photograph, but is derived from the whole or part of a photograph or pseudo-photograph (or a combination of either or both). Section 6 extends the reach of the Protection of Children Act 1978, although the relative effectiveness appears to be focused on the phrase 'derived from'. The proliferation of online

---

[31] Available at: http://www.justice.gov.uk/publications/non-photographic-depictions.htm. The consultation period ran from 2nd April 2007 to 22nd June 2007.

[32] Ibid. Page 1.

[33] Ibid. Page 4.

virtual worlds had led to an increase in virtual indecent images of children; however to fall within this new section and for a person to be found guilty it appeared that this image needed to be derived from, or be a tracing of a real photograph or pseudo-photograph. The difference between a person who creates an indecent virtual image of a child from their imagination and a person who bases their virtual persona on a photograph of a child is negligible, yet the person who created the image from their imagination would arguably not be found guilty, while the person who used a photograph as the basis of their virtual image would be found guilty of an offence. It thus appeared that the loophole that had previously existed for virtual indecent images of children had not been fully closed.[34]

Coroners and Justice Act 2009

The loophole (relating to virtual indent images of children not derived from a photograph), still in existence despite the provisions within the Criminal Justice and Immigration Act, seems to have been overcome by the Coroners and Justice Act, which creates a new all-encompassing offence within Section 62.[35] The new offence is of being in possession of prohibited images of a child.[36] Section 62(2) continues by stating that an image is prohibited if it is pornographic, or is grossly offensive, disgusting or otherwise of an obscene nature. Section 62(3) states that an image will be pornographic if it can be reasonably assumed from its nature that it has been produced for the purpose of sexual arousal. This is a question for the jury to decide. Section 62(6) is more explicit and states that an image will be prohibited if it focuses solely or principally on a child's genitals or anal region, while section 62(7) lists a number of acts which, if depicted within the image, will lead to the photograph being prohibited.[37] The critical aspect of this Act is, however, how the term 'image' is defined. Section 65(2) refers to an image as a moving or still image (produced by any means), or data (stored by any means) which is capable of conversion into an image. The phrase 'produced by any means' is of utmost importance as this closes the loophole left after the amendment by the Criminal Justice and

---

[34] For a criticism of this offence see: Johnson, M *Camera Obscura – the CJIA 2008 and Virtual Pornography* (19th July 2008) Justice of the Peace, volume 172, number 29.

[35] Available at: http://www.opsi.gov.uk/acts/acts2009/ukpga_20090025_en_1.

[36] Coroners and Justice Act 2009, Section 62(1).

[37] The acts included in Section 62(7) (a–f) are sexual intercourse with, or in the presence of a child, an act of masturbation by, of, involving or in the presence of a child, penetration of the vagina or anus of a child with a part of a person's body or with anything else, an act of penetration, in the presence of a child, of the vagina or anus of a person with a part of a person's body or with anything else, the performance by a child of an act of intercourse or oral sex with an animal (whether dead or alive or imaginary), and the performance by a person of an act of intercourse or oral sex with an animal (whether dead or alive or imaginary) in the presence of a child.

Immigration Act, as a virtual indecent image of a child which is simply derived from a person's imagination can now be found to be illegal under the provisions of the Corners and Justice Act.

Section 64 of the Coroners and Justice Act does provide some defences for a person who is accused of an offence under Section 62. First of all, that the person had a legitimate reason for being in possession of the image concerned, secondly that the person had not seen the image concerned and did not know, nor had any cause to suspect it to be a prohibited image of a child, and thirdly that the person was sent the image concerned without any prior request having been made by or on behalf of the person, and did not keep it for an unreasonable time. If a person does not have a legitimate defence and is found guilty of an offence, Section 66 states that they shall be liable for a maximum prison sentence of three years.[38]

Concluding thoughts

The United Kingdom appears to have a wide range of legislation to tackle both extreme or obscene pornography and online indecent images of children. Although there is a strong argument to suggest that this legislation is robust enough to tackle hardcopy and virtual images, difficulties still exist in ensuring that this type of image will be permanently removed from the Internet. There are a number of key reasons for this. First of all, much of the material exists in other jurisdictions, which makes detection and prosecution much more difficult.[39] The Internet Watch Foundation reported in October 2009 that it received 27,000 calls in the ten months up to October 2009. Out of these calls, 5,742 were confirmed as being images depicting child sexual abuse, yet over 99 per cent of these images were located on a server outside of the United Kingdom's jurisdiction and therefore often out of the reach of the legislation. International co-operation amongst law enforcement agencies is improving however, as was seen in the well-publicised case of Ian Green, who in August 2010 was sentenced to four years' imprisonment after admitting 24 charges of making, possessing and distributing indecent images of children. He used the social networking site Facebook to share up to 100,000 indecent images of children. This case involved the police from the United Kingdom, Australia, Canada, South Africa and Switzerland.[40] Secondly, even if the material is

---

[38] For more on the provisions of the Coroners and Justice Act in relation to prohibited images of children please see: Johnson, M *Picture Perfect – the Coroners and Justice Bill and illegal images of children* (15th September 2009) Solicitors Journal, volume 153, number 34.

[39] See: Internet Watch Foundation News *Public reports help remove child sex abuse images* (14th October 2009). Available at: http://www.iwf.org.uk/about-iwf/news/post/268-public-reports-help-remove-child-sexual-abuse-images.

[40] See: BBC News *Facebook child abuse images ringleader jailed* (26th August 2010). Available at: http://www.bbc.co.uk/news/uk-england-11101149?print=true.

located and based within the United Kingdom it can be very difficult for the law enforcement agencies to track down those responsible and they often need to rely on techniques such as tracing credit card details.[41] One example of this was the police operation 'Operation Ore', which commenced in 1999 and led to almost 1,500 convictions. Perhaps one way of seeing a greater reduction in these images will be more self-regulatory activity. For instance, in September 1996 the Internet Watch Foundation was established by the United Kingdom's Internet industry.[42] The organisation operates a telephone hotline for members of the public to contact them with reports of online indecent images of children. The Internet Watch Foundation agreed to extend their hotline to non-photographic images of children from April 2010 to cover the provisions contained in the Coroners and Justice Act.[43] Once the accuracy of this report has been verified, the Internet Watch Foundation will inform the Internet Service Provider that it is hosting the illegal content and ask them to remove it. Once an Internet Service Provider has been notified they are deprived of the legal excuse contained within Articles 12–14 of the E-Commerce Directive that they were unaware of the relevant material. This means that they will be liable for the images online if they do not take proactive steps to remove the material the Internet Watch Foundation has requested them to remove. The Internet Watch Foundation asserts that the requests they make to Internet Services Providers to remove content are always adhered to and that the material is often removed within 24 hours.[44]

Online harassment

The nature of the Internet provides new means of bullying or harassing people. This could include sending threatening emails or damaging viruses,

---

[41] See: BBC News *UK probe into online porn* (14th April 2004). Available at: http://news.bbc.co.uk/1/hi/uk/3625603.stm and Arthur, C *When will we know whether Operation Ore was a success?* (17th May 2007) The Guardian. Available at: http://www.guardian.co.uk/technology/2007/may/17/guardianweeklytechnologysection2. A key way in which the police were able to track perpetrators was through their credit card usage. Although Operation Ore was successful in many ways, it was not without its criticism, particularly in relation to the way the police gathered evidence, criticism of testimony obtained from the United States of America and dubious forensic techniques. See: Leppard, D *Child porn suspects set to be cleared in evidence 'shambles'* (3rd July 2005) The Sunday Times. Available at: http://www.timesonline.co.uk/tol/news/uk/article539974.ece.

[42] See: http://www.iwf.org.uk.

[43] See: Internet Watch Foundation Coroners and Justice Act 2009. Available at: http://www.iwf.org.uk/hotline/the-laws/non-photographic-child-sexual-abuse-images/coroners-and-justice-act-2009.

[44] Internet Watch Foundation News *Public reports help remove child sex abuse images* (14th October 2009). Available at: http://www.iwf.org.uk/about-iwf/news/post/268-public-reports-help-remove-child-sexual-abuse-images. There is an element of controversy in their powers. Towards the end of 2008, instead of blocking just the image, they blocked an entire page on Wikipedia, which contained an indecent image of a child. See: Fullman, S & Imrie, A *IWF: Wikipedia blocked for illegal image* (January 2009) E-Commerce Law and Policy, volume 11, issue 1, pages 8–9.

impersonating someone online, subscribing another person to mailing lists, making disparaging comments anonymously on blogs or message boards and misuse of social networking sites.

Legislation dealing solely with harassment in the online world does not currently exist. Instead, interpretation of older legislation, which was enacted to deal with more 'traditional' forms of bullying, is often broad enough to ensure applicability to the Internet. The legislation that this section will consider includes the Protection from Harassment Act 1997, the Malicious Communications Act 1988 and the Communications Act 2003.

Protection from Harassment Act 1997

This legislation was enacted at the time when the Internet revolution was just beginning. It was not enacted in response to this development, although was a response to a number of 'stalking' cases where the defendant had been acquitted. It aimed to protect persons from harassment and other similar conduct. Section 1 of the Act sets out the general prohibition, which is that a person may not pursue a course of conduct which amounts to the harassment of another and which the perpetrator knows, or ought to know that the behaviour amounts to harassment of the other. Section 125(2) of the Serious Organised Crime and Police Act 2005 insets section 1A into the Protection of Harassment Act and says that a person may not pursue a course of conduct which involves the harassment of two or more persons, and which he knows or ought to know involves harassment of those persons, and by which he intends to persuade any person (whether one, some or all in question) not to do something that he is entitled or required to do, or to do something that he is not under any obligation to do. In discerning whether the person knew or ought to have known that the behaviour amounted to harassment of the other an objective test is employed in section 1(2); specifically, would a reasonable person in possession of the same information think that the course of conduct amounted to harassment? Harassment is defined in Section 7(2) of the Act and includes alarming a person or causing them harm or distress[45], while a 'course of conduct' is defined in Section 7(3) as being two or more occasions. The finding of a course of

---

[45] In the case of **R v Colohan** [2001] 2 FLR 757 the court was asked to address whether the characteristics of the accused should be taken into account when deciding whether they ought to have known that their conduct amounted to harassment. In this case, the accused was a schizophrenic who had sent a number of abusive letters to a Member of Parliament. He was convicted of an offence under Section 2, but on appeal, he argued that the judge had misdirected the jury by not informing them that they needed to consider whether a reasonable person suffering from schizophrenia would have known that their behaviour amounted to harassment. He further submitted that based on his illness he had an adequate defence in that his behaviour was reasonable (as contained within Section 1(3)(c)). Despite the existence of this illness, the court rejected the appeal arguing that the defence does not allow provision for the insertion of phrases such as 'reasonable person' or allow for the court to consider the characteristics of the accused.

conduct is central to a successful prosecution under this Act, yet the legislation is limited on the guidance it provides to define this term.[46] Accordingly, the common law has taken the lead in clarifying the definition of this term. In **Lau v DPP**[47] the defendant appealed against his conviction for harassment arguing that there was not a sufficient course of conduct, as the two events (the first was slapping his previous girlfriend and the second was threatening a friend of his former girlfriend) were four months apart. The court held that the four month gap meant there was insufficient evidence for the harassment claim to be proved and continued by suggesting that the fewer the number of incidents there were and the greater the amount of time between the incidents the less likely it would be that a course of conduct could be found. The decision in Lau was applied immediately afterwards in the appeal in **R v H (Gavin Spencer)**[48] where two incidents over a six month period were held to be insufficient to count as a course of conduct. The appeal was also allowed as there had been a reconciliation between the couple between the two incidents. At the opposite end of the timescale spectrum, in the case of **Kelly v DPP**[49] the court held that three abusive telephone calls that were made in five minutes was sufficient to be a course of conduct. Even though the recipient of the call did not pick up, there were messages left on the voicemail system, which the court considered to be sufficient for a prosecution under Section 2.[50] Finally, in **R v Patel (Nitin)**,[51] which again relied on the judgment in Lau, the Court of Appeal held that for incidents to be included within a course of conduct there does need to be a sufficient nexus. In order to find this connection, due regard needs to be given to the location, the time (both between the acts and the duration) and the nature of the act. This is a non-exhaustive list, but it is clear that simply because two incidents exist, these alone are insufficient for a course of conduct to be found.[52]

Section 2 of the Protection from Harassment Act sets out the offence and according to Section 2(1), a person who pursues a course of conduct in breach of Section 1 is guilty of an offence. The maximum criminal sentence available under this heading is six months' imprisonment or a fine.[53] Section 1(2) lists

---

[46] Aside from the fact that it needs to be on two or more occasions, as outlined in Section 7(3), the Act states in Section 7(4) that it can include speech.

[47] [2000] Crim L. R. 580.

[48] [2001] Crim L. R. 318.

[49] [2002] EWHC 1428 (Admin).

[50] For more on this case see: Tausz, D & Ormerod, D C *Harassment: whether leaving three abusive and threatening phone calls on the victim's voice mail, which were listened to at one time, is capable of constituting a course of conduct* (January 2003), Criminal Law Review, pages 45–47.

[51] [2004] EWCA Crim 3284.

[52] For more consideration on the connection between incidences leading to a course of conduct see: Finch, E *Stalking the Perfect Stalking Law: an evaluation of the efficacy of the Protection from Harassment Act 1997* (September 2002) Criminal Law Review, pages 703–719.

[53] Section 3 also sets out that the victim can pursue a civil claim and damages can be awarded for (amongst other things) loss of earnings or anxiety. An injunction may also be awarded to prevent any further conduct, which amounts to harassment.

three defences which the accused must prove on the balance of probabilities. It will be a defence if the course of conduct was pursued for the purpose of preventing or detecting a crime, or it was pursued under any enactment or rule of law, or finally that in the particular circumstances the course of conduct was reasonable. A more serious offence is set out in Section 4, which states that a person whose course of conduct causes another to fear on at least two occasions that violence will be used against him is guilty of an offence.[54] Again, an objective test is deployed in Section 4(2) to decide whether the alleged perpetrator knew or ought to have known that his course of conduct would have caused another person to fear that violence would be used against them. Again, the course of conduct needs to be two or more occasions and the maximum sentence available for this offence is five years or a fine.[55] Section 4(4) does provide three defences (which effectively replicate those in Section 1(2)), on which the accused can try to rely. First of all, that the course of conduct was pursued for the purpose of preventing or detecting a crime, secondly that the course of conduct was pursued under an enactment or rule of law and thirdly that the course of conduct was reasonable for the protection of himself or another or for the protection of property belonging to himself or another. The burden is on the accused to prove the validity of the defence on the balance of probabilities.

Malicious Communications Act 1988

The Malicious Communications Act[56] makes it an offence to send a letter, electronic communication[57] or another article, which contains an indecent or grossly offensive message,[58] a threat or information which is false and known or is believed to be false by the sender, or any other article which is indecent or grossly offensive with the intention of causing anxiety or distress.[59] A person guilty of an offence under this section is liable to a fine and a maximum prison

---

[54] The issue was considered in **Kelly v DPP** [2002] EWHC 1428 (Admin) (considered above). The victim received three voicemail messages from her former partner. She listened to them consecutively. The court found that there had been a course of conduct, as there had been more than two distinct telephone calls, although they could not find the defendant guilty of a Section 4 offence as the victim had only been put in fear of violence being used against her once. The principle that to be successful in a Section 4 offence the prosecution need to show that the victim was put in fear of violence on more than one occasion was confirmed in the case of **Courti v DPP** [2002] Crim L. R. 131.

[55] Section 4(5) states that if a jury find a defendant not guilty of an offence under Section 4, they may still find him guilt of an offence under Section 2.

[56] Available at: http://www.opsi.gov.uk/ACTS/acts1988/Ukpga_19880027_en_1.htm.

[57] 'Electronic communication' was added to the Act by Section 43 of the Criminal Justice and Police Act 2001. Section 2A defines an electronic communication as: any oral or other communication by means of a telecommunication system or any communication (however sent) in electronic form.

[58] See: **Connolly v DPP** [2008] 1 WLR 276.

[59] Malicious Communications Act 1988, Section 1(1).

sentence of six months. A defence is contained in Section 1(2) and it provides that a person shall not be found guilty if the threat was made to reinforce a demand which the sender believed he had reasonable grounds for sending and he thought that the threat was a proper means of reinforcing the demand. This Act was used in the high-profile incident involving Christopher Pierson, who, in the aftermath of the 2004 tsunami, sent 35 emails from a bogus email address to different people who had posted pleas on a news website, saying that their friend or relative had been killed. The emails appeared official and he had spent some time designing the emails to make them appear as if they were sent by the Foreign and Commonwealth Office. He was sentenced by Bow Street Magistrates to six months' imprisonment.[60]

Communications Act 2003

Under Section 127, a person is guilty of an offence if he sends, by means of a public electronic communications network, a message or other matter that is grossly offensive or of an indecent, obscene or menacing character, or causes any such a message or matter to be sent. Further, a person is guilty of an offence if, for the purpose of causing annoyance, inconvenience or needless anxiety to another, he sends by means of a public electronic communications network, a message that he knows to be false, causes such a message to be sent, or persistently makes use of a public electronic communications network. If a person is found guilty under this section they shall be liable to imprisonment for a maximum term not exceeding six months or a fine, or both. As this section makes reference to public electronic communication networks, it is clear that the provisions cover material sent over the Internet. The main case considering the exact scope of the Section 127 offence was **DPP v Collins**[61] in which the DPP appealed against an earlier decision which found Collins not guilty of making offensive telephone calls to his Member of Parliament. The calls (or messages left) contained racially offensive comments, but the recipients to the calls were not members of an ethnic minority. Accordingly, the court at first instance held that there had been no offence as the comments were not 'grossly offensive' to the recipient. The DPP appealed arguing that the defendant would know that the words would be grossly offensive to those to whom they related, or that they could be taken so. The House of Lords accepted the appeal and held that the purpose of the Act was not to protect people from undesirable or offensive comments, but to prohibit the use of a public electronic communications network for sending such messages. Section

---

[60] See: BBC News *Man jailed over tsunami emails* (24th January 2005). Available at: http://news.bbc.co.uk/1/hi/england/lincolnshire/4201775.stm.
[61] [2006] 1 WLR 2223.

127(1) criminalises the sending of grossly offensive or indecent messages and it follows that the message does not need to be received. The court also held that it is a question of fact (taking into account the United Kingdom's open and multiracial society) to decide whether a message is grossly offensive and decided that the comments made by Collins were indeed grossly offensive.[62] More recently, the Communications Act was used to prosecute Paul Chambers, who posted a message on the social networking site Twitter threatening to blow up Doncaster airport following their cancellation of his flight to Ireland. He was fined £385, plus costs.[63]

A final comment on Section 127 is that it criminalises the sending of a grossly offensive or indecent message through an electronic public communications network. This means that Internet Service Providers are excluded from being held liable for comments made. This is confirmed by Article 12–14 of the E-Commerce Directive 2000/31/EC (implemented by the E-Commerce Regulations 2002[64]), which provides that an Internet Service Provider shall not be liable if they merely act as a conduit, or are hosting or caching the comment. This principle has been strengthened in terms of hate speech against a person regarding their sexual orientation or religious beliefs. The Electronic Commerce Directive (Hatred against Persons on Religious Grounds or the Grounds of Sexual Orientation) Regulation 2010[65] updates and strengthens the provisions in the E-Commerce Regulations by ensuring that Internet Service Providers and other providers of digital services are exempt from liability for religious and sexuality-based hate speech over their systems.[66] The view of the government was that Internet Service Providers could at no stage have the intent to stir up hate speech and so should be absolved of all responsibility for these offences.[67]

---

[62] For more on this case see: Ormerod, D *Telecommunications: sending grossly offensive message by means of public electronic communications network* (January 2007) Criminal Law Review, pages 98–100.

[63] See Claburn, T (Information Week) *Twitter Bomb Joke Convicted* (10th May 2010) available at: http://www.informationweek.com/story/showArticle.jhtml?articleID=224701387 and Leydon, J (The Register) *Twitter bomb joker found guilty* (10th May 2010). Available at: http://www.theregister.co.uk/2010/05/10/twitter_bomb_joker_guilty/. At the time of writing it is believed that this is the first time that a person has been convicted of a crime for a Twitter post. The Communications Act has also been used to prosecute an individual who has used wireless broadband without permission. See: OUT-LAW.COM News *UK war driver fined £500* (25th July 2005). Available at: http://www.out-law.com/page-5938.

[64] Statutory Instrument 2002/2013.

[65] Available at: http://www.opsi.gov.uk/si/si2010/draft/ukdsi_9780111490402_en_1.

[66] The 2010 regulations replace The Electronic Commerce Directive (Racial and Religious Hatred Act 2006) Regulations.

[67] For more see: OUT-LAW.COM News *E-Commerce Regulations updated to exempt ISPs from hate speech charges* 14th January 2010). Available at: http://www.out-law.com/page-10664.

Key points:

- The Internet allows undesirable images to be freely available and transportable across the world. The challenge for legislatures is to ensure that images which are indecent, offensive or obscene are adequately legislated against.
- The Obscene Publications Act 1959 and Section 63 Criminal Justice and Immigration Act 2008 deal with obscene publications and extreme pornography respectively.
- Online indecent images of children have a much wider body of legislation starting with the Protection of Children Act 1978, which makes it an offence to make, or permit to be taken, possess or distribute an indecent image of a child.
- This offence has been widened more recently, for example by extending the definition of photographs to extend to pseudo-photographs and by raising the age of a child from 16 to 18.
- The Criminal Justice and Immigration Act 2008 sought to close the loophole that existed for virtual indecent images of children, which did not appear to be covered by the legislation. Such an image became prohibited where it was a tracing, or derived from a real photograph, or pseudo-photograph. This meant that virtual indecent images of children created from a person's imagination were still above the law.
- The Coroners and Justice Act 2009 seems to have closed this loophole by making illegal the possession of prohibited images of children. The key definition within this Act is that of 'image', which can be 'produced by any means'.
- There are a number of ways in which a person can be stalked electronically. Perpetrators can make use of telephone, email and social networking sites.
- The United Kingdom has a wide body of legislation to tackle online harassment and other forms of online bullying.
- The Protection from Harassment Act 1997 makes it an offence for a person to pursue a course of conduct that leads to the harassment of another, or causes another to fear that violence will be used against them on at least two occasions.
- The Malicious Communications Act 1988 makes it an offence to send an indecent or grossly offensive message, while the Communications Act 2003 makes it an offence to use a public communications electronic network service for sending an indecent or grossly offensive message.
- Internet Service Providers are provided with exemption from liability through Articles 12–14 of the E-Commerce Directive. This protection has been strengthened by the provisions in the Electronic Commerce Directive

(Hatred against Persons on Religious Grounds or the Grounds of Sexual Orientation) Regulations 2010.

Further reading:

- Akdeniz, Y *Possession and dispossession: a critical assessment of defences in possession of indecent photographs of children cases* (April 2007) Criminal Law Review, pages 274–288.
- Akdeniz, Y and Ellison, L *Cyberstalking: The Regulation of Harassment on the Internet* (1998) Criminal Law Review Special Edition, pages 29–47.
- Basu, S and Jones, R P *Regulating Cyberstalking* (2007) Journal of Information, Law and Technology, volume 2.
- Edwards, L & Waelde, C *Law and the Internet* (2009) Hart Publishing, chapter 20 (by Lilian Edwards) *Pornography, Censorship and the Internet.*
- Geach, N & Haralambous, N *Regulating harassment: is the law fit for the social networking age?* (2009) Journal of Criminal Law, volume 73, issue 3, pages 241–257.
- Klang, M & Murray, A *Human Rights in the Digital Age* (2005) Routledge-Cavendish Publishing, chapter 3 (by Marie Eneman) *The new face of child pornography.*
- Kohl, U *Who has the right to govern on-line activity? A criminal and civil point of view* (2004) International Review of Law, Computers and Technology, volume 18, issue 3, pages 387–410.
- McGlynn, C & Rackley, E *Criminalising extreme pornography: a lost opportunity* (2009) Criminal Law Review, issue 4, pages 245–260.
- Nair, A *Internet Content Regulation: Is a Global Community Standard a Fallacy or the Only Way Out?* International Review of Law, Computers and Technology (2007), volume 21, number 1, pages 15–25.
- Nair, A. *'Caveat Viewer!': The rationale of the possession offence* (2008) International Review of Law, Computers and Technology, volume 22, numbers 1–2, pages 157–164.
- Rowbottom, J *Obscenity laws and the internet: targeting the supply and demand* (February 2006) Criminal Law Review, pages 97–109.
- Thomas, D A *R v Smith (Christopher): Sentencing – sexual offences prevention order – downloading indecent images from the internet* (2009) Criminal Law Review, issue 8, pages 600–602.

Questions for consideration:

11.1.   How does the Internet facilitate the sending of indecent images or increase the opportunity for a person to harass another?

11.2. Chart the development of the legislation set up to tackle indecent images of children from the Protection of Children Act 1978 through to the Coroners and Justice Act 2009.

11.3. To what extent did the Criminal Justice and Immigration Act 2008 plug the loophole within legislation relating to virtual indecent images of children? Is the loophole completely closed off by the Coroners and Justice Act 2009?

11.4. Explain the difference between the Section 2 and Section 4 offences in the Protection from Harassment Act 1998.

11.5. How have the courts defined a 'course of conduct' for both the Section 2 and Section 4 offences?

11.6. To what extent do you agree with the view that the legislation relating to online harassment is adequate for the Internet age?

11.7. 'The legislation within the United Kingdom that is designed to tackle online indecent images of children is broad and robust enough to ensure that these undesirable images will soon be removed from the Internet.'
To what extent to do you agree with this point of view?

11.8. Following a nationwide police investigation into the activities of an online paedophile ring on a social networking site, the police have been monitoring the activities of Paul, Liz and John. These three people had been communicating on this system for some time and their communications caused the police sufficient concern to raid their respective houses.

In Paul's house the police search the contents of his computer and find a large number of pornographic photographs of children. These had all been taken with a digital camera.

On Liz's computer the police find a computer software package that is able to alter and modify other images. On closer inspection they find other folders with indecent images of children which have been modified by the use of the same computer software.

Finally, in John's flat they find a number of drawings and paintings of children in sexually explicit positions. John argues that the pictures are artistic and that he has been working on them during his post-graduate art class.
Outline any possible charges and evaluate the likelihood of a successful prosecution.

11.9. After graduating from University, Timothy split up with his girlfriend Angela. They had been going out with one another for approaching 18 months, but Timothy believed that their lives were going to be taking a different direction, so it was an appropriate time to end their relationship. Timothy had also been struggling with Angela's recreational drug use and autistic tendencies.

Angela took the break up badly and so set about trying to win Timothy back. She continually posted messages on his personal social networking site and also contacted him by telephone at least five times a day. She also sent a large number of text messages. The majority of the messages were sexually explicit, while others used very graphic and indecent language. There were also a few messages where Angela threatened to kill herself if he did not go out with her again.

Timothy contacted the police about Angela's behaviour and she has now been arrested. Advise Angela on the likelihood of her being successfully prosecuted under any relevant online harassment legislation.

11.10.   The UK has various measures it can adopt to combat cyber-stalking however, they each have limitations, the biggest of which is their limited jurisdiction. The nature of the Internet means that without a piece of global legislation the problem of cyber-stalking will always be with us.

Undertake a critical evaluation of this statement.

All weblinks mentioned in the text can also be found at:
http://www.palgrave.com/law/rogers

Glossary

Avatar	A representation of a person in a virtual world.
B2B	Business to business.
B2C	Business to consumer.
Bandwidth	The amount of data that can be sent through a modem connection.
Banner advertisement	An advertisement that appears on webpages you are viewing. They are often strategically placed.
Behavioural advertising	The building-up of a profile of a user to allow advertisers to target advertisements that are relevant to the user.
Blog	An online journal regularly updated by the author and intended to be viewed by members of the public.
Bluetooth	Short-range technology which allows Bluetooth-enabled devices to communicate with each other.
Cloud computing	Computer networks that allow users to access information anywhere in the world. A social networking site is a good example.
Cyberspace	A word used to describe the online world of computers.
Cybersquatter	A person who registers a domain name to prevent a more legitimate owner from using it.
Cookie	Files which attach themselves to the hard drive of a computer and monitor and track the usage of the Internet by the user. They are said to form the 'memory' of the Internet.
ta controller	The person who determines the grounds for processing personal data under the Data Protection Act 1998.
subject	The person who is the subject of the personal data.
l of ` attack	The continual sending of information to a system to clog the system up and prevent it from operating effectively. An example is sending a large number of emails to

	prevent the inbox from receiving or sending any further communications.
Domain name	The address that identifies a website.
Dot com	The colloquialism given to an online business.
E-commerce	Electronic commerce, the carrying out of business online.
Encryption	A security device where a message is scrambled and 'locked' and can only be opened by a person with the relevant decoding key.
Grooming	An offence under the Sexual Offences Act 2003 where a person over the age of 18 (having met or communicated with a person under the age of 16 on at least two earlier occasions) intentionally meets, or travels with the intention of meeting the person under the age of 16, with the intention of committing an offence against the minor.
Hacking	Unauthorised access to a computer system.
Happy slapping	The filming of an assault by mobile phone. Often this film is either circulated or placed online.
HTML	Hyper Text Markup Language
HTTP	Hyper Text Transfer Protocol
Hyperlink	A word or phrase which, when clicked, directs you to a different webpage or website.
ICANN	The Internet Corporation for Assigned Names and Numbers – the body responsible for handing out top-level domain names.
Information Commissioner	The independent authority set up to regulate a range legislation relating to privacy, data protection and fre of information.
Instant Messaging	Real time communication between two or more using text.
Internet Watch Foundation	Operates a hotline allowing members of the p report online indecent or illegal images.
M-commerce	Mobile commerce
Malware	A contraction of the words 'malicious' a software designed to enter computers computer system.

Netiquette	An informal system of etiquette on the Internet.
Open source	Material, such as computer code or an article which is freely available online.
Pop-ups	A form of online advertising, where advertisements appear in new windows on the screen.
Pharming	The redirection of a user to a false website in order to secure their personal information.
Phishing	A communication (normally an email) purporting to come from a recognised bank or other institution requesting details such as username, password and bank account information.
Search engine	An online index of websites.
Social network site	An online community where users can communicate and share information, such as photographs and videos.
Spam	Unsolicited commercial email sent in bulk.
Spoofing	The alteration of information (such as an email address or subject line) to make the communication appear as if it is coming from a different source.
Trojan horse	A computer programme that looks authentic, but when accessed will damage the computer's hard drive.
Web 2.0	The user-generated content era of the Internet.
Website	A location on the Internet often made up of a number of webpages.

Index